On Dangerous Ground

As a rule, countries consider clearly defined international borders to be paramount for their survival and prosperity. Most borders gain definition peacefully and, once they do, these definitions stick (i.e., the border remains settled). The failure to define borders, however, produces protracted, geopolitical, militarized competitions (or rivalries) between neighboring countries. Rider and Owsiak model this failure as a particular type of bargaining problem – namely, bargaining over territory that affects the distribution of power between neighboring states significantly – that undermines efforts to resolve border disagreements peacefully. Countries must then overcome this bargaining problem or risk falling into a protracted rivalry, which then needs to be addressed with more resources. The authors develop a theory of how borders settle. They then explore the consequences of the failure to settle, theoretically connecting it to the onset of rivalries. This leads to the process that helps rivals overcome the bargaining problem, resolve their border disagreement, and terminate their rivalry.

TOBY J. RIDER is Associate Professor of Political Science at Texas Tech University. His work has appeared in *The Journal of Politics, International Studies Quarterly, Journal of Conflict Resolution, and Journal of Peace Research*, among other publications.

ANDREW P. OWSIAK is Associate Professor of International Affairs at the University of Georgia. He coauthored *International Conflict Management* (with J. Michael Greig and Paul F. Diehl, 2019), and his work has appeared in *The Journal of Politics, British Journal of Political Science, International Studies Quarterly, Journal of Conflict Resolution*, and *Journal of Peace Research*, among other publications.

On Dangerous Ground

A Theory of Bargaining, Border Settlement, and Rivalry

TOBY J. RIDER
Texas Tech University

ANDREW P. OWSIAK
University of Georgia

CAMBRIDGE
UNIVERSITY PRESS

CAMBRIDGE
UNIVERSITY PRESS

Shaftesbury Road, Cambridge CB2 8EA, United Kingdom

One Liberty Plaza, 20th Floor, New York, NY 10006, USA

477 Williamstown Road, Port Melbourne, VIC 3207, Australia

314–321, 3rd Floor, Plot 3, Splendor Forum, Jasola District Centre, New Delhi – 110025, India

103 Penang Road, #05–06/07, Visioncrest Commercial, Singapore 238467

Cambridge University Press is part of Cambridge University Press & Assessment, a department of the University of Cambridge.

We share the University's mission to contribute to society through the pursuit of education, learning and research at the highest international levels of excellence.

www.cambridge.org
Information on this title: www.cambridge.org/9781108794541

DOI: 10.1017/9781108885713

First published 2021
First paperback edition 2022

A catalogue record for this publication is available from the British Library

ISBN 978-1-108-84034-7 Hardback
ISBN 978-1-108-79454-1 Paperback

Dedicated with love to my spouse, Jill, and children, Alex and Sam.

Toby J. Rider

To Ash, Paula, Andrew, and Doris. You know what you did.

Andrew P. Owsiak

Contents

Figures

Tables

Preface

A project like this undergoes a transformation as it develops. It began as a series of articles about the relationship between border settlement and interstate rivalries – a relationship that we thought existed, and for which we had a solid theoretical explanation. Those articles, published in the *Journal of Politics* (2013) and the *Journal of Peace Research* (2015), however, did not grant us the space we needed to tell a full story. They covered why unsettled borders lead to rivalry onset, as well as how settling borders alters the rivalry relationship. Yet they left a crucial question unanswered: how do rivals reach border settlement in the first place?

We intended a third article to answer this final question, but presentations of it in draft form generated deserved criticism. Our audience wanted to know how border settlement happened generally (not merely in rivalries), what conceptual foundations underlay our argument, and how any third article would fit into a coherent whole with our previous work. At that point, we realized the necessity of a book, not only to insert the piece of the story missing thus far but also to develop further the pieces that existed in published form and to tie them together into the larger story we were telling.

As with any new project, early momentum energized us, and the Peace Science Society (International) generously supported a workshop for our book in 2015 at its annual meeting, held that year at the University of Mississippi. Glenn Palmer and Jeff Carter proved instrumental in orchestrating that workshop for us, and we therefore owe them our gratitude. Numerous individuals – including K. Chad Clay, Michael Colaresi, Paul Hensel, Marc Hutchison, Sara McLaughlin Mitchell, and Scott Wolford – read an early draft of the manuscript at that time and provided us with crucial feedback and (re)direction. The project greatly improved, and adopted a new structure, in the aftermath of our collective conversation. In the years that followed, we then called on Scott Wolford and Chad Clay repeatedly for still further advice. Each of the colleagues listed here donated significant time and effort to improve our work. We cannot thank them enough, and hasten to acknowledge that we accept responsibility for any shortcomings that remain.

Our gratitude extends beyond this initial group to five additional groups as well. First, research assistants contributed significantly to the data underlying our analyses. In 2011, we set out to gather data on the process by which neighboring states settle(d) their borders, including the various conflict management tools they employ(ed). This task proved challenging, laborious, and larger than we initially expected. Thus, between 2011 and 2017, myriad graduate and undergraduate students contributed to data collection, archiving, cleaning, and analysis. Doug Atkinson, Allison Cuttner, Patrick Howell, Josh Jackson, Cody Knapp, and John Willingham provided the in-depth research that allowed us to compile the initial dataset. We owe a special thanks to Josh Jackson, however, who supervised a team of graduate and undergraduate research assistants at the University of Georgia in 2017 to check the accuracy of the full dataset. This research team included Cheikh Faye, Caroline Gustavson, George McCall, Lucas Nussbaumer, Christian Pedraza, and Garrett Shrader. Without the combined assistance of these individuals, we would – no doubt – still be searching for, reading, writing, and coding myriad historical narratives. An introduction to the dataset appears in *Conflict Management and Peace Science* (2018), co-authored by Andrew P. Owsiak, Allison Cuttner, and Brent Buck.

Second, our universities – Texas Tech University and the University of Georgia – supplied funding that allowed us not only to present our work to colleagues at academic conferences but also to hold writing retreats. The latter may seem odd, but proved especially valuable. With family obligations, teaching schedules, and university service commitments competing for our attention (including during the summer!), the chance to meet in person for days at a time gave us bursts of momentum that would otherwise not have been possible. We also found it more efficient to work simultaneously at the same physical location (when possible) to resolve concerns that arose, even though technology allows for virtual meetings. We hope other universities will recognize and support scholars similarly, particularly young ones.

A series of locations comprise the third group. Our writing road show did not prove terribly exciting, but we spent many hours writing at the Cartel Coffee Lab (Tempe, Arizona), the Franklin House Cafe (Athens, Georgia), Starbucks (various), the Tempe Mission Palms (Tempe, Arizona), and Walker's Pub (Athens, Georgia). The fourth group emerged as we moved the project toward its final form and across various procedural checkpoints. Paul Diehl, Sara Mitchell, Cas Mudde, John Vasquez, and Scott Wolford offered us valuable insight into the book publication process, sharing their collective experience with us. That made navigating the process less opaque, which helped tremendously. We also thank our editors at Cambridge University Press, Robert Dreesen and Sara Doskow, who showed confidence in the project and guided it through the publication process. Finally, we owe Jill and Ash a special thanks.

At multiple times, we each announced that we would – well, asked if we could – disappear for a few days to advance the project. The most notable occasions involved a week in June 2018 (Tempe, Arizona) and roughly another week in February 2019 (Athens, Georgia). Our absence often made more work for them, but they kindly adapted and supported us.

One final note: to stave off the questions of curious readers – and ensure they focus on the book's content, as opposed to peculiar details – we note that a coin flip determined author order on this project.

1

Introduction

> The very important role of international boundaries in modern times is underlined by the prolonged negotiation and hard bargaining which often precede their settlement, and also by the promptness with which States react or, at least, are expected to react, against the violation of their territorial sovereignty.
>
> A. O. Cukwurah

1.1 INTRODUCTION

After the establishment of the People's Republic in 1949, the Chinese government set out in earnest to sign treaties that clarified its mutual borders with many of its neighbors – and with good reason. Among the many, diverse states in the international system, China boasts three of the longest interstate land borders in existence (with Russia, Mongolia, and India) and more neighbors (fourteen) than any other country. Settling these borders therefore became important, not merely because state security requires escaping – or at least, productively managing – external threats like territorial challenges, but also because the borders had regularly been disputed, altered, and partially settled at various points in history. The Chinese understood interstate borders to be a source of conflict, one highly salient to the state generally and to the regime's survival in particular.

Puzzlingly, the path to settlement, as well as the success achieved along this path, diverges markedly across China's negotiations with its many neighbors. Two broad outcomes regularly occurred. On the one hand, China engaged in serious confrontations with a handful of neighbors. After failed negotiations to establish a permanent boundary in 1959, for example, India and China began deploying troops, building outposts, and increasing patrols in their disputed border region. Their activities culminated in a Chinese military offensive in

October 1962.[1] Russian and Chinese territorial expansion after 1917 likewise led to decades of border clashes and militarization, including a seven-month crisis in 1969, which started when Chinese troops ambushed Soviet border guards on Zhenbao Island. Finally, the China–Vietnam border followed this path, too. In the aftermath of the Vietnam–United States and Vietnam–Cambodian wars, a series of military engagements occurred in the late 1970s and early 1980s. Among other concerns, China accused Vietnam of both shifting border markers to favor the Vietnamese and occupying its land. The crisis escalated into a brief border war in 1979. In all three cases, disagreements along shared boundaries resulted in multiple crises, troop deployments, repeated military skirmishes, and decades of mutually hostile foreign policies (e.g., geopolitical competition and elevated threats of war). In one of the cases – the Chinese–India border – the status of the boundary remains unsettled, providing a flashpoint for contemporary conflict.[2]

In contrast, China uncontroversially resolved its borders with many other neighbors. Between 1960 and 1963, for example, it signaled an interest in settling its borders with Burma, Mongolia, North Korea, Pakistan, and Afghanistan. Not only did it achieve these settlements through relatively quick rounds of negotiation, but the process also unfolded without violence and, in some cases, with China making significant concessions (Fravel 2008).[3] What explains these two different settlement paths – one relatively peaceful and the other full of repeated violence and stalemate? Why did settlement proceed relatively smoothly in some cases and prove more difficult in others? We argue that the key to explaining these divergent outcomes lies in the characteristics of the exact border under dispute, which affects how easy bargaining over the border's delimitation proceeds, as well as the likelihood that bargaining succeeds.

Interstate borders serve as one of the foundational institutions in modern international relations. Although often taken for granted today, the territorial state – defined through clearly delineated boundaries – is a relatively recent phenomenon in human history. Early hunter-gatherers had conceptions of territory and borders, but these varied greatly across groups and geographic locations (Diener and Hagen 2012). The emergence of empires and city-states

[1] As Ganguly and Pardesi (2020) note, "militarized incidents have come to the fore again. According to the Indian government, the Chinese military crossed into Indian territory 1,025 times between 2016 and 2018." The most recent militarized incident occurred in May 2020. See "Why We Should Worry about China and India's Border Skirmishes," available online at `https://foreignpolicy.com/2020/05/23/india-china-border-skirmishes/` (last accessed May 27, 2020).

[2] Tensions remained high along the Chinese–Indian border as we sent the book to print. US President Donald Trump even offered to mediate in late May 2020. See "Trump Offers to Mediate 'Raging' India-China Border Dispute," available online at `www.usnews.com/news/world/articles/2020-05-27/trump-offers-to-mediate-raging-india-china-border-dispute` (last accessed May 27, 2020).

[3] Evidence suggests that China was also willing to settle with – and make significant concessions to – India at the same time (Fravel 2008; Lamb 1964).

in the ancient world afforded territorial domains greater structure; even then, though, borders often remained ambiguous and likely to overlap. The concept of the state subsequently expanded further still, presumably because of its reliance on land (i.e., agriculture) and people (i.e., a tax base) for its authority. As it did, it came into contact with other expanding states, creating an urgent need to clarify the territorial jurisdictions of geographically proximate states.

The Treaty of Westphalia in 1648 serves as the watershed moment for the modern interstate system – and the territorial state. To be fair, the system it established evolved over centuries. Weaknesses in the various governing systems, such as the feudal system that dominated medieval Europe between the ninth and fifteenth centuries, likely facilitated its arrival (Spruyt 1994; Tilly 1992); yet the Treaty codified the idea of geographic sovereignty – that is, the notion that states hold distinct territories within which they can govern as they see fit, free from the external interference of others. This not only established sovereigns as the highest authority in domestic matters (i.e., within their respective states), but also extended that right to foreign policy interactions as well (i.e., relations between states; see Shaw 2014). Sovereigns gained the exclusive power to make war, peace, and other agreements with their counterparts abroad. The resources with which they could wage these wars (e.g., treasure, people, and taxes), as well as enrich their own well-being, depended intimately on what land belonged to them. The need to define interstate borders thereby gained greater importance.

Despite the salience of borders to the interstate system, little research looks at how states bargain over the placement of their borders, what causes them to fail at border settlement, or what the consequences of that failure are. What, for example, differentiates the borders that China settled relatively easily – and with generous concessions – from those that not only remained unsettled, but also produced protracted, militarized, and violent conflict? Our book addresses this puzzle by answering three interconnected questions. First, what factors facilitate or inhibit the likelihood that neighboring states successfully delimit their mutual, territorial border(s)? Second, should neighbors fail to settle their border(s), what effect does this have on their relationship? Do unsettled borders increase the odds that neighbors develop a hostile competition with one another? And, finally, how do states locked into such hostile competitions eventually settle their disputed borders, and what happens to their relationship when they do?

Revisiting the example of China and her neighbors offers hints at potential answers, ones that we develop throughout the entirety of the book. Most interstate borders settle peacefully, and indeed, Chinese negotiations with Burma, Mongolia, North Korea, Pakistan, and Afghanistan follow this path. Its more intransigent border negotiations, however, reveal a curious trend: the disputed territory in these cases frequently contained a militarily strategic position or economically valuable resources. Much of the border conflict between Russia and China, for example, derives (in part) from the strategic importance of securing possible invasion points along the Amur and Ussuri rivers, protecting transportation routes (e.g., port and railway access), and controlling mountain passes along the China–Mongolia border. India and China likewise dispute border regions in Sikkim and Arunachal Pradesh, the latter of which represents a critical geographical point that India perceives to be essential for the defense of its homeland. And although some of the China–Vietnam border skirmishes relate to Vietnam's conflict with Cambodia, the Sino-Vietnamese conflict over the Paracel and Spratly islands concerns access to the sea and oil resources.[4]

In the end, whether the disputed territory contains a militarily strategic position or economically valuable resources – what we call power endowments – constitutes a major factor that separates cases into the two paths that Chinese border settlements take. Neighboring states that dispute territory lacking power endowments follow the less intransigent settlement path, while those disputing territory that contains power endowments more often experience repeated, protracted bargaining failure. This occurs because power endowments introduce a unique bargaining obstacle: the commitment problem. When combined with other characteristics that accompany bargaining over territorial issues, the commitment problem generates interstate rivalries – that is, intense, hostile relationships in which states perceive one another as threats, enemies, and competitors. After rivalries begin, states must then overcome the commitment problem in order to settle the border and, consequently, to terminate the rivalry that the unsettled border created and sustained.

1.2 THE MAIN ARGUMENT

The book asks two broad questions related to interstate cooperation. First, under what conditions are neighboring states likely to cooperate over their shared borders, and relatedly, under what conditions will cooperation be prone to break down? Second, if cooperation fails and a boundary consequently remains unsettled – defined here as the absence of (an) interstate agreement(s) that delimit(s) the entirety of neighboring states' shared boundary – then what consequences follow?

Questions like these strike at the heart of what it means to be a state in the modern international system. Territorial boundaries define the limits of the sovereign state, determining which state's laws and authority govern a people's daily activity. Moreover, most interstate interactions – including both conflict and cooperation – occur across these borders between neighboring, as opposed to nonneighboring, states. As a result, states hold strong incentives to delimit their borders clearly. Doing so removes a highly salient, contentious issue from their foreign policy agenda with neighboring states, thereby making them

[4] As we note in Chapter 2, we focus on land borders between contiguous states throughout this book. Future work might modify and extend the book's argument to maritime borders, a possibility we discuss in Chapter 9.

more secure and allowing them to divert resources to other policy priorities. It also resolves jurisdictional ambiguity so that economic activity flourishes (e.g., tourism, travel, trade, and investment).

As long as borders remain unsettled, then, states pay numerous direct and opportunity costs. They must defend their claim to disputed land diplomatically, which requires that they prioritize the border over other policy initiatives. Because a competing claim threatens to take a piece of the state, leaders also divert significant resources into the military, fearing that the territorial competition will turn violent (i.e., that one of them will turn to the "outside option" to bargain via war). Whether to prepare for a potential conflict or to deter the adversary from encroaching on its perceived sovereign rights, the state needs a strong military. And finally, when sovereign jurisdiction in the disputed area remains unclear, trade and investment suffer (Simmons 2005). Without a clear understanding of which rules do (or will) govern their activity, economic actors cannot form accurate expectations about what consequences their behavior will have. Economic activity therefore remains depressed – a potentially significant opportunity cost – until the neighboring states sort out the matter.

Given the high potential costs of undelimited (i.e., unsettled) borders, why do borders remain unsettled, sometimes for decades? One theoretical answer derives from the bargaining and enforcement problems that arise when states negotiate over border territory (Fearon 1998). It begins with the above motivations, which encourage neighboring states to work earnestly and quickly to establish their mutual border(s). The involved states encounter two interrelated, common obstacles during this work: a bargaining problem and an enforcement problem. States care about the distribution of the disputed good and bargain hard to ensure they get at least their minimum preferred share. They also want reassurances that any signed agreement will be enforced, although knowing the agreeing must be honored reinforces states' incentive to bargain harder to ensure a favorable deal (Fearon 1998). Bargaining and enforcement concerns are present in any interaction that tries to resolve a disagreement, and scholars have specifically identified information and commitment problems as issues that add friction to these interactions. Our study's main contribution novelly applies bargaining theory to border settlement and rivalry, focusing on the commitment problems that impede the settlement process because they incentivize one party not to honor the agreement in the future. Information-based bargaining problems arise in the border settlement as well, and we consider them as a potential alternative explanation for rivalry development and termination.

An information problem emerges when actors negotiate over the distribution of a good (like border territory), and they each want to maximize their share of it. Whether in business or international relations, how much each negotiator receives depends on its power relative to its counterpart – that is, the costs it will bear in pursuit of the object, how willing it is to forego settlement altogether (i.e., its next best option), and its chances of winning the good via other means (e.g., war; Fisher, Ury, and Patton 1991). Under such conditions, negotiators hold incentives to misrepresent their interests, intentions, strength, and resolve. If a negotiator successfully convinces a counterpart that it has a stronger bargaining position than it actually does, then it should receive better settlement terms. Each side knows this, however, and all negotiators consequently engage in the same behavior. Gaining credible, shared information becomes the key challenge.

A second obstacle concerns the commitment problem. Bargainers that identify an acceptable way to divide the disputed good in question next think about how those settlement terms will be implemented. Any concerns about the implementation phase then, working backwards, affect states' willingness to sign onto the settlement terms they find acceptable (Fearon 1998). The largest such concern includes a rapid, large, potential shift in future power that threatens to undermine the settlement. When a power shift of this type occurs, one state strengthens at the expense of the other. The rising state cannot credibly promise not to renege on the agreement after the settlement shifts power in its favor. If it reneges, it can renegotiate better settlement terms for itself from its position of newfound strength. The declining state, however, anticipates that incentive. Barring protections against the strengthened state reneging and reopening the bargaining process, the weaker state elects to forego settlement altogether, creating an impasse. Nonviolent bargaining fails, settlement stalls, and the bargainers turn to alternative means of managing their dispute – namely, war.

When we apply the logic of information and commitment problems to the border settlement process, two general paths emerge. In the first, neighbors primarily face an information problem. Although a common, noteworthy obstacle to settlement, information problems need not be insurmountable. They complicate negotiators' ability to both find the bargaining range (i.e., the set of all settlement terms that both sides prefer to reaching no settlement at all) and agree upon precise settlement terms that fall within this range. Yet conflict management tools increase the (credible) flow of information between negotiators, thereby offering a way forward. Bilateral negotiation, mediation, and even sometimes war serve this purpose.[5] As the negotiators exchange offers and counteroffers, their assessment of one another's strength theoretically converges, which increases the probability that they reach a settlement.

Three characteristics define this settlement path. First, states employ conflict management, particularly negotiation and mediation, repeatedly. Their efforts may fail, especially early in the process when negotiators must sift through a greater amount of inaccurate information. Each iteration, though, theoretically

[5] Consistent with international relations research, we include good offices, fact-finding, and conciliation under the umbrella of mediation (Greig, Owsiak, and Diehl 2019). International law scholars adopt a different approach (see, e.g., Merrills 2005).

inches the negotiators closer to settlement. Second, the settlement process is less protracted along this path than the second one (described subsequently). This need not imply that settlement proceeds smoothly; indeed, it often moves in fits and starts, with stalled progress along the way. Nevertheless, the larger point remains: this path generally proves easier to travel than the second one. Finally, states along this settlement path resort infrequently to violence. Because negotiators achieve progress at the bargaining table, the need for violence arises less often. Stated differently, as long as negotiators clarify incomplete information via nonviolent conflict management, their need for violence to achieve the same goal declines. Moreover, when violence does arise, it remains isolated and infrequent – used to clarify incomplete information.

The second settlement path arises when bargainers encounter the commitment problem. Numerous circumstances theoretically put the commitment problem's logic in motion (Powell 2006), but we focus on situations in which states bargain over an object that itself contains a source of power (Fearon 1996). Border territory often possess this characteristic. In particular, some territory contains a militarily strategic position (e.g., a valley, high ground, or straits) or economically valuable resources (e.g., natural resources or populations) – what we call "power endowments." These power endowments worry states. A settlement necessarily (re)distributes border territory and, therefore, any power endowments it contains (i.e., at least one side will need to make concessions in order to resolve a competing territorial claim). When the disputed territory lacks power endowments, states expect that a settlement will produce no noteworthy change in their relative power; the redistributed territory carries no accompanying, significant redistribution of power endowments. In contrast, when the disputed territory contains power endowments, states predict that power will quickly (re)distribute after they sign and implement a settlement, and so a commitment problem emerges. Settlement advantages one state, making it more powerful in the post-settlement period. Because a stronger bargainer should get better settlement terms, that state cannot credibly promise not to renege on and renegotiate the settlement from its position of greater, future strength. At the same time, settlement disadvantages the other state, which then fears the vulnerability that a settlement creates, seeks to avoid that vulnerability, and therefore refuses to sign any settlement – even if it finds the settlement terms generally acceptable. The settlement process then stalls.

The characteristics defining this settlement path differ markedly from those that define the first path. Conflict management efforts still occur, as states try to reach a settlement; yet these efforts generally do not move states meaningfully closer to settlement. Negotiation and mediation increase information flows. Because bargainers do not primarily face an incomplete information problem along this path, however, conflict management proves less helpful, unless it can overcome the commitment problem mechanism – that is, unless it prevents a power shift from occurring or reduces the likelihood that a state reneges on a signed settlement. Most, but not all, conflict management efforts fail to address this logic, leaving settlement consistently beyond the disputants' reach.[6]

Scholars posit that, when peaceful conflict management fails, states resolve a commitment problem via war (Powell 2006). This avenue, however, may be neither feasible (e.g., when states are not prepared to fight) nor desirable. To solve a commitment problem via war, states need to destroy the source of power (i.e., prevent the power shift), conquer the territory (i.e., prevent a need to renegotiate for more of the disputed territory later), or remove the foreign government (i.e., the actor who might try to renegotiate later). Problems arise with each option. States do not want to destroy the power endowments, but rather to acquire and hold them; the (modern) international system does not recognize conquest as an appropriate way to acquire territory; and, setting aside the international legal ramifications, replacing a foreign government proves costly – often prohibitively so. Neither conflict management nor the alternatives (e.g., war) move states toward settlement, so the bargaining process becomes protracted and states turn to threats, displays, and uses of violence. Some of this violence escalates to war, but war does not definitely resolve the issue. More often, states engage in aggression and violence short of war; although intended to defend each neighboring state's claim to the disputed territory, these behaviors also sour the neighbors' relationship.

This second path motivates our other question about interstate cooperation: what consequences follow for neighboring states' interactions when border settlement fails? Scholars typically argue that states use war to resolve the bargaining failure that commitment problems create. As we note earlier, however, war may not be possible in the border settlement process – at least, not as a way to *solve* the commitment problem. We therefore derive a novel, alternative policy that states use in such circumstances: a rivalry. When neighboring states dispute power-endowed border territory, they face a commitment problem (i.e., lie along the second settlement path discussed earlier). Nonviolent bargaining fails, and war seems either undesirable or unacceptable. The states still find the territory highly salient, though, and want both to defend their claim to it and to deny their adversary uncontested control over it. They therefore begin a long-term geopolitical competition with each other – conceptualized here as a rivalry (Colaresi, Rasler, and Thompson 2007; Diehl and Goertz 2000). The rivalry offers states a means to continue competing over the disputed territory. It marshals resources and allows states to maintain their defenses, to prepare for any violence that might occur, and to bolster their bargaining power for future negotiations, all while trying to erode the adversary's strength (or bargaining power). Moreover, rivalry results naturally from the recurring violence that lies along the commitment–problem-driven settlement path. This recurring violence creates feelings of threat, enmity, and competition – the hallmarks of interstate

[6] Legal approaches, which increase the cost of reneging on a settlement, constitute an important exception. See Section 1.3.

rivalry. To escape this path (and the related rivalry), states then need to settle their border, which requires overcoming the commitment problem.

1.3 THE ROADMAP

The book follows a path commensurate with the above argument. The first part considers how states navigate the border settlement process generally. It shows that some states reach settlement more easily than others, as well as the conditions under which they do so. The second part of the book then follows the states that struggle to settle their mutual borders. It asks, in particular, what happens to neighboring states' relationship as they try and fail repeatedly to settle their borders. We argue that these states disproportionately encounter a commitment problem, and they initiate a rivalry as a policy response to that problem. Finally, the third part of the book investigates how rivals with unsettled borders can move toward settlement and what happens to their relationship when they succeed. Once again, we propose that rivals with unsettled borders disproportionately face a commitment problem that they find difficult to overcome. Some, but not all, conflict management tools help states surmount this obstacle, and once they clear it, the states' relationship changes fundamentally, from a hostile to a more benign one.

Before delving into the chapter details, we wish to clarify the overall research strategy that guides our investigation. The book presents a causal theory, but does not claim to test that theory or engage in causal inference. It starts with an empirical puzzle – namely, that neighboring states experience divergent outcomes when attempting to settle their borders with one another. It then offers a theoretical argument that makes sense of that puzzle. Finally, we review the data to ascertain whether the patterns that the argument suggests generally and robustly appear there. In other words, although our theory identifies causal relationships, our empirical analysis does not attempt to establish causality.[7] We therefore use causal language when advancing the theoretical argument (or mechanisms), but avoid causal language when discussing the empirical strategy and data analyses. In these latter cases, we instead adopt language that notes whether the patterns within the data are, or are not, consistent with the theoretical arguments' expectations.

Each chapter contributes to the larger theoretical story, developing the detail underlying it and using the above empirical strategy to search for evidence consistent with it. Two important concepts provide the foundation for the entire story: border settlement and commitment problems. In order to ensure conceptual clarity, Chapter 2 first defines and justifies our use of these two concepts. Border settlement, for example, means different things in scholarly research – sometimes "mutual satisfaction" and sometimes "mutual agreement." Mutual

[7] For a discussion of the various ways to pair data with theory, beyond merely theory testing, see Clarke and Primo (2012).

satisfaction, or de facto settlement, exists when neighboring states are content with the current distribution of a given border territory. In contrast, mutual agreement refers instead to de jure settlement, which exists when neighboring states have signed a treaty (i.e., a formal, interstate agreement) that settles their mutual border's delimitation under international law.

Our argument concerns de jure border settlement, measured through the lens of border delimitation agreements, rather than mutual satisfaction with a border's territorial distribution. That decision rests on three considerations. First, mutual satisfaction remains impossible to observe empirically. It is true, for example, that satisfaction demands a lack of conflict, but a lack of conflict itself does not necessarily imply satisfaction. Rivals (e.g., the United States–Soviet Union during the Cold War, or Syria–Israel or India–Pakistan today) often experience periods without active conflict, even though the status quo does not satisfy them (i.e., they are involved in intense, hostile competitions with one another). We therefore cannot use the absence of conflict to track "satisfaction," and we would not want to do so. Because the theoretical relationship between unsettled borders and rivalry – itself correlated with interstate conflict – interests us, measuring unsettled borders through conflict (or its absence) creates a tautology that would undermine the study. We instead need a measure of settlement that does not depend on conflict. No such reasonable measure of de facto settlement exists, so we turn to de jure settlement to achieve that goal.

Second, all neighboring states are preoccupied with the placement of their borders and sign agreements to delimit their respective jurisdictions. The delimitation process therefore appears within all neighboring states' histories, and the public process of reaching and signing agreements places information about de jure settlement prominently in the public domain. Indeed, we have narratives of the border settlement process for most contiguous dyads over the past 200 years.[8] Finally, although other scholars proxy mutual satisfaction, we can directly observe delimitation efforts and outcomes. We prefer a direct approach, as it better ensures that the observed behavior (i.e., the delimitation process) aligns with the concept we wish to capture (i.e., settlement). These considerations lead us to distinguish between de jure border settlement – that is, signing international border agreements that function as international law – and de facto settlement, or satisfaction with the territorial distribution. We adopt the former, which connects our work with the subfields of international law (through interstate treaties and agreements) and international conflict management (through the delimitation process).

The second half of Chapter 2 then centers on our use of a bargaining framework. This framework emphasizes the commitment problem mechanism, which operates when one state expects that its adversary will likely experience

8 We created these narratives for the book project. They are available from the authors upon request.

a large, rapid, future shift in power. Settlement terms depend on the relative power balance between bargainers, including their capability and resolve (Fearon 1995). If, therefore, a state predicts that the relative power balance will change substantially and quickly after signing a settlement, then it expects the settlement itself to be unstable. Once the power shifts in the post-agreement period, the state that the power shift benefits cannot credibly promise not to renege on and renegotiate the settlement terms from a place of newfound strength. This, after all, would give it better terms. The state that the settlement disadvantages, however, knows such an incentive exists. Predicting that it will be vulnerable to the strengthened state's attempts to renegotiate the settlement in the near future, the weakened state therefore foregoes any settlement today. It prefers either to prevent the power shift from happening, or to fight a war over the matter before the power shifts and its prospects for winning deteriorate.

Powell (2006) identifies three types of commitment problems, and we focus on one of these: a power shift that results from bargaining over a good that itself contains a source of power (Fearon 1996). When the disputed good has such a power source, any redistribution of the good – that is, a settlement that necessarily involves concessions from one or more bargainers – will, by definition, shift power. Numerous disputed goods possess such a characteristic, and border territory often does. More specifically, when disputed border territory possesses a militarily strategic position or economically valuable resources – that is, power endowments – then a settlement involving that territory threatens to create a significant, rapid power shift between the bargaining states. This produces a commitment problem that causes bargaining over border territory to break down. To surmount that obstacle, many contend that states go to war; we propose, however, that the same logic results in the emergence of a protracted, geopolitical competition – or an interstate rivalry.

Why would states choose to form a rivalry, rather than go to war, as a means of resolving the commitment problem? Two main reasons exist. First, states may be unable to go to war. Solving the commitment problem requires preventing an expected power shift or precluding a strengthened actor from reneging and renegotiating in the post-settlement period. Scholarship argues that war solves the commitment problem because it does the former. It destroys the source of power, thereby removing the possibility that a power shift occurs. States do not want power endowments destroyed, however; they want to acquire those endowments for themselves. War would not achieve that goal, unless the state could conquer its neighbor, either in part (i.e., the disputed territory) or in whole (i.e., remove the foreign government), and take the disputed territory intact. Historically, this proved a viable option, but the international community refuses to recognize territorial conquest as a legitimate way to manage sovereignty disputes – a trend that has only strengthened over time.[9]

[9] For a historical review, see Hathaway and Shapiro (2017).

With conquest off the table, states need another way to compete over border territory. Rivalry offers one such option.

States may also not be prepared to fight a war in the immediate aftermath of a bargaining failure. War is a costly gamble, with no guarantee of victory, especially among states relatively equal in power. Moreover, states need time to prepare for war – that is, to marshal the material wealth and assets of the state, and to convince relevant domestic and international audiences that war is a worthwhile policy to pursue. They therefore seek alternative means of confronting and hurting their adversary, and rivalry offers them such a means. Since it is a long-term competition, rivalry forces opponents to commit significant resources to a dispute and to adopt costly domestic and foreign policies (e.g., to prioritize the rivalry over other policy initiates, to invest resources in ways they would not otherwise choose, etc.). It also forestalls the need to reach any settlement that might trigger the power shift that states fear.[10] Our theory therefore predicts that when border regions remain unsettled, particularly regions containing power endowments that trigger bargaining failures through the commitment problem logic, the likelihood that neighboring states develop a rivalry increases significantly.

Chapter 3 next theorizes the first step in the book's story arc. It builds a theory of border settlement that relies heavily on the concepts we introduce in Chapter 2. The chapter begins with a review of the vast research on interstate territorial (i.e., border) disputes. This research advances knowledge substantially; nevertheless, it has yet to produce a rigorous theory of how bargaining over borders occurs and why that bargaining succeeds or fails. The argument we subsequently present offers such a theory. It conceptualizes the border settlement process as a standard bargaining game (Fearon 1995; Hopmann 1996). In this game, strong incentives exist for states to reach a settlement; indeed, unsettled borders generate significant opportunity costs that motivate a settlement – and as soon as possible (i.e., actors forego the mutual gains from settlement, which include trade, investment, economic development, tourism, and security). Two prominent bargaining problems, however – information problems and commitment problems – often interfere with states' ability to reach such a settlement.

We explore both of these problems, as well as how conflict management efforts and various dyadic characteristics theoretically (do not) address them. To overcome an information problem, states must find the bargaining range and agree on settlement terms that reside within this range, even as their desire to secure the best deal possible encourages them to misrepresent their true position. Signaling or conveying credible information becomes key in this

10 On some occasions, a rivalry immediately escalates to war. Most often, it does not, however, instead producing a competition in which war remains an outside option to pursue in the future. Wars also rarely end in outright conquest, leaving rivalries (and their disputed issues) to fester, even after war occurs.

process, and we propose a series of factors that might assist in it. These include repeated conflict management (e.g., negotiation and mediation), along with similarity in regime type (e.g., democracy), the relative power distribution, and alliance ties between the bargaining states.

The commitment problem presents a different logic and, consequently, requires a different solution. As we note earlier, some disputed border territory possesses power endowments, which then induce a commitment problem. To resolve such a problem, states must either prevent settlement from shifting relative power – a difficult task with power endowments at stake – or reduce incentives for the state the settlement strengthens to renege and renegotiate after the settlement takes effect. Most conflict management does neither, so the presence of a power endowment generally increases the likelihood of failed settlement (or conversely decreases the likelihood that settlement occurs).

Chapter 4 executes an empirical analysis to establish whether the patterns the above theory suggests generally hold. It starts with a detailed discussion of the border settlement data, including descriptive statistics on patterns of border settlement across space (i.e., region) and time (i.e., 1816–present). It then outlines an empirical strategy for evaluating whether the patterns in the data align with the theory's expectations. That evidence cumulatively yields three main conclusions. First, the patterns we uncover are generally consistent with our theoretical expectations. Neighboring states who primarily face an information problem can overcome it through iterated conflict management, most notably negotiation and mediation. Second, alternatives to our theoretical argument do not seem consistent with the empirical patterns we observe. Border settlement, for example, occurs more often among democratic neighbors, but a small set of cases drives these results (Gibler and Owsiak 2018). Similarly, neither allies nor power-asymmetric dyads are persistently more likely to settle their borders, as theory might predict. Dyadic characteristics alone, in other words, offer a poor avenue through which neighboring states share credible information.

Third, and most importantly for our argument, the regularities that the commitment problem story suggests appear prominently in the data. When disputed territory contains (a) power endowment(s), the probability of bargaining failure – that is, the likelihood that borders do not settle – increases. This result generally holds regardless of how much conflict management occurs, a fact that further supports our argument. Negotiation and mediation primarily promote the exchange of information. Because the commitment problem logic does not stem from incomplete information, though, these conflict management efforts theoretically prove less valuable when commitment problems dominate the bargaining process, no matter how many times states use them. In contrast, legal approaches – that is, arbitration and adjudication – provide a means through which to surmount the commitment problem. Arbitration and adjudication create a legal ruling under international law. States can subsequently violate such a ruling, but not without incurring some material or repetitional costs.

Legal approaches, then, interfere with a state's ability to renege on a settlement in the future, even if that settlement shifts power in its favor. In so doing, these approaches, although not a perfect solution, increase the likelihood that states reach a border settlement. Because states turn to legal approaches infrequently, however, this does not negate our larger point: when neighboring states dispute power-endowed border territory, they are significantly less likely to settle their borders.

The end of Chapter 4 raises a natural question: what happens when states fail to settle their borders? Chapter 5 supplies an answer. In particular, we develop a theoretical argument that links unsettled borders – through the same commitment problem logic – to the formation of interstate rivalries. When a border region contains a potential source of power (i.e., a power endowment), the risk increases that a commitment problem emerges, which then undermines settlement progress. Fearing that a settlement reached today will be unstable tomorrow, states eschew signing a settlement altogether. This leaves borders unsettled, and states invest in various foreign policy tools to compete over the insecure, contested, and valuable unsettled border region, in the hopes of gaining a bargaining advantage that will allow them to achieve a more favorable and durable settlement should they eventually clear the commitment problem. Through such a competition, a rivalry relationship develops between the neighboring states.

Chapter 6 presents the empirical strategy that assesses this portion of our argument. Once again, three main patterns emerge. First and foremost, unsettled borders increase the likelihood of rivalry onset. Such a finding is broadly consistent with our argument, but admittedly leaves the causal mechanism unexplored. The analysis therefore delves further and finds power endowments appear more often when a neighboring dyad has unsettled, as opposed to settled, borders. This demonstrates that power endowments and border (un)settlement go hand-in-hand, exactly as our argument predicts. It is the first step in linking unsettled borders to the causal mechanism we advance, although that causal mechanism admittedly remains untested. Finally, neighboring states are more likely to form rivalries when contesting territory that contains (a) power endowment(s). In the aggregate, such findings coincide with the expectations of the commitment problem argument. Because alternative theoretical arguments once again perform poorly, we have greater confidence that the results obtain because of the mechanism we propose.

Once we know that unsettled borders lead – via a commitment problem – to interstate rivalries, two additional questions arise. How do rivals navigate the border settlement process? Because rivalries constitute a unique interstate relationship, their path to settlement may look similar to that of other dyads (see Chapters 3 and 4), but not necessarily so. Furthermore, once rivals reach a border settlement, what happens to their relationship? It seems likely that the relationship would change fundamentally at this point, since the underlying (commitment) problem that created and sustained the hostile relationship disappeared. Nevertheless, this need not be theoretically true. Rivals link many issues together (Dreyer 2010; Vasquez 2009) and institutionalize their relationship within the policy-making apparatus. A valid argument therefore exists that the rivalry will continue. In response to both questions, further investigation seems warranted.

Chapter 7, the final theoretical chapter, explores these questions, extending the bargaining framework specifically to the rivalry context. We argue that states initiate a rivalry to compete over disputed border territory when nonviolent bargaining fails and they find war either undesirable, unacceptable, or unavailable (Chapters 5 and 6). The incentives to obtain a border settlement, however, do not disappear. States consequently work toward settlement, even as they engage in a rivalrous competition with one another. Nonviolent bargaining efforts generally continue to fail because they do not resolve the commitment problem. Nevertheless, two potential, alternative avenues toward a settlement emerge. On the one hand, legal approaches raise the costs of reneging on a settlement. This undermines the incentives to violate an agreement in the future, thereby increasing the odds of reaching a border settlement today. On the other hand, rivalry itself alters states' calculations. Through building military capacity, rivalry raises the cost of war and mitigates concerns that a (re)distribution of the disputed territory will change relative power significantly. This, in turn, bolsters a potential settlement's stability, thereby encouraging states to sign it. Both avenues require time to unfold. States will turn to legal approaches only after exhausting other options, since these approaches significantly limit their control over the dispute's management and outcome. Similarly, for states to feel secure, they need time to devote and accumulate significant resources to be used for winning the competition. We therefore expect rivalries driven by commitment problem logic to be longer and more violent than other types of rivalries (i.e., rivals disputing power endowments will take longer to settle their borders and have longer rivalries).

Once they settle their borders, however they do so, we next argue that rivals' relationship fundamentally changes. Resolving the commitment problem mechanism (i.e., reaching border settlement) necessarily removes the force that produced and sustained the rivalry. Absent this force, the motivation for the rivalrous competition dissipates, creating space for less hostile relations to develop. In this way, border settlement increases the likelihood that a rivalry ends. Yet even if it does not immediately end, the removal of the same force should change rivals' behavior toward one another fundamentally. Any disputes that arise among the rivals after border settlement should be less frequent, shorter, and less severe.

In Chapter 8, we develop a modeling strategy and report empirical patterns related to this portion of the argument. The myriad yield five broad conclusions consistent with our theory. First, rivals disputing power-endowed territory are less likely to reach border settlement. This aligns with both general models of border settlement (see Chapters 3 and 4) and the expectation that rivalries form because of the commitment problems that power-endowed territory generate (see Chapters 5 and 6). Second, although negotiation and mediation generally help rivals settle their borders, they only do so when rivals dispute territory that lacks power endowments (i.e., face an information problem). The introduction of power endowments – that is, the commitment problem – renders these tools relatively unhelpful in the settlement process, as our theory would predict. Third, legal approaches, which interfere with the commitment problem's logic, *can* help rivals achieve border settlement when they dispute power-endowed territory. These approaches still prove more helpful when states dispute territory that lacks power endowments, but their usefulness for addressing the commitment problem stands in stark contrast to that of the alternative conflict management tools available (e.g., negotiation and mediation).

Fourth, if rivals overcome their commitment problem – that is, they obtain border settlement, however they do so – the likelihood rises that the rivalry ends. We connect this finding to the expectations of the commitment problem logic as well. Rivalries end less frequently when power endowments are present; thus, border settlement fosters rivalry termination when states have cleared the commitment problem that plagues their bargaining. And finally, even if a rivalry persists after border settlement, the disputes that the rivals experience are significantly shorter and less severe. These regularities in the data are, in aggregate, consistent with expectations that border settlement fundamentally transforms rivalry relationships – indicating, once again, that the commitment problem we identify in certain (i.e., power-endowed) border territory fosters and may sustain the rivalries we study throughout the book. Resolving that bargaining obstacle alters how neighboring states interact and behave.

Chapter 9, the concluding chapter, then ties everything back together again. It first supplies a more detailed overview of the theoretical argument, as well as the various empirical patterns consistent with it – drawn largely from the summary tables that conclude each empirical chapter. Next, it establishes five prominent paths forward for future research. These include theorizing the border settlement process further, identifying the other paths to rivalry, explaining why some rivalries persist after border settlement, exploring the logic behind legal approaches' effectiveness in greater detail (including alternative logics), and extending the argument to maritime borders. The chapter then ends with a discussion about the policy implications of our study.

PART I

THE SETTLEMENT OF BORDERS

2

Conceptual Foundations

> [W]hile resolution is unattainable, a decisive military victory is equally unattainable.... Consequently, the parties are trapped between their ongoing interest in maintaining the rivalry and avoiding a compromise resolution, and their inability to impose a favorable outcome on each other.
>
> G. Blum

2.1 INTRODUCTION

Two concepts form the core of the theoretical argument that we present throughout this book: settled borders and commitment problems. The concept of border settlement appears frequently in research on territorial interstate conflict.[1] It can, however, encompass either mutual agreement on *or* mutual satisfaction with (i.e., acceptance of) a territorial border division, and scholars sometimes slip between these two meanings. Our argument relies on a conceptualization of border settlement as the mutual *agreement* of a border's delimitation under international law (Owsiak 2012; Owsiak, Cuttner, and Buck 2018). The first part of this chapter discusses the evolution of research on interstate borders, explains the rationale for defining settled borders as we do, and examines the implications of adopting our definition.

We also argue that the lack of border settlement contributes to interstate rivalry via a commitment problem, and this, too, requires explication before we advance our argument. The study of rivalry constitutes a prolific research program.[2] We offer an innovation within this program by connecting rivalries to the bargaining model of war. In particular, we argue that many unsettled

[1] See, for example, Gibler (2012), Huth and Allee (2002), Kocs (1995), Owsiak (2012), Simmons (2002, 2005), and Vasquez (2009).

[2] For overviews and foundational works, see Diehl and Goertz (2000, 2012), Colaresi, Rasler, and Thompson (2007), and Valeriano (2012).

borders are the product of a commitment problem. Scholars generally believe that commitment problems are one type of negotiating obstacle that results in bargaining breakdown and violent conflict – particularly war (Fearon 1995; Powell 2006); yet we propose that states might manage commitment problems through interstate rivalries as well. The second part of the chapter therefore explains the origins of commitment problems and why initiating and maintaining a rivalry might be a valid method for managing certain subsets of them.

2.2 CONCEPTUALIZING SETTLED BORDERS

Scholars frequently proclaim the dangers of territorial conflict, and the evidence in favor of their position is overwhelming.[3] States involved in a territorial claim are at increased risk of militarized (low-level) conflict. Once militarized, territorial disputes then tend to recur, involve higher levels of severity, and escalate to war more often than nonterritorial disputes (Hensel 1996; Quackenbush 2010; Senese and Vasquez 2008). Importantly, these empirical tendencies dominate the entire post-Westphalian history; indeed, territorial issues underlie the majority of all wars between 1648 and 1989 (Holsti 1991, 308). In short, territorial disagreements regularly evoke interstate violence, whether low-level militarized conflict or war.

As the research program on territorial conflict matured, it moved beyond these general, foundational observations to examine different *types* of territorial conflict, under the assumption that not all territorial disagreements are alike. This work produces a consensus that interstate borders, as a subset of all possible territory, embody the fault lines at most risk of interstate conflict (Gibler 2012; Kocs 1995; Owsiak 2012; Vasquez (1993, 2009). To be fair, this position is not entirely new. It often appears implicitly in much earlier international relations research. Boulding (1978, x), for example, discusses the emergence of stable peace among states, noting that "in peace, we refrain from doing a great number of physically possible things which we do not refrain from doing in war, like bombing cities or invading territories." In addition, he observes the dangers of territorial expansion specifically (44), as well as mobilizing forces to the "frontier" (i.e., border; 35). Two implicit assumptions underlie these various observations: (i) that states can clearly define the frontiers to which troops mobilize or across which they invade and (ii) that conflict will occur at these frontiers, for state expansion will be possible only until another state impedes it. Similarly, Morgenthau ([1948]1985, 125–126) compares the security that predetermined, natural borders afford states (e.g., the United Kingdom's separation from Europe via the English Channel or Italy's separation from Europe via the Alps) to the insecurity that accompanies borders without predetermined natural features (e.g., the French–German border or Russia's

[3] For an overview of this research, see Tir and Vasquez (2010).

European borders). Although not his main point, Morgenthau underscores that conflict results when actors cannot agree – through geographic focal points or other means – on the limits of their respective sovereign jurisdictions.

Recent research discusses the dangers of unsettled borders more explicitly. From an empirical perspective, Kocs (1995), Huth (1996), and Owsiak (2012) each define territorial disagreements as largely involving contests over the placement of interstate borders.[4] Any subsequent analysis of these disagreements then necessarily becomes about interstate borders.[5]

From a more theoretical perspective, numerous scholars advance theories of interstate conflict in which border contestation plays a critical role. Three prominent examples highlight this trend. First, Vasquez (2009) proposes a steps-to-war theory that rests on territoriality – or the tendency of humans to divide the world into and defend geographic political units (see also Senese and Vasquez 2008). Such a tendency necessarily produces territorial disagreements among states, and these disagreements militarize because states (have) learn(ed) that aggression (e.g., military force and violence) is the most effective way to manage them. Given these premises, the theory predicts that interstate conflict will occur most frequently between political units (i.e., states), generally along the boundaries where their jurisdictions collide. Once neighboring states agree upon the placement of their mutual borders, though, conflict becomes significantly less prevalent.

Gibler (2012) subsequently builds on Vasquez's work, as well as theories about war-making/ state-making.[6] He argues that unsettled borders constitute a highly salient, external threat. To address it, a state both militarizes to prepare for successful aggression and centralizes decision-making authority in the executive to ensure efficient protection against the threat. When the external threat disappears (i.e., the border settles), the nondemocratic pressures ease. The state no longer can justify high levels of militarization easily. The rationale for strong militarization ceases to exist, citizens demand other benefits for their continued taxation, and, as a result, the state must deploy resources differently to meet their demands. At the same time, other institutional actors place greater constraints on executive authority, producing a more decentralized decision-making process. Democracy therefore finds a more fertile environment in which to grow after border settlement occurs. In this way, (un)settled borders contribute to both conflict/peace and regime type (i.e., non/democratic governments).[7]

4 See also Huth and Allee (2002) and Hensel et al. (2008).

5 Distinctions exist between territorial claims and disputes on the one hand, and border settlement on the other. We discuss this more subsequently and use "disagreement" as a broader term to cover the general contestation over territorial issues.

6 See, for example, Tilly (1992) and Rasler and Thompson (2012).

7 A lengthy body of research explores the nexus between territorial/border disagreements, interstate conflict, and democratization. See, for example, Gibler (2012), Park and James (2015), and Owsiak (2019).

Finally, Simmons (2005), Carter and Goemans (2011), and Abramson and Carter (2016) propose that borders are institutions – or "set[s] of rules, compliance procedures, and moral and ethical behavioral norms designed to constrain behavior" (Simmons 2005, 827). When borders are settled, the involved states know and agree upon the rules, procedures, and norms associated with these borders. This reduces both jurisdictional uncertainty (i.e., which rules apply in a given situation) and policy uncertainty (i.e., whether actors might abruptly change or misapply the rules). As uncertainty falls, political and economic behavior gains predictability; thus, after border settlement, interstate trade rises, as investors and traders hold clearer expectations about what will happen in their transactions (Simmons 2005), and militarized conflict falls, as neighboring states fear fewer highly salient threats to their jurisdictional sovereignty (Carter and Goemans 2011; Owsiak 2012). Moreover, this reduced uncertainty persists because border settlement serves as a focal point, locking-in the stability associated with it. Indeed, territorial claims fall after border settlement (Owsiak, Cuttner, and Buck 2018), particularly if that settlement follows a historical precedent (Carter and Goemans 2011).

Theoretical arguments like those presented earlier each depend on knowing when states have settled their borders, thereby removing contestation over border territory from their foreign policy agenda. As we show subsequently, however, border settlement is conceptually challenging to unpack, and some slippage often exists between what scholars argue theoretically and what they study empirically. We therefore believe that (re)conceptualizing border settlement not only aids in understanding our argument but also demonstrates how our work contributes to existing research on territorial conflict, international cooperation, international conflict management, and interstate rivalries.

2.2.1 Unpacking Border Settlement

Theoretical arguments involving "border settlement" generally maintain that border settlement exists when neighboring states agree upon and accept their respective sovereign jurisdictions. Agreement and acceptance, however, are two distinct matters. Agreement constitutes de jure settlement – that is, settlement grounded in international law. The current international legal system recognizes states as the highest organizational unit of the system and accordingly bestows key rights upon them – namely, that of sovereignty, which "expresses internally the supremacy of the governmental institutions and externally the supremacy of the state as a legal person" (Shaw 2008, 487). Numerous consequences follow from this right (Shaw 2008). States must first determine the limits of one another's sovereign jurisdictions. This requires a territorial distribution – for the state, as a unit, cannot exist independently of territory, and territory unattached to a state has no autonomous international legal standing (Sharma 1997; Shaw 1982, 2008). Once states divide territory among themselves, they must subsequently recognize and respect one another's territorial integrity, remaining out of one another's affairs. Were they to do otherwise, they would critically undermine the sovereignty norm and, therefore, their foundational right. Lastly, states must preserve and protect the larger territorially defined system they create (Shaw 1982), as each individual state's rights necessarily depend on the system's survival. Because of these consequences, territorial distribution plays a prominent, foundational role in the international legal system, and neighboring states execute agreement over territorial distributions via a legal (i.e., de jure) instrument: international boundary treaties. States also cannot unilaterally abrogate these treaties under international law – at least not easily.[8] This makes de jure settlement irreversible under international law in the absence of mutual consent, a point to which we return subsequently.

In contrast to de jure settlement, acceptance of sovereign jurisdiction concerns de facto settlement – that is, settlement based upon actors' satisfaction with a territorial distribution. A state's satisfaction with a border delimitation exists independently of any de jure settlement, although the two are related. One would expect, for example, that those creating and signing international border agreements accept the territorial distribution to which they agree. Although generally true, states – including a state's leadership or its citizenry – occasionally become dissatisfied with previous agreements, as Ecuador did after discovering the Cenepa River system along its Peruvian border in the wake of the 1942 Rio Protocol (see also China–Vietnam; Day 1987). In this case, Ecuador signaled de facto dissatisfaction, even though it could not renege on its de jure agreement.[9] At other times, citizens ignore legal (de jure) boundaries because the resources that traverse an interstate border matter more to their daily lives than international legal issues. Thus, the nomadic people in the Ogaden region historically received special permission in treaties to cross (or in a sense, ignore) the legal border between Ethiopia and British Somalia.[10] Finally, those involved in intrastate conflict frequently use legal borders strategically to mount attacks on other governments (e.g., see Democratic Republic of the Congo–Rwanda), or citizens cross borders to escape such conflicts (e.g., Afghanistan–Iran or Ghana–Togo). This creates de facto instability in the border region (Gibler 2012; Owsiak, Diehl, and Goertz 2017). In each of these cases, although the motivation varies, at least one actor does not accept the legal border in practice – that is, the border lacks de facto settlement.

If border settlement concerns agreement on (i.e., de jure settlement) and acceptance (i.e., de facto settlement) of interstate border delimitations, then

8 See Article 62(2) of the 1969 Vienna Convention on Law of Treaties. See also Kocs (1995) and Cukwurah (1967).

9 Ecuador argued that it *could* renege on its de facto settlement. The Guarantor nations to the Rio Protocol, however, declared Ecuador's arguments invalid (see Day 1987, 420–425), and the Vienna Convention on the Law of Treaties (1969) supports the Guarantors' position.

10 See also winter pasture issues along the Afghanistan–Iran border (Biger 1995; Day 1987).

the primary question for conceptualizing border settlement becomes: what *defines* the agreement and acceptance of border delimitation? Paradoxically, most scholars to date answer this question indirectly – focusing not on manifestations of acceptance and agreement, but rather on what constitutes the *rejection* of interstate border delimitations. Simmons (2005) offers an illustration. She proposes that interstate borders function as institutions and that institutional certainty (i.e., border agreement) facilitates trade. To test this argument, she relies on territorial claim data from Huth (1996), which identify instances when states actively contest one another's sovereign jurisdiction – not when they agree on and accept it. Similarly, Vasquez (2009) argues that more peaceful interstate relationships follow when neighboring states agree on the placement of their interstate border; he then uses data on militarized interstate disputes (MIDs) that occur over territorial issues to identify the dyads that do *not* agree upon and militarily contest the territorial status quo.

Using "rejection" to capture either "agreement" of "acceptance" is inappropriate in the context of border settlement. It assumes causal symmetry – that is, that the absence of factors that cause "not agreement" (i.e., rejection) necessarily means "agreement" exists (Goertz and Mahoney 2012).[11] On a conceptual level, this is not logically true. If, for example, a group deciding where to eat dinner chooses not to reject a restaurant option, we would not automatically conclude that they *agreed on* that option; we would instead conclude that the option remained on the table for a *possible* agreement, which had yet to occur. Empirical data confirm such causal asymmetry in the context of interstate borders. Territorial claims data derive from official, public statements in which two or more states contest sovereignty over a particular piece of land (Frederick, Hensel, and Macaulay 2017; Huth and Allee 2002). These claims, in other words, capture rejections of a border.[12] Were rejection and agreement (or acceptance) two sides of the same coin, one would expect active claims to exist always and only when neighboring states have not signed international agreements that delimit their mutual border. Owsiak, Cuttner, and Buck (2018) show that does not happen. Claims do not always exist where borders remain unsettled under international law (e.g., see Kenya–Sudan or India–Bhutan), and they occasionally arise after border settlement occurs (e.g., Ecuador–Peru or China–Vietnam).[13] A failure to reject the territorial status quo (i.e., initiate a territorial claim) is therefore not identical to having achieved border settlement. Likewise, possessing de jure border settlement does not imply that actors cannot raise territorial claims. Agreement and acceptance

[11] An empirical illustration of causal asymmetry appears in Owsiak, Diehl, and Goertz (2017).

[12] Most territorial claims involve border territory. In fact, Huth and Allee (2002) largely define them this way.

[13] On this point, see also Cukwurah (1967).

of border delimitation, on the one hand, and the failure to reject border delimitation, on the other, are not equivalent.[14]

A similar problem arises with respect to militarized disputes. An MID occurs when one state displays, threatens, or uses force against another state in the international system (Palmer et al. 2015). States use the military in pursuit of their foreign policy goals – that is, to manage an issue on their foreign policy agenda. Nevertheless, militarization is not the dominant tool through which states manage their territorial disagreements. Hensel et al. (2008) gather data on the management of territorial claims and report that MIDs appear in a mere 3.17% of their territorial claim-year observations; stated differently, of the 10,041 total years in which two states contest ownership of territorial space during the period 1816–2001, states use the military to manage their territorial disagreements in only 318 of those years (see also Owsiak, Cuttner, and Buck 2018). Owsiak (2012) obtains a similar finding with respect to de jure border settlement. Of the 2,790 contiguous dyad-years that lack border settlement, only 256 (9.18%) contain MIDs. Whether we define rejection of the territorial status quo as active contestation of territorial sovereignty (i.e., the existence of a territorial claim) or the absence of de jure border settlement, using MIDs to track this rejection misses 90–97% of the "rejection cases" that other scholars believe exist. This occurs because rejection of the status quo and how to pursue that rejection are two distinct matters. Thus, even if we set aside the issue of causal asymmetry noted earlier, MIDs alone cannot appropriately or accurately track the failure to accept or agree upon the territorial status quo.

Gibler (2012) provides an exception to the above critique, thereby coming closest to capturing the "acceptance," as opposed to "rejection," of interstate borders. He conceives border settlement as a function of focal points.[15] According to Schelling (1960, 70–71), a focal point is a "particular outcome" with "intrinsic magnetism," which derives from "intuitively perceived mutual expectations." Faced with a strategic situation in which bargaining actors must find a mutually acceptable solution among a range of possibilities, Schelling proposes that some solutions possess inherent appeal because they appear more likely to be accepted than the alternatives – for example, meeting at noon in a prominent location when those meeting have not specified time or place in advance and cannot communicate further with one another.

[14] Quantitative social scientists will recognize that this sounds similar to discussions about how to interpret null results. As Greene (2012, 109) notes: "Not rejecting the null hypothesis is not equivalent to 'accepting' it – though the language might suggest so."

[15] Gibler (2012) frequently uses the term "border stability," but also regularly mentions "border settlement." For example, he writes that "As a result of settling their borders, neighbors should experience greater chances of both having a peaceful relationship and becoming democratic" (Gibler 2012, 114). This summarizes his territorial peace argument, and we therefore conclude that his argument rests on border settlement (i.e., acceptance), which he then measures through border stability (i.e., focal points). The underlying assumption is that stability facilitates settlement.

Gibler applies this same logic to border settlement, identifying the factors that might create or alter the acceptance (i.e., de facto settlement) of interstate borders – operationalized through focal points. For example, he argues that, inter alia, geographic features like mountains (Gibler 2007) or differences in colonial parent states (Gibler 2007, 2012) coordinate and sustain the acceptance of borders – the former because they offer a geographically noteworthy landmark and the latter because the agreements among colonial parent states created a focal point for future borders as they divided colonial spheres of influence (on the latter, see also Carter and Goemans 2011). In contrast, relative capabilities of the involved states, the age of the border under consideration, militarized conflict, civil war, and territorial transfers threaten to change existing border focal points (Gibler 2012, 117–123). A state that gains power relative to its counterpart may seek to redistribute territory, while a state losing power might anticipate and seek to forestall such a redistribution (e.g., the Paraguayan war of 1864; Weisiger 2013). Militarized conflict, including civil wars, may not only upset the existing territorial status quo but suggest a new one instead (e.g., the changing hands of Alsace-Lorraine between France and Germany). And border focal points might entrench as the border ages (e.g., Spain–Portugal), while territorial transfers substitute a new focal point for a previous one (e.g., the Colombia–Venezuela acceptance of a 1922 arbitral award). In this way, Gibler uses indirect measures (i.e., proxy variables) to capture focal points, which he argues affect de facto settlement.

Focal points undoubtedly play a prominent role in the border settlement process, and two potential theoretical relationships exist, corresponding to two distinct coordination problems.[16] The first coordination problem involves where to place the border. Focal points *facilitate* border settlement here. Gibler's (2012) work envisions such a relationship, which explains why he measures border settlement through various factors that produce and sustain border focal points. Because his indirect measurement is not ideal for our purposes, however, we pursue an alternative that both better captures the concept of border settlement and avoids the criticisms we raise (see the subsequent discussion). The second coordination problem concerns how actors behave after border settlement occurs – that is, whether settlement subsequently coordinates political, social, and economic behavior. In this case, border settlement (e.g., an agreement) might itself *become* a focal point that reduces jurisdictional uncertainty, thereby encouraging greater cooperation. This makes a border settlement likely to persist if it exists, since it will be costly to change jurisdictional boundaries once in place.

Despite any potential relationship between focal points and border settlement, we disagree with how Gibler (2012) approaches the relationship between focal points and border settlement. Proxy (i.e., focal point) variables do not cleanly capture de facto settlement. They theoretically identify settlement terms

[16] We thank Scott Wolford for suggesting this organization.

that states are more likely to use than others, but do not indicate whether states actually *agree on* or *accept* those terms in practice. Focal points, by definition, raise the likelihood of agreement or acceptance and even predict the content of settlement agreements.[17] They also suggest that certain terms, if chosen, will be difficult to change and therefore relatively stable. After all, although "the rationale may not be strong at the arbitrary 'focal point,' ... at least it can defend itself with the argument 'If not here, where [else]?'" (Schelling 1960, 70). This theoretical argument, however, misses the point. It answers the question "what form will *de facto* settlement likely take?" but not "did de facto settlement occur?"[18] This distinction matters greatly because the theoretical arguments linking border settlement and conflict depend on the answer to the latter question, not the former. If scholars posit that accepted and agreed upon borders change behavior, then one needs to know whether that agreement and acceptance took place, not whether it would be stable if it existed.

To be fair, Gibler (2012) takes an indirect approach to studying de facto settlement for solid theoretical reasons. He correctly concludes that the acceptance of borders (i.e., de facto settlement) cannot be easily observed empirically. After all, states satisfied with a territorial distribution do not repeatedly profess or act on that satisfaction in observable ways. Moreover, he wishes to avoid using conflict (e.g., MIDs) or territorial disputes to identify (un)settled borders (as other researchers do), primarily because he wants to study the effect of settled borders on conflict and recognizes that measuring the former through the latter would preclude this possibility. We understand and appreciate these concerns, fully aware that Gibler's work has provided substantial theoretical and empirical insights into the relationship between border settlement, interstate conflict, and democratic regimes. Nonetheless, we believe that an indirect approach like his is not necessary when the possibility of directly capturing border settlement exists.[19] We return to this point subsequently.

We also disagree with Gibler's (2012) exclusive focus on de facto settlement, at the expense of de jure settlement. We can observe de jure settlement

17 Many rivers and mountain crests become interstate borders for exactly this reason (Cukwurah 1967; Schelling 1960). Border areas commonly contain multiple focal points, however. If one were to use a river as an interstate border, for example, the focal point could be the thalweg (i.e., the middle of the principal navigable channel) or either bank of the river (e.g., see the Nicaragua–Costa Rica border, as described in "Dispute Regarding Navigational and Related Rights (Costa Rica v. Nicaragua)," judgment of July 13, 2009, International Court of Justice (ICJ), available online at `www.icj-cij.org/docket/files/133/15321.pdf`). In such cases, states might select one of the focal points based on precedents set in other border delimitations (see Clay and Owsiak 2016). Regardless, the delimitation terms should arise from *one* of the focal points more often than not.

18 Rasler and Thompson (2011) note that Gibler's measures focus on border *instability* (i.e., the de facto rejection of borders). If true, then our earlier critique applies – namely, that causes of border stability and border instability are not necessarily symmetric (see earlier discussion; Goertz and Mahoney 2012).

19 For a similar critique, see Owsiak (2012) and Rasler and Thompson (2011).

directly for *all* neighboring states in the international system. Because territorial jurisdiction forms the foundation of the international system, all neighboring states either delimit their borders via public interstate agreements or recognize the importance of eventually doing so. In other words, de jure settlement is a universally applicable, directly observable concept – one that explicitly captures whether two states *actually agree* on their border's delimitation. De facto border settlement is nearly impossible to observe empirically, but de jure settlement is not.

The threat that underlies many theoretical arguments – including, inter alia, Gibler (2012), Simmons (2002, 2005), and Vasquez (2009) – also depends on de jure settlement, as opposed to de facto settlement. When Simmons, for example, theorizes about the importance of jurisdictional clarity for increasing economic activity, that clarity results from de jure border settlement; it allows economic actors to know precisely "who has the authority to make, apply, and adjudicate rules within a particular territory," which provides a conducive environment for economic activity to flourish (Simmons 2005, 823). Similarly, Vasquez (2009) argues that territoriality motivates states to divide the world into territorial units. Focal points (e.g., geographically salient characteristics, such as a river) facilitate this division but are neither necessary nor sufficient for it to occur (Vasquez 2009, 155–156). Settlement therefore must depend on more than focal points alone; indeed, Vasquez seemingly has de jure settlement in mind, for he discusses the challenges that emerge when revolutionary states try to change "existing boundaries."[20] Most states treat boundaries as "in existence" once de jure settled (i.e., delimited via interstate agreement), even when colonial powers settled the border before newer states gained independence.[21] In the end, de jure settlement seems to align closest with the arguments that scholars advance.

Finally, focal points may behave differently before and after de jure border settlement. Gibler (2012) examines two sets of characteristics: those likely to produce a focal point (e.g., the colonial heritage of the involved states, which proxies whether a colonial power previously drew a clear border) and those likely to disrupt an existing focal point. The latter characteristics are "behavioral indicators of conditions likely to affect the legitimacy of *previously drawn borders*" (emphasis ours; Gibler 2012, 120). These include the relative capabilities and militarization levels of the involved states, age of the border under examination, whether territorial transfers or territorial disputes exist between the involved states, and whether the involved states experience a civil war. Empirical evidence suggests that the effects of these factors may vary across

[20] See also Maoz (1989).

[21] This is the principle of *uti possidetis* (see Shaw 2008, 525–528). Based on this principle, Gibler's reliance on colonial heritage to proxy whether borders are "defined" essentially means that he uses de jure settlement (i.e., delimitation under international law) to proxy de facto settlement (i.e., acceptance of the territorial distribution). We agree with giving de jure settlement priority over de facto settlement, for the various reasons outlined here, and adopt this position throughout the book.

the pre- and post-de jure settlement periods. Territorial transfers, for example, become less common after de jure settlement. Those that occur also result less frequently from conquest, involve less violence, and concern significantly less territorial area (Owsiak, Cuttner, and Buck 2018). We consequently need to know the status of interstate borders under international law before considering focal points further.

Given the earlier discussion, we propose that de jure settlement – that is, agreement on the delimitation of interstate borders under international law – constitutes the appropriate conceptual focus for our study. Although de facto border settlement – that is, satisfaction with, or mutual acceptance of, the territorial distribution – cannot be directly observed empirically, de jure settlement can, for every contiguous dyad in the interstate system during the last 200 years. Moreover, the factors that affect de facto border settlement often affect de jure settlement (e.g., colonially drawn borders) too or require that we know the border's de jure settlement status first (e.g., territorial transfers, or changes in relative capability). We therefore prioritize de jure settlement, and for the remainder of the book, we use the term "border settlement" to refer to "de jure border settlement" specifically.

Defining Characteristics of Border Settlement

Border settlement exists when a pair of neighboring states (i.e., a "contiguous dyad") has delimited the entirety of its mutual border(s) through one or more international agreements. We operationalize this definition in detail in Chapter 4. In this section, however, we entertain two additional theoretical questions that our conceptualization generates. First, why focus on the delimitation of interstate borders, as opposed to their demarcation? Second, do border agreements function as focal points, making agreed upon delimitations subsequently difficult to change?

Delimitation and demarcation are related, but distinct, processes (Cukwurah 1967, 27–29). States delimit a border when they (or third parties) determine a border's location on a map. In contrast, they demarcate a border when they mark that border physically in the field, usually by placing relatively permanent pillars, markers, or signs on the earth's surface. Delimitation therefore almost always precedes demarcation, for states cannot place markers in the field before they understand where the border should be.

Our conceptualization stresses delimitation, as opposed to demarcation, for both theoretical and empirical reasons. On a theoretical level, politics play out more heavily in the delimitation than the demarcation process. During delimitation, political leaders negotiate the details of where the border will be placed. These negotiations can be contentious, often stalling and failing, which results in borders that remain undelimited for decades. In fact, state leaders worry so much about being "locked into" a particular border delimitation that they opt to sign an explicitly designated, temporary agreement – such as a *modus vivendi* (i.e., a provisional arrangement concerning the border) –

instead of a border delimitation agreement when they expect that they cannot live with a given border delimitation indefinitely.[22] As a result, when states sign a delimitation agreement, we can more easily conclude that they not only have agreed on the border's placement, but also intended their agreement to govern that placement permanently, since border treaties cannot be unilaterally changed under international law. Delimitation of a border's entirety therefore constitutes a transformative moment in border relations. Prior to this, neighboring states disagree about the placement of at least a part of their mutual border; afterward, however, they agree on where the entire border should be.[23] This "full agreement" aligns delimitation with the concept of border settlement (see earlier discussion), making it an appropriate way to conceptualize border settlement in practice.

One might nonetheless still ask whether demarcation requires agreement as well? Although it does, using demarcation agreements to capture border settlement will be inferior to using delimitation agreements. States treat demarcation as a function of delimitation – that is, demarcation involves the "laying down" of an already "mutually defined" (i.e., delimited) line on the ground (Cukwurah 1967, 28). Delimitation agreements reflect this subservient relationship, for they regularly contain instructions asking a field team to execute a delimitation agreement's terms (e.g., see Colombia–Peru agreement of 1851; Ireland 1938, 197). Demarcation therefore flows from delimitation and cannot deviate substantially from it unless a major misstep occurs during the delimitation process. Although a distinct possibility if political leaders or third parties delimit borders without fully understanding the border area's typology, even when such missteps arise, states tellingly halt demarcation and return to delimitation. For example, Argentina and Bolivia attempted to delimit their border in 1891, but "the line described in 1891 proved very difficult actually to locate on the ground, because of the geographical misconceptions which it perpetuated," including where to find the referenced ridges (e.g., "the highest") in the border area and how ravines emptied into one another (Ireland 1938, 6–7). As a result, they halted demarcation and returned to delimitation, ultimately signing additional delimitation treaties (e.g., in 1925). Such behavior suggests that delimitation constitutes a higher, more primary political hurdle than demarcation, with the latter applying a delimitation agreement states have already reached. To the extent that we wish to know when states have successfully navigated the political process associated with reaching *agreement* on the border's placement (i.e., border settlement), delimitation, rather than demarcation, seems to be the appropriate benchmark.

[22] For illustrations of this behavior, see, for example, Ireland (1938) on Latin America.

[23] We discuss partial delimitation in Chapter 4. We consider a border "settled" when states have delimited it in full.

On a more empirical level, states also explicitly sign delimitation treaties. Besides being well-publicized, these empirically observable documents give borders international legal recognition (Shaw 2008; see also 1969 Vienna Convention on the Law of Treaties). Separate demarcation treaties, however, are rarer. States do not ignore the demarcation in public venues; they often signal when demarcation has ended and that its results are agreeable, usually through an exchange of diplomatic notes or the release of a demarcation commission report.[24] These notes do not carry the same status as treaties under international law. Moreover, they are less well-publicized than, prove more difficult to locate than, and may, consequently, be more absent from historical accounts than delimitation treaties. The empirical danger to using demarcation to denote border settlement, then, is that we often will not know when demarcation agreement exists for many pairs of neighboring states. The same challenge does not arise with delimitation agreements.

In the end, we believe that delimitation comes closer than demarcation to capturing what scholars mean conceptually by border settlement. Not only does delimitation precede and generate the subsequent demarcation process, but states must also sign treaties to delimit borders. These treaties widely broadcast the involved states' commitments to one another and carry international legal obligations, thereby reducing states' ability to feign agreement or sign agreements frivolously. When we observe a delimitation treaty, we can therefore conclude that states have successfully and indefinitely negotiated their border's placement. Their border is settled under international law.

A second question that stems from our conceptualization of border settlement is whether border delimitation agreements function as focal points. We conclude that they do. A focal point helps actors' expectations converge on a mutually acceptable outcome when many outcomes are possible. Schelling (1960, 71) proposes that "any element that qualitatively distinguishes ...[an outcome] from surrounding" ones can create a focal point. A border delimitation agreement does this. It "defends itself with the argument": if we do not agree that the border belongs here, where else should we draw it? (Schelling 1960, 70). Given an infinitely available number of ways to draw a border, an existing agreement focuses states' attention on a much smaller subset of possible outcomes – making the terms of the agreement stand out from the alternative options available. Through this characteristic, delimitation agreements increase jurisdictional certainty, which encourages greater political, social, and economic cooperation.

Numerous empirical regularities support this broad theoretical claim. To begin with, when a state leader signs a delimitation agreement but her legislature then fails to ratify it – that is, border settlement fails, but proceeds far in the process – the leader returns to many of the same agreement terms in later

[24] On the former, see Colombia–Panama. On the latter, see the Argentinian–Paraguayan exchange in 1921–1925 (Ireland 1938; United States Department of State 1966).

attempts to delimit the border, albeit with some adjustments.[25] When third parties enter the delimitation process, they, too, follow the same behavioral pattern. For example, when Colombia and Venezuela asked the Swiss Federal Council to delimit their border via an arbitral ruling in 1922, the Swiss adopted much of the earlier (1891) Spanish arbitral award dealing with that same border (Ireland 1938, 217–219). Similarly, the ICJ uses historical agreements as a foundation for its delimitation rulings, even if it must first interpret unclear provisions of those agreements (e.g., see *Libya* v. *Chad* 1989). In short, once agreed upon, a given delimitation entrenches somewhat. It consequently stands out from the alternatives (i.e., is a qualitatively distinct and, therefore, appealing option), thereby promising greater stability and certainty.

A second empirical observation further underscores how border agreements function as focal points: states often use similar provisions in their border treaties with different neighbors. Clay and Owsiak (2016) propose that this occurs because states use a border agreement with one neighbor to signal acceptable delimitation terms to other neighbors with whom they have yet unsettled borders.[26] The terms might concern the use of specific geographical features (e.g., the thalweg of a river or the crest of a certain mountain range) or more general principles. Chinese border agreements in the 1960s illustrate the latter (Clay and Owsiak 2016, online appendix). In these, the Chinese continually rejected the colonially drawn borders and proposals (e.g., the McMahon Line) as imperial and, therefore, inappropriate for postcolonial states. Nevertheless, they often accepted these borders in practice. What they rejected, then, was the public adherence or reference to imperial precedents (Lamb 1964). This characterizes China's approach to settling its border with Afghanistan, Burma/Myanmar, and Pakistan.[27] Lamb (1964) even suggests that China used these various agreements to show India how to settle *their* mutual border; when India kept insisting, however, that the British had already delimited the border, China had no room to negotiate, for it could not accept reference to British imperial actions (see also Fravel 2008). Whether or not the principle extends to Sino-Indian border relations, the broader point remains: states seemingly apply similar provisions across their multiple border negotiations, suggesting that border agreements create focal points that transcend the individual borders in which they first appear. States seek to transfer the certainty and stability these terms carry to other contexts in which they are needed.

Finally, states use historical border delimitation agreements as the foundation for their legal arguments about where a border should be. We observe this most readily in cases that appear before the ICJ, where claimant states must advance a detailed legal position in writing and the court issues an

25 Compare, for example, the articles of the 1858, 1883, and 1884 border agreements between Costa Rica and Nicaragua (Ireland 1971, 12–17).

26 This causes border agreements to cluster geographically. See also Gibler and Tir (2014).

27 See Lamb (1964), Whittam (1961) and United States Department of State (1964, 1968, 1969).

argument-based, legal ruling in response (see also Huth, Croco, and Appel 2013). In such cases, historical agreements offer one way that states can build a case for sovereign rights over a disputed territory (Shaw 2008). Although other ways also exist – such as occupying disputed land not belonging to a state, exercising effective sovereign control over a disputed area, or demonstrating that citizens' self-determination grants one sovereign control (e.g., see Libya's position in its 1989 case against Chad; Shaw 2008) – many ICJ case filings and rulings about territorial sovereignty build upon, rather than ignore, existing delimitation agreements.[28] In fact, the ICJ argues in *Libya* v. *Chad* (1989) that border delimitations, once agreed upon, persist *even if the agreement producing the delimitation ceases to exist.*[29] Border delimitation agreements therefore set permanent focal points under international law that states cannot escape. This fosters the stability and certainty that political, social, and economic actors crave.

Implications

Four main implications follow from building a theory around our conceptualization and definition of border settlement. These concern: (i) a position on the relevance of international law to interstate behavior; (ii) the limitation of the theory's spatial domain to land contiguous (i.e., neighboring) states; (iii) the relationship between territorial claims, which are well-studied, and border settlement, which is not; and (iv) the relevance of border settlement in contemporary politics. In this section, we develop each implication in brief detail. This not only addresses some of the theoretical critiques of our study, but also highlights the explanatory power of the theory we present in later chapters, as well as how it differs from existing scholarly work.

First, our conceptualization of border settlement necessarily depends on both the permanence and the efficacy of international law. For us, border settlement rests entirely on international border agreements – that is, whether neighboring states have signed one or more agreements that delimit the entirety of their mutual border. States frequently find these agreements challenging to obtain, in part because signatories cannot unilaterally revoke them under international law (Article 62(2) of the 1969 Vienna Convention on Law of Treaties). As a result, states do not sign border agreements frivolously but rather do so only when committed to executing a given border delimitation's terms (Fearon 1998). Border agreements, in other words, provide a behavioral indicator that states have resolved a highly salient, contentious issue with finality – an event that we later connect theoretically to other interstate behavioral changes.

[28] See, for example, *Burkina Faso* v. *Mali* 1983, *Libya* v. *Chad* 1989, or *Costa Rica* v. *Nicaragua* 2005. Documents for these cases appear on the website of the International Court of Justice, www.icj-cij.org/.

[29] See judgment of February 3, 1994, in Case concerning the territorial dispute (*Libyan Arab Jamahiriya/Chad*), available online at www.icj-cij.org/docket/files/83/6899.pdf.

The potential Achilles heel to such a conceptualization concerns the sense of finality that we attribute to border agreements – and through them, to border settlement. International relations scholars occasionally posit the impermanence and inefficacy of international law. Some argue, for example, that the interstate agreements that constitute international law do not independently constrain state behavior; instead, these agreements – and international law more broadly – result from states maximizing their interests at a particular moment in time (e.g., see Goldsmith and Posner 2006; Mearsheimer 1994/1995; Posner 2014). If or when state interests shift, the previously produced international agreements collapse or change significantly in response. This, if true, precludes the possibility that states resolve any issue via international agreement with any sense of finality. Border settlement then becomes epiphenomenal – a temporary respite in an ongoing territorial struggle.

Such a position derives from the legal principle of *rebus sic stantibus*, which permits states to terminate their obligations under an international agreement if a "fundamental change in circumstances" occurs (see 1969 Vienna Convention on Law of Treaties). If one places the bar low enough, then states can always find a "fundamental change in circumstances," thereby undercutting the permanence of interstate agreements. The "strictest interpretation" of *rebus sic stantibus*, however, is "the most widely used and hotly contested" of the various "grounds for terminating treaties and agreements prior to their originally agreed-upon expiration date" (Kegley and Raymond 1990, 89–90). Lissitzyn (1967) offers a more moderate interpretation of the principle, arguing that states can only abrogate their obligations if they can demonstrate that certain knowledge they lacked at the time of signing a given agreement would have altered their intentions while crafting that agreement (see also Shaw 2008, 950). Although a significantly higher standard, it may not be high enough in the case of border treaties. Article 62(2) of the 1969 Vienna Convention on the Law of Treaties maintains that "a fundamental change of circumstances may not be invoked as a ground for terminating or withdrawing from a treaty: (a) if the treaty establishes a boundary." Thus, it would seem that the widely accepted, alternative legal principle of *pacta sunt servanda* – that is, "treaties are binding upon the parties to them and must be performed in good faith" (Shaw 2008, 903) – applies more often to border agreements than *rebus sic stantibus* (see also Guzman 2008).[30] This aligns with the position of many scholars, who argue

[30] See also *Chad* v. *Libya* (1989) at the ICJ. The Court reviewed and based its decision on a 1955 treaty (i.e., agreement) between the claimants that dealt with a large number of interstate issues, including border delimitation. Despite the fact that this agreement contained both an expiration date and the right for parties to terminate the treaty unilaterally, the court found that: (a) there was "nothing in the 1955 Treaty to indicate the boundary agreed was to be provisional or temporary"; (b) "[the boundary] bears all the marks of finality"; and (c) "A boundary established by treaty thus achieves a permanence which the treaty itself does not enjoy. When a boundary has been the subject of agreement, the continued existence of that boundary is not dependent upon the continuing life of the treaty under which the boundary is agreed." See judgment of February 3, 1994, in Case concerning the territorial dispute (*Libyan Arab Jamahiriya/Chad*), available online at `www.icj-cij.org/docket/files/83/6899.pdf`.

that border agreements and, therefore, border settlement cannot be "undone" under international law (e.g., see Cukwurah 1967; Kocs 1995; Shaw 2008).

Of course, if agreements are epiphenomenal, states might still ignore legal principles altogether and renege or behave as they please. And yet, they do not.[31] As states negotiate, they recognize that a border delimitation agreement will likely persist indefinitely. They therefore bargain hard, as opposed to signing *any* agreement; prefer explicitly designated, temporary agreements (e.g., *modus vivendi*) when unprepared to delimit their borders with finality; and avoid reneging on border delimitation agreements they sign. Ecuador offers the most notable exception to the latter point, but it also underscores the argument we make here. Ecuador argued that the discovery of the Cenepa River system along its Peruvian border in the wake of the 1942 Rio Protocol rendered the protocol void. Tellingly, however, the international guarantors to the protocol – Argentina, Brazil, Chile, and the United States – refused this interpretation and held Ecuador to the agreement for over fifty years, despite Ecuador's dissatisfaction. In other words, the international community rejected the idea that states can abrogate border agreements; it instead holds its members to the commitments they make through such agreements.

Were one to disagree still with our interpretation of border agreements under international law, we would simply note that the signing of border delimitation agreements is a behavior – one that we argue in subsequent chapters signifies a turning point in how conflictive or cooperative neighboring states behave toward one another.[32] One cannot, however, study the effects of such agreements on conflict behavior if conflict itself – or its absence – defines the period of (non)agreement. As a result, we focus on de jure border settlement (i.e., border delimitation agreements) to ground our conceptualization of border settlement in international legal theory and imbue the concept with a sense of legal finality. If we are incorrect about the permanence or constraining effect of these agreements, we will find evidence that interstate relations do not shift significantly between the pre- and post-border settlement periods. Existing empirical work, the results presented throughout this book, and the narratives we constructed of the de jure border settlement process, however, suggest the opposite and support our interpretation.

A second implication of our conceptualization of border settlement concerns its spatial domain. Only states that share a border with one another (e.g., the United States and Canada) have a border to settle via interstate agreement.[33] A theoretical argument built upon de jure border settlement therefore cannot

[31] There is, however, a plausible alternative to the constraining effects of international law on interstate behavior. After border settlement, states invest in territory on their side of the border. This could make reversion to an unsettled status too costly, thereby leading states to change their preferences with respect to (un)settlement. We thank a reviewer for noting this possibility.

[32] See Gibler (2012), Owsiak (2012, 2013), Simmons (2002, 2005), and Vasquez (2009).

[33] Major (e.g., colonial) powers and intergovernmental organizations assist with the border settlement process. For a discussion of how we code the border settlement variable, see Chapter 4.

explain the behavior between distant states (e.g., Mexico and Mali). Moreover, we propose – as have other scholars (e.g., see Gibler 2012; Kocs 1995; Owsiak 2012) – that the theoretical argument we advance applies only to states sharing an inland or river boundary, rather than only a maritime one (e.g., the United Kingdom and France). States find land-based borders more salient than maritime ones and, therefore, a significantly greater source of interstate tension (Hensel et al. 2008). Neighboring states also must settle the de jure status of their land borders before doing the same for their maritime ones, as the former affects the latter (see Klein 2011; Kraska 2011; Shaw 2008). Maritime borders consequently do not fit into the theoretical story we tell here – a fact supported through supplemental analysis.[34] As a result, the border settlement concept we use in this book focuses entirely on neighboring states that share an inland or river boundary.

The third implication of our conceptualization of border settlement addresses whether it allows us to learn anything new about interstate relations. A significant amount of work studies territorial claims,[35] and critics could argue that territorial claims and border settlement merely occupy two sides of the same coin. Theoretical and empirical considerations do not support such a position. A territorial claim exists when leaders belonging to two or more states officially contest sovereign jurisdiction over a specific piece of territory (Hensel et al. 2008; Huth and Allee 2002). In contrast, border settlement relies on interstate agreements that delimit borders. Territorial claims should be theoretically more likely when borders are undelimited (or unsettled) and less likely after delimitation (or settlement); states should, in other words, contest borders over which they disagree and not contest borders over which they agree. Nevertheless, states can make official statements contesting sovereignty regardless of a border's delimitation status. The two concepts do not perfectly overlap.

Owsiak, Cuttner, and Buck (2018, online appendix) find empirical support for this position. Although they note that territorial claims are less likely after, as opposed to before, border settlement, they also demonstrate that border settlement captures information that territorial claims miss, marking the concepts as distinct. Their various findings underscore this point. First, territorial claims occasionally appear after border settlement. Of the contiguous dyad-year observations that contain border settlement, 17.73% also include a territorial claim; if conceptually identical, we would not expect to see territorial claims in these cases, since the involved states had previously delimited their borders. Similarly, neighboring states do not always actively contest sovereignty where they have not settled their borders. Of the

34 Future research might theorize about and investigate maritime borders further. We return to this idea in Chapter 9.

35 See, inter alia, Hensel (2001), Hensel et al. (2008), Huth (1996), Huth and Allee (2002), Huth, Croco, and Appel (2013), James, Park, and Choi (2006), Lee and Mitchell (2012), Owsiak (2019), Park and James (2015), Simmons (2002, 2005), and Wiegand (2011).

contiguous dyad-year observations that lack border settlement, 23.83% contain no territorial claim; if conceptually identical, we would expect claims to be present in these cases because the borders remain undelimited. Finally, territorial claims in the pre- and post-border settlement periods differ significantly from one another. After border settlement occurs, territorial claims become significantly shorter, contain less violence, involve island territory more frequently, and concern colonial possessions less frequently. Such findings suggest that a border's delimitation status constitutes a unique context in which interstate behavior takes place. They also support the conclusion that border settlement and territorial claims are conceptually related but distinct concepts.

The final implication derived from our conceptualization of border settlement concerns its – and therefore, our theoretical argument's – relevance in contemporary politics. State independence patterns mean that the majority of international borders have existed for decades. In addition, scholars propose that various factors encourage neighboring states to settle their borders sooner rather than later, including opportunities to increase security (e.g., see Gibler 2012; Owsiak 2012; Vasquez 2009), to make economic gains (e.g., see Simmons 2002, 2005), and to increase the likelihood of developing more stable, democratic regimes (e.g., see Gibler 2012; Owsiak 2013). Combined with the fact that borders, once settled, remain settled indefinitely under international law, one might expect most borders to have settled by now – and to remain so. It is therefore reasonable to ask whether border settlement still happens in today's world, and as an extension, whether a theory built upon border settlement remains relevant to contemporary international politics.

To inform our answer to this question, Table 2.1 lists the nineteen borders whose delimitation remains ongoing (i.e., unsettled) as of the end of our analysis (2001), as well as the end of 2015. These data miss a few cases, particularly in the former Soviet Union's sphere of influence (see Owsiak, Cuttner, and Buck 2018). Nevertheless, the list of unsettled borders in the table contains numerous high-profile, conflict hot-spots in the world, including Guyana-Suriname, Cyprus-Turkey, Russia-China, Ghana-Togo, Syria-Israel, India-Pakistan, and the Korean Peninsula. Any theory that helps us explain – even in part – how these relationships emerged, sustain themselves, and might be transformed into more cooperative ones offers significant insight into how to manage some of the longest lasting, resource-draining conflicts in the international community. The list also highlights that border settlement proceeds slowly. Of the nineteen borders unsettled in 2001, only two were settled by December 2015, even though settlement attempts occur frequently (Owsiak, Cuttner, and Buck 2018). This may result from states' unwillingness to make concessions or their desire to leverage territorial disputes for other benefits (Wiegand 2011). Our study contributes to a larger discussion about how one might help states overcome such incentives and dispense with a highly salient, violence-prone issue on their

TABLE 2.1. *Contemporary unsettled borders*

Dyad	Ongoing as of 12/31/2001	Ongoing as of 12/31/2015
Belize-Guatemala	Yes	Yes
Venezuela-Guyana	Yes	Yes
Guyana-Suriname	Yes	Yes
Cyprus-Turkey	Yes	Yes
Russia-China	Yes	No
Ghana-Togo	Yes	Yes
Kenya-(South) Sudan	Yes	Yes
South Africa-Lesotho	Yes	Yes
Syria-Israel	Yes	Yes
Saudi Arabia-Yemen	Yes	Yes
Afghanistan-Pakistan	Yes	Yes
Tajikistan-China	Yes	Yes
China-India	Yes	Yes
China-Bhutan	Yes	Yes
North Korea-South Korea	Yes	Yes
India-Bhutan	Yes	Yes
India-Pakistan	Yes	Yes
India-Bangladesh	Yes	No
Malaysia-Singapore	Yes	Yes

foreign policy agenda – border settlement. We therefore conclude that our theoretical argument has much value in our contemporary world.[36]

2.3 RIVALRY AND COMMITMENT PROBLEMS

Interstate rivalries – that is, dyadic interstate relationships defined by perceptions of threat, enmity, and competition, as well as a heightened likelihood of militarized conflict – are costly and inefficient (Colaresi, Rasler, and Thompson 2007; Diehl and Goertz 2000). Rivals expend many resources over an extended period of time to prepare for hostilities, protect their interests, and undermine their opponents' attempts to gain an advantage. The perceptions driving such behaviors do not emerge from nowhere. Rather, rivalries typically begin because states cannot resolve a disagreement over a salient, interdependent issue. Border territory constitutes one such issue, as it often creates a commitment problem that causes states to prefer rivalry to a negotiated settlement.

Our application of the commitment problem logic is novel – both to the bargaining model research, which typically views war as the solution to commitment problems as opposed to rivalry, and to the rivalry literature, which generally avoids theorizing about the links between the bargaining models of

[36] We detail the policy implications of our argument and findings in Chapter 9.

war and rivalry relationships. Given this novelty, we lay the conceptual foundations for our argument in this section. We begin with an examination of the bargaining model research, which explores why rational actors would choose inefficient outcomes to resolve their disagreements. This research identifies three possible explanations for such behavior – one of which is a commitment problem. Next, we justify our focus on the commitment problem explanation and examine its three potential sources. Our review concludes that commitment problems can arise when states dispute a good that contains a source of power. A certain subset of border territory typifies this situation. Finally, we end with a discussion about why states might prefer to manage their commitment problem over border territory through a rivalry, instead of fighting the war that traditional bargaining model research envisions.

2.3.1 Bargaining Failure as a Cause of War

A key question underlying much of international relations research is: "why war?" The motivating puzzle has intuitive appeal: why are rational leaders unable to find peaceful settlements to their disagreements short of war? War is an inefficient means of dividing goods. A prewar settlement would make both parties better off, because war shrinks the total pie they are dividing (i.e., it carries significant costs), and a prewar bargain would therefore allow the parties to receive more of the disputed good. Nonetheless, although probabilistically rare, war does occur. Why? Any theory of war, then, must explain why actors where unable to come to terms when a division of goods surely existed that would have made them better off (Wagner 2007). Scholars identify at least three answers to this puzzle: private information with incentives to misrepresent (Fearon 1995), how the benefits and costs of war are distributed among domestic actors (Debs and Goemans 2010), and commitment problems (Powell 2006).[37]

The first mechanism – information problems – proposes that the distribution of capabilities or resolve between actors informs negotiated settlements, at least in part. Actors anticipate that their share of a disputed good will reflect their power (e.g., capabilities) or willingness to endure costs (e.g., resolve) relative to the other, bargaining actors. A more powerful actor, or one willing to bear greater costs, expects to receive more of the disputed good – in proportion to the power or resolve advantage it holds. The true distributions of relative power and resolve, however, are not always public knowledge. States hold private information about their true levels of each. They also have an incentive to lie about these levels because convincing an opponent that they hold more power or resolve means obtaining a greater share of the disputed good for themselves.

[37] Fearon (1995) identifies indivisible issues as a potential answer to this puzzle as well, but Powell (2006) argues that issue indivisibility operates as another form of commitment problem, rather than a separate mechanism. We therefore treat it as such here.

Thus, uncertainty over capabilities and resolve emerge, which leads states to demand more than they should or reject reasonable offers from their counterparts. When this occurs, bargaining breaks down and violent conflict begins.[38]

A second mechanism for bargaining failure focuses on the domestic costs and benefits of war. State leaders that bargain over a good must determine which divisions of a disputed good are acceptable to the state and which divisions necessitate war. A leader could, in theory, concede all of the disputed good, but such an outcome will likely be unacceptable to that leader's domestic audience. Moreover, the costs and benefits of any settlement may fall disproportionately on different domestic groups, and the leader must be aware of how any settlement terms affect those keeping her in office.[39] When a domestic audience finds a leader's settlement proposal unacceptable and has the capacity to punish the leader for it, the leader potentially faces domestic backlash. Leaders forced from office because of failed foreign policies (e.g., giving away too much of a coveted good or losing a war over that good) experience divergent consequences. Some merely lose elections, while others experience a violent removal or death. Because they wish to avoid any such consequences, leaders account for the likelihood that a particular bargaining outcome will affect their tenure in office, as well as how they might be removed from and fare after holding office, when making decisions that concern peace and war.

The final mechanism posits war as the consequence of a commitment problem, which exists when states do not expect an agreement made today to be honored in the future. This expectation arises when one actor anticipates a large, rapid, future power shift to benefit its adversary. Powell (2006) identifies three potential sources of future power shifts that trigger commitment problems and war: exogenous power shifts, first-strike advantages, and bargaining over a source of power. Regardless of the exact trigger, the theory expects that the state benefiting from the future power shift will renege on and renegotiate the agreement from its stronger, future bargaining position. Mindful of the benefiting state's incentives, the state that the power shift would weaken eschews an agreement today; it prefers to fight a war in the present, rather than fight or renegotiate an agreement in the future against a stronger adversary.

Our study focuses on the commitment problem mechanism. This decision does not imply that we find the other mechanisms irrelevant for the question we investigate. Each mechanism represents a viable explanation for international

38 States have tools at their disposal for credibly conveying information to adversaries during crisis bargaining, thereby helping them overcome these types of information problems (e.g., see Fearon 1997; Slantchev 2011). Although not a key part of our story, we touch on this briefly in the next chapter.

39 Scholars refer to the group that keeps a leader in office as a winning coalition (Bueno de Mesquita et al. 2003). These coalitions exist in both democratic and nondemocratic states, although their characteristics and size will depend on specific domestic institutions. The discussion we present here therefore applies to all types of states.

conflict and enjoys empirical support.[40] Complex social phenomena, like those we engage in this book, are also likely to be multicausal. States bargaining over salient territorial issues face multiple obstacles to peace, including information asymmetries (see Rider 2009, 2013) and the fact that the costs and benefits of territorial revision do not distribute equally across domestic groups (see Spruyt 2005).

Nonetheless, we isolate the commitment problem mechanism because we think it is particularly prevalent in the context of border territory and rivalry, applies to a significant number of prominent rivalries, is oddly neglected in the theoretical and empirical literatures, and has the potential to explain the entire process through which interstate relationships transition – from issue emergence to rivalry onset to the settlement of contested issues to the termination of hostile relations. By focusing on this single mechanism, we gain a better opportunity to scrutinize the theoretical logic and the robustness of empirical patterns. This, in turn, allows us to build a far more complete picture of the border settlement and rivalry process than we could otherwise do – or at least, more so than if we attempted to engage multiple theories and empirical strategies simultaneously.

2.3.2 Bargaining over a Source of Power

According to Powell (2006, 180), three logics exist through which a commitment problem can arise and lead to war: preventive war, preemptive war, and bargaining over a good that contains a source of power. The expectation of a large, rapid, future shift in power underlies all three logics; only the source of the power shift differs. Preventative war results from an exogenous power shift – that is, a shift in power whose source does not derive from the good(s) over which the states are bargaining. These exogenous sources exist in many forms (e.g., rapid economic growth). A preventive war only occurs, however, if the war's initiator believes it can destroy the source of the power shift. It fights the war, in other words, to prevent the power shift from taking place.

Alternatively, incentives for a preemptive war result when an overwhelming first-strike advantage exists. In this case, states perceive the first-strike advantage as the source of a potential power shift. This type of commitment problem arises when two conditions hold: (i) a state finds the benefit of attacking first so great as to almost guarantee the attacker's victory, and (ii) neither side can credibly commit not to take advantage of that opportunity. War occurs through this logic because one of the involved states moves to take advantage of striking first, in the hopes of doing so before the other state. The states aim, once again,

[40] On information revelation, see Fearon (1994b), Schultz (2001), and Werner and Yuen (2005). On domestic institutional configurations, see Bueno de Mesquita et al. (2003), Chiozza and Goemans (2011), and Debs and Goemans (2010).

to destroy the source of the power shift (i.e., to remove a standing first-strike advantage).

Finally, two states might bargain over an object that itself contains a source of power (Fearon 1996). Any redistribution of the object necessarily changes the distribution of power between the involved states, thereby producing an expected shift in power capabilities. Imagine, for example, two states bargaining over such a good. One state, the status quo state, prefers the current division of the good. The second state, the revisionist state, demands some more, perhaps even all, of the good. Redistribution of the good from the status quo state to the revisionist state promises to increase the power of the revisionist state and decreases the power of the status quo state. Even if the status quo state wishes to transfer control over the good to the revisionist state to avoid a war today, the revisionist state cannot credibly promise not to use the newly acquired power gained through the redistribution to demand more in the future. The status quo state consequently refuses to transfer any portion of the good, even if it means fighting a war today; it would rather do that than face a stronger revisionist state in the future.

All three commitment problem logics can theoretically lead to war; yet, the third logic proves most relevant for a study about borders and interstate rivalry. A rivalry is a long-term process, in which two states come to see one another as threats, competitors, and enemies. Entering a rivalry requires each involved state to orient their foreign policy around addressing this threat over many years, if not decades. Rivals therefore spend significant energy mobilizing their economies, building and buying arms, and establishing reliable alliances. In contrast to this long-term perspective, preemptive and preventive war each carry a short policy time horizon. The incentives for preemptive war dissipate once a first-mover attacks. It seems unlikely that those incentives will persist for many years, especially when each involved state feels pressure to take advantage of the immediate strategic situation. Incentives for preventive war derive from similar, albeit less immediate, time-sensitive dynamics. States do not then have the luxury of using the long-term preparation characteristic of rivalry relations to confront the logics that drive preemptive and preventive war. Moreover, states engage in preemptive and preventive war to destroy the source of the potential power shift. Because rivalry offers a path for states to sustain competition over a good, however, it represents an unreasonable policy through which to accomplish that goal. Thus, although preemptive and preventive war logics can arise within the context of rivalries, these mechanisms inadequately account for the onset and maintenance of rivalry relationships.

Once we set the preemptive and preventive war logics aside, the third logic remains: bargaining over goods that contain a source of power. With this type of commitment problem, a power shift does not occur until states redistribute the disputed good, whenever that might be. This releases the power shift from a dependence on time (see preemptive and preventative war mechanisms), thereby opening the option for states to engage in long-term rivalry competitions, rather than war, to manage their disagreement. In the next two sections, we explain why bargaining over a source of power fits well with what we know about border territory and interstate territorial disputes. We also connect the process of bargaining over a source of power specifically to rivalry relations through the commitment problem mechanism. Scholars traditionally use commitment problems to explain why war occurs, rather than the life cycle of rivalry relationships. We propose, though, that bargaining over border territory that contains a source of power triggers a commitment problem, and this explains why many contiguous states' struggle to settle border territory, as well as why long-term, competitive rivalries develop as a result of their struggle.

2.3.3 Border Territory as a Source of Power

We contend that border territory possesses characteristics capable of generating a specific type of commitment problem, and these characteristics inhibit border settlement. The inability to settle then produces and sustains rivalry relations. To build this argument, we first must establish that certain types of border territory can generate the particular type of commitment problem we envision – one that results when states bargain over a source of power. To be clear, not all border territory will produce such a commitment problem. Only if a given territory grants the holder a potential source of power would we expect the commitment problem to arise, failed settlement to persist, and rivalry to emerge.

Three specific border characteristics, when present, provide such a source of power. First, states find some territory militarily important because it provides a strategic advantage to the controlling state. This advantage takes many forms, such as high ground from which invaders can more easily observe or attack, as well as critical avenues for military invasion or resupply (e.g., straits). Status quo states that control the territory will want to both continue holding the territory and deny the territory to adversaries. Revisionist states, in contrast, have strong incentives to gain control of the territory to increase their own security or to enhance their bargaining leverage. Israel, for example, has noted the strategic value of both the Sinai and the Golan Heights as a justification for refusing to return these lands to Egypt and Syria respectively. The Khyber Pass, connecting Afghanistan and Pakistan, similarly leads to persistent conflict because it sits at a critical juncture for moving troops and resupplying any invading armies.

Second, territory houses populations that offer the state economic labor, a source of tax revenue, or conscripts for military service. Losing people consequently threatens to decrease the economic or military power of a state vis-à-vis its competitor.[41] Parts of Kashmir, for example, remain well-populated,

[41] Questions of ethnicity may also fall under this broad heading. Note, however, that only one side usually justifies its position based on ethnic claims. For example, Biger (1995) notes that the Burkina-Faso/Mali border dispute involved access to fresh water, although Mali also made ethnic claims. States may use ethnicity to prevent losing other benefits associated with a given

which may (partially) account for the intractability of this dispute. Third, disputed territory may contain natural resources necessary for sustaining life or a population's general economic welfare and prosperity. These resources include lakes or rivers – which provide access to fresh water for drinking and irrigation (e.g., Mali-Burkina Faso) or facilitate trade (e.g., Iran-Iraq) – as well as oil (e.g., Argentina-Uruguay or the Spratly Islands), an economic good valuable for trade, industrialization, and military applications.

Conceptually, when border territory has either a strategically valuable location or (an) economically valuable resource(s) that promises to increase the controlling state's power, we refer to the territory as containing "power endowments." Border territory with power endowments specifically threatens to trigger a commitment problem, as the transfer of some, or all, of it could shift power between the disputing states. As a result, the revisionist state makes demands, but the status quo state prefers not to offer any concessions. The border then remains unsettled. In contrast, when border territory lacks power endowments, the probability of bargaining breakdown declines. Commitment problems appear significantly less often, and the likelihood rises that neighboring states settle their mutual border.

If power-endowed territory increases settlement failure, what happens when borders remain unsettled? According to standard bargaining models, commitment problems cause failed negotiations, after which disputing states turn to war to settle their disagreement. We do not challenge that war occurs because of commitment problems. We do, however, propose that war represents only *one* means through which states compete over a disputed good. War carries high costs; it necessitates the investment of significant resources without guaranteeing a victorious outcome. Because the power shift we entertain only occurs when territory changes hands, states experience no immediate need to launch a war to forestall the power shift. They therefore search for less costly, less risky means of competition. Rivalry offers such an alternative means. It allows states to avoid or delay the costs of war, while still preventing the power shift that they fear.

2.3.4 Why Rivalry, Rather than War

Scholars traditionally use the commitment problem mechanism to explain why war occurs, particularly when less costly, non-violent processes might yield the same outcome (Fearon 1995; Powell 2006). Yet the commitment problem may also lead states to engage in long-term, inefficient competitions (e.g., rivalry). To build that case, we discuss several reasons why states might choose rivalry over war as a means of attempting to resolve their commitment problem. In doing so, we do not argue against war as a logical solution to the

territory. For other cases of one-sided ethnic claims, see Cambodia-Vietnam or the Falkland Islands dispute (Biger 1995; Day 1987; Huth and Allee 2002).

commitment problem. We simply posit that states occasionally have incentives to choose an alternative, nonwar tool (like a rivalry) to address it and its effects.

As we note earlier, a rivalry is a dyadic relationship in which two interdependent states perceive one another as threats, enemies, and competitors (Colaresi, Rasler, and Thompson 2007; Diehl and Goertz 2000). Rivals consequently orient their foreign policy around confronting one another, which institutionalizes their competition. This locks the rivalry in for an extended period of time, thereby encouraging rivals to engage in long-term policy planning about the rivalry.[42] It also offers a way to hurt an adversary without going to war. Through the rivalry process, states push their adversaries to adopt policies and invest resources in ways they would not otherwise choose. Moves to increase armaments or seek allies often necessitate the adversary to reciprocate. These tit-for-tat advancements could escalate to war, but need not do so. Indeed, states often hope to deter, outcompete, or outlast their rival.

When a first-strike advantage or exogenous power shift generates a commitment problem, states work to destroy the source of the power shift. When, however, they bargain over a good that contains a source of power, they prefer to possess, rather than destroy, the good. Moreover, any power shift will not occur unless states agree to or one compels the other to redistribute the good. Compellence being unavailable in territorial disputes, especially in modern times (Hathaway and Shapiro 2017), states need to reach agreement. Yet they also fear the power shift that results if they do. Rivalry offers them a third policy – a way to compete over the good, while also forestalling an agreement that would trigger a power shift and avoiding a risky, high-cost war that only *potentially* prevents the power shift.

Three considerations explain why rivalry may be a reasonable, logical consequence when states bargain over issues that contain a source of power. First, states face uncertainty over whether war offers them a practical means of resolving their commitment problem. In many commitment problem logics, war destroys the source of power, thereby resolving the commitment problem that the power source creates (i.e., preemptive and preventive war). Such an approach proves impossible or undesirable when bargaining over a good that contains a source of power. In the context of border territory, for example, it would be challenging to destroy the militarily strategic advantage that accompanies some land, such as a narrow mountain pass, high ground, or straits. Even if it could be done, it would be counterproductive. States want to seize or hold the valuable good, not destroy it.

War can achieve such goals, but the record shows that it fails more often than it succeeds. India and Pakistan, for example, have fought three wars, and their border remains unsettled. Similarly, Israel and its neighbors have participated

42 According to data by Thompson and Dreyer (2012), the median rivalry exists for sixty-two years.

in a series of wars against one another (Sarkees and Wayman 2010). Despite these wars, numerous unsettled borders persisted for long periods of time, and those that settled typically did not do so via war itself (e.g., see Egypt-Israel). In short, war does not guarantee a solution to the commitment problem (Werner 1999b). Rational states expect this. War's characteristics (e.g., cost, inefficiency, uncertainty) prompt them to consider less costly strategies instead (e.g., rivalry).[43]

Second, states find it difficult to select war as a policy, even as they need a way to compete over the disputed good. Setting aside whether war achieves its goals, internal and external constraints can prohibit a state from choosing to go to war – constraints that need not prevent it from engaging in a rivalry. Few state leaders make decisions unilaterally. Instead, they face veto players (e.g., elites, the military, or the public), who differ in their preference for war over other policies. Leaders must convince these actors about the necessity of war. This will be a tall task when the adversary possesses similar capabilities (common among neighboring states), and the state must not only capture and hold the disputed land, but also prevent future, renewed fighting from setting back any gains it makes (i.e., it must fully defeat, if not capture and replace, the adversarial government). These features raise the cost of war significantly, making it less likely that key domestic groups will support going to war. Rivalry then becomes a viable alternative.

External constraints similarly interfere with a state's ability to launch a war. At a broad level, the international system condones neither war (generally) nor territorial conquest (specifically). States that engage in either therefore risk material (e.g., sanctions) or reputational consequences. Whether those consequences materialize depend on numerous considerations, including a state's relationship with other states. Influential powers (e.g., systemic or regional hegemons), for example, serve as gatekeepers to war. They possess strong incentives to restrain their proteges' involvement in interstate conflict – in order to preserve the status quo or avoid involvement in a costly war themselves. Protégés may then need an influential power's permission to go to war, or face the loss of aid, sanctions, or even wider condemnation. For these protégés, rivalry offers an appealing alternative to war; it avoids placing the relationship with the influential power or international community under tension, circumvents the punishment that accompanies war, and still allows an outlet through which to pursue the disputed good.

Third, a state may initially lack the preparation needed to fight a war, and rivalry offers a way to deter the adversary, while also postponing a war until war preparations improve. Preparing for war requires significant domestic and international policy changes. Domestically, a state needs to increase defense

43 Wars most often occur *within* the context of rivalry (Colaresi, Rasler, and Thompson 2007; Diehl and Goertz 2000). That is, by the time war occurs, the rivalry has already begun.

spending, accelerate arms acquisitions, and recruit for the military (whether through volunteers or conscription). Internationally, it may seek alliances, whether for outright protection, the aggregation of capabilities in an expected fight, or the easier deployment of forces (e.g., basing rights, flyover approval, or port access). Adopting any such policies requires a long(er)-term time horizon. Military spending and alliance building necessitate the reallocation of budgeted resources; depending on the state's regime type, this process can be complex and time-consuming, as domestic groups debate and approve various policies. Similarly, ordering, building, delivering, and training on weapons systems takes years, as does the process of recruiting (or conscripting) and training additional military personnel. Finally, the process of reorienting foreign policy and resources to address a threat demands rallying relevant domestic audiences. This, too, requires time.

The rivalry process offers states the time and the context necessary to accomplish the earlier policy changes. It clearly identifies a threat and reorients foreign policy toward combatting that threat. Along the way, the rivalry process institutionalizes the threat within the state's foreign policy apparatus, which justifies the resource reallocation to domestic actors and lays the foundation for adopting sustained, long-term policies. Reorientation and institutionalization, for example, together lock-in the expectation that a threat will continue for the foreseeable future. This shifts decision-makers' time-horizon and compels them to develop a long-term strategy for managing the threat (i.e., rival), thereby opening space to adopt policies that take time to implement (e.g., alliance building or arms acquisitions). In short, the emergence of a rival prompts a state to put itself on what can best be described as a "war-footing," for a war is its worst case scenario. These preparations may deter war, but if the state desires war in the future, they also lay the practical groundwork necessary for engaging in a successful war on the timeline that the state prefers.

In the end, states often cannot turn to war when disputing a good, like border territory, that contains a source of power. They therefore need an alternative policy – one that keeps the competition alive, prevents the adversary from unilaterally consolidating its hold on the good, and leaves war available as a future option. Rivalry provides such a policy. Because it is a long-term competition, states expend significant resources on confronting their rival(s) over an extended period of time, but in doing so, they also force their adversary to respond in kind. This susses out the adversary's resolve (Rider 2009, 2013) and tests whether the adversary has the capabilities to compete (Kydd 2000). As this competitive process of burning resources unfolds, one state may determine it cannot outspend or mobilize sufficient resources to defeat its adversary. Such a conclusion promises to force one side to capitulate without ever having to fight an actual war. If a war comes, however, the rivals have laid the material and institutional groundwork needed to fight it.

2.4 CONCLUSION

Any good theoretical argument must clarify its conceptual foundations. In this chapter, we consequently provide the origins, characteristics, and implications of two central concepts that underlie the remainder of our work: border settlement and the commitment problem. Research repeatedly notes the dangerous role of unsettled, interstate territorial issues generally and – more recently – unsettled borders in particular. Yet scholars do not always agree on what border (un)settlement conceptually is. For example, "border settlement" might involve either the agreement on border delimitation (i.e., what we label de jure border settlement, as a result of its dependence on interstate legal agreements) or the acceptance of border delimitation (i.e., what we label de facto border settlement).

We consider a border "settled" after the two involved states (i.e., the dyad) sign (an) international agreement(s) that delimit(s) the entirety of their mutual border(s). This places us squarely within the de jure border settlement camp, which proves more advantageous than the available alternatives. Not only does a de jure conceptualization align with how we believe most scholars use the broad term "border settlement" in their theoretical arguments, but it also exists prior to any de facto settlement, can be observed empirically, and is used universally by all neighboring states during the period of our study. Of course, adopting such a conceptualization carries a series of implications as well. In particular, it depends upon the idea that international law constrains state behavior and restricts our theoretical argument to the states with an opportunity to settle their borders via agreement – namely, neighboring (i.e., contiguous) states. These, however, are not major limitations. Our research shows that states behave as if border agreements constrain them, and the vast majority of interstate rivalries – the relationships we seek to explain – appear within contiguous dyads. Moreover, we demonstrate that exploring de jure border settlement offers great promise, for not only does it provide us insights that existing studies of territorial claims alone cannot, but it also sheds light on some of the most violent rivalries in the contemporary world (e.g., Syria-Israel, India-Pakistan, China-India, or the Koreas) and the locations at greatest risk for potential future conflict.

Our second central concept, the commitment problem, theoretically connects unsettled borders with rivalries – that is, the dyadic relationships we seek to explain, defined through mutual perceptions of threat, enmity, and competition, as well as a high likelihood of militarized conflict. A commitment problem occurs when states cannot reach an agreement today because they fear that a foreseen, large, future shift in their relative power will undermine such an agreement. Scholars identify the commitment problem as one reason rational states choose war over a negotiated solution that might offer them the same outcome with fewer costs. We propose, however, that a rivalry relationship may be yet another inefficient outcome that rational states prefer to a negotiated agreement when a commitment problem exists.

A commitment problem theoretically stems from one of three sources: exogenous power shifts, a first-mover advantage in military action, or an object that itself contains a source of power. States can resolve the first two of these by destroying the source of power (i.e., preventive and preemptive war, respectively). As a result, these sources infrequently produce rivalries; the strategic situation incentives states to resolve the commitment problem in the immediate future, not enter a protracted competition. The third source, however, contains the seeds for rivalry. When states bargain over an object, like border territory, that contains a source of power (or what we call a "power endowment"), they want to *possess* that salient object, not destroy it. Because both states find the object salient, both pursue exclusive possession of it, mindful that not possessing it places them at a relative disadvantage.

As existing research notes, war offers states one path through which to escape this commitment problem – that is, to determine the object's ultimate possessor. Yet there are a few problems with doing so. Unless one state fully conquers the other, a prohibited behavior under international law, this type of commitment problem will likely persist even after a war. Because the territory is highly salient, even a weakened, vanquished state will merely bide time before pursuing the object once more (e.g., see Alsace-Lorraine). War also costs states much in material and personnel – costs they must bear immediately at the time of fighting. Finally, states may be unprepared to fight a war or face external or internal constraints that impede their ability to do so. Given these considerations, a rational state may pursue border territory through a rivalry, as opposed to a(n) (absolute) war. This allows them not to concede the disputed, salient territory; to prepare politically and militarily for a potential, future militarized conflict; to spread the costs – both of preparing for war and of maintaining a combative posture – over a longer period of time; and to test one another's resolve over the disputed object within the confines of a less costly context.

The next few chapters put these concepts into action. We begin by advancing a general theory of how states settle their borders – and explaining how a rivalry relationship (plagued by a commitment problem) complicates this settlement process. Then, we return to the outset of a dyad's history – that is, where the border settlement process begins – and argue that the persistence of unsettled borders leads to rivalries because it produces commitment problems over border territory that contains sources of power. Finally, we propose that if the commitment problem drives rivalries, then the settling of borders will hasten rivalry termination. Each component of this larger argument finds support in the chapters that follow.

3

A Theory of Border Settlement

> The most popular vision of peace is of nations living independently, each respecting the rights and territories of others....
>
> G. Blainey

3.1 INTRODUCTION

Well-established borders constitute one of the defining features of the modern state – and by extension, the international system. As Cukwurah (1967, 29–32) notes, border delimitation is itself an act of sovereignty, clarifies sovereign jurisdiction, allows states to exercise the rights afforded to them by virtue of their being states (i.e., to possess and use sovereignty), and yields the idea that states are equal to one another (i.e., that they have the *same* sovereign rights). The principle of sovereignty therefore closely intertwines with interstate borders; it holds that states possess near-absolute authority over their lands and people, with borders establishing the legal domain of that power. Unsettled borders then create uncertainty about where one state's legal jurisdiction ends and another state's begins. This jurisdictional ambiguity invites conflict between sovereigns and generates high opportunity costs. States not only fight about who exercises authority over the territory and population of the disputed border region, but they also often forego the benefits of cooperation while borders remain unsettled – losing both security (through alliances and territorial threat) and economic gains (through lower trade, tourism, and the joint exploitation of resources in the disputed region).

Given the potential for conflict and the opportunity costs that accompany unsettled borders, states have strong incentives to mutually agree on a border's location. It is therefore not surprising that most borders in the international system are indeed now settled. Yet, to look backward from today's vantage point often obscures the difficulty with which borders settled. Some states struggled for decades to achieve a full delimitation of their mutual border (e.g., see Colombia–Venezuela), and some continue to struggle today (e.g., see Table 2.1). This subset of states disproportionately represents the international system's most violent and protracted conflicts between neighbors. And it raises a critical question: what differentiates those states who can settle their borders (more easily) from those that cannot?

In the previous chapter, we defined what it means conceptually to have a settled border. We also extended the theoretical insights from commitment problem logic – that is, that these problems lead to bargaining failures that arise when actors bargain over a source of power – from the war context to that of border settlement and rivalry. In this chapter, we develop a general theory of border settlement that answers one key question: what factors influence whether neighbors will successfully agree on the mutual distribution of border territory? Because this question remains understudied, we approach an answer to it by linking together disparate theories of bargaining and conflict management, and by novelly applying the commitment problem logic outlined in the previous chapter to the border settlement context.

Our theory begins by conceptualizing border settlement as a straightforward bargaining process, wherein states have competing incentives to reach a settlement and to procure as large a division of the disputed territory as possible for themselves. Drawing on bargaining theories, we identify information and commitment problems as the most common obstacles to concluding border delimitation negotiations successfully (Fearon 1995; Powell 2006). Information exchange can be facilitated by numerous mechanisms; to address commitment problems, however, we need to theorize explicitly about the value of disputed territory, which drives the commitment problem itself (see Chapter 2). We therefore identify two broad categories of border territory: territory that contains a power endowment and territory lacking it. The presence of these power endowments, we argue, represents a unique challenge to border settlement that states struggle to overcome.

With this foundation, we next integrate expectations from theories of conflict management. In particular, we ask: to what extent do conflict management strategies – bilateral negotiations or third-party conflict management, such as mediation, arbitration, or adjudication – affect neighboring states' ability to settle their borders?[1] We argue that these conflict management strategies address

[1] International relations scholars organize conflict management strategies differently than some international law scholars. The former often combine conflict management strategies into broader categories, particularly for quantitative analysis. Good offices, fact-finding missions, and conciliation, for example, commonly appear under the broader umbrella of mediation (Greig, Owsiak, and Diehl 2019), for both theoretical (i.e., these various tools share many traits) and empirical (i.e., third parties rarely use some of these tools) reasons. Arbitration and adjudication also combine into a larger category (e.g., binding third-party tools, or legal approaches). Certain legal scholars, in contrast, discuss these tools separately (e.g., see Merrills 2005). We follow the international relations approach throughout this book, using the aggregate categories of mediation and legal approaches.

bargaining challenges differently. Bilateral negotiations, for example, can help surmount the challenge of incomplete information, but cannot easily allay the fears that underlie commitment problems (see, e.g., Walter 2002). Third parties, in contrast, may help with either challenge – with some strategies (e.g., binding third-party conflict management, like arbitration and adjudication) better able to help with overcoming commitment problems than others (e.g., nonbinding conflict management, like mediation; see Beardsley 2008; Gent and Shannon 2010; Mattes and Savun 2009). Conflict management can therefore facilitate border settlement, but we note that this is not easy, quick, or guaranteed. Disputing states may need time to understand the conflict management process, to prepare their domestic constituency for a settlement, and to determine the incentives of any third parties involved (see Greig and Diehl 2006).

The value of the disputed territory itself may also undercut conflict management, even among states like democracies that are theoretically predisposed toward it (see Park and James 2015). We therefore outline expectations for border settlement conditional on both conflict management and power endowments. The theory we advance predicts that conflict management techniques will be much more likely to produce settlement in the absence of power endowments. Such cases present smaller hurdles to settlement that third parties can more easily address. We break with much previous research, however, to argue that the commitment problem – expected and exacerbated when power endowments are present – will make states reluctant to settle their borders, even with the help of third-party conflict managers.

3.2 THE SALIENCE OF BORDER TERRITORY

States disagree over many issues; nonetheless, disputes over territory are particularly dangerous. Territorial disputes are more likely than disputes over other issues to become militarized (Senese and Vasquez 2008; Vasquez and Henehan 2001), to recur (Hensel 1994), and to escalate to war (Holsti 1991; Vasquez 2009). Despite this general trend, however, not all territorial disputes are alike. In particular, disagreements over the delimitation of mutual borders (a subset of territorial disputes) may produce much of the conflict associated with the broader category of territorial disputes (Gibler 2012; Holsti 1991; Huth 1996; Kocs 1995; Owsiak 2012; Vasquez 2009).

A review of recent research confirms this latter point. Neighboring states that have not delimited their mutual borders, for example, experience a disproportionately high likelihood of interstate conflict. These dyads (i.e., pairs of states) are significantly more likely to become involved in MIDs – that is, to threaten, display, or use military force against one another (Ghosn, Palmer, and Bremer 2004; Palmer et al. 2015) – to experience wars (Gibler 2012) and to develop rivalries with one another (Colaresi, Rasler, and Thompson 2007). Furthermore, studies hint that the status of these borders drives the conflictive behavior we observe. Once these dyads settle their border(s) – by signing an international agreement that delimits the entirety of their mutual border(s) – they are subsequently less likely to fight over any issue, even nonterritorial ones (Owsiak 2012). And as we demonstrate in Chapters 7 and 8, the settlement of a rival dyad's border fundamentally transforms their relationship; after border settlement, rival dyads are significantly more likely to end their rivalry or, if the rivalry persists, to behave substantially more peacefully toward their perceived enemy in both interstate crises and disputes.

Such findings suggest two noteworthy implications. First, states (will) find threats to border territory especially salient. The security of the state depends on having well-defined, defended borders, free from proximate threats, particularly for those citizens living in or near the border region. Indeed, border threats are often seen as threats to the sovereignty or survival of the state itself (on this point, see, e.g., Ireland 1938, 275). Moreover, border territory is also sometimes endowed with characteristics over which states want control, such as natural resources, populations, or militarily strategic or historically significant space. These characteristics obviously provide value to the state that holds the territory. Yet states also worry that *not* holding the territory may put them at a disadvantage relative to a neighbor that has control over it – something existing research does not fully consider. If, for example, border territory contains a militarily strategic position (e.g., the Golan Heights), the state not holding it might be at a military disadvantage relative to the state that holds it. The advantaged state could then issue (further) demands for territorial or policy concessions to the disadvantaged state. Its advantage, in turn, increases the likelihood that the disadvantaged state offers a concession, which perhaps (further) enhances the advantaged state's position, leading to additional demands. Thus, whether for existential reasons or because of a territory's characteristics, leaders often treat border disputes as highly salient.

Second, states should want to settle border disputes, since substantial opportunity costs accrue when borders remain unsettled. Uncertain sovereign jurisdictions, for example, significantly undermine trade, as economic actors are unclear what rules apply to their entities and transactions (Simmons 2005). Threats to and militarization of border regions also disrupt or inhibit cross-border interactions, from tourism to cultural exchanges to trade (Blum 2007; Simmons 2005). As we argue later, these salient security threats often produce protracted conflict too, requiring states to reorient their domestic resources to address the threats. Indeed, such threats theoretically increase the influence of hawkish elements in government (Vasquez 2009), the centralization of the state (Gibler 2012), and arms expenditures (Rider 2009) – each of which augments the military posture of the state, thereby diverting resources toward addressing the border dispute and away from the pursuit of other foreign and domestic policy goals (Gibler and Miller 2014). Finally, unsettled borders can complicate bargaining over other, often unrelated, issues between the involved states.[2] All of these outcomes carry significant opportunity costs, and because border disputes often persist for decades (see, e.g., Ireland 1938; Kocs 1995), these costs can be large.

The idea that states generally want to settle their borders is not merely a theoretical one. States behave and speak in ways consistent with this idea. Whittam (1961, 175), for example, notes that Burma's leaders "had been concerned about the boundary with China ever since they first assumed office [at independence]." This motivated them to quickly press for a border settlement agreement with China. Similarly, numerous Latin American states reveal a strong desire to settle their borders. These states entered the international system without clearly defined borders; upon independence, they then immediately engaged one another repeatedly in an attempt to settle these borders, with some even going so far as to recognize the need for a *modus vivendi* that reduced jurisdictional uncertainty and the potential for violence while they negotiated further about a more permanent delimitation (e.g., see the September 1905 Colombia–Peru agreement over the Putumayo Region; Ireland 1938, 191). And African states regularly display this general behavioral pattern as well – namely, a desire to settle borders quickly after independence, along with concrete attempts to do so (see Kornprobst 2002).

Anecdotal evidence therefore supports theoretical expectations. States find borders salient and want to settle their borders' delimitation. Moreover, they often continue trying to do so, even after repeated failures. This occurs because states cannot reduce or escape the threat surrounding their unsettled border by manipulating their geopolitical environment – that is, by changing their neighbors or inserting new unoccupied lands as a buffer. Rather, they may only choose between two broad policies at each point in time: settling the border's delimitation or paying the costs associated with unsettled borders. These costs, as well as the incentives noted earlier, motivate leaders to continue working toward the settlement of their outstanding border disputes, even when these efforts generally fail. But this raises a critical question: if there are such strong incentives for states to settle their borders, why do border issues fester between states, particularly for long periods of time? We now turn our attention to this question.

3.3 THEORETICAL FOUNDATIONS

For the sake of simplicity, let us assume two neighboring state actors exist: State A and State B. Each state controls a piece of territory of a certain size, with its own resources and population. The states are unclear, however, on the limits of

[2] For example, see Blum (2007), who outlines India–Pakistan cooperation in the shadow of the Kashmir dispute. Complications for other negotiations arise more acutely if states break off diplomatic relations because of border disputes (e.g., see, inter alia, Bolivia–Paraguay or India–Pakistan).

their jurisdictional control relative to one another. They would therefore like to agree upon the exact location of a mutual border between their territories, which would define the legal jurisdiction of their respective governments. As they work toward this goal, we will make a few additional assumptions about how they behave. First, we assume the leaders of these states are rational – to the extent that they have preferences over the border's placement, can identify their most and least preferred outcomes over the border's placement, and will act in a manner consistent with those preferences. Second, leaders care about the distribution of the good being disputed – in our case, the territory to be divided; more specifically, they want as much of the territory as possible (Fearon 1995; Hopmann 1996; Schelling 1960), which makes them self-interested actors.[3] Note that because there exist only two states and a border must be drawn somewhere, all land will be allocated to either State A or State B, meaning that any gains in territory distributed to State A will necessarily reduce the area available for distribution to State B (and vice versa). Thus, the involved states have competing preferences, and the possible outcomes can be conceptualized as a continuum (running from 0 to 1, or equivalently, 0% to 100%), with any given point along the continuum denoting the fraction of the disputed good going to State A (x) and State B ($1 - x$) if a settlement were reached at that point (x).

Given these assumptions and the characteristics that accompany the border settlement process, two implications follow. The first concerns the timing of settlement: states will prefer to settle their borders sooner, rather than later, as delays in settlement increase the costs they incur. Delays forestall gains from cooperation, divert resources toward defense and away from other policy goals, and increase the likelihood of violent conflict. Importantly, the costs accumulate as unsettled borders persist; minimizing these costs therefore encourages states to seek as early a settlement as they can get.[4]

Despite such an incentive, there exists a countervailing consideration as well: border settlements cannot be abrogated or changed unilaterally under international law (Cukwurah 1967; Shaw 2014). States consequently expect any settlement reached to endure *indefinitely*, for they are unsure whether or when they will be able to alter the agreement in the future. This long time horizon encourages them to bargain hard over border delimitation – in the sense that they actively strive for the best possible terms and do not sign border settlement agreements frivolously (Fearon 1998). Note that this does not undercut states' incentive to settle borders early. They still wish to do so. Yet they are unwilling to accept *any* terms simply to reach *a* settlement. Instead,

[3] For simplicity, we assume actors want to maximize their share of territory. As some scholars have noted, however, actors can have limited aims (Schultz and Goemans 2019) and these limited versus unlimited aims may have an effect on the probability of war.

[4] In other words, border settlement displays positive duration dependence.

they push for an early settlement that grants them the substantive terms that they find (at least minimally) acceptable for the foreseeable future.

Finally, because unsettled borders prove costly and states are rational actors, there exists some settlement that both states prefer to unsettled borders (Fearon 1995). The costs of conflict – whether in war, rivalry, or even simply prolonged delays in border settlement – eat into the overall benefits the involved states can receive once a distribution of the disputed territory occurs.[5] Knowing this, rational states should find an agreement mutually preferable to conflict before that conflict sets in, settle the border with one another, and thereby maximize their utility (i.e., minimize the costs accumulated through unsettled borders and maximize the benefits that result from settled borders). In a world of rational actors, this expectation holds as long as the costs of conflict are greater than zero. And it means, simply put, that rational states will generally be better off settling the border than engaging in protracted conflict over its placement.

3.3.1 Negotiating about Unsettled Borders

Although leaders may be motivated to settle outstanding border issues, this does not imply that settlement will be quickly or easily attained. In fact, empirical evidence suggests the opposite; neighboring states often struggle to delimit their mutual borders. For example, they regularly participate in numerous rounds of bargaining, which produce agreements that deliberately postpone a final border delimitation (i.e., modus vivendi; e.g., see Colombia–Peru), settle only a fraction of their outstanding border claims at a time (e.g., see Afghanistan–Iran), or propose a final delimitation that domestic institutions subsequently reject (e.g., the Colombia–Venezuela dispute described earlier). The frequent failure to produce agreements that settle interstate borders fully, quickly, and comprehensively implies that states face obstacles when negotiating over border territory. Examining the phases of the bargaining process highlights the origins of these obstacles.

The bargaining process begins when actors recognize that they are interdependent with respect to some issues – for example, sovereignty over disputed territory. Schelling (1960, 5) refers to these as strategic situations, in which "the ability of one participant to gain his ends is dependent to an important degree on the choices or decisions that the other participant will make" (see also Ramsbotham, Woodhouse, and Miall 2011). Because actors within such situations cannot unilaterally obtain their goals, they must bargain with one another if they hope to get what they want. As they do so, they proceed through a three-stage process (Hopmann 1996). In the first stage, actors search for the bargaining range. Each disputant holds a set of settlement terms that it

[5] In addition to the costs discussed earlier, conflict can destroy a disputed territory's strategic or economic value as well. Conflict can therefore directly reduce the value of the good being disputed.

prefers to continued disagreement (i.e., its "win set"). The bargaining range merges the disputants' win sets; it contains the set of all possible joint solutions (i.e., negotiated agreements) that the disputing actors *both* prefer to having no solution (i.e., no agreement, or continued conflict). Thus, the acceptable alternatives to a negotiated agreement define the limits of the bargaining range, as these alternatives restrict the range of joint solutions that the actors will find mutually acceptable.[6] In some circumstances, these alternatives – if attractive enough – may render negotiation unnecessary. Imagine, for example, a State X that wants to upgrade its nuclear power technology by trading with a State Y that has this technology. Were the trade to fall through, State X's nuclear power plants could continue functioning – just with less modern technology. This alternative reduces State X's dependence on State Y, thereby bolstering State X's bargaining position and allowing State X to walk away from negotiations easily if the terms do not match what it wants.

Borders, however, do not typically present these types of alternatives to negotiation. In particular, any alternative that involves failing to reach an agreement carries significant costs that continue to mount over time (see earlier discussion). These costs ensure that a bargaining range for a border's placement necessarily exists for rational states (Fearon 1995), although this does not guarantee that the actors will find it. Actors can still disagree over the location of this range (i.e., contest which possible divisions of the disputed territory lie within the bargaining range).

Once they find the bargaining range, actors next need to agree upon a specific solution that constitutes a point within that range – that is, an exact distribution of the disputed good (e.g., territory). A challenge, however, exists here as well. A bargaining range typically contains many specific distributions that actors would find mutually preferable to no agreement. Yet because different distributions necessarily divide the good's benefits differently, actors' preferences over these distributions diverge, requiring them to negotiate over the exact distribution that should be chosen. Finally, if they clear this hurdle, actors must next ensure compliance with the distributional agreement reached as well – that is, there is an implementation phase. This last stage cannot entirely be divorced from the preceding ones. Actors frequently account for compliance concerns when negotiating agreements to their disputes (Downs, Rocke, and Barsoom 1996; Fearon 1998). These concerns may be particularly acute when actors bargain over an issue – such as territory – that either potentially sets an undesirable precedent for additional claims that could whittle away the state (thereby threatening state identity; see Walter 2006) or that might permit its counterpart to demand further concessions from a place of increased power if the agreement's terms enter into force (Powell 2006).

6 Fisher, Ury, and Patton (1991) refer to these limits as the best alternative to a negotiated agreement (BATNA). See also Lebow (1996).

3.4 OBSTACLES TO BARGAINING

Based on the negotiation process outlined earlier, we identify two mechanisms that complicate bargaining over border delimitations: incomplete information and commitment problems (Fearon 1995; Powell 2006).[7] Various factors increase the probability that these two obstacles arise, which in turn alters the likelihood that border settlement occurs. The most theoretically pertinent of these factors concerns power endowments. In the previous chapter, we defined power endowments as border characteristics capable of altering state power – most notably, by offering the state that holds the territory either a militarily strategic advantage or highly desirable economic resources.

As we argue subsequently, border territory without power endowments primarily faces the obstacle of incomplete information. States want as big a piece of the proverbial pie as possible. To get this, they must convince one another that a militarized conflict would end in a settlement that favors them. Whether this reflects an objective assessment does not matter; so long as the opponent *believes* a state will get more in a conflict, it will be willing to offer concessions consistent with that expectation. This creates strong incentives for each state to misrepresent their true levels of capabilities (i.e., the resources at its disposal) and resolve (i.e., the costs it is willing to bear in pursuit of its goals). During negotiations, for example, a state will attempt to convince its counterpart that it is more powerful than the counterpart perceives, and that if negotiations break down into militarized conflict, it is more likely to win. Similarly, a state may try to convey that it has a stronger will, meaning that it is prepared to pay much higher costs for the disputed border than the counterpart expects. These misrepresentations obscure the true bargaining range, thereby complicating settlement; in particular, they present the alternatives to a negotiated settlement as more favorable to a disputant, which changes what the involved actors think is the true location and size of the win-set(s) and, therefore, bargaining range. If the counterpart believes the state's misrepresentations, they also shift the potentially agreed upon distribution in the state's favor. This possibility of obtaining more of the disputed good makes the risk of missing the bargaining range altogether (or continued nonagreement) acceptable. The challenge, then, is to discover better information about the disputants' capabilities and resolve.

In contrast, border territory with power endowments will inhibit border settlement via the commitment problem mechanism. When territory contains power endowments, the full value of these endowments cannot be realized while the territory remains disputed. Once delimitation occurs, however, the state that holds the endowed territory controls the advantages it offers. Because these advantages, by definition, can potentially shift the balance of power

[7] Fearon (1995) raises the possibility that indivisible issues constitute a bargaining obstacle among rational actors as well. He dismisses this, however (Fearon 1995), and Powell (2006) subsequently argues that indivisible issues merely constitute another form of the commitment problem. We therefore do not consider indivisible issues as a separate bargaining obstacle here.

between disputants – causing one neighbor to increase in relative power, while the other decreases – the gaining state cannot credibly commit *not* to use its newfound position of strength to demand further concessions from the now weaker state. Foreseeing this, the state who expects to lose foregoes border settlement, decreasing the likelihood that any type of conflict management will successfully produce a final, comprehensive settlement. In this way, the power endowment makes settlement challenging, even if states possess the information to find the bargaining range. Implementation concerns undermine the possibility of a stable distributional agreement.

In the sections that follow, we discuss the logic underlying these two mechanisms in greater detail. We also derive numerous hypotheses from these logics, each of which offers predictions about the conditions under which we expect the likelihood of border settlement to change. To date, few studies explore border settlement as the outcome we discuss here (see Chapter 2; for an exception, see Gibler and Owsiak 2018). Our discussion therefore draws on disparate bodies of research as an initial attempt to understand how and when border settlement occurs.

3.4.1 Border Territory and Information Problems

The first negotiating obstacle – incomplete information – makes a bargaining range difficult to locate or, if found, the precise terms to adopt difficult to agree upon. The ability to credibly convey information is critical for successful conflict resolution. In highly salient, interstate disputes, the most pertinent information becomes the balance of military power between disputing states and how much these states value a given, disputed issue (i.e., their resolve).[8] These two factors inform how to divide the disputed good. A militarily stronger state, *ceteris paribus*, expects to fare better if it must fight a war – the default policy option if peaceful conflict management fails and a solution must be reached. Given this, it demands a more favorable pre-war distribution of the disputed good. Similarly, a state that places a higher value on the disputed good will, *ceteris paribus*, pay greater costs to obtain it. Such a state will fight longer and devote more resources to any related war; this ensures that a war will be more costly to its counterpart and, therefore, a less attractive outcome. Moreover, if an agreed distribution cannot be had, a more resolved state will fare relatively better under the nonagreement status quo; its greater cost acceptance allows it to hold out for more favorable terms, until the state valuing the good less concedes. These considerations encourage it to demand a more favorable pre-war distribution of the disputed good too.

The importance of the above information in the bargaining process also proves to be its Achilles' heel. If a state can convince its counterpart that it

[8] Other factors matter to the extent that they alter these characteristics – for example, military technology, public opinion, alliance relationships, and so on.

is stronger militarily or has greater resolve than the counterpart thinks, it can demand more favorable settlement terms – regardless of whether these characteristics accurately reflect reality. To complicate matters further, information on military capabilities or resolve is typically private, meaning that a state usually knows its own capabilities and resolve (more or less) perfectly, but its opponent's capabilities and resolve incompletely. Thus, private information, as well as incentives to misrepresent it, constitute a notable obstacle to resolving interstate disagreements short of war (Fearon 1995).

States can overcome this incomplete information problem by using mechanisms that facilitate the credible transmission of information.[9] Often, this involves sending signals, particularly those that impose costs on the sender (Fearon 1997). Signaling is an attempt to let others know what *type* of actor one is – for example, whether an actor is bluffing or being truthful (i.e., expressing serious intentions or accurate information). Schelling (1966) explores this theme at length with respect to United States (US)–Soviet Union cold war deterrence. In this discussion, he notes that the credibility of information depends not on words, but on particular kinds of actions:

> It is hard to make [intentions] believed.... Just saying so won't do it.... What we have to do is get ourselves into a position where we cannot fail to react as we said we would – where we just cannot help it – or where we would be obliged by some overwhelming cost of not reacting in the manner we had declared. (Schelling 1966, 43)

The key, then, is to recognize that signaling cannot be done verbally, for "words are cheap, not inherently credible when they emanate from an adversary, and sometimes too intimate a mode of expression" (Schelling 1966, 150).[10] Instead, a signaling actor who wants to credibly convey information to an adversary must find actions that a "serious" type would pay for, but a "bluffing" one would not. These actions "prove something; significant actions usually incur some cost or risk, and carry some evidence of their own credibility. And actions are less ambiguous [than words] ...." (Schelling 1966, 150). Actions like these fall broadly into two types: tying hands (i.e., a leader cannot help but to act as she signaled she would, as that produces significant, unacceptable costs for her) or sunk costs (i.e., paying significant costs up front that make a change in policy seem wasteful; on both types, see Fearon 1997). Indeed, states can actually take actions that generate both types of costs (Slantchev 2005). Military action, like mobilizing troops or deploying carrier groups, can sink costs because actors will pay those regardless of the outcome of crisis. These actions also potentially affect war payoffs by impacting the distribution of

9 Revealing credible information may help states reach an agreement that avoids conflict. Some evidence suggests, however, that such an effect is conditional on the beliefs that the states hold before the information revelation occurs (Arena and Wolford 2012).

10 For an example of when just talk, or what some call "cheap" talk, can be effective at transmitting credible information that helps states avoid war see Bils and Spaniel (1917).

power and likely war outcomes, which affectively ties states' hands by altering their preferences over war and peace (Slantchev 2011).

The importance of credible signaling has motivated scholars to investigate the various characteristics thought to foster or impede it. From this research, we identify three state/dyadic-level characteristics within the adversaries' relationship that theoretically affect signaling during the border settlement process: audience costs, (a)symmetry in military capabilities, and alliance ties. The first of these – audience costs – receives significant attention because of its ties to democratic peace research (on the latter, see Russett and Oneal 2001). Audience costs are a form of "tying hands." Essentially, a state's leader invokes audience costs – accidentally or purposively – by publicly stating demands or threatening escalatory actions, thereby making these known to both the opponent and the leader's own domestic constituency. If the leader then fails to follow through on these public demands or threats, domestic publics could choose to punish the leader for damaging the state's honor, obligations, or diplomatic reputation, or for being imprudent or incompetent in executing policy (Schelling 1966, 49).

A relatively recent, prominent illustration of this idea follows from US President Barack Obama's "red line" statement on Syria. In August 2012, Obama proclaimed that "we have been very clear to the Assad regime ... that a red line for us is we start seeing a bunch of chemical weapons moving around or being utilized. That would change my calculus.... We have put together a range of contingency plans."[11] Assad reportedly used chemical weapons on his citizens after this warning, and Americans therefore expected the president to respond. An NBC news survey reported in August 2013 that a majority of US respondents had heard about Syria's use of chemical weapons, but were not sure that military strikes were appropriate. Nonetheless, if asked specifically about whether they would support air strikes on chemical weapons units and infrastructure, respondents' support for military action improved significantly. By 2016, 72% of respondents favored military strikes, and 57% expressed support for sending special operations forces to Syria.[12] These opinions affected how Americans evaluated Obama's job performance. During the period 2012–2015, the approval rating of Obama's handling of foreign affairs slid from a stable 49% through the 2012 election to a low of 31% at the end of 2014.[13] It recovered by the end of his term in 2016, but these data suggest that his Syria

[11] James Ball 2012. "Obama Issues Syria a 'Red Line' Warning on Chemical Weapons." *Washington Post*. Available online at www.washingtonpost.com/world/national-security/obama-issues-syria-red-line-warning-on-chemical-weapons/2012/08/20/ba5d26ec-eaf7-11e1-b811-09036bcb182b_story.html.

[12] Dina Smeltz, Craig Kafura, and Kelhan Martin. 2016. "Americans Support Limited Military Action in Syria Against ISIS." The Chicago Council on Global Affairs. Available online at www.thechicagocouncil.org/publication/americans-support-limited-military-action-syria-against-isis.

[13] Justin McCarthy 2016. "Americans' Approval of Obama on Foreign Affairs Rises." Gallup. Available online at http://news.gallup.com/poll/194624/americans-approval-obama-foreign-affairs-rises.aspx.

policy – or lack thereof – cost him. Had he been eligible for re-election at the nadir of his approval rating, the Syrian policy might have impacted his chances of re-election.

This example underscores three noteworthy points about audience costs. First, audiences must be *able* to punish their leader. Democratic elections offer a routinized, institutional opportunity for the punishment of democratic leaders, but as in the example above, audiences must wait for these elections. Leaders of nondemocratic states, in contrast, can be removed from office at any point, although it is more difficult to do so. Second, audience costs do not guarantee a leader's punishment; rather, they make it more costly for the leader to change direction from any publicly stated commitments. These costs ultimately provide credibility to the leader's public statements – a costly signal of what she intends to do.

Finally, although audience costs exist in democratic (Fearon 1994a) and nondemocratic states (Weeks 2008), scholars associate them more with the former. Bueno de Mesquita et al. (1999), for example, argue that goods like national security or a better economy – both externalities of border settlement – may matter more to democratic than nondemocratic leaders. The former must satisfy a larger group of supporters (i.e., a larger winning coalition) than the latter. This, in turn, has foreign policy implications. Nondemocratic leaders can lean more on the provision of private goods to secure their winning coalition's support; relatively fewer supporters make such direct benefits a viable, and perhaps desirable, policy (e.g., direct payments, government positions, or other benefits). Democratic leaders, however, must generally rely more on public goods (e.g., overall security or economic growth) to influence their winning coalition. Not only do democratic institutions foster less loyalty to leaders, but the larger number of winning coalition members also renders public goods the most efficient and effective mechanism for securing support. Given these institutions, democratic leaders will only fight wars they believe they can win, since losing a war means they will necessarily fail to provide a public good (e.g., national security), and they cannot effectively compensate their winning coalition members with private goods to offset this failure. A democracy that escalates a dispute therefore sends a credible signal about the information it holds about either its resolve (i.e., how willing it is to fight) or its prospects of winning a potential conflict (but see also Chiozza and Goemans 2011). Pairs of democracies then share an advantage over other dyads, since both democratic dyad members can signal effectively in this way.

Democracies might also signal a second way: via opposition parties. In democratic states, citizens expect opposition parties to criticize the government and its policies. This not only keeps the government accountable, but also helps the opposition parties build a platform from which to launch successful election bids. They argue that government policy is misguided and an alternative government – which usually just happens to include them – will correct the government's mistakes. Given this general expectation, when opposition parties *support* a government policy, then one might anticipate the government to be more likely to enact that policy (Schultz 1998). As an illustration, foreign states will find a Republican United States president's threats of militarized conflict more credible when the Democratic party supports those threats too (e.g., the United States threat to Afghanistan in response to 9/11). In such cases, the audience costs noted earlier still operate; the opposition party's support, however, intensifies them.

Audience costs can be difficult to observe, but research generally finds both that they exist (Partell and Palmer 1999) and that any such costs we observe may be understated (Schultz 2001). Thus, despite some empirical measurement challenges, scholars conclude that audience costs can significantly increase the possibility of a leader's punishment. This threat of punishment ultimately supplies credibility to a leader's public statements. A bluffing leader that faces high audience costs would unnecessarily put her job at risk; she would be unwilling (i.e., lack the resolve) or unable (i.e., lacking the capability) to fight militarily, so misrepresenting her true capabilities or resolve becomes a less attractive option. If she tries to bluff and her opponent challenges her, she would back down, at which point supporters (i.e., the domestic audience) would punish her. Knowing this, she prefers to avoid bluffing in the first place.

Stated more generally, as the (institutional) potential for audience costs rises, the veracity of leaders' statements about their capabilities and resolve increases as well (along with the threats and concessions these statements promote in the bargaining process).[14] The audience costs help distinguish serious statements from bluffs. Because democratic leaders, on average, confront greater (potential) audience costs than nondemocratic leaders (see earlier discussion), it stands to reason that two democratic states interacting – each of which has higher audience costs than nondemocratic states – bargain at an advantage over other dyads (i.e., pairs of states). They more easily reveal to one another the credible information needed to overcome the bargaining obstacle caused by uncertainty over power or resolve. This allows them to reach a border settlement more easily than dyads containing at least one nondemocratic state.

Beyond audience costs, a democratic dyad may experience a second advantage during the border settlement process: a shared norm for resolving political disputes peacefully. This norm manifests itself through elections, but permeates the broader policy-making process as well. Dixon (1994, 15) labels this the "norm of bounded competition," in which "political actors, whether inside or outside of government, agree not to employ physically coercive or violent means to secure a winning position on contentious public issues" (see also Maoz and Russett 1993; Russett and Oneal 2001). When a democracy confronts another democracy over an issue, each *expects* the other to follow the norm of bounded political competition; that is, each knows the other values the

[14] Audience costs are a function of institutional arrangements by which the leader obtains and sustains support. See preceding discussion and Bueno de Mesquita et al. (2003).

nonviolent resolution of political issues. It therefore channels the dispute into nonviolent conflict management mechanisms (e.g., negotiation or mediation) and away from violence. Moreover, neither general misunderstanding nor the break-down of nonviolent processes leads to violence at rates as high as in other types of dyads; expectations of nonviolent conflict management persist.

In contrast, a democratic state facing a nondemocratic one understands that the latter does not generally abide by the norm of bounded competition. If it prioritizes and pursues nonviolent conflict management while the nondemocracy stresses violence, then the nondemocracy may take advantage of it and gain the upper hand. Although commonly mischaracterized as "peace at any price" (on this point, see Bell 2007), Chamberlain's policy of appeasement illustrates the logic behind this argument. Exhibiting a preference for nonviolent conflict management if at all possible, Chamberlain pushed negotiation and mediation in 1938, unaware that Hitler participated in these diplomatic initiatives while simultaneously preparing to fight an imminent war. When Hitler's plans later became clear to him, Chamberlain felt deceived and cheated (Bell 2007).

A democracy that engages diplomatically, while its nondemocratic counterpart does not, faces more than a personal affront, however; it also may experience a military attack for which it would be either unprepared, significantly weakened, or placed at a disadvantage. Israel, for example, frequently moves to military action when contesting issues with its nondemocratic neighbors. It regarded Egypt's closing of the Straits of Tiran in 1967 as an act of war worthy of a military response (Reiter 1995), the possibility of a nuclear Iran or Syria as an impetus for a military strike against nuclear facilities there (in 1981 and 2007, respectively), and refuses to cede the Golan Heights to Syria. The reasons for its behavior are complex; yet a contributing factor is that the various involved states do not all share the norm of bounded competition. Violence remains a real possibility, and to prevent being placed at a disadvantage, the democratic state (e.g., Israel) adopts the political norms of the nondemocratic states (e.g., Egypt, Iran, or Syria) when interacting with them – namely, not constraining its behavior with the norm of bounded competition. This makes it more difficult for such dyads – and relatedly, dyads composed of two nondemocratic states – to settle their borders successfully.

These various logics lead to the following general expectation:

***Hypothesis* 3.1.** Democratic, neighboring states are more likely to settle their borders than other dyadic regime pairs of neighbor states.

This hypothesis rests heavily on a well-established body of research: democratic peace theory (Russett and Oneal 2001). It is worth noting, however, that recent studies question the connection between democracy, territory (especially borders), and peace that underlies the hypothesis's logic (see Gibler 2012). On the one hand, some scholars note that almost all democratic dyads settle their borders before both states in the dyad become democracies (Gibler and Owsiak 2018; Owsiak and Vasquez 2019); according to these authors, shared democratic norms and institutions therefore cannot affect the border settlement process, as they did not exist during it.[15] On the other hand, numerous scholars note that democratic dyads do not necessarily bargain more peacefully than their counterparts over territory (James, Park, and Choi 2006), including borders (Gibler 2012; Owsiak 2019). These findings contradict others in the field (see, e.g., Hensel et al. 2008). The discrepancy may result from issue salience; as Park and James (2015) show, democratic dyads handle territorial claims more peacefully than nondemocratic dyads, but only if the territory under dispute has low salience to them. As the salience of the territory grows, so does the disputatiousness of the democratic dyad. Within intermediate to high levels of territorial claim salience, democratic dyads then behave like their counterparts. Whether the arguments presented here hold merit is an empirical question; as such, our analysis allows us to weigh on this contemporary discussion.

To determine the share of a disputed good (e.g., territory) that it believes it should receive through bargaining, a state estimates the adversary's capabilities, compares that estimate with its own capabilities, and uses the resulting indicator of relative strength to develop ideas about the appropriate distribution of the good. Generally speaking, states expect the disputed good's distribution to align with the distribution of relative power between them. Relative equals, for example, split a good evenly, while a state twice as strong as its adversary receives twice as much of the disputed good. The logic behind this thinking derives from how states expect to fare in war should bargaining break down and a military fight to distribute the good be necessary.

States consequently make, accept, and reject bargaining offers based on their calculation of relative military power. At the extremes, these calculations are easier to make. When, for example, a large asymmetry in military capabilities exists between two states, little debate ensues about who is stronger, and the amount of the discrepancy between them matters marginally less. A state's assessment of its situation changes little if an adversary is seven, as opposed to eight, times stronger. Large power asymmetries therefore foster greater confidence in state's calculation of battlefield outcomes (i.e., relative power). Consequently, they gain confidence in their assessment of the appropriate distribution of the disputed good as well.

In contrast, as states approach equality (i.e., parity) in relative power, who will win a military contest becomes murkier. Any small advantage tips the scales, so factors like military strategy, logistics, the quality of soldiers and leaders, and the support of the domestic population play a greater role. These factors, however, are more difficult to assess in enemies than estimating the quantity and quality of military hardware (e.g., guns, or land, air, and naval

15 Gibler and Owsiak (2018) review the democratic dyad cases in depth. Their analysis suggests that democratic norms and institutions played a minimal role in the border settlement process within these dyads.

forces). In addition, disputants' incentives to misrepresent their capabilities and resolve increase as they approach power parity – with deleterious effects. Determining whether one faces a serious or bluffing adversary constitutes a main challenge in the bargaining process (see earlier discussion). Bluffing, however, becomes less of an issue as power asymmetry grows. If State A is ten times stronger than State B (in military capabilities), for example, then State B bluffing about its military capabilities will not likely overcome that objective fact to change the bargaining dynamic; the distance is too wide. As power approaches parity, the situation changes. Bluffs hold greater promise. A disputing state could more easily be wrong about the true power distribution, which then carries real consequences if a military battle ensues. This uncertainty raises the probability that bluffs will achieve their goal: to convince the adversary to concede more. And these benefits encourage more states to *try* bluffing in the first place. Unsure of whether they face a bluffing or serious adversaries, states then bargain more inefficiently.

Power parity therefore brings greater uncertainty about the type, strength, and resolve of the adversary. This uncertainty clouds the bargaining process and therefore increases the probability that bargaining breaks down (Reed 2003). In other words, we expect that:

***Hypothesis* 3.2.** Neighboring states are less likely to settle their borders as they approach relative power parity.

A third factor that affects the signaling of military capabilities and resolve is alliances. States sign alliances for numerous reasons – one of which is capability aggregation (for an overview, see Morrow 1991). By adding the military capabilities of multiple states together, allies intend to deter attacks from adversaries or, if this fails, to win any military battle that occurs. They attempt this deterrence through signaling about both military capabilities and resolve. On the one hand, an alliance possesses greater military capabilities than any individual member. It therefore becomes more costly for an adversary to attack, since it must attack a (now) stronger entity. On the other hand, engaging an alliance partner demonstrates greater resolve. Allies are weary of fighting proxy battles on one another's behalf. An ally is therefore unlikely to join a partner's conflict if that partner chooses not to fight. Moreover, appealing to an ally for assistance and then backing down – or alternatively, trying to convince an ally that one is serious about fighting when not (i.e., bluffing) – carries consequences. The ally may prove less reliable when subsequently needed in a future dispute. An alliance can therefore signal a state's greater capabilities and resolve, in an attempt to both convince an adversary that the costs of conflict are higher than it expects and, relatedly, obtain a larger share of the disputed good.

Alliance logic typically applies to an adversary outside the alliance. Yet existing theories of alliance formation suggest that alliances facilitate the credible signaling of information – and the reduction of uncertainty – between alliance members as well. Alliances serve their deterrent purpose when actors are confident that alliance partners will fulfill their obligations to one another (Morrow 2000). An alliance's greater military capabilities, for example, mean little to an adversary if the allies do not actually plan to assist one another. Everything hinges on the alliance partners' collective reliability.

It is therefore not the mere signing of an alliance that signals information and achieves deterrence. Were this true, states would always sign alliance agreements, and the ability of alliances to signal would therefore lose value. Rather, a useful signal must convey information that helps states distinguish between adversary types (e.g., resolved or bluffing). The best signals are those that impose costs on the sender – costs a resolved adversary would pay, but a bluffing one would not. Alliances impose two such costs: requiring the coordination of security policy and military action. The coordination of security policy ensures that alliance partners do not operate at cross-purposes and that they work politically toward common goals. The North Atlantic Treaty Organization (NATO), for example, has common policies that address a number of threats, from Russia to cyberspace. In exchange for greater security through the alliance, members cede some autonomy over their policy (although the autonomy ceded may vary across alliance members; see Morrow 1991, 2000). The coordination of military action subsequently ensures that the alliance is ready for the need to use force. Any multi-national force faces command, control, logistic, and tactical issues that ideally must be worked out before the need for the force arises. Joint military exercises offer a highly visible form of this coordination, although it runs much deeper than these exercises alone. Such costs signal members' commitment not only to adversaries, but also to one another. States uninterested in either the alliance or making good on the obligations they contain are unlikely to pay the costs associated with the coordination that the alliance requires.

The above coordination affects bargaining in intra-alliance disputes. In particular, it reduces information asymmetries between alliance partners in two ways. First, close coordination over policy and military matters reduces uncertainty over the resolve of (i.e., the intentions) and the distribution of capabilities between partners, respectively. Addressing command and control issues, conducting joint training exercises, discussing tactics, and procuring equipment for collaborative action provides allies with an inside look at their partners' militaries. Similarly, coordinating security policy gives alliance partners insight into one another's resolve (i.e., the costs for conflict that partners can stomach and sustain). This complicates the alliance partners' ability to exaggerate their capabilities or resolve in the hopes of receiving a larger share of the disputed good. Second, a breakdown in bargaining – and the outbreak of conflict between alliance partners – diminishes the deterrent ability of the alliance. Not only are resources used up on the internal squabble, rather than addressing adversaries external to the alliance, but these adversaries are also less likely to believe that alliance partners will reliabily fulfill commitments to help one another. Adversaries can therefore exploit intra-alliance turmoil to time an attack and achieve their goals. Alliance partners know this, however, and will consequently only make demands of one another when they are highly resolute. In other words, a state will only issue demands over a good disputed with an alliance partner when it is willing to risk the alliance partnership to win its perceived share of that good. This makes demands between alliance partners more credible, thereby facilitating the settlement of intra-alliance disputes.[16]

Based on the above logic, we therefore anticipate that:

***Hypothesis* 3.3.** Neighboring states are more likely to settle their borders when allied to one another, as opposed to when they lack a shared alliance.

3.4.2 Border Territory and Commitment Problems

The second negotiation obstacle involves implementation concerns. As actors negotiate, they think ahead to the implementation phase – to ascertain whether any agreement they reach is likely to be short-lived (Fearon 1998). The expectation of a short-lived agreement develops when actors believe that one of the negotiators' incentives will change in the aftermath of the agreement, causing it to renege on the agreement's terms. These credible commitment concerns underlie much international behavior; here, however, we focus on a particular variant: the commitment problem (Powell 2006), which arises when negotiators cannot credibly promise to abide by an agreement reached today – that is, not to renegotiate or impose a new solution – if they become relatively more powerful in the future. Mindful both that implementation would fall short and that power will shift between them, negotiators (particularly the actor likely to weaken in the agreement's wake) eschew agreement altogether. The problem becomes particularly acute when negotiators bargain over a good (e.g., border territory) that itself contributes to the shift in power that would undermine the very agreement reached.

We focus on this latter commitment problem scenario – where states are bargaining over a good that is itself a source of power (see Chapter 2). Redistribution of the good in this case, by definition, alters the relative power between disputants. As an illustration of the problem and its logic, assume two states, State A and State B, who control x and $1 - x$ proportion of a given border territory, respectively (see previous discussion for the assumptions and underlying foundations). State A prefers the status quo; it wants the distribution to remain as it is. State B, the revisionist state, wishes to increase its own share of the territory (i.e., increase $1 - x$), which necessarily means decreasing State A's share (i.e., to increase the quantity $1 - x$, the value of x – or A's share of the territory – must fall). Now assume further that the territory contains a source of power uniformly distributed over it (i.e., the source of power appears in

[16] See Gartzke, Li, and Boehmer (2001) for a similar argument regarding trade, information, and conflict.

all parts of the territory equally).[17] In this scenario, redistributing the territory according to State B's proposal will alter the relative power between States A and B. State A, the status quo state, will be made weaker by transferring all or part of the territory to State B; it loses the power (resources) contained within the territory it transfers to State B. In contrast, State B will be made stronger because it gains not only territory, but also the power that territory contains.

Losing territory seems like a bad deal for State A, but there are conditions under which it is willing to lose *some* territory. Its primary concern, however, has to do *not* with the exact re-distribution proposed by this agreement, but rather, with State B's future intentions. State A understands that State B will become stronger relative to it after taking control of the newly transferred territory. At that point, it worries that State B will use its new, stronger position to revise the agreement further – to wrestle even better terms for State B from State A (e.g., additional territorial concessions). Because State A will be weaker at that future negotiation, it may not be able to stop State B's revision attempt. Thus, State A prefers to forego settlement with State B today, rather than renegotiate with a stronger State B in the near future. This results in the breakdown of the bargaining process, and the border remains unsettled [18]

In the context of interstate border negotiations, the situation outlined earlier is most likely to occur when the disputed border territory contains power endowments – that is, a strategically important position (e.g., an offensive or defensive military advantage) or significant economic value (e.g., exploitable resources). Transferring territory with power endowments shifts the relative power between the involved states. Thus, even though leaving the border unsettled generates opportunity costs, such a policy will often be preferable to reaching an agreement today, strengthening an opponent (or, alternatively, weakening oneself), and permitting the opponent to renegotiate today's agreement terms from a future, stronger bargaining position. These incentives increase the likelihood of bargaining breakdown when border territory contains power endowments. Border territory that lacks these power endowments, however, does not produce this same commitment problem and, therefore, a similar collapse of the bargaining process.

Based on this reasoning, we expect that:

***Hypothesis* 3.4.** Neighboring states are less likely to settle their borders when the border territory contains power endowments, as opposed to when it does not.

[17] This simplifies the discussion greatly.

[18] Chadefaux (2011) argues that states can generally find ways to avoid commitment problem-driven wars by negotiating over power. Trade-offs can be made such that the rising state gives up sources of power to alleviate the declining states' concerns about future renegotiation. War, or rivalry in our case, is still possible, however, when negotiations are complicated by a significant overlap between the benefits being split and capabilities. Which is exactly the type of scenario we are modeling.

3.4.3 The Role of Conflict Management Tools

Protracted disagreement – particularly over a highly salient issue – sours disputing states' relationship and erodes confidence between them. In particular, these states develop concerns about the willingness or ability of one another: to provide accurate information about their needs, interests, and positions (i.e., not to bluff or misrepresent to gain an advantage); to make the necessary concessions to reach an agreement; to deliver their domestic constituency so that any potential agreement does not collapse; and to commit credibly to the implementation of the agreement (e.g., see Ghosn 2010; Greig 2001, 2005; Greig and Diehl 2006). The border settlement process therefore requires that neighboring states address and (if necessary) overcome these concerns, and we note two potential methods by which they might do so. First, as states interact with one another diplomatically – through repeated negotiations – they should clarify one another's positions, learn about one another's intentions, understand better what the negotiation process and an agreement look like in practice, and generally build a relationship defined by increasing levels of trust (Axelrod 1984; Bo 2005; Greig and Diehl 2006). Second, where negotiators struggle to achieve these tasks on their own, third-party involvement may help (Greig and Diehl 2006). In particular, third parties can act as (perhaps more credible) conduits of information (Kydd 2003), accept (some) responsibility for unpopular concessions (i.e., shield leaders from domestic backlash; on this argument, see Allee and Huth 2006), propose specific settlement terms, settle the dispute outright (e.g., in arbitration), or guarantee an agreement that the disputants reach (see Walter 2002).

The first conflict management tool – (repeated) negotiations – reveals information about states' capabilities and resolve. Negotiations occur when disputants sit down with one another (in the absence of a third party) to bargain nonviolently about a way to resolve their disagreement. The negotiation process therefore demands that actors share information with one another about what they want and why (Fisher, Ury, and Patton 1991; Hopmann 1996). Misrepresentation may still rear its head, but through repeated exchanges, negotiations help sort fact from fiction. As they search for the bargaining range and the mutually acceptable terms to agree upon within it, for example, disputants offer proposals, monitor one another's reactions to these proposals (e.g., rejections, acceptances, and counteroffers), and track the overall trend in the proposals (e.g., whether bargainers' positions are moving closer, whether concessions on a given issue are increasing, etc.). Through this back-and-forth, disputants test the boundaries of one another's positions (i.e., determine whether a given position is firm or flexible), explore where concessions can be made (or not), and gather research to assist their bargaining exchange (e.g., intelligence, which helps them verify the veracity of one another's statements; for evidence that negotiations iterate, see Ghosn 2010). All of this helps reduce the informational uncertainty about the disputants' relative capabilities and resolve (for an overview of the field, see Druckman and Wall 2017).

***Hypothesis* 3.5.** As the number of bilateral negotiations addressing a border's delimitation increases, the likelihood rises that the involved neighboring states will settle that border.

The remaining conflict management tools – mediation and legal approaches – involve third-party conflict managers (for an overview, see Bercovitch and Jackson 2009).[19] In mediation, a third party helps disputants negotiate. The third party can play any number of roles as a mediator, which range from facilitative (i.e., handling the logistics of negotiation, or controlling the communication between disputants; often called "good offices") to fact-finding (i.e., independently gathering information about the disputants' positions, capabilities, and resolve) to directive (i.e., making specific, substantive proposals about how disputants should resolve their dispute; often called "conciliation"). This process is voluntary for both the third party and disputants; each can walk away at any time, even if a proposal sits on the table merely awaiting their signature (see Greig and Diehl 2012). As a result, mediation succeeds at producing an agreement of any kind less than half of the time; it yields a comprehensive peace agreement in fewer than 10% of mediation attempts (Greig, Owsiak, and Diehl 2019).

In legal approaches, the voluntary aspect of mediation fades. Disputants agree at the outset – via either a specific, special agreement related to the dispute at hand (i.e., the *compromis* that begins the arbitration process) or a general, standing agreement (i.e., recognition of a court's jurisdiction, which opens the door to adjudication) – to allow a third party to decide how to resolve the dispute and to abide by the third party's decision (i.e., award or ruling).[20] For this reason, scholars label legal approaches "binding" (see Gent and Shannon 2011). Nonetheless, the binds involved are not absolute. States may reject legal awards that they do not like – more so from arbiters than from international courts.[21]

We mention compliance issues because, at first glance, the binding aspect of legal approaches suggest that they should succeed more often than mediation.

[19] Following other research, we include good offices, fact-finding missions, and conciliation under the larger mediation umbrella (Greig, Owsiak, and Diehl 2019). For detailed definitions of our conflict management strategies, as well as what strategies our data contains, see Chapter 4.

[20] We include post-war conferences under legal approaches as well (see Chapter 4). In these conferences, the international community often redraws the map (e.g., after the world wars). The treaties involved give the conference proceedings legal status, while those affected often have little choice but to follow (i.e., the agreements are binding). These are the essential characteristics of legal approaches.

[21] China's behavior in the recent South China Sea Arbitration demonstrates this well (2013–2016). It rejected the arbitration panel's jurisdiction, refused to participate in the arbitration process (even returning the tribunal's mail), and does not recognize the tribunal's award. In contrast, international courts experience high compliance rates. Disputing states comply with over 90% of ICJ awards that involve territorial, river, or maritime claims (Mitchell and Owsiak 2017), and with over 80% of the World Trade Organization's Dispute Settlement Mechanism awards (Reich 2017).

Indeed, a legal approach, once started, virtually guarantees an award – especially since it is designed to do so in the presence of recalcitrant disputants. Yet legal approaches do not provide a one-and-done solution to unsettled borders. Variation across legal approaches helps explain why. Of the legal approaches available to disputants, arbitration proves the most attractive for numerous reasons (Gent and Shannon 2011; Owsiak and Mitchell 2019). First, disputants can select the arbiter, giving them control over who decides their case. Adjudication, in contrast, requires states to use standing courts; since each court's jurisdiction is limited (e.g., by region or issue area), the number of courts that can hear any given case is small.[22] Second, disputants can direct the arbiter, through the *compromis*, to focus on specific issues, documents (e.g., treaties), or legal principles. Arbiters work within these constraints because the *compromis* forms the basis of their authority. Courts, however, cannot be similarly directed to focus on some treaties, to the exclusion of the wider body of international law (see Shaw 2014, 774). Finally, because the *compromis* narrows the issues, actors, and legal principles involved, violating an arbitration award carries fewer reputation costs than violating an international court award (on reputation in international law, see Guzman 2008). This is not to say that non-compliance with an arbitration award carries no reputation costs; rather, defying an arbiter is, *ceteris paribus*, less costly than defying an international court and the larger international legal system they support. The latter triggers the interests of a much wider, global audience. In the end, disputing states' preference for arbitration over adjudication may result from a greater willingness to violate an arbitral award's terms, although they theoretically will still violate these terms less often than similar terms that arise through the mediation process. Legal approaches, like mediations, may therefore need to be repeated as states work toward border settlement (see Colombia–Venezuela example discussed subsequently).

Third parties – whether employing mediation or legal approaches – facilitate the exchange of information in numerous ways. First and foremost, when disputants do not trust one another, third parties provide a more credible source of information. This can be done as a producer or conduit of information (or both). As a producer, third parties create independent information that verifies disputants' negotiating positions, capabilities, or resolve. Fact-finding offers an illustration of this behavior, but the production of independent information extends beyond it alone. For example, international institutions – and other bureaucracies for that matter – develop "expert authority" (Barnett and Finnemore 2004), which allows them to generate more reliable, unbiased information and make it available to the wider international community (Keohane 1984). It is this type of information that proves vital for reducing uncertainty during bargaining (see also Fisher, Ury, and Patton 1991). As a conduit, the third party also provides a channel through which disputants

[22] Forum shopping among the available courts, however, may still occur. See Busch (2007).

communicate with one another. Here, bias may help. As Kydd (2003) notes, an unbiased mediator that merely wants peace has an incentive to say anything to obtain peace; disputants may therefore be hesitant to accept these mediators' statements as truth. In contrast, Kydd argues that a disputant will find a biased mediator – that is, a mediator with closer ties to itself – more credible. The biased mediator has an incentive to be truthful because its interests are intertwined with the disputant's interests.[23] Consistent with this argument, much research finds that biased mediators (e.g., those that share a similar regime type, alliance ties, or significant trade ties with one or more disputants) not only mediate more often than less biased mediators, but succeed more at it as well (see Crescenzi et al. 2011; Melin 2011; Owsiak and Frazier 2014; Svensson 2009). Nonetheless, evidence suggests that unbiased mediators may outperform biased ones (Rauchhaus 2006). Regardless of how this debate unfolds, both sides claim that mediators supply information that helps disputants bargain more effectively.[24]

A second way that third parties promote the exchange of information is through iteration. If disputants could solve their disagreement on their own, they would. Including a third party proves more costly than negotiating with the other disputant(s) alone. It introduces additional negotiators, who bring along their own substantive interests that must now be addressed; reduces the disputants' level of control over the disagreement's management and outcome, giving it to the third party instead; and slows down the settlement process. Disputants would prefer to avoid these costs, only involve a third party when they can not make further progress alone. Thus, third parties will be disproportionately involved in managing disputes that are more difficult to resolve – the ones that disputants could not handle (i.e., a selection effect exist).

The difficulty of the disputes, in turn, suggests that iterations of conflict management will be necessary, rather than single, isolated attempts. These iterations "soften disputants up" for settlement (Greig and Diehl 2006). Each conflict management attempt familiarizes disputants with the third party, its role, its interests, and how it will behave (e.g., will it exercise coercion to push disputants toward a settlement), as well as the conflict management process itself. Moreover, the iterations necessarily reveal information about the disputants' positions, interests, capabilities, and resolve. In mediation, for example, the disputants will need to share this information to move toward a settlement; whether they share this with the mediator (acting as a conduit) or directly with the other disputants does not matter. Information flows. Similarly, disputants lay out their argument for arbiters or adjudicators, which explains

[23] This raises a separate issue: how to find a mediator that *both* sides trust. Kydd (2003) does not provide an answer, but Rauchhaus (2006) does; by arguing that unbiased mediators prove more effective than biased ones, Rauchhaus removes third-party bias from disputants' calculations altogether.

[24] For a more critical perspective on the ability of mediators to help states overcome information problems, see Fey and Ramsay (2010).

their positions on the disputed issues. Since these legal processes take years to unfold, however, disputants have time in which to learn about one another's capabilities and resolve and – with this information – to bargain "in the shadow" of the court (Bilder 1987; Mnookin and Kornhauser 1979). The logic for this behavior parallels states' pursuit of negotiation while contemplating and perhaps preparing for war, for as Lebow (1996, 20) notes:

> The pursuit of multiple strategies can be a cost-effective means of coping with uncertainty; if bargaining fails, there is a ready alternative. Development of multiple options also puts pressure on the other party to be more accommodating. Is it the sensible thing to do when there are doubts that bargaining will lead to a successful outcome.

A legal approach provides the pressure that Lebow identifies because it threatens to produce an award unless the disputants mutually agree to stop it. Moreover, legal processes are more effective than mediation at wringing concessions from all disputants (Beardsley and Lo 2014). These characteristics incentivize disputants to negotiate a solution with renewed vigor – before the legal process finishes – and supplies them with a back-up solution should they fail.

Importantly, three broad pieces of evidence indicate that iterations of third-party conflict management affect interstate disputes in accordance with the theoretical argument we outlined earlier. First, studies repeatedly note that conflict management predicts further conflict management (Beardsley 2011; Greig and Diehl 2006; Greig and Regan 2008; Hensel et al. 2008; Melin 2013; Melin and Svensson 2009). Greig (2005), for example, finds that the likelihood of mediation rises as the number of previous mediations increases. Mediation therefore seems to repeat itself, likely because it is being used to address difficult conflicts. In Greig's (2005) study, repeated negotiations reduce the likelihood that third parties will offer to mediate, but increase the likelihood that disputants ask them to do so. Third parties, in other words, do not offer to assist while disputants appear to make progress; as repeated negotiations fail to resolve a disagreement, however, the disputants increasingly turn to third-party mediators for help. Similar evidence appears in research on legal processes (Gent and Shannon 2011; Powell and Wiegand 2010, 2014).

Second, iterations may produce the proposed "softening up" process. Powell and Wiegand (2010), for example, find that disputants who "win" in legal processes employ those processes again. Self-interest informs this behavior, but it necessarily does so with any softening up logic. Once disputants understand that conflict management can be beneficial to them, they employ it more often to address their disputes. Finally, iterations of third-party conflict management enhance bilateral negotiations. Disputants withdraw approximately 18% of ICJ cases and 60% of World Trade Organization cases before the legal process produces an award – often because they reach an out-of-court settlement (Busch and Reinhardt 2002; Mitchell and Owsiak 2017).

Given the logic connecting (repeated) third-party conflict management to effective bargaining, as well as the general evidence in support of it, we therefore expect that:

***Hypothesis* 3.6.** As the number of mediations addressing a border's delimitation increases, the likelihood rises that the involved neighboring states will settle that border.

***Hypothesis* 3.7.** As the number of legal processes addressing a border's delimitation increases, the likelihood rises that the involved neighboring states will settle that border.

The previous conflict management hypotheses – negotiation, mediation, and legal processes – related primarily to border territory that does not contain power endowments. When the (re)distribution of disputed territory will not alter the relative power between the disputants, the commitment problem does not arise; in such cases, the main bargaining obstacle becomes about disputants' ability to obtain accurate information about one another's capabilities and resolve. Conflict management assists disputants with overcoming this information problem.

If disputed territory triggers a commitment problem, however, conflict management will be less effective. Repeated bilateral negotiations, for example, reduce information asymmetries; yet they struggle to allay the concern that an adversary will exploit a more powerful, future position created by the redistribution of the disputed, endowed territory. Similarly, a third-party mediator that provides credible information about disputants' positions or encourages them to share this information with one another cannot forestall any power shift that a settlement creates. One might insist that this argument is undermined by the fact that conflict management iterations can build trust between disputants. We do not deny that this can occur, but even in the instances where it does, the commitment problem likely lingers. The stakes are high. Not only do unsettled borders concern a highly salient issue (i.e., territory), but with power endowments present, their settlement threatens to redefine the disputants' relationship fundamentally, placing one in a vulnerable position at the hands of the other. Moreover, there exists no lifeline should the weaker state need it. The international community decries interstate aggression and has, on occasion, acted to reverse full invasions of a state (e.g., the response to Iraq's invasion of Kuwait in 1990). It does not, however, generally react as strongly to minor border adjustments or incursions. A weakened state knows that it most likely faces the strengthened state alone, especially if its entire existence does not hang in the balance.

In short, we propose that the effectiveness of negotiation and mediation is conditional on the type of bargaining problem the disputants are facing. In the absence of power endowments, disputants primarily encounter an information problem. Negotiation and mediation should increase the likelihood of border settlement in these instances, as they primarily assist with information problems (see earlier hypotheses).[25] When power endowments are present, however, the

[25] Mediators could, in theory, guarantee an agreement – that is, promise to enforce the terms of an agreement to prevent a power shift in the post-agreement implementation phase – at which point

commitment problem presents itself, making negotiation and mediation less successful at producing border settlement; they are not equipped to overcome this obstacle to bargaining. In other words:

***Hypothesis* 3.8.** Bilateral negotiations will be less likely to facilitate border settlement when power endowments are present than when they are not present.

***Hypothesis* 3.9.** Mediation will be less likely to facilitate border settlement when power endowments are present than when they are not present.

Unlike negotiation and mediation, legal approaches may generally be able to help surmount commitment problems. The critical question is: how (if at all) can a legal award either (a) prevent the power shift associated with a redistribution of border territory from occurring, or (b) decrease the ability of the strengthened state to renegotiate the award's terms after the disputants implement the award and their relative power shifts?

A legal award is unlikely to prevent a power shift altogether for two reasons. First, legal awards will, *ceteris paribus*, necessarily redistribute (some) border territory and, therefore, power between disputants. An award either redistributes border territory or reinforces the status quo distribution (i.e., does not redistribute territory). If it redistributes the disputed border territory, then the award *ensures* a power shift, rather than impeding it. Alternatively, if it reinforces the status quo, it leaves the disputants' relative power unchanged. Predicting the general effect of legal approaches on power redistribution therefore hinges on the relative balance between these two broad outcomes. Unfortunately, there is no a priori theoretical reason to suspect that legal awards tilt one way more than another. Research suggests, however, that redistribution of some type is likely to occur. As Sumner (2003, 1806–1807) notes:

> When the [International Court of Justice, the main adjudicative body with jurisdiction over border disputes,] lacks guidance from treaties, *uti possidetis*, or effective control, it is most likely to proceed in equity *infra legem* and halve the difference between the litigants' positions. The court – somewhat ironically – prefers prescribing an equitable solution over entertaining justifications based on geography, economics, culture, history, elitism, or ideology.

Given this preference, a redistribution of territory, and therefore power, seems more likely than not; thus, legal awards encourage power shifts. Second, even if they wanted to do so, international legal awards cannot prevent a power

mediation could then overcome the commitment problem. To our knowledge, there exists no data to effectively evaluate this proposition in interstate disputes, although it seems anecdotally possible (e.g., guarantors hold the 1942 Ecuador–Peru Rio Protocol together for nearly fifty years). We note, however, that this should not alter our argument or findings about mediation writ large. Guarantees occur rarely (e.g., see Walter 1997); this suggests that, in general, our argument about mediation will be accurate.

shift during the award's implementation phase. Legal awards require self-enforcement (i.e., the disputants must enforce them). The ICJ, for example, does not concern itself with implementation issues (i.e., compliance issues; see Shaw 2014). Similarly, arbiters do not implement or enforce their awards, but merely issue them. After receiving an award, what disputants ultimately do with it is up to them.

This leads to the second consideration: can legal approaches decrease the possibility of an award's renegotiation after it is issued? The answer, *ceteris paribus*, is yes. Once a legal process produces an award, two related factors work to lock in its terms. The first concerns the status of legal awards. A legal award itself is part of international law. Awards concerning border territory may therefore "constitute roots or sources of legal title to territory" (Shaw 2014, 359), which are then impossible to change unilaterally under international law. Moreover, these awards are not subject to appeal. The ICJ, for example, permits disputants to ask for an interpretation of its awards, but not an appeal (and rehearing) of that award's terms (Mitchell and Owsiak 2017). In a similar vein, even when an arbitration process fails – that is, the disputants immediately reject an award after it is issued – they often return to that award's provisions in the future. Colombia and Venezuela demonstrate this well. After many negotiations, they asked the Spanish monarch to arbitrate their border dispute in 1891. The Spanish award left them each unsatisfied, however, and the dispute continued. In the early 1900s, they then agreed to allow the Swiss Federal Council to arbitrate again, and the Swiss award largely reinforced the Spanish award (albeit with arbitrated demarcation as well; Ireland 1938; Scott 1922). In this way, legal awards – whether for purely legal or practical reasons, or both – function as focal points (Schelling 1960); among myriad possible distributions, legal awards identify and prefer one distribution over the alternatives.

International law as a focal point does not alone explain why a state would comply with a legal award's terms. Schelling (1960) notes that focal points answer one critical question: if not these (distributive) terms, then which alternative terms will we choose? A state strengthened by a legal award's redistribution of territory has the answer; it dictates more favorable terms for itself to the weakened state and compels the weakened state to comply. Why, then, would we expect the strengthened state to respect international law?

The answer to this question engages a lengthy debate on the independent value of international law (e.g., see Chayes and Chayes 1993; Downs, Rocke, and Barsoom 1996; Goldsmith and Posner 2006). The scholars involved in this debate begin with the assumption that states are rational, self-interested actors and ask when it would be in these states' interest to comply with international law. Pessimists conclude that states break international law at will (i.e., compliance with international law is epiphenomenal), while optimists maintain that international law meaningfully constrains state behavior – at least somewhat.

The constraints behind international law primarily derive from a cost–benefit calculation. A rational state will comply with international law when it concludes that compliance offers it a better outcome than noncompliance. For a state strengthened by a legal award, there are a handful of considerations that help determine which path to choose. First, it receives benefits from the current legal award; border settlement generally facilitates jurisdictional certainty, which enhances both economic activity and state security (Simmons 2005). This factors lightly into its calculations, for it is not choosing between unsettled and settled borders, but rather two manifestations of border settlement (i.e., different territorial distributions). Second, it knows it can get additional benefits if it uses its position of newfound strength to renegotiate the legal award's terms. This realization motivates the commitment problem. Finally, there are costs to renegotiating legal awards unilaterally – most notably, reputation costs. Border settlement terms, however reached, are public and part of international law. If the strengthened state violates the legal award's terms, then its actions as a violator of international law are readily known to other states. This, in turn, can affect its future cooperative endeavors. Guzman (2002), for example, argues that a reputation for failing to abide by one's international commitments can cost a state in future deals (to varying degrees, dependent on a variety of factors; see also Goemans 2000); other states will be less cooperative with a known cheater than with an honest counterpart (for limitations to this argument, see Brewster 2009; Downs and Jones 2002).

There are, however, more immediate and concrete consequences as well. Violating a negotiated agreement will be of primary concern to the negotiating parties (i.e., disputants). Violating a mediated agreement adds the concern of a third-party mediator. Yet violating a legal award does more than simply introduce the third-party conflict manager's concerns. The international legal system rests on expectations that states abide by their commitments to one another (i.e., *pacta sunt servanda*; Shaw 2014, 66–69). Thus, unilaterally renegotiating a legal award prompts involvement from the broader set of states that rely on international law; it therefore carries international audience costs. States can – and do – sanction one another in a variety of ways for violating international law (Guzman 2002).

None of this guarantees that a state will not renegotiate a legal award's terms after gaining power through the redistribution of territory. Indeed, sanctions for violating international law – whether reputation or material – are rarely optimal, thereby undermining the likelihood of perfect compliance (Guzman 2002). These sanctions, however, alter a rational, self-interested state's willingness to renegotiate a legal award's terms. In so doing, it interferes with the commitment problem logic and creates room for legal approaches to facilitate border settlement, even when territory contains power endowments. We therefore expect:

***Hypothesis* 3.10.** Legal approaches will facilitate border settlement both when power endowments are present and when they are not present.

The preceding hypothesis admittedly rests on the optimist's interpretation of international law – namely, that international law constrains state behavior. Mindful of this, two caveats are in order. First, the argument we present does not demand that states *never* renegotiate legal awards during the awards' implementation phase. Rather, it simply requires that this renegotiation is, on average, less likely to occur after a legal award as opposed to after an agreement produced through negotiations or mediation. That seems a reasonable conclusion to reach from the argument presented earlier. Second, the optimist argument produces a testable hypothesis. If the pessimists are correct instead, then we would not expect to find corroborating patterns in the data. We therefore do not ignore the possibility that the pessimist view is correct.

3.5 CONCLUSION

Neighboring states have numerous incentives to settle their border's delimitation; yet some borders move easily toward settlement, while others do not. What factors separate these two groups of cases? What influences whether border settlement successfully occurs (or not)? This chapter offers, to our knowledge, the first explicit theory of the border settlement process – one that integrates insights from disparate research on border (i.e., territorial) disputes, interstate bargaining, and conflict management.

Our theory conceptualizes border settlement as a straightforward bargaining process, in which states encounter competing pressures. On the one hand, they want to reach a settlement so that they can access the economic and security benefits associated with settled borders. On the other hand, they would like to obtain as much of the disputed territory as possible for themselves, so not just *any* settlement terms will do. These countervailing pressures both pull disputants toward border settlement and push them away from it. As they navigate these currents, two main bargaining obstacles interfere: information problems and commitment problems. Information problems impede bargaining by obscuring disputants' positions, intentions, capabilities, and resolve. Without accurate information on these various dimensions, the disputants cannot locate the terms that they both prefer to the unsettled status quo. In contrast, commitment problems arise when a settlement's terms threaten to shift the relative power between the disputants, thereby allowing the strengthened state to force the weakened state into a (near-)future renegotiation and revision of that agreement's terms – to the strengthened state's advantage. The weakened state anticipates this, however, and consequently refuses to settle in the first place. Knowing that a settlement today merely strengthens and therefore makes itself vulnerable to its adversary tomorrow, it chooses to forego settlement altogether.

Numerous factors help disputants overcome information problems. Shared democratic regimes, shared alliances, and asymmetric power distributions increase disputants' ability to clarify one another's positions, intentions, capabilities, and resolve. Where these characteristics are wanting, iterated negotiations allow disputants to exchange (repeated) proposals to clear up any uncertainty. Finally, if disputants cannot convey information credibly between themselves, third-party mediators, arbitrators, and adjudicators can assist them, acting as independent sources or conduits of information.

Commitment problems prove more difficult to surmount. In the context of border disputes, these problems arise when border territory contains power endowments – that is, resources capable of shifting the relative power between the disputants. Any redistribution of this type of territory necessarily gives one actor greater power, while taking it from the other. This torpedoes the border settlement process. Negotiation and mediation, we argue, cannot facilitate border settlement in such cases. The stakes are too high; not only is the issue (i.e., territory) highly salient, but the potentially weakened state will not want to make itself vulnerable and (perhaps) risk its security. The only path forward for border settlement involves disrupting either the power shift – which is impossible if territory will be redistributed – or the strengthened state's incentive to renegotiate the settlement. Legal approaches to conflict management (e.g., arbitration or adjudication) may do the latter and, therefore, help states overcome the commitment problem – to the extent that violating (i.e., unilaterally renegotiating under threat of force) a legal settlement carries significant costs (e.g., reputation or material). These costs encourage the strengthened state to abide by the legal award, even if it could renegotiate the terms. And if the settlement terms stabilize, then the potentially weakened state has an incentive to bargain once again.

In the next chapter, we outline an empirical strategy for determining whether the patterns in the data are consistent with these expectations. As we expect, information problems feature prominently in the border settlement process, but it is commitment problems that sharply distinguish the borders that settle easily from the ones that do not.

4

An Empirical Evaluation of Border Settlement

> [E]very border, all other factors being equal, is going to be contested at some point in the history of two neighbor[ing states], although the contesting may not necessarily be violent.
>
> J. A. Vasquez

4.1 INTRODUCTION

Under what conditions does border settlement occur? The current chapter investigates this broad question, with particular attention given to the hypotheses we advanced in the previous chapter. Because we offer one of the first explicit attempts to model the border settlement process empirically, this chapter contains significant detail about our study's research design – to clarify the scope conditions governing our results.[1] The first part of the chapter describes our variables – some explicitly collected for this project, and many that we use throughout the book – and justifies a key sampling choice we make – namely, a decision to focus not on all dyads (i.e., pairs of states), but rather on land contiguous (i.e., neighboring) dyads only. The second part of the chapter then implements our research design, presenting the evidence that allows us to evaluate the predictions made in Chapter 3 and understand the border settlement process better. Finally, we end the chapter with a synthesis of our main findings, which offers a jumping off point for the remainder of the book: what happens when states struggle to settle their borders?

[1] Studies of territorial claim resolution exist (see, for example, Hensel et al. 2008; Huth 1996; Huth and Allee 2002), but territorial claims and border settlement are not identical concepts. See Owsiak, Cuttner, and Buck (2018), as well as our discussion in Chapter 2.

4.2 DESIGNING THE EMPIRICAL STUDY

To examine how and when border settlement occurs, we need to observe the behavior of neighboring states (i.e., units) over time. We first use EUGene[2] (Bennett and Stam 2000) to create one observation for each year that any unique pair of states (hereinafter, a dyad) are both members of the international system and share a contiguous land border.[3] Thus, all analyses are restricted to *land contiguous dyads*, based on the theoretical premise that two states must share a border in order to settle a border.[4] The Correlates of War (COW) Project's Direct Contiguity data identifies these land contiguous dyads (Stinnett et al. 2002). Our unit of analysis is therefore the contiguous dyad-year during the period 1816–2001 (e.g., the United States–Canada 1921, the United States–Canada 1922, etc.).[5]

Critics might object to our unit of analysis, on the grounds that we should evaluate the importance of contiguity more directly, rather than assuming it. Were we to include all dyads (i.e., both contiguous *and* noncontiguous) in our model and interact each independent variable with a contiguity variable, they might propose that we could directly uncover and highlight the difference between neighboring dyads and those whose members sit at a greater distance from one another. Park and Colaresi (2014) adopt such an approach when studying the effect of settled borders on dyadic interstate conflict and the emergence of dyadic democracy. Two considerations, however, preclude us from relying upon a similar approach here. First, this approach fails to address the theoretical point that noncontiguous states do not share borders that they settle. Research on interstate borders generally recognizes this scope limitation (for example, see Gibler 2012; Goemans and Schultz 2017; Owsiak 2012), and we concur. Second, as theory anticipates, data on border settlement do

[2] The Expected Utility Generation and Data Management Program. This program is available at `www.eugenesoftware.org/`. A second-generation version of the program is also now available at `www.newgenesoftware.org/`.

[3] State system membership derives from the Correlates of War data, available at `http://correlatesofwar.org`. For a discussion about using dyads to study international relations, see Diehl and Wright (2016). Because borders are dyadic phenomena, this is the appropriate unit for our study.

[4] The study therefore excludes dyads in which water (e.g., the Mexico–Madagascar dyad) or other states (e.g., the Mexico–Canada dyad) separate a dyad's members. Future studies could extend our argument to maritime borders – a matter we discuss further in Chapter 9. Because evidence suggests that states treat land borders differently than maritime borders (our own analysis [not shown]; see also Hensel et al. 2008), however, we exclude maritime border settlement from this study. For more information on maritime border settlement, see Asgeirsdottir and Steinwand (2018) and Prescott and Schofield (2004).

[5] The temporal range of our analysis depends on data availability. The year 1816 marks the beginning of the Correlates of War (COW) Project and Issue Correlates of War (ICOW) Project datasets, while the data we employ for territorial claims – data that provides essential components of our analysis – currently do not exist after 2001.

not exist for noncontiguous dyads.[6] These dyads would therefore fall from our analysis (i.e., through list-wise deletion).[7] In the end, these theoretical and empirical considerations lead us to focus exclusively on land contiguous dyads. An analysis we present later in this chapter confirms the appropriateness of our decision.

4.2.1 Dependent Variable: Border Settlement

Our dependent variable in this chapter is *border settlement*. We operationalize this dichotomously, using data from Owsiak, Cuttner, and Buck (2018). A border is settled (a value of 1) in the year after which neighboring states have signed an international agreement that delineates the entirety of their mutual border(s). Since this variable becomes a key independent variable of interest in later chapters and underlies the argument of the entire book, we digress briefly to explain exactly what the variable captures and describe some of its key characteristics.

Four coding decisions underlie the border settlement variable, thereby providing scope conditions on the results we present throughout the book (Owsiak 2012; Owsiak, Cuttner, and Buck 2018). First, border settlement occurs through the signing of international agreements (see also Kocs 1995). It is therefore a purposive act – and importantly, as our research shows, one rarely done under duress. Moreover, although it often occurs in phases, we do not consider a dyad's border "settled" until it delimits all parts of its mutual border through whatever series of agreements accomplishes that task. As an illustration, Afghanistan and Iran settled their border through four separate agreements in 1872, 1889, 1905, and 1935; border settlement then exists beginning in 1936 (Biger 1995; Prescott and Triggs 2008). The United States–Canada border also settles in segments; the Root–Bryce Treaty of 1908 provided the final, complete delimitation of the boundary line, meaning that the border is settled as of 1909 in our data (Ireland 1971, 272). This decision aligns best with the conceptualization of border settlement presented earlier (see Chapter 2). For a border to be settled, dyad members must have agreed on (and therefore, minimally accepted) the delimitation of a given border; if

[6] Park and Colaresi (2014) circumvent this issue by relying upon proxy indicators of border settlement, as Gibler (2012) does. We argue in Chapter 2, however, that these proxy variables are less desirable than the more direct measure we employ, and this leaves us with missing data for border settlement in noncontiguous dyads.

[7] We could prevent this, assigning a value to the border settlement variable for noncontiguous dyads. This creates additional problems, though, when interpreting the results. If we count noncontiguous dyads' fictitious borders as "settled," then we have two types of settled borders in the data: one that occurs because an opportunity and a willingness to settle exists (i.e., in contiguous dyads) and one in which the opportunity (and through it, the willingness) to settle never arises (Most and Starr 1989). Because we know the factor that differentiates these two types (i.e., contiguity), theory encourages us to set aside the latter case type empirically.

any outstanding disagreement about a border's delimitation persists, regardless of how large or small a segment remains disputed, then the concept suggests that the border should be considered unsettled. Our coding captures this sentiment.

A couple of challenges arise empirically when using border agreements to determine settlement dates. On the one hand, historical narratives occasionally conflict. Examples include the Chad–Libya border, as well as the Austria–Germany border. In the former, Biger (1995, 148–149) considers the border fully delimited via a 1955 Libya–France agreement; Huth and Allee (2002, 346 and 361), however, believe the border remains unsettled until the ICJ issues its 1994 ruling. Similar divergence among experts occurs with respect to the Austria–German border. Kocs (1995) believes it – or more accurately, the Austria–Bavaria border, as it was known then – to be delimited under the Munich Treaty of 1816; in contrast, Biger (1995, 49–50) notes that border delimitation occurs at the end of the Austro-Prussian War in 1866. Whenever disagreements like these arise, the earliest date serves as the border settlement date. This derives from our desire to reduce the years during which neighboring states have unsettled borders, for such a decision biases the data against our argument; in particular, reducing periods of unsettled borders makes it more difficult for conflict and rivalry to occur when borders are unsettled (i.e., the events of interests must fall, if at all, in a narrower time period; see Chapters 5 and 6). Any findings we obtain with the current data would be strengthened were we to relax this coding decision and use a later settlement date instead.

On the other hand, border agreements may not exist in specific, individual cases. China and Tajikistan offer a case in point. As Biger (1995, 167–168) notes, "The southern section of the boundary [between these states], has never been determined by treaty. Nevertheless, since 1884 there have been no boundary disputes in the area and since Tajikistan's independence there have been no conflicts concerning its alignment." Given the coding rule discussed earlier, we classify such borders as *unsettled*. This may seem counterintuitive, since no active disputes exist along such borders, but our variable relies upon the signing of interstate agreements – *not* on whether the dyad members actively contest the unsettled border territory (e.g., the Saudi Arabia–Yemen border) or not (e.g., the China–Tajikistan border).

This approach preserves uniformity in the variable's coding rules – or more accurately, prevents us from making ad hoc amendments to the data based on our own subjective reading of specific cases. Ad hoc amendments potentially introduce bias into the analysis, and the need to protect against that bias outweighs any benefits obtained through re-classifying some of the unsettled cases. Moreover, our approach also avoids tautology. We argue later that unsettled borders produce interstate rivalry – that is, mutual feelings of threat, enmity, and competition, which are accompanied by a high probability of militarized conflict. These feelings do not arise without cause; rather, disputes of some kind underlie them.[8] If we rely exclusively on active disputes to identify (un)settled borders, then we risk relating rivalry, disputes (and conflict), and border settlement definitionally, and any findings we obtain might be misleading.[9] It is therefore of paramount importance for us to keep disputes and border settlement conceptually and empirically distinct. Finally, our decision again biases the data against our hypotheses. It creates cases in which borders are unsettled (i.e., no agreement exists) and no dispute occurs. Our theory anticipates that unsettled borders increase the likelihood that a dispute arises, which then fosters a rivalry (see Chapters 5 and 6). Adding cases where states do not contest their unsettled borders introduces observations to the analysis that run counter to our theory's predictions. If we uncover significant findings despite the current data's coding, then amending our data (e.g., reclassifying the cases noted here as instances of settled border dyads that do not fight each other) will only strengthen those findings.

The second coding rule concerns domestic politics. Some states experience internal disagreement over whether border settlement is advantageous for the state. Consequently, a state's leader will negotiate and sign a border agreement, only to quickly reverse course. This pattern generally arises when another domestic actor, one with veto authority over the settlement process, encourages the leader to reverse course after signing an agreement – a phenomenon particularly common in Latin America. Bolivia and Paraguay, for example, signed negotiated border agreements in 1879, 1887, and 1894, but after each, at least one of the two states' legislatures failed to ratify the agreement (Ireland 1938, 66–69). Similarly, Colombia and Venezuela submitted their border dispute to the Spanish monarch for arbitration in 1883; when the Spanish Queen Regent issued her ruling in 1891 and the Colombian government subsequently signed an agreement that ceded land to Venezuela, the Colombian Congress rejected the settlement (Biger 1995, 174; Ireland 1938, 211–213).

Another, related domestic obstacle results from discord between the leader and her negotiators in the field. A foreign minister, for example, might sign an agreement on behalf of the state, only to have the executive reject the terms he negotiated. Colombia and Venezuela offer an illustration of this as well. The two states' foreign ministers signed an agreement on April 24, 1894, in which disputed border areas received greater clarification. The Venezuelan government "did not accept this treaty [outright] but [instead] proposed twenty-four modifications," prompting Colombia to suggest modifications as

[8] That is, rivalries form for a reason. See Diehl and Goertz (2000) and Colaresi, Rasler, and Thompson (2007).

[9] More formally, (a) unsettled borders would contain disputes by definition (if we amend the rule discussed here); (b) rivalries already contain disputes by definition; and, therefore, (c) rivalries would contain unsettled borders by definition. Any association between unsettled borders and rivalry could then derive merely from definitions, rather than a real empirical relationship. For a similar point, see Gibler (2012).

well (Ireland 1938, 212–213). Negotiations therefore continued for another thirty years, as both sides searched for a mutually acceptable delimitation.

To address situations like these, the coding rules consider a border settled only if a domestic actor holding veto power over the agreement does not explicitly reject it. Most often, the vetoing actor is the legislature, which must ratify the signed agreement. Failure to ratify in such cases then leaves the border unsettled until the legislature approves a signed agreement (e.g., see El Salvador–Honduras; Day 1987, 425–428). Similarly, borders remain unsettled when a minister negotiates an agreement that his government subsequently does not endorse.

The third coding rule accounts for the unique process through which post-colonial states enter the international system. Colonial states never possessed interstate borders in the modern sense, but that is not to say they had no borders. Spain, for example, defined administrative districts in the Americas that subsequently became independent states; their districts, then, had boundaries, albeit poorly defined ones within a single empire. Similarly, great power states regularly attempted to delimit the borders between their respective colonial holdings, laying down a series of treaties intended to be, in effect, "interstate borders" (see Rich 1992). In each case, whether within or across colonial empires, post-colonial states inherited a type of border – again, with variation existing around how well parent states defined those borders in practice (see Carter and Goemans 2011). As a result, a question arises about how to classify such cases: should we consider these borders settled because colonial parents drew borders for their colonial territories, or alternatively, should we classify them as unsettled because the colonial states did not themselves explicitly agree to their borders via interstate agreements?

Our border settlement variable adopts a coding strategy that sits between these two alternatives. It begins from the premise that the international system prefers territorial integrity – or the continuation of interstate borders – to territorial revision (Hathaway and Shapiro 2017; Shaw 2014; Zacher 2001). This preference affects not only existing states, but also ones born into the international system – through the principle of *uti possidetis*. According to the ICJ, *uti possidetis* is a "time-hallowed," "general principle of international law," whose "essence ... lies in its primary aim of securing respect for the [existing] territorial boundaries [of a state] at the moment when independence is achieved."[10] If parent states settled the borders of their colonial states prior to the latter attaining independence, then these borders would remain settled under international law after independence.[11]

[10] See ICJ, Judgment of December 22, 1986, in the case between Burkina Faso and Mali. Available at www.icj-cij.org/files/case-related/69/069-19861222-JUD-01-00-EN.pdf. Last accessed July 17, 2017.

[11] Great powers therefore play an indirect role in border settlement. Our data and analysis capture their efforts.

Some challenges interfere with a strict application of *uti possidetis* to post-colonial states. As we note earlier, colonial parents might draw unclear boundaries, as Spain did throughout Latin America. In such cases, borders appear settled, but overlapping territorial claims arise immediately when new states enter the system and try to interpret the unclear boundaries they inherited. In addition, many would argue that the borders that colonial powers drew often reflected and served those powers' interests, not those of the colonial states. Major powers, for example, frequently met and divided colonial lands among themselves, without consulting the people living in the affected lands (e.g., see the 1884–1885 Berlin–West Africa Conference; Rich 1992, 237–242). Should the newly independent states subsequently be compelled to accept these borders as settled with finality, one might question whether the settlements violated the post-colonial states' right to self-determination – that is, whether settlement impeded the peoples of the new states from "freely determining their own political status" (Shaw 2014, 188).[12] On these grounds, myriad states initiate a territorial claim immediately upon independence, either because they inherited an active border claim from their colonial parent (e.g., see Guatemala–Belize/the United Kingdom or Ghana–Ivory Coast/France) or because they independently chose to contest their border (e.g., see Poland–Czechoslovakia, Oman–United Arab Emirates, or Cambodia–South Vietnam; Huth and Allee 2002).

The coding rule underlying our variable balances the two competing principles – *uti possedetis* and self-determination. It considers a new state's border settled with a given neighbor if: (a) a parent state settled that border in its entirety via interstate agreement (or via internal administrative documents if the border previously laid within a colonial empire) and (b) the new state does not raise a territorial claim along the border within the first year of its independence. If a claim fitting the latter characteristics arises, however, it then classifies the border as unsettled until the new states sign one or more agreements that delimit all outstanding, disputed sections of the border. As an illustration of how the coding words, consider the Saudi Arabia–Oman border. Saudi Arabia laid claim to the Buraimi Oasis along its border with Oman, perhaps as early as 1934.[13]

[12] Shaw (2014, 377–380) explains in depth how the principles of *uti possidetis* and self-determination reconcile under international law. Of note, "Self-determination cannot be used to further larger territorial claims in defiance of internationally accepted boundaries of sovereign states, but it may be of some use in resolving cases of disputed and uncertain frontier lines on the basis of the wishes of the inhabitants" (Shaw 2014, 379). These latter, disputed cases generally arise at independence, often pre-dating it. See also Prescott and Triggs (2008).

[13] The uncertainty in dates derive from discrepancies between Biger (1995, 412–413), Huth and Allee (2002, 365), and Day (1987, 253–254) about when the dispute began. Day places the Buraimi Oasis dispute (without dates) in the Saudi Arabia–United Arab Emirates dyad. Biger and Huth and Allee show the Buraimi Oasis dispute connected to both the Saudi Arabia–United Arab Emirates and the Saudi Arabia–Oman dyads – the difference being that Huth and Allee believe Saudi claims begin in 1934, while Biger considers the start to be 1949. Regardless of when it started, however, Saudi Arabia claimed the area prior to Oman's independence, and

The dispute primarily concerned Saudi Arabia and Britain, which then acted on behalf of the United Arab Emirates. When Oman became an independent state, it asserted its own claims to the Buraimi Oasis and surrounding areas. After a series of negotiations, the two states signed a security pact in 1982 – in which they agreed to resolve their border disputes – followed, in 1990, by a border delimitation agreement. Because Oman raised claims within the first year of its independence (i.e., 1971), our variable considers the Oman–Saudi Arabia border to be unsettled from 1971 to 1990 and settled from 1991 onward (Biger 1995, 412–413; Huth and Allee 2002, 365).

A one-year window of opportunity for newly independent states to raise a territorial claim is highly restrictive. Indeed, given that our unit of analysis is the contiguous dyad-year, the one-year window is the smallest one we can create. Nevertheless, we believe it is appropriate because, once again, it biases the data against our argument. Newly independent states that raise claims after one year will have settled borders in our data.[14] This, for example, occurs in the cases of the Kazakhstan–Kyrgyzstan and Sudan–Egypt borders; in both, claims arise two years after independence, but a combination of parent and independent states (China–Russia and Britain–Egypt, respectively) negotiated a full delimitation before the second state along the border achieved independence. Similarly, Libya claimed the Aozou Strip along its border with Chad, but these claims appear to emerge more than one year after Chad's independence (largely, in 1972, when Libya occupies the Aozou Strip militarily) and follow a 1955 Libyan–French agreement that delimited the Chad–Libya border in full.[15] In each of these cases, our variable labels the border as settled at the time the dyad comes into existence. Thus, any conflict that might arise in such cases would provide evidence contrary to our argument's prediction (i.e., that settled borders reduce the likelihood of interstate conflict generally, and rivalry in particular; see later chapters) in our analysis. Any significant relationships we identify in this study would only strengthen were we to relax this criteria and admit additional unsettled, conflict-ridden borders into the analysis.

The fourth, and final, coding rule concerns states that leave and re-enter the international system, usually as a result of the world wars. Occasionally, states use this opportunity to raise (or resurrect) territorial claims against their neighbors. Yugoslavia, for example, issued a claim against Italy to Trieste and its surrounding areas from 1945 to 1975, even though the Treaty of Rapallo (1920) and the Pact of Rome (1924) had previously resolved the border between the two states (Biger 1995; Day 1987; Huth and Allee 2002). In such

various sources agree that Oman joined the Buraimi Oasis dispute when it advanced its own claim upon independence.

14 On all examples provided here, see Biger (1995) and Huth and Allee (2002).

15 For a similar interpretation of the 1955 Libyan–French agreement, see the ICJ's Judgment of February 3, 1994, in the Case Concerning the Territorial Dispute between Libyan Arab Jamahiriya and Chad. Available at www.icj-cij.org/files/case-related/83/6899.pdf. Last accessed July 17, 2017.

cases, the variable's coding does not allow states to "unsettle" their borders, regardless of why they do so or on what grounds they issue their new claim. To see why, consider an analogous case: Russia and Turkey. After World War II (from 1945 to 1953), the Soviet Union laid claim to the areas of Ardahan and Kars, along the modern Georgia–Turkey and Armenia–Turkey borders, respectively. Russia and Turkey resolved these claims, however, in the 1878 Treaty of Berlin and reaffirmed the border's status in the 1921 Treaty of Moscow (Biger 1995; Huth and Allee 2002). Under the coding rules presented earlier, as well as the position we adopt under international law (i.e., that border agreements are permanent unless altered mutually and nonviolently; see Shaw 2014), Russia could not unsettle its Turkish border in 1945. The only difference between this case and that of Italy–Yugoslavia is that the Axis powers invaded and occupied Yugoslavia during World War II, causing it to exit the international system as an independent state in 1941 and re-enter the system in 1944. That occupation, though, neither alters Yugoslavia's international agreements nor provides a justification for territorial changes, even as states might believe otherwise.[16] As long as the involved states settled their mutual border in accordance with the first three coding rules presented earlier, the border therefore remains settled if the signatory states leave and re-enter the international system. As elsewhere, this biases the data against our argument – making it more likely that conflict would occur during periods when borders are settled, as opposed to when they are not. The cumulative weight of these coding decisions therefore establishes the most difficult empirical context through which to evaluate our argument.

Border Settlement Data Characteristics

Our concept and measure of border settlement depends entirely on the signing of interstate agreements. Because these agreements – and therefore, border settlement – cannot be reversed under international law (Cukwurah 1967; Shaw 2014) and states feel pressure to settle their borders,[17] it is theoretically possible for border settlement to be a historical phenomenon of little importance today. We partially address this point in Chapter 2; as we note there, a number of borders remain unsettled, and these borders appear within well-known conflict hot spots (see Table 2.1), which demonstrates that border issues remain relevant in contemporary international relations. We now, however, offer more evidence on this point. The data indicate that the act of border settlement itself – and relatedly, the process that yields it – is not a spatially or temporally bounded phenomenon; rather, it occurs consistently throughout the entire time period our study covers. Figure 4.1 illustrates this point graphically. It tracks the

[16] Indeed, Yugoslavia based its claim (in part) on the fact that Italy committed acts of aggression against it in World War II, lost that war, and "snatched" the territory from Yugoslavia in the past (quoted in Day 1987, 73–74).

[17] For expressions of this sentiment, see Ireland (1938) and Whittam (1961).

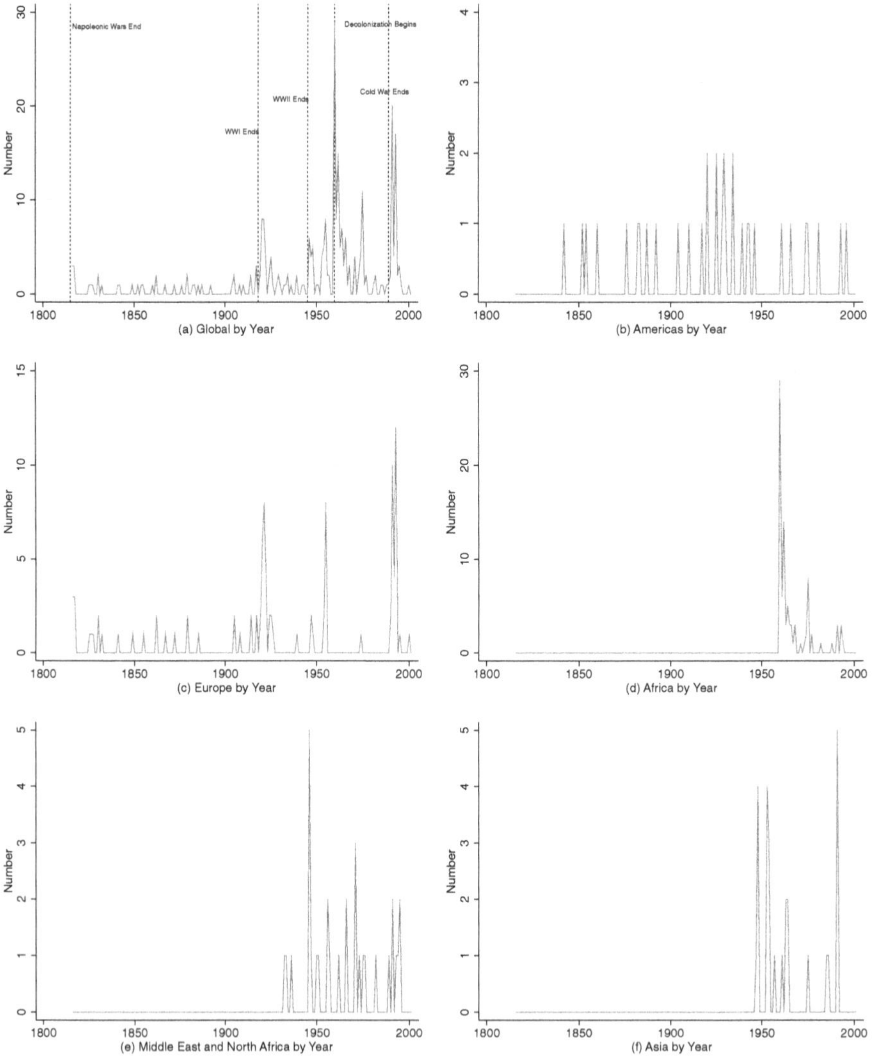

FIGURE 4.1. Number of dyadic border settlements by region, 1816–2001

Notes: Y-axes do not share a common scale so that variation can be observed in panels with lower numbers of settlements per year.

frequency with which borders are (fully) settled by year during the period 1816–2001 – first for the entire world (panel a) and then for five regional subgroups, including the Americas (panel b), Europe (panel c), (sub-Saharan) Africa (panel d), the Middle East and North Africa (panel e), and Asia and the Pacific (panel f).[18]

[18] We classify states/dyads into regions according to the following process. Each state receives a number 0–999 from the Correlates of War State System Membership data. Combining these

The panels in Figure 4.1 offer numerous insights about the border settlement data.[19] Border settlement occurs consistently throughout the entire 1816 – 2001 period. Panel (a) demonstrates this well. Although a border settlement does not appear in every year the study covers, a lack of *any* settlement rarely persists for extended periods of time. Indeed, the longest period without a border settlement runs for eleven years (from 1888 to 1903). The second longest period lasts eight years (1833–1840), and the vast majority of such periods exist for five years or less, even in more recent times.

The data also identify settlement "waves" (i.e., spikes in the time series data). These waves correspond with key international events – for example, the world wars, decolonization, and the end of the Cold War (see labels in panel a). Disaggregating the data further reveals how the waves vary by region (note: the y-axes differ across the panels in Figure 4.1, so that readers can more easily observe variation in the panels with fewer settlements per year – for example, the Americas, which experience a maximum of two border settlements in any given year). Distinct settlement waves ripple through the Americas (1920–1935), Europe (1919–1925, 1955, and 1991–1993), sub-Saharan Africa (1960–1962 and 1974–1975), the Middle East and North Africa (1946, 1971, and 1991–1995), and Asia (1948–1954, 1963–1964, and 1991).

We might expect settlement waves like these to occur for four reasons: independence, interdependence, accommodation, and diffusion. Independence waves appear when groups of states enter the international system and adopt their colonially settled borders under the principle of *uti possidetis*. This explains the sharp spike in the African panel (d) in 1960 – a phenomenon that produces the spike observed in the global data at that time as well (marked "decolonization" in panel a); indeed, the panels in Figure 4.1 suggest that *uti possidetis* operates most strongly in the sub-Saharan Africa region, although it appears elsewhere too (e.g., Asia; see also Figure 4.2 and its discussion subsequently).[20]

Interdependence drives settlement waves via a slightly different mechanism. It emerges when the terms used to settle one border affect another border. Colombia illustrates this mechanism well. It could not settle its border with either Peru or Brazil without settling its border with the other.[21] As a result of these linkages, two of the three states would achieve progress in their border settlement process, only to have the third scuttle it. Colombia, for example,

yields widely used, dyad identifier numbers that range from 0 to 999999, where the first three numbers correspond to one state and the latter three numbers to the other – with the smaller of the two state numbers listed first. In general, the dyad identifiers place dyads into the following regions, which we use throughout the chapter: 0–199999 Americas, 200000–399999 Europe, 400000–599999 (sub-Saharan) Africa, 600000–699999 the Middle East and North Africa, and 700000–999999 Asia (and the Pacific).

19 See also a related discussion in Owsiak, Cuttner, and Buck (2018).

20 We reach this conclusion through a comparison of the magnitudes of sharp spikes across the various regional charts, as well as the discussion of Figure 4.2 that follows.

21 Colombia's border settlement with Peru also affected its Ecuadorian border, creating still more interdependence.

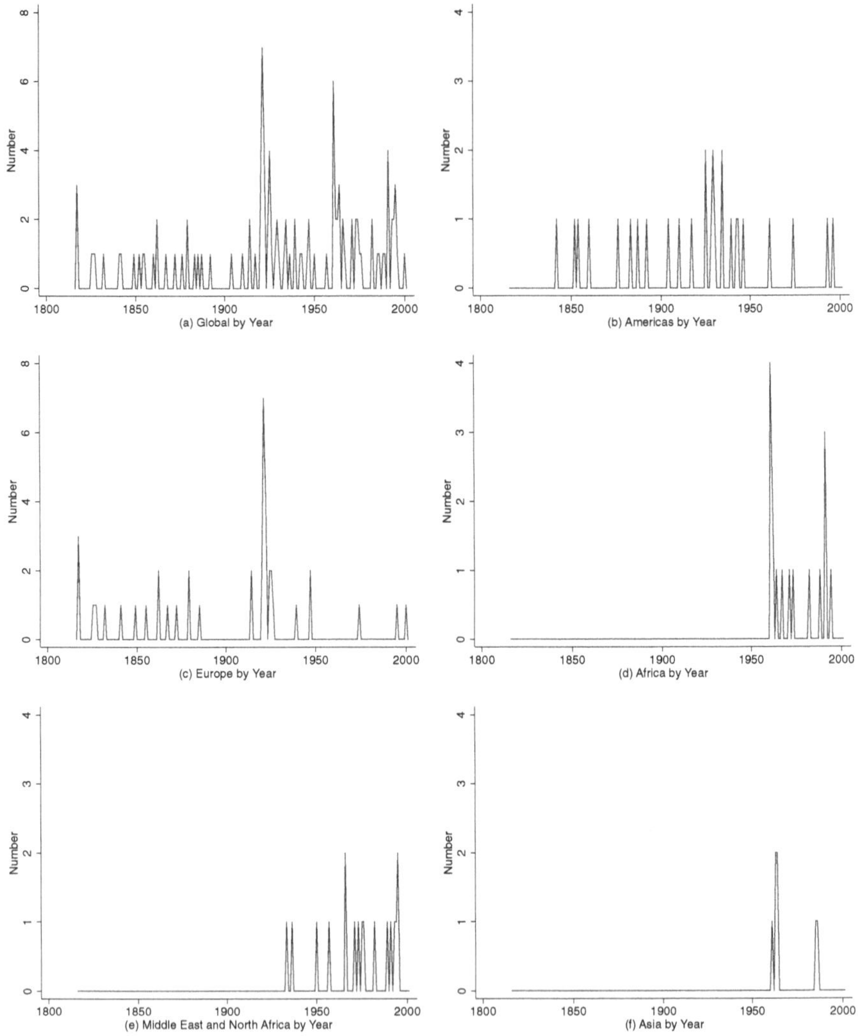

FIGURE 4.2. Dyadic border settlements by region, 1816–2001 (independence cases removed)

Notes: Y-axes do not share a common scale so that variation can be observed in panels with lower numbers of settlements per year.

protested the Brazil–Peru border progress to Peru in 1866 and 1869, as well as to Brazil in 1875 and 1876 (Ireland 1938, 187–190; see also Huth and Allee 2002, 442–444). Other protestations occurred as well, and eventually, Peru proposed a general conference in 1894, where all the involved states – Brazil, Colombia, Ecuador, and Peru – could negotiate together. Unfortunately,

Ecuador declined to both attend the conference and approve the convention that the other three states produced, thereby undermining the latter's collective efforts. Then, in 1924, after over a century of repeated, failed negotiations, Colombia finally reached a settlement with Peru, only to have Brazil lodge a formal complaint that it, too, had unaddressed interests at stake in the Colombian–Peruvian settlement. The United States subsequently mediated at Colombia's request, Brazil withdrew its complaint, and the three neighbors settled their borders in 1928 (Biger 1995, 172–173; Ireland 1938, 196–199). In short, these various border negotiations were intricately linked and therefore required settlement processes that moved in tandem.

The final two causes of waves focus on state leaders' motives. Accommodation produces border settlement waves when a given state possesses the incentive to settle many outstanding borders quickly. Fravel (2008) highlights this mechanism within China; he argues that threats to regime survival within China (most notably, during 1960–1964 and 1990–1999) encouraged the Chinese government to accommodate neighboring states with whom China had territorial disputes. These accommodations allowed China to address its internal threats better, by reducing ethnic agitation and external influence in border regions, as well as permitting a different distribution of military resources throughout the country. In contrast, diffusion occurs when a state uses the terms in a border settlement with one neighbor to signal both its willingness to settle and its preferred settlement terms to additional neighbors with which it wants to settle. Clay and Owsiak (2016) find strong evidence of this process; although it relates to the other wave mechanisms (e.g., accommodation), they find that diffusion explains unique behavior that accommodation cannot.[22]

Although settlement waves originate from all four sources, independence has the largest effect on the data. Figure 4.2 highlights this conclusion. To create it, we reproduce Figure 4.1 but remove all cases in which a new border appears in the international system that a parent state settled prior to a new state's independence. The revised figure therefore excludes instances where post-war conferences produce new states (e.g., when major states create Czechoslovakia after World War I), as well as instances where states immediately adopt previous administratively or colonially drawn borders at independence – under the principle of *uti possidetis* (e.g., the Guinea-Bissau border with Senegal, which France and Portugal settled in 1886; see Biger 1995).

The differences between Figures 4.1 and 4.2 therefore capture the effects of independence. Two of these differences warrant particular attention. First, the revised figure reports waves smaller in magnitude than those in the original figure. Sub-Saharan Africa demonstrates the starkest effect; the 1960–1962 wave falls from a maximum of nearly 30 border settlements to 4. A similar effect appears in Europe (1991–1993), sub-Saharan Africa (1974–1975), the Middle East and North Africa (1946), and Asia (1948–1954 and 1991),

[22] On diffusion processes, see Simmons, Dobbin, and Garrett (2008).

although these are admittedly less pronounced. Trends in the global data also adjust in response to changes in the underlying regional data.

Second, independence affects the Americas minimally. This seems surprising at first, but it aligns with well-known regional patterns. Cukwurah (1967, 112–116) traces the origin and history of the *uti possidetis* principle. It first arose in Latin America as a way to prevent border disagreements from festering. Yet, it had the opposite effect there; although states could agree to accept the administrative boundaries as their international ones, the administrative boundaries themselves lacked sufficient clarity to prevent alternative interpretations of them from arising. Consequently, states agreed *in principle* to accept administrative boundaries, but *in practice*, Latin American borders produced a series of overlapping claims anyway. These claims then festered.

Based on these data, we conclude that independence generally – and the principle of *uti possidetis* in particular – plays a large role in border settlement processes throughout the world. Its role seems largest in sub-Saharan Africa, and almost nonexistent in the Americas. The distinct regional experiences, however, underscore the value of both settled borders and border agreements. *Uti possidetis* works well when parent states sign an agreement that delimits a border in detail (e.g., in sub-Saharan Africa); in contrast, it functions poorest where parent states produce delimitations that lack sufficient clarity (e.g., the Americas). In either case, the principle only applies where border agreements – and therefore, border settlement – already exist.

Another prominent characteristic of the border settlement data is that it necessarily follows a stepwise function.[23] A border transitions from unsettled to settled when states fully delimit it through interstate agreement(s), and it never transitions in the reverse direction (under international law or our coding decisions; see Cukwurah 1967; Shaw 2014). This implies that the proportion of unsettled borders in the international system generally only decreases over time – or alternatively, that the proportion of settled borders only increases over time – the exception being that the addition of new states may introduce unsettled borders that then require settlement. Indeed, this trend, an artifact of our variable's coding structure, appears in Figure 4.3, which calculates the proportion (or percentage) of interstate borders settled per year both globally (panel a) and across the various regions (panels b–f).

The figure reveals a few noteworthy characteristics. First and foremost, we see the stepwise function that the coding should produce. The percentage of neighboring states with (fully) settled borders climbs slowly over time – from 17.6% in 1816 to 44.4% in 1850, 56.3% in 1900, 81.8% in 1945, 86.9% in 1990, and 92.9% in 2001 (the last year in our study). Relatedly, then, unsettled borders fall across this same period from 82.4% in 1816 to 7.1% in 2001

[23] See Spivak (1994, 275).

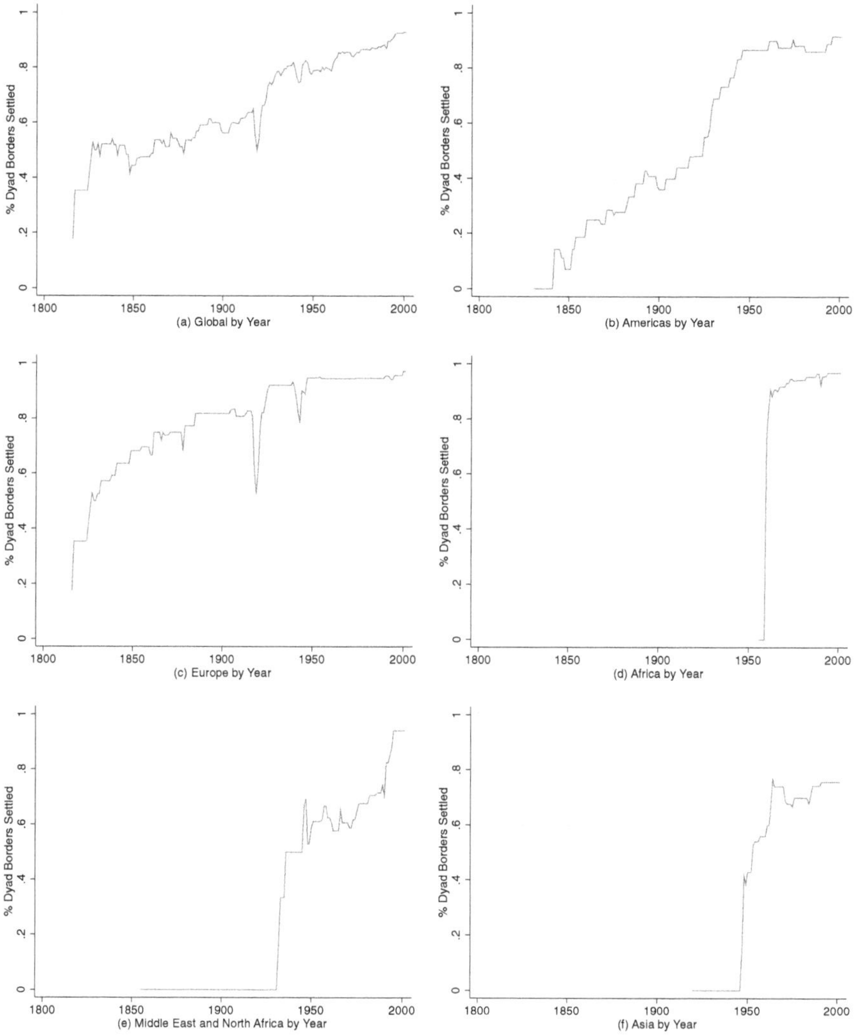

FIGURE 4.3. Percentage of dyadic borders settled by region, 1816–2001
Notes: Dyads on which we are missing data are removed from these calculations.

(global data, panel a).[24] Despite this general upward trend, brief moments of reversal occur, where the percentage of settled borders falls. These setbacks correspond with times when new states – and therefore, new borders – enter the international system. In Europe, for example, there are two sharp changes

[24] "Unsettled borders" is the inverse of "settled borders," so the percentage of unsettled borders for a given year is equal to 100% minus the percentage of settled borders for that year.

that emerge at the end of the world wars. The percentage of settled borders in Europe first falls from 80.6% in 1917 to 52.3% in 1919, before later returning to 82.0% by 1922. The addition of new states throughout Eastern Europe after World War II and their settling of border issues in the years following the war causes such a pattern. Similarly, the percentage of settled borders in Europe falls from 93.3% in 1939 to 88.9% by 1946, before quickly reversing course. Other regions contain similar – albeit unique – reversals, and the global data reflects the aggregation of these regional effects.

If unsettled borders threaten international peace, as we later argue in greater detail, then Figure 4.3 also offers an indication of where the greatest threats to peace lie. Border settlement in Asia-Pacific and the Middle East–North Africa historically lag behind other regions, suggesting that the main danger lays in these two regions. In the 1990s, however, the Middle East–North Africa experienced border settlements that now place it on par with most other regions. Indeed, as of 2001, almost every region boasted border settlement rates upward of 94%, except one: Asia. The Asia-Pacific region had only 75.7% of its borders settled as of 2001. Relatedly, 47.0% of the contemporary unsettled borders (or 8 of 17, as of December 2015) reside in the Asia-Pacific region (see Table 2.1). The starkness of this figure magnifies when we consider that the Americas and sub-Saharan Africa tie for the region with the next most contemporary, unsettled borders – at only 17.6% each (or 3 of the 17 unsettled borders as of 2015). This suggests that the Asia-Pacific region faces the greatest risk of contemporary international conflict – particularly conflict involving India or China, who dispute 75% of the contemporary unsettled borders in the Asian region (or 6 of 8; see Table 2.1).

Figure 4.4 offers yet another perspective on the trends that appear in Figure 4.3. Rather than focus on contiguous dyads, we shift the focus slightly in this figure to *individual* states. For every year during the period 1919–2001, we determine how many states exist in the international system, the total number of borders each state has, and how many of these borders states have settled according to the coding criteria outlined earlier.[25] With this information, we next calculate the percentage of each state's borders that it had settled prior to each year of its existence during the period 1919–2001. As a final step, we then average the percentage of *all* states' settled borders in each year – for all states in the international system (panel a), as well as for the five distinct regions (panels b–f). To illustrate this process more concretely, five states neighbored Peru in 1928, and Peru had settled its borders with three of them, yielding a settled border percentage of 60% for that year. Averaging similar calculations for all other states in the Americas lead to the conclusion that Latin American states'

25 We calculate this measure for a narrower time period (1919–2001) than the dyadic data (1816–2001). Because of changes to contiguity over time, as well as historical missing data (on the latter, see subsequently), it is difficult to make accurate state-level calculations before World War I. For more information, see Owsiak, Cuttner, and Buck (2018).

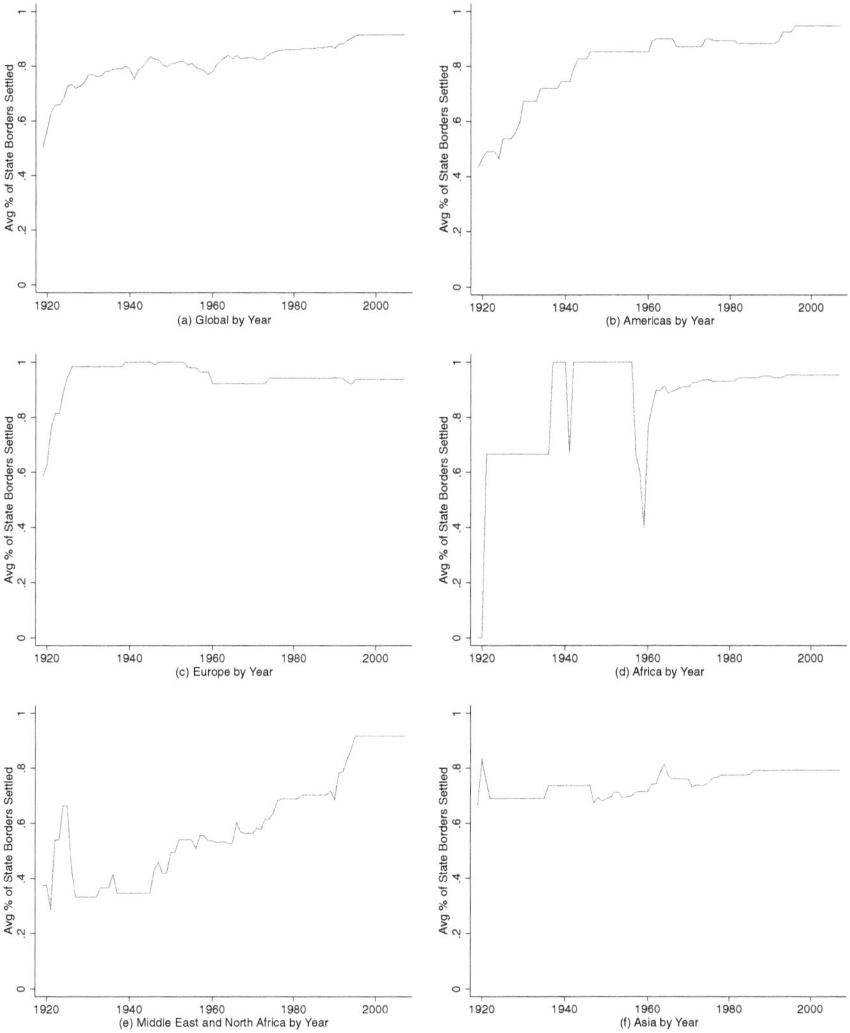

FIGURE 4.4. Average percentage of a state's borders settled by region, 1919–2001

Notes: The unit of analysis is the state, rather than the dyad. The time period is restricted because it is harder to generate state-level settlement data prior to 1919. See Owsiak, Cuttner, and Buck (2018).

had settled an average of 56% of their borders in 1928 – a figure graphed explicitly in panel (b) and that contributes to the global value for 1928 in panel (a).

The data in Figure 4.4 yield conclusions similar to those derived from Figure 4.3. Regardless of whether we consider the entire world or individual regions, the percentage of states' borders that are settled, on average, increases over time. In 1919, for example, states had already settled an average of approximately 50% of their borders (panel a). Around World War II, this value increased to roughly 80%, hovered between 80% and 85% as decolonization unfolded (1955–1975), and began climbing slowly again in 1975. By 2001, states had settled an average of about 91% of their borders. Most states, then, have settled the vast majority of their borders – a finding that results partially as a function of measuring border settlement through international law and partially from the incentives states hold for removing contentious issues with those immediately around them.

Nonetheless, as Figure 4.4 demonstrates, individual regions vary significantly, particularly with respect to the speed and timing of border settlement. By speed, we mean how rapidly or slowly settlement occurs over time – or the slope of the line at any given point in the figure. Sharper slopes indicate faster increases in the average rate of border settlement, while flatter slopes suggest slower increases. In sub-Saharan Africa, for example, a sharp uptick in border settlement takes place in 1960 (panel d). A few new states enter the region with unsettled borders in 1957–1959, and because few sub-Saharan African states exist during this time, each one has a rather large effect on the region's average percentage of states' settled borders. The percentage of settled borders therefore falls markedly during the period 1957–1959. In 1960, however, a large number of sub-Saharan African states enter the region and adopt their colonially settled borders (through the principle of *uti possidetis*). This, in combination with negotiated border settlement processes, causes sub-Saharan African states' average percentage of settled borders to jump from 40% in 1959 to 76% in 1960, 84% in 1961, and 90% in 1962. Similar increases appear throughout the various panels in Figure 4.4, although no other region experiences an increase as severe as the one highlighted here.

Timing addresses a slightly different issue: when the increases in border settlement actually occur – that is, the year(s) in which the slope increases. As an illustration, the average percentage of states' settled borders in the Middle East and North Africa rises from 35% in 1945 to 54% in 1952, after which it levels off until the mid-1960s (panel e). A similar settlement wave then occurs in the region between 1990 and 1995 – when the average percentage of states' settled borders increases from 69% to 92%. In contrast, states' average level of border settlement seems to rise most sharply in the Americas over the period 1920–1940 (panel b), in Europe prior to 1925 (panel c), and in Asia during the mid-1960s (panel f). Different regions, in other words, experience the border settlement process in distinct ways – with respect not only to the speed with which border settlement happens, but also to when settlements cluster in time.

Figure 4.4 also underscores our earlier findings on the dangerousness of the Asian region. As of 2001, Asian states report the lowest percentage of settled borders, sitting just shy of 80%. All other regions boast an average percentage greater than 91% – with some as high as 95%. If, therefore, unsettled borders significantly foster militarized conflict and rivalry, as we argue in later chapters, then the Asian region possesses more conflict potential than any other region.[26]

The conclusions we discuss throughout this section and the remainder of the book all rest on the accuracy and thoroughness of the border settlement data we employ, and one limitation of their generalizability therefore merits attention: missing data. Simply put, in certain cases, we do not have data on a border's status. These borders fall into two groups. The first group contains historically independent states that later merged into a cohesive whole. Baden, Bavaria, Hanover, Hesse Electoral, Hesse Grand Ducal, Mecklenburg Schwerin, Prussia, Saxony, and Wuerttemburg were individual German states that unified into a greater German state in the period 1866–1871. These states had borders with one another, as well as additional, non-German states. Our research uncovered information on some of these borders, but not all – particularly the historical border agreements between the individual German states. A similar issue arises with the Italian states that unify in 1860–1861. Together, these cases account for 41% of the missing settled border data.

A second group concerns newer states that result from the breakdown of larger ones. When a new state emerges, we search for information on whether the parent state had settled the new state's borders through either internal, administrative documents or a treaty with a foreign state. In most cases, we obtain this information, but for a few, we do not. The latter most often stem from the break-up of the Austro-Hungarian Empire and the Soviet Union, when new states appear and their borders remain unclear. These two empires each account for an additional 15% of the missing border data.[27]

To get a more macro-level view of how missing border settlement data might affect our analyses, Figure 4.5 tracks the proportion of contiguous dyad-years for which border data are missing over the period of our study (1816–2001). An examination of this figure reveals that missing data declines substantially over time. At the outset of the data series, when data are harder to obtain, we lack settled border data on 53% of contiguous dyad-years. This results from a combination of the small number of independent states in the international system in 1816 and a lack of border settlement information on the individual German and Italian constituent states.[28] By the late 1800s, the percentage of dyads for which we are missing settled border data falls to just under 15%. It then hovers between 15% and 20% until 1900, drops below 10% after World War I, plummets to 1% by 1950, and then rises to 11% in the post–Cold

[26] We discuss this implication further in Chapter 9.

[27] We continue making efforts to gather these data, and thank the many research assistants that have contributed to this effort (see Acknowledgments).

[28] To illustrate the point more concretely, we lack settled border data on 19 dyads in 1816. Fifteen of these (or 70%) are German or Italian states, while Austria-Hungary accounts for two more (another 11%).

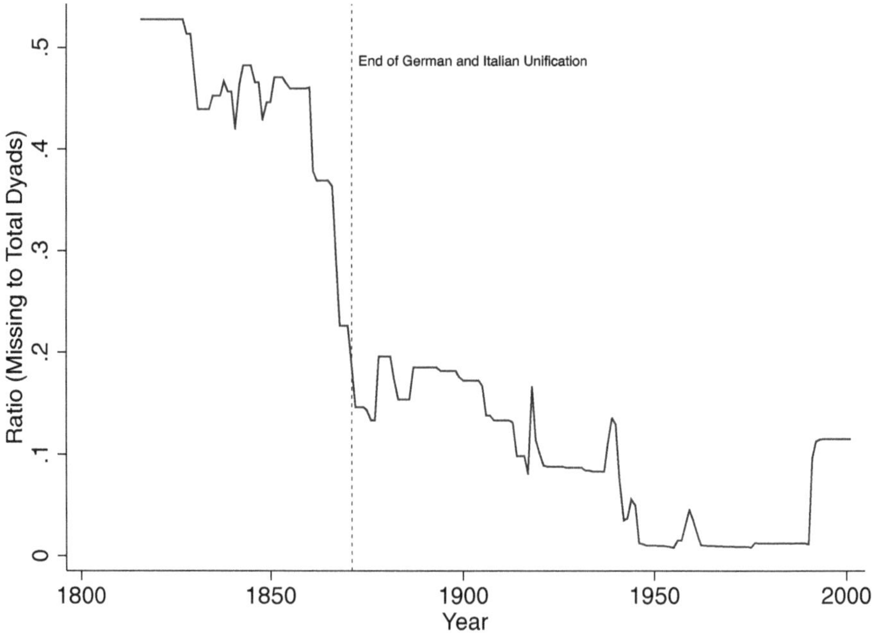

FIGURE 4.5. Percentage of settled border missing data dyads, 1816–2001

War world – the latter largely as a result of post-Soviet states entering the international system.[29]

A drastic, noteworthy decline in the proportion of missing data also appears around the period 1860–1871, when missing data falls from nearly 46% in 1860 to under 15% in 1872. This corresponds with German and Italian state unification and indicates that we have greater border data on the later, unified states than we do on their earlier, constituent parts. Nevertheless, missing data persists throughout the time period our study covers, although its source (from German and Italian states historically to post-Soviet ones in modern times) and magnitude vary.

Missing border settlement data is not problematic for our study. Researchers typically worry about missing data because it has the potential to bias their results; in particular, if the sample from which researchers draw their data miss, overreport, or underreport characteristics that exist in the population, then missing data skews their results. For example, if survey respondents that identify with a specific political party choose not to answer foreign policy questions more often than other respondents, then conclusions about foreign policy derived from the survey will insufficiently account for their viewpoint.

29 More specifically, post-Soviet states account for thirty-two of thirty-five dyads (91%) on which we are missing settled border data in 2001.

When one then generalizes back to the population – where those political party members both exist *and* have opinions on foreign policy issues – the conclusion reached through analyzing the survey data will be inaccurate, biased toward the opinions of the respondents who actually answered the questions.

We, however, do not rely on a sample. Our study uses the universe of *all* neighboring pairs of states throughout the period 1816–2001, not a sample of them from which we generalize. Thus, missing data in our case simply means that the inferences we reach throughout this book *may* not apply to the subsets of the population for which we lack border settlement data – most notably, pre-1872 Germany and Italy or post-1992 former Soviet states. Our research continues to reduce these missing data, expand the population being studied, and therefore minimize the limitations that missing data exert on our conclusions. We hasten to note, though, that the cases for which we are missing data are rare, systemic events. If our conclusions do not apply to such cases, little explanatory power will be lost.[30]

In the end, there are 398 contiguous dyads during the period 1816–2001 – some of which lack contiguity over the entire period, as states emerge or dissolve. Of these, we have border settlement data on 312 contiguous dyads (or 78.39%). Table 4.1 breaks these aggregate figures apart further to indicate the data's coverage by region. In almost every region, we have border settlement data on 80–100% of the contiguous dyads that exist during the period 1816–2001. Europe proves the only exception – largely because the rare, systemic events that we know to affect our data (e.g., German and Italian unification, as well as the break-up of the Soviet Union) occur predominantly within this region. Nevertheless, as the table demonstrates, our data coverage suggests that our study can provide conclusions that will, on average, apply to states throughout the world.

4.2.2 Key Theoretical Variables

Establishing whether the hypothesized patterns outlined in Chapter 3 generally appear in the data requires three groups of theoretically motivated independent variables. Each either evaluates our argument's expectations or accounts for possible alternative explanations. The first group captures dyadic

[30] Data imputation can help overcome missing data generally, but not in our case. The border settlement data are not missing at random. Rather, they are temporally and spatially clustered, and we know the factors influencing these clusters. This makes multiple imputation inappropriate (see King et al. 2001). A simpler imputation method, "single imputation" (Honaker and King 2010), is also inappropriate. We could, for example, assume that a lack of information on a given border means it is unsettled (i.e., we never found the border agreement because it does not exist). Such a position would allow us to classify the missing data as instances of unsettled borders, but this solution produces two types of unsettled borders in the data: those that we *know* are unsettled and those that *might* be unsettled. Any conclusion we reach with such data must therefore be tempered by the potential error that the imputed data would introduce.

TABLE 4.1. *Border settlement data coverage by region, 1816–2001*

	All Contiguous Dyads	Contiguous Dyads with Settled Border Data	Data Coverage (%)
Americas	37	36	97.30
Europe	176	105	59.66
(Sub-Saharan) Africa	94	93	98.94
Middle East and North Africa	43	38	88.37
Asia (and Pacific)	48	40	83.33
Total	398	312	78.39

characteristics that could influence border settlement through their ability to increase or decrease the information problem; the second group concerns a characteristic of the disputed territory, which influences the likelihood that a commitment problem emerges; and the final group focuses on the conflict management process itself. We address each group in turn.

Dyadic Characteristics: Information Problems

Various theoretical arguments predict that certain, prominent, dyad-level characteristics affect border settlement by altering the ability of disputants to exchange credible information with one another. Some scholars, for example, argue that democratic dyads (i.e., those composed of two democratic states) may be better equipped than other dyads to reach negotiated settlements to their disputes (Dixon 1994; Huth and Allee 2002; Mitchell 2012). A dichotomous variable, *joint democracy*, considers this possibility. It denotes whether both dyad members scored +6 or higher on the Polity IV Project's Democracy–Autocracy Index (Marshall and Jaggers 2009).[31] This measure accords with what is popularly used in the field.

The relative power between dyad members can affect the border settlement process as well. As two bargaining states approach power parity, they face greater uncertainty over one another's type, strength, and resolve (Reed 2003) – and misrepresentation therefore promises more significant marginal effects on the bargaining process. It is, for example, hard to bluff an adversary about one's likelihood of winning a conflict when the adversary holds a large, asymmetric power advantage; closer to power parity, however, bluffs prove more convincing (or at least, more plausible), and therefore, of greater benefit. To address these dynamics, we construct a variable to track the effect of relative military capabilities (i.e., a measure of power parity) on border settlement. This continuous variable measures the ratio of the stronger to the weaker state's

[31] We use the Polity2 variable score, which adjusts the index for states experiencing foreign occupation, internal conflict, or regime transitions (Marshall and Jaggers 2009, 15–16).

capabilities (Singer, Bremer, and Stuckey 1972).[32] To account for diminishing effects near extreme values of the ratio, we use the natural log of the ratio in the analyses.[33]

Finally, states allied to each may be able to more credibly signal information to each other, increasing the likelihood that attempts to settle the border will succeed. The need to coordinate security and military policy reduces uncertainty over resolve and capabilities between partners. Moreover, an increased risk of escalation between allies decreases the deterrent capability of the alliance. It reorients resources that should deter a common adversary toward an alliance partner instead, and the target of any intra-alliance threat will increasingly question whether its alliance partners might fight together against it. These various considerations theoretically encourage alliance ties among the disputants to facilitate and incentivize a peaceful settlement. With this in mind, a dichotomous variable captures whether a contiguous dyad's members have any *alliance* obligations with one another during each year of their existence. The Alliance Treaty Obligations and Provisions (ATOP) dataset supplies these data (Leeds, Ritter, and Mitchell 2002).

Power Endowments

The second group of key independent variables involves *power endowments*. We argue that the presence of these endowments increases the probability that a commitment problem emerges. This, in turn, interferes with the neighboring states' ability to settle their borders via negotiation and mediation, and increases the likelihood that protracted and potentially violent conflict occurs. What might these power endowments look like in practice? Theory provides an answer. Powell (2006, 185–186), for example, notes that a "commitment problem can arise when states are bargaining over issues that are themselves a source of military power, ... [This includes territory with a] strategically important geographical feature, such as a mountain pass, ridge, or river, the control of which gives the state a military advantage." Fearon (1995, 408) uses similar language when discussing power shifts:

> The objects over which states bargain frequently are themselves sources of military power. Territory is the most important example, since it may provide economic resources that can be used for the military or be strategically located .... [B]oth sides might prefer some package of territorial concessions to a fight, but if the territory in question is strategically vital or economically important, its transfer could radically increase one side's future bargaining leverage (think of the Golan Heights).

If we combine their sentiments, Powell and Fearon propose that the power shifts capable of producing a commitment problem derive from strategically

32 See Carroll and Kenkell (2019) for a discussion of the limitations of capability ratios as a measure of relative power and a suggested alternative.

33 *Capability Ratio (ln)* = ln(stronger state CINC score/weaker state CINC score), where CINC is the Composite Index of National Capabilities (Singer, Bremer, and Stuckey 1972).

and economically valuable territory. Any territory that contains these characteristics – that is, power-endowed territory – theoretically *can* produce a commitment problem. In contrast, any territory that lacks these characteristics – that is, nonpower-endowed territory – theoretically cannot.

The Huth and Allee (2002) and ICOW territorial claims data capture this information, allowing us to distinguish between nonpower-endowed and power-endowed territory. They code the strategic and economic value of disputed territory as follows:

- The strategic value of border territory is "coded 1 if bordering territory is strategically located and 0 otherwise." Strategic value includes land: (a) in close proximity to shipping lanes/straits, (b) in close proximity to an opponent's military base(s), (c) that provides access to the sea for an otherwise landlocked state, (d) used as a military base by the target, (e) that could be used to open a second front against the target, or (f) that might block the primary attack route of the opponent Huth (1996, 256). In addition to these markers of strategic value, Huth and Allee (2002, 67) also consider territory to possess strategic value if it contains (or is believed to contain) "natural resources that were used by the state in the production of military weapons systems." ICOW employs a similar coding strategy (Frederick, Hensel, and Macaulay 2017).
- The economic value of border territory is "coded 1 if bordering territory was of economic value to the challenger and 0 otherwise." Economic value depends entirely on a given land's "resource endowment." The variable takes a value of 1 in years for which the land in question contained (or was believed to contain) – within 50 miles of the disputed area – any of the following resources in an amount that would permit the land's holder "to generate export earnings": "oil, manganese, iron ore, lead, titanium, bauxite, sulfur, copper, nickel, chromium, cobalt, tin, tungsten, zinc, phosphate, gold, silver, uranium, diamonds," or in arid climates, water (Huth 1996, 257). ICOW follows a similar coding process (Frederick, Hensel, and Macaulay 2017).

These coding rules include the exact endowments that theoretically threaten to shift the distribution of power between disputants significantly, thereby sowing the seeds of a potential commitment problem. On the strategic side, the indicators capture any feature that gives the territory's holder a military advantage (e.g., control over straits and shipping lanes, primary attack routes, or military bases; resources that might enhance military weapons; and land that permits new military fronts to open). On the economic side, they encompass access to natural resources that will permit the territory's holder to generate substantial revenue; this, too, supplies it with a greater opportunity to shift the distribution of power between it and its adversary – albeit over a somewhat longer time horizon than for strategic territory. Through these variables, we can consequently isolate the territory that scholars expect will lead to a commitment problem.

Scholars do not distinguish between the effects of strategically and economically valuable territory.[34] The commitment problem logic operates the same when land contains either (or both) characteristics (see earlier discussion; Fearon 1995; Powell 2006). We consequently combine these two characteristics into a single, dichotomous variable that indicates whether the disputed territory possesses either (or both) power endowment(s). Power endowments, then, are present (a value of 1) when the disputed territory contains either militarily strategic or economically valuable land (or both); in contrast, they are absent (a value of 0) if the disputed territory lacks both characteristics. Of note, we create two distinct versions of this variable: one derived from the Huth and Allee (2002) territorial claims data (covering 1919–1995) and the other from the ICOW Project's territorial claims data (covering 1816–2001; Frederick, Hensel, and Macaulay 2017).[35] Use of these two different datasets allows us to check for and speak further about the robustness of our findings.[36]

Conflict Management

Peaceful conflict management, or diplomatic, attempts to settle the delimitation of interstate borders dominate the border settlement process. To obtain data on these attempts, we reviewed numerous historical and academic resources, and constructed narratives for the border delimitation process between each pair of neighboring states.[37] Using these narratives, we then noted: (a) each conflict management attempt that addressed the unsettled border (including the specific strategy used; see subsequent discussion), (b) the years in which these attempts occurred, (c) the outcome of each attempt (i.e., whether it produced an agreement of some sort),[38] and (d) the identity of any third-party actor involved

34 For an exception, see Dal Bo and Powell (2009). Their model focuses exclusively on economically valuable territory.

35 On the conceptual and operational differences between (un)settled borders and territorial claims, see Owsiak, Cuttner, and Buck (2018).

36 Powell (2006) proposes that researchers quantify the power shift responsible for a commitment problem. We find this task impossible, for reasons we lay out elsewhere (see Chapter 6). Nevertheless, Powell argues that territory with power endowments has a higher probability of generating a power shift than territory without them (see also Fearon 1995). Our variable captures this expectation; it permits a comparison of territory with power endowments to territory without them. We therefore think the variables outlined here offer the best way to evaluate the implications of our argument empirically, given data limitations.

37 See Owsiak, Cuttner, and Buck (2018) for a sample narrative. The sources used to construct these narratives vary by dyad, but include, inter alia, Biger (1995), Brownlie (1979), Day (1987), Huth and Allee (2002), Ireland (1938, 1971), Kocs (1995), and Prescott and Triggs (2008), as well as news stories and the International Boundary Study series created in the Office of the Geographer at the United States Department of State.

38 These agreements can be: partial or full delimitation efforts; modus vivendi — that is, agreements that foster peaceful relations while the involved parties work to settle the disputed issue; formalized, documented intentions to submit a dispute to arbitration; and agreements to meet again about the matter in the future.

in each attempt. These roughly correspond to questions of what form conflict management takes, when it occurs, what result it achieves, and who exactly participates.

Any conflict management effort requires the use of a particular conflict management strategy, which identifies the form that effort takes. Five such strategies are commonly used during attempts to manage border disagreements.

- Bilateral negotiations: the disputing parties meet to discuss and settle the disputed issues, exchanging proposals of the settlement terms that they find acceptable during their discussions (Hopmann 1996).
- Mediation: the disputing parties voluntarily permit a third party to facilitate the logistics of their negotiations (i.e., good offices), help them communicate better with one another, investigate the issues under dispute and ascertain the facts (i.e., fact-finding missions), or offer specific settlement terms they might adopt (i.e., conciliation; on mediation, see Greig and Diehl 2012). Third-party mediators need not be impartial, and in many cases, they are not (Princen 1992). Moreover, because the process is voluntary, an individual disputant or the third party can end a mediation process at any time.[39]
- Arbitration: the disputing parties agree to allow a third party to review the facts concerning the disputed issues and rule on the terms that will settle these issues. In most cases, the disputants decide exactly who has their permission to arbitrate the case, as well as the principles and evidence on which the third party must make its ruling (and by extension, the principles and evidence the arbiter cannot consider). Disputants also agree ex ante to abide by the arbiter's ruling, although states occasionally violate this principle and reject arbitration rulings.
- Adjudication: a standing court (e.g., the ICJ) hears the disputants' case and – following the statues that concern the court's litigation process – creates a ruling that settles the disputed issues. As part of its process, an international court requires that at least one disputant submit an application that initiates the case. It then ascertains whether it has jurisdiction to hear the case, and if it does, hears evidence, deliberates, and rules on the merits of the case. The international community expects states to comply with court rulings, and they overwhelmingly do, especially on territorial issues like the border delimitation disagreements we consider in this study.[40]

39 Following some international relations research (Frazier and Dixon 2006; Greig, Owsiak, and Diehl 2019), we include good offices, fact-finding missions, and conciliation within our mediation variable. In effect, this mirrors other scholars' use of a "non-binding third-party conflict management" variable (see, for example, Gent and Shannon 2010; Powell and Wiegand 2014). For an example of research that breaks these various strategies apart, see Owsiak and Mitchell (2019).

40 On states' compliance record with ICJ rulings, see Mitchell and Owsiak (2017).

TABLE 4.2. *Conflict management strategies in contiguous dyad-years, 1816–2001*

Strategy	Frequency in Data (Number)	Strategy % in Data	Frequency in Owsiak et al. (2016)
Negotiation	590	74.49	1,340
Mediation	66	8.33	90
Arbitration	53	6.69	100
Adjudication	29	3.66	33
Post-war conference	43	5.43	124
Plebiscites	7	0.89	14
Administrative decrees	4	0.51	228
Total	792	–	1,929

- Post-war conference: victorious powers or disputants redraw the map in the aftermath of a war, causing state border births and border changes that the conference settles. [41]

These five strategies offer different processes through which states can find the concessions needed to settle their borders. As one moves down the above list, the disputants' control over both the conflict management process and the substantive outcome that derives from that process decreases, while conversely, that of third parties increases. For example, disputants retain complete control in bilateral negotiations; they determine when to meet, how to communicate, and what settlement terms to propose and accept. Disputants cede some control to third parties through mediation and arbitration, with the exact concession depending on the role the third party plays. Finally, disputants lose control almost completely within adjudication and (often) post-war conferences, where a third party determines both the process and the final substantive outcome.

Table 4.2 displays the frequency with which these five strategies appear in our data (first column) as well as their relative frequency in the data when compared to one another (second column). (Bilateral) negotiations, for example, occur in 590 of our contiguous dyad-years, or 74% of all conflict management attempts within our data. The table reveals similar information for the other conflict management strategies. The last column then displays the total number of each strategy found within the Owsiak et al. (2016) International Border Agreements Dataset, which we revised since that publication.

A few conclusions emerge from Table 4.2. First, states prefer to maintain control over their border delimitations (see also Owsiak and Mitchell 2019).

[41] After World War I, for example, the Paris Peace Conference carved the Czechoslovakian state out of Austria in the Treaty of St. Germain-en-Laye and determined both the Czechoslovakian and Austrian states' borders. See the Treaty of Peace between the Allied and Associated Powers and Austria. (1919) United Kingdom Treaty Series, No. 11. Available at `http://treaties.fco.gov.uk/docs/pdf/1919/TS0011.pdf`. Last accessed August 7, 2017.

Negotiations far outnumber the use of any other strategy, and the voluntary cession of almost complete control over the delimitation process and outcome occurs rarely (e.g., adjudication; 3.66% of our conflict management efforts). Second, states rely on certain conflict management strategies infrequently in our data – most notably, plebiscites and administrative decrees. In the context of border delimitation, a plebiscite solicits a popular vote to determine the state to which the people living in a specified geographic area want to belong. In contrast, actors impose administrative decrees to divide geographic spaces within a larger state (e.g., Sudan–South Sudan), federation (e.g., the Soviet Union), or colonial empire (e.g., Spain in Latin America).

These two strategies appear often in the Owsiak, Cuttner, and Buck (2018) data, but drop from our study because of the unit of analysis we employ: the contiguous dyad-year (see final rows of Table 4.2). Each contiguous dyad-year requires the existence of two states that neighbor one another along an inland territorial or river border. Most plebiscites and administrative decrees, however, occur before a state enters the international system, when its own dyad-year observation does not exist. As a result, we do include plebiscites or administrative decrees in the analyses that follow, although they still influence it indirectly. The criteria for border settlement, for example – namely, a border fully delimited via agreement – can be met through the principle of *uti possidetis*, and administrative decrees prove instrumental in determining when this principle applies.

Finally, as comparisons between the first and third columns of Table 4.2 indicate, we use a subset of the full border settlement conflict management data. The omitted conflict management attempts generally concern parent states settling colonial boundaries with each other or other independent states (e.g., Britain's behavior in South China). Because these parent states are contiguous neither to one another (e.g., the United Kingdom-France dyad) nor to the independent states with which they negotiate (e.g., the major powers settling borders with states in Africa, the Middle East, or Asia), their efforts will not explicitly appear in the study. As before, however, they indirectly affect border settlement, as they determine the states to which *uti possidetis* applies. We mention these points here to be transparent about exactly what the analysis includes and excludes.[42]

Given the differences in conflict management tools, and the conditions under which we expect them to work, we estimate models with a number of different variable codings. In some models, we consider *all conflict management efforts*,

[42] Major states (e.g., as mediators or arbiters) and intergovernmental organizations (e.g., as mediators, arbiters, or adjudicators) can assist neighboring states in the border delimitation process. To the extent that they do, our conflict management data captures their efforts. We also have data on pre-independence (often, colonial) efforts at border settlement, which only enter our analysis indirectly (i.e., through the principle of *uti possidetis*; see the coding rules discussed earlier). How (colonial) parent states work toward border settlement constitutes a different research question that remains beyond the scope of this work.

an aggregation of all five strategies. In other models, we seek to understand better whether disputants work through border settlement alone or with assistance, and if the latter, what form third-party assistance takes – particularly when power endowments are present. This produces four additional variables: (bilateral) *negotiations*, *any third-party* involvement (i.e., mediation, arbitration, adjudication, and post-war conferences), *mediation* (alone), and *legal approaches* (i.e., arbitration, adjudication, and post-war conferences). The first variable tracks disputants' independent efforts, while the later three variables capture the involvement of third parties – whatever their role may be.

Each of these conflict management variables consists of a running sum of the number of conflict management attempts that occurred in the dyad's border delimitation process prior to the dyad-year in question. A running sum best represents the logic underlying many theories of conflict management, which propose that conflict management efforts accumulate. In other words, no single conflict management attempt proves decisive, but rather, the cumulative conflict management effort affects the probability of dispute resolution (see Chapter 3; Greig and Diehl 2006). Anecdotal evidence within dyadic border settlement processes offers *prima facie* support for this logic (e.g., see Blum 2007; Ireland 1938). We therefore create five running sum variables: all conflict management, negotiations (only), any third-party conflict management (mediation and legal approaches), mediation (only), and legal approaches (only).

4.2.3 Control Variables

In addition to the variables noted above, we include two control variables that influence the dyadic border settlement process – that is, that affect both the likelihood that conflict management occurs and the achievement of full border settlement. The first accounts for differences between major and minor states. Major powers exert two effects on settlement processes. On the one hand, they increase the likelihood of conflict management. Major powers, by definition, hold interests (and historically, territory) all over the world. This places them in a position to negotiate – and therefore, settle – borders more often than other states, especially as empires collapse. On the other hand, major states might forestall conflict management efforts when they themselves dispute territory with a less powerful state (for this argument, see Zawahri and Mitchell 2011). In these instances, the major power thinks it can get a better deal by limiting conflict management efforts, or perhaps directing efforts toward an approach that grants them more control over the management process and outcome (e.g., negotiation, as opposed to mediation or arbitration). The states qualifying as *major powers*, and the periods during which they do so, come from the Correlates of War Project's (2008) State System Membership List.

The second control variable concerns ethnicity. Border placement frequently involves attempts to (re)unite ethnic kin within a single state (e.g., see the Italy–Yugoslavia, Greece–Turkey, Benin–Niger, India–Pakistan, or Korean disputes).

When activated, this issue potentially undermines settlement efforts more than other motivations for disputing border territory. Protecting ethnic kin is neither a divisible issue, nor one on which domestic groups favor concessions. Disputes involving ethnic kin therefore drag on, and as they do, efforts at conflict management may accumulate without producing a settlement. We control for border territory that contains concerns about ethnic kin with a dichotomous variable, *ethnic linkages*, that indicates whether, in each year of its existence, a contiguous dyad disputes border territory and at least one dyad member holds concerns about its ethnic kin living in that disputed territory. The Huth and Allee (2002) and ICOW data (Frederick, Hensel, and Macaulay 2017) supply these data (separately).

4.2.4 Modeling

In essence, we model the time until an event occurs – in this case, border settlement. Scholars often conduct such an event history analysis with hazard models. We employ the conditional logistic regression model, which is "a special case of the Cox [hazard] model for discrete grouped duration data" like ours (Box-Steffensmeier and Jones 2004, 88). Our decision to use this, as opposed to the Cox model, derives from a desire to present our results in a form accessible to the widest audience possible. Logistic regression, being used more often than hazard modeling (in international relations research, if not elsewhere), will be more readily interpretable to a broader readership. Moreover, interpreting the interaction terms needed to evaluate our arguments becomes easier with logistic regression, as opposed to hazard, models. We can, for example, talk about a variable's effects on the predicted probability of border settlement, rather than changes to the hazard rate. This results in a more intuitive discussion.

Our dichotomous dependent variables make (conditional) logistic regression an appropriate statistical modeling technique, and we therefore employ it throughout the entire book. The conditional component arises from each model being conditioned on a null value of the dependent variable in the previous dyad-year. In this chapter, for example, the model predicts the likelihood of border settlement in a dyad-year, given that the border remained unsettled in the previous dyad-year. This makes theoretical sense, since a dyad cannot settle a border that it has already settled. Similar conditions underlie the models in Chapters 6 and 8 (on rivalry onset and termination, respectively).

The models control for temporal interdependence through the use of time polynomials (labeled *dyad life*, *dyad life*^{2}, and *dyad life*^{3}; see Carter and Signorino 2010), which measure the life of the dyad. The inclusion of linear, square, and cubic terms allows the effect of time to vary nonlinearly over the dyad's life. If, for example, older dyads – as a result of conflict weariness – or newer dyads – because of the desire to dispense quickly with a highly salient issue after independence – are more likely to settle their borders than middle-aged ones, the polynomials will capture such effects.

We also note that the temporal domains differ somewhat across our various models. Our general models predict border settlement between land contiguous dyads during the period 1816–2001. When we incorporate the Huth and Allee (2002) data on power endowments and ethnic linkages, the analysis restricts to the period 1919–1995 because their data cover only this narrower timeframe. We overcome any limitation this might create through using the ICOW data as well. ICOW offers an alternative method for measuring the variables we borrow from Huth and Allee and covers the entire 1816–2001 period (Frederick, Hensel, and Macaulay 2017). We retain the Huth and Allee (2002) data, though, despite its narrower temporal domain, to evaluate the robustness of our results.

4.2.5 Does a Contiguous Dyad Specification Make Sense?

Although we focus solely on (land) contiguous dyads in our study, do noncontiguous dyads belong in the analysis too? As we note earlier, including them seems theoretically indefensible and empirically impossible. Noncontiguous dyads have no borders to settle, so our theoretical argument cannot possibly apply to them. Moreover, because noncontiguous dyads lack borders, there exists no settled border data on them. To include them, we would therefore need to make assumptions and research design decisions that would muddy the study's inferences substantially. It seems better, in our opinion, not to do this.

Empirical evidence supports our decision. The appendix to this chapter contains an analysis of rivalry onset that includes contiguous and noncontiguous dyads. It strongly suggests that the causal path to rivalry onset and maintenance – a main argument of this book – differs significantly across these two types of dyads. Contiguous states develop rivalries than often than noncontiguous states. Beyond this general observation, however, a series of interaction terms indicate that contiguous dyads behave entirely differently than noncontiguous ones in the rivalry onset process. Joint democracy (i.e., whether both members of a dyad are democratic states), for example, significantly inhibits rivalry formation in noncontiguous dyads, but often *encourages* it in contiguous dyads. Alliances among dyad members produce the opposite effect, suppressing rivalry in contiguous dyads, despite their tendency to promote it in noncontiguous dyads. In the end, contiguous and noncontiguous rivalries demonstrate disparate effects across many variables and appear to follow two distinct causal pathways to rivalry – each likely to require a unique causal argument. We provide one argument for why rivalries form among contiguous states and save causal arguments for how noncontiguous dyads form rivalries for future researchers to develop.

4.3 EMPIRICAL FINDINGS

We begin the empirical analysis with a description of diplomatic attempts to settle interstate borders. Table 4.3 provides this information for all contiguous

TABLE 4.3. *Conflict management and the border settlement process, 1816–2001*

Unit of Analysis: Contiguous Dyad-Years Containing Unsettled Borders Only ($n = 3,852$)				
All conflict management	6.96%			
Negotiation		4.92%		
All third-party conflict management		1.97%		
Mediation			0.75%	
Legal strategies			1.22%	
Arbitration				0.47%
Adjudication				0.29%
Post-war conferences				0.47%

dyad-years in which borders remain unsettled. This is the condition underlying the statistical models that follow. Unsettled borders are the key theoretical population that we need to model. Once a dyad settles its border, it drops from the analysis. We therefore restrict the description to dyad-years in which settlement is possible, as these observations alone underlie the models that follow.[43]

As Table 4.3 indicates, diplomatic settlement attempts do not dominate the data. A new diplomatic settlement attempt begins in approximately 7% of the contiguous dyad-year observations with unsettled borders. The vast majority of these dyad-years (over 97%) therefore see *no* active attempts to settle dyadic borders. This aggregate finding masks significant variation, however. The table therefore unpacks the aggregate variable, to summarize every other variable we use in the analysis. Aggregate variables appear in italics, with their subcomponents nested beneath them. Arbitration, adjudication, and post-war conferences, for example, constitute the larger *Legal Strategies* category. Variables disaggregate as one moves down the table and right, with the lowest of any nested category appearing in nonitalicized text.

The disaggregation of conflict management in Table 4.3 yields a key conclusion that other scholars commonly find: states prefer to maintain control of the management of highly salient issues like border territory (Owsiak and Mitchell 2019). In the border settlement process, states use negotiation the most (in almost 5% of contiguous dyad-years with unsettled borders). Negotiation allows dyad members (i.e., the disputants) the greatest control over the conflict management process and outcome. They determine when and where to meet

43 The Owsiak, Cuttner, and Buck (2018) data contain some diplomatic attempts after settlement occurs. These include reaffirmations of an existing delimitation, demarcation agreements, and attempts to revise existing border settlement terms. Neighboring states, for example, that use the principle of *uti possidetis* to determine their borders at independence may mutually agree to revise their borders. Activities like these are qualitatively different than those focused on border settlement in the first place. See also Chapter 2.

(if at all), what to discuss, and what terms to propose and accept. Third parties play no role in these efforts.

States next rely most on mediation, which appears in 0.75% of contiguous dyad-years with unsettled borders. Mediation introduces a third-party actor, who not only brings its own preferences and interests to the table but also can influence the settlement process. Mediators may provide a venue for the mediation, control communication between disputants, propose settlement terms, or manipulate the likelihood of an agreement – by increasing the benefits of an agreement or the costs of nonagreement. Disputants therefore lose some control over conflict management, depending on the exact functions the mediator performs.

Individual legal strategies cause disputants to lose even greater control, and they therefore use such strategies less often still. In arbitration, disputants agree to both let a third party decide how to settle the contested issues and abide by the third party's decision. Despite binding them to this decision, however, disputants retain some control. They can still choose the arbiter, determine what principles and evidence the third party considers, and partially define the arbitration process through the *compromis*. Adjudication takes this control away. The choice of third-party actor restricts to the courts with the jurisdiction to hear the case at hand. Moreover, disputants can neither select the full panel of judges that will hear the case nor control the court's process, which follows pre-established statutes. Finally, in a post-war conference, the major power victors typically control the settlement process, giving less weight to disputant positions than adjudication would (e.g., on the Paris Peace Conference of 1919, see MacMillan 2001). This loss of control once again affects disputants' choice of conflict management strategy. They employ arbitration in 0.47% of the contiguous dyad-years with unsettled borders and adjudication in 0.29% of these dyad-years. Post-war conferences, which disputants often have little choice to permit, appear in 0.47% of the contiguous dyad-years with unsettled borders.

4.3.1 Border Settlement in Land Contiguous Dyads

Our first three hypotheses identify dyadic characteristics that theoretically help disputants overcome information problems during the bargaining process: joint democracy, power parity, and alliance ties between the disputants. Models 1–3 of Table 4.4 evaluate these characteristics' effect on border settlement. Among the three characteristics, only joint democracy exerts a consistent, statistically significant effect on border settlement. Hypothesis 3.1 proposes that jointly democratic dyads share a bargaining advantage; whether because of shared democratic institutions or norms, democratic dyads signal and exchange information between members more credibly than nondemocratic dyads. The results support this prediction. When both dyad members are democratic states – as opposed to at least one dyad member being a nondemocracy – the

TABLE 4.4. *Border settlement in contiguous dyads, 1816–2001*

	Model 1	Model 2	Model 3
Hypotheses	3.1–3.3 Baseline	3.4 Huth & Allee Claims	3.4 ICOW Claims
Joint democracy	1.037** (0.367)	1.813*** (0.412)	1.608*** (0.394)
Capability ratio (ln)	−0.107 (0.074)	−0.097 (0.077)	−0.169* (0.073)
Allied	0.328 (0.222)	0.866*** (0.245)	0.335 (0.232)
Major power	0.144 (0.249)	0.018 (0.244)	−0.102 (0.236)
Power endowments	–	−2.161*** (0.410)	−1.568*** (0.239)
Ethnic linkages	–	−1.406*** (0.414)	−0.618 (0.331)
Dyad life	−0.114*** (0.029)	−0.152*** (0.026)	−0.108*** (0.023)
Dyad life^2	0.002** (0.001)	0.003*** (0.001)	0.002*** (0.000)
Dyad life^3	−0.000* (0.000)	−0.000*** (0.000)	−0.000*** (0.000)
Constant	−2.351*** (0.277)	−1.772*** (0.274)	−1.583*** (0.257)
N	3,821	3,701	3,821

Notes: Conditional logistic regression; standard errors in parentheses; * $p < 0.05$, ** $p < 0.01$, *** $p < 0.001$.

dyad is significantly more likely to experience border settlement in a given dyad-year. This holds across all three models in Table 4.4, as well as each of the models presented in Tables 4.5 and 4.6.

The coefficients attached to the *joint democracy* variable indicate that its relationship to border settlement is positive and statistically meaningful. Yet they do not explain how much joint democracy affects the likelihood of border settlement. As Long and Freese (2006, 157) note, "the estimated parameters from the BRM [i.e., the binary regression model, including a logistic regression] do not provide directly useful information for understanding the relationship between the independent variables and the outcome [of interest].... [S]ubstantively meaningful interpretations are based on predicted probabilities." Understanding substantive significance therefore requires an additional step: calculating the predicted probability of the outcome of interest (here, border settlement) under different values of the independent variable (here, joint democracy). As we proceed through the empirical discussions in this book, we calculate and present these probability estimates, each of which necessarily contains some uncertainty and, therefore, a confidence interval. A change in probability from pr_0 to pr_1 is considered "statistically significant" if the 95% confidence intervals surrounding pr_0 and pr_1 do not overlap – that is, if we are reasonable certain that the two estimates differ from one another.

In Models 1–3 (Table 4.4), the effect of joint democracy translates into a roughly 150–400% increase in the likelihood of border settlement, from a base probability of 0.027 for nondemocratic dyads to a probability of 0.071–0.130 (probability results not shown). The exact effect depends on the model used to make the prediction. Model 1 predicts that the probability of border settlement is 0.071 for jointly democratic dyads (a 165%, statistically nonsignificant increase over the base probability), while Model 3 predicts a probability of 0.130 (a 380%, statistically significant increase). Model 2's estimation lies between these two extremes.

These probabilities suggest that joint democracy exerts a strong effect on border settlement. We, however, endorse such a conclusion cautiously. Gibler and Owsiak (2018) show that, in the vast majority of cases where democratic dyads settled their borders, democracy itself played little role in the settlement process. Instead, they argue that post-war conferences (e.g., in the case of the Austria–Czechoslovakia border), major power intervention (i.e., the United States or Soviet Union; e.g., in the case of the Poland–Czechoslovakia border or the independence of Namibia), and legal approaches (e.g., in the case of the Chile–Argentina border) pushed democratic dyads' borders toward settlement without assistance from the disputants' democratic regimes. Because the cases on which they base their conclusions are the same as those that drive our joint democracy results, a word of caution seems wise. If Gibler and Owsiak are correct, then our models simply capture a mistaken statistical relationship. Nonetheless, our models consistently indicate that joint democracy may help facilitate border settlement. We therefore conclude that Hypothesis 3.1 has empirical support; the strength of that support, however, depends on whether joint democracy itself produces the effect we observe. That debate lies beyond the scope of the current project.

Power parity is a second characteristic that potentially affects the credible exchange of information between disputants. Disputants' inability to obtain reliable information about one another's intentions, capabilities, and resolve often leads to bargaining breakdown. Certain conditions theoretically exacerbate this problem. As power distributes more asymmetrically between the disputants, for example, the missing information affects their calculations – and therefore, bargaining outcomes – less. They know who is stronger, although they may still disagree about intentions and resolve. Closer to power parity, in contrast, they fail to agree on who is stronger as well. Moreover, incentives to bluff increase because a disputant can theoretically gain the upper hand by convincing its opponent that it is the stronger disputant – a tactic undermined by large power asymmetries. This suggests that power parity hinders border settlement, while power asymmetry promotes it (Hypothesis 3.2).

The results in Models 1–3 of Table 4.4, as well as those in Tables 4.5 and 4.6, provide no support for this hypothesis. Power parity occurs at the minimum value of the *capability ratio* (ln) variable. Were the hypothesis accurate, we would consequently expect positive and statistically significant coefficients on that variable. Yet we do not observe this in any model. The coefficients are not only generally statistically insignificant, but they are also negatively signed. Contrary to Hypothesis 3.2, then, the likelihood of border settlement increases as a dyad's members approach power parity; or conversely, the probability of border settlement falls as the relative power distribution between dyad members becomes increasingly asymmetric.

Predicted probabilities illustrate the trend substantively (based on Model 3, Table 4.4). When one disputant is 1.87 times stronger than the other (the 25th percentile for the relative capabilities ratio values in the data analyzed), the probability of border settlement is 0.035. This probability falls to 0.031 when one disputant is 3.80 times stronger than the other (the median value) and to 0.026 when it is 11.30 times stronger (the 75th percentile). These changes, however, are never statistically significant; the 95% confidence intervals for the probability estimates overlap, even for the estimates associated with the 25th and 75th percentile values of the capability ratio variable. In short, relative capabilities exert no statistically or substantively meaningful effect on border settlement.

Alliance ties also theoretically alter the credible flow of information between disputants. Allies coordinate security policy – to a greater or lesser extent, depending on the exact commitments made. This requires that allied states not only share information with one another, but also build a reputation for sharing *credible* information in particular. If allies confront unsettled borders, then this relationship helps them overcome the information problem that might plague their bargaining (Hypothesis 3.3).

Our empirical results provide mixed support for this hypothesis. In Model 2 (Table 4.4), for example, alliances demonstrate the predicted effect. The positive, statistically significant coefficient on the *allied* variable indicates that a shared alliance increases the likelihood of border settlement. Substantively, the probability of border settlement among non-allies in a given dyad-year – all else equal – is 0.024; for allies, this probability rises to 0.052 – a 119%, statistically significant change. Models 6 (Table 4.5) and 7 (Table 4.6) reveal a similar effect.

In the remaining models, however, the alliance variable has a positive sign (as expected), but does not obtain statistical significance (contrary to

Hypothesis 3.3). What explains these inconsistent findings? Two possibilities exist. The first relates to the time period being analyzed. Of the three models where alliances exert a statistically meaningful effect on the likelihood of border settlement, two involve the Huth and Allee claims data (Models 2 and 7). These data restrict our analysis from the larger 1816–2001 period to the narrower 1919–1995 period. It is possible, then, that the effect of alliances is stronger in the post-World War I period. If true, we would not be the first to discover that alliances behave differently across the nineteenth and twentieth centuries (e.g., see the discussion in Vasquez 2009). The second possibility concerns the relationship between alliance formation and border settlement. Gibler (1996) argues that alliances often accompany (or logically, follow) territorial settlements. The high salience of unsettled territorial issues, along with the hostility that accompanies their management, hinders the formation of alliances. Assuming an alliance did form, this same salience and hostility also might overwhelm the ability of alliance relationships to convey information credibly between alliance partners. The net effect would not necessarily lead to a reduced likelihood of border settlement, only interfere with the positive effect that Hypothesis 3.3 proposes.

Whatever the reason, the effect of alliances on border settlement remains inconsistent across our models. Occasionally, an alliance between dyad members increases the likelihood of that dyad settling its borders, as Hypothesis 3.3 predicts (three of eight models). Most often, however, alliance relationships exert no statistically significant effect on whether dyadic border settlement occurs (five of eight models). These results cumulatively offer mixed support for Hypothesis 3.3.

Our fourth hypothesis shifts the focus from the role of information problems to that of commitment problems in the border settlement process. We argue that a commitment problem arises more often when border territory contains power endowments than when it does not. The commitment problem, in turn, complicates the border settlement process; fearful that border settlement will produce a power shift (and greater vulnerability for one of them), the involved states avoid reaching a border settlement in the first place (Hypothesis 3.4).

Models 2–3 of Table 4.4 consider this possibility directly – first using the Huth and Allee territorial claim data (Model 2) and then the ICOW territorial claim data (Model 3). Regardless of which data we use, the likelihood of border settlement falls significantly when a dyad disputes territory containing power endowments. The negative, statistically significant coefficients on the *power endowments* variable yield this conclusion. In substantive terms, changing a territory's characteristics from the absence of to the presence of power endowments reduces the likelihood of border settlement by 77% with the ICOW data (from 0.052 to 0.012) and 87% with the Huth and Allee data (from 0.039 to 0.005); both of these substantive decreases are statistically significant (see Figure 4.6, which presents these results graphically). Such findings provide strong empirical support to Hypothesis 3.4 – an important result given the

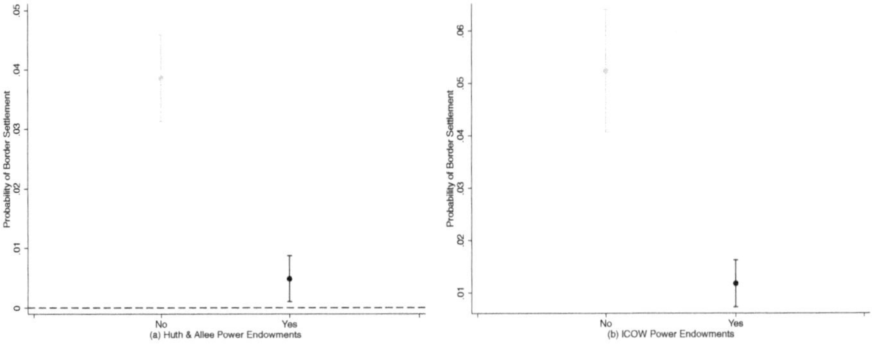

FIGURE 4.6. Power endowments and border settlement, 1816–2001

Notes: Derived from the results in Models 2–3, Table 4.4; mean prediction (dot) and 95% confidence interval (vertical line). Y-axes differ to best illustrate results.

prominent role that the commitment problem plays in the remaining chapters of this book.

The control variables in Table 4.4 offer three additional insights into the border settlement process. First, dyads containing a major state are no more or less likely than dyads lacking a major state to settle their borders. This result holds not only across the three models in Table 4.4, but also across every model presented in Tables 4.5 and 4.6 as well. Second, when disputed territory involves concerns about ethnic kin, the likelihood of border settlement declines significantly, but only when we use the Huth and Allee data (Model 2). The same effect does not emerge when we use the ICOW data (Model 3; for a similar result, see also Models 7–8 in Table 4.6). This discrepancy may result again from the narrower time period that the Huth and Allee data capture. Nevertheless, we note that controlling for ethnic concerns does not alter the conclusion we reach about the relationship between territory containing power endowments and border settlement.

Finally, the probability of border settlement changes over a dyad's life. The quadratic and cubic terms, as well as the vast range in dyads' ages, complicate the interpretation and presentation of this relationship. Figure 4.7 therefore depicts the relationship visually. At each year of a dyad's existence, it plots both the mean value of border settlement and the 95% confidence interval around this value. For example, the probability of border settlement in a given dyad-year sits at 0.063 when a contiguous dyad first enters the international system – although the 95% confidence interval indicates that this value may be as high as 0.085 or as low as 0.042. Because border settlement first trends downward, we enter a dotted line at the value 0.042; this line runs horizontally through the figure and marks the low end of the initial estimate's confidence interval. If an estimate and its entire confidence interval fall below this line, then we know a statistically significant reduction in border settlement has occurred.

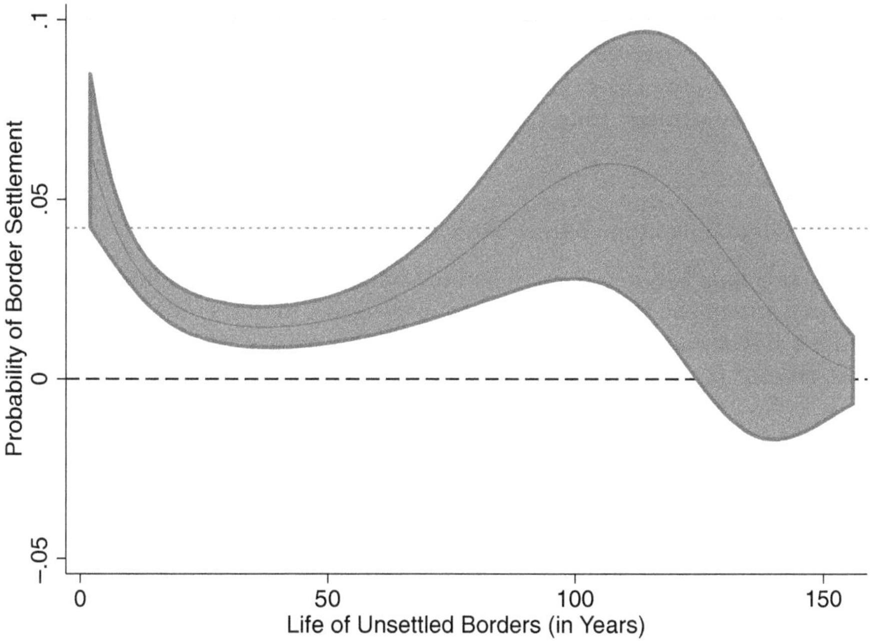

FIGURE 4.7. Border settlement over a contiguous dyad's life

Notes: Derived from Model 3, Table 4.4; mean prediction (dark line) and 95% confidence interval (lighter area).

A statistically significant reduction manifests itself when a dyad turns ten years old. At this age, the estimated probability of border settlement is 0.034 (95% confidence interval: 0.027–0.041). Yet the probability of border settlement does not stop falling there; it continues declining until a dyad reaches the age of 38 ($pr_{38} = 0.014$), at which point it reverses course and begins increasing. By age 73, it regains the initial probability with which it entered the international system ($pr_{73} = 0.030$, but the confidence interval once again crosses the horizontal, dotted reference line at 0.042). It then continues climbing until hitting a peak of 0.060 when a dyad is 107 years old. Finally, it falls once again; by age 155, a dyad's likelihood of border settlement sits at 0.003.

Figure 4.7 shows the dangers and effects of the bargaining obstacles we identify. Easy cases settle fast and early (e.g., those employing *uti possedetis*). Information and commitment problems, however, complicate border settlement in a number of cases, and the likelihood of border settlement subsequently falls as dyads encounter these problems. Given sufficient time to bargain – and perhaps third-party assistance (see next section) – dyads overcome the information problems, which explains why the probability of border settlement rises in a dyad's mid-life. Yet the probability does not stabilize at a high value because the cases in which older dyads bargain over unsettled borders likely contain commitment problems – something that repeated bargaining (and time alone) cannot overcome. The probability of border settlement therefore plummets toward zero. The next section sheds further light on these suppositions, examining in greater detail how dyads bargain during the border settlement process.

4.3.2 Bargaining in the Border Settlement Process

Our remaining hypotheses consider how conflict management efforts affect the border settlement process. Table 4.5 investigates the general effects of these efforts (Hypotheses 3.5–3.7), while Table 4.6 explores whether and how the presence of power endowments alters these general effects (Hypotheses 3.8–3.10). We begin with the general effects.[44] Of the various models presented in Table 4.5, Model 6 is of most direct interest to our hypotheses, since it separates the effects of negotiations, mediations, and legal approaches from one another. Nonetheless, the aggregate variables used in Models 4 and 5 are worth discussing briefly. In Model 4, iterated conflict management significantly increases the likelihood of border settlement. Panel (a) of Figure 4.8 shows the substantive effects behind this finding.

Without conflict management efforts ($x = 0$), the likelihood of border settlement in a given dyad-year is 0.024. The 95% confidence interval around this estimate suggests that this value might be as high as 0.028, and we consequently set a dotted horizontal reference line at this value in panel (a) for comparison purposes. When, if at all, does the likelihood of dyadic border settlement rise above that reference line? This occurs at the fourth conflict management effort, when the probability of border settlement hits 0.041 (95% confidence interval: 0.030–0.051). After that ($x > 4$), the mean probability of border settlement continues rising steadily through successive conflict management iterations, but the confidence intervals also widen, as fewer dyads experience each successive round of conflict management. Nonetheless, these confidence intervals (i.e., the vertical lines) always end above the dotted reference line, indicating that the repeated attempts at conflict management significantly increase the likelihood

44 Concerns about selection effects bedevil all social science research. In our study, actors must agree to participate in bilateral or third-party conflict management efforts. This raises the concern that any relationships we uncover between conflict management tools and border settlement results primarily from the disputing states' willingness to resolve their disagreement in the first place (i.e., the conflict management tools exert no independent effect on the probability of border settlement). Such an argument would manifest empirically as straightforward, consistent, positive correlations between conflict management tools (of any type) and border settlement, a pattern we do not see in the data. Instead, the data show significant variation in the success of conflict management tools in the border settlement process, depending on time, the type of tool, and the issues under contention. These patterns suggest that our results do not derive from selection effects alone, especially not actors simply choosing to settle their borders and, therefore, engage in conflict management.

TABLE 4.5. *Conflict management and border settlement, 1816–2001*

	Model 4	Model 5	Model 6
Hypotheses	Baseline	3.5	3.5–3.7
Any conflict management	0.143*** (0.036)	–	–
Negotiations	–	0.092 (0.062)	0.115 (0.064)
Any third party	–	0.256** (0.089)	–
Mediation	–	–	−0.105 (0.137)
Legal	–	–	1.032*** (0.203)
Joint democracy	1.021** (0.370)	0.886* (0.376)	0.791* (0.371)
Allied	0.340 (0.228)	0.317 (0.231)	0.464* (0.229)
Major power	0.315 (0.254)	0.351 (0.255)	0.482 (0.265)
Capability ratio (ln)	−0.100 (0.075)	−0.099 (0.074)	−0.112 (0.075)
Dyad life	−0.123*** (0.031)	−0.126*** (0.030)	−0.125*** (0.025)
Dyad life^2	0.002** (0.001)	0.002** (0.001)	0.002*** (0.001)
Dyad life^3	−0.000* (0.000)	−0.000* (0.000)	−0.000*** (0.000)
Constant	−2.410*** (0.282)	−2.381*** (0.281)	−2.472*** (0.272)
N	3,821	3,821	3,821

Notes: Conditional logistic regression; standard errors in parentheses; * $p < 0.05$, ** $p < 0.01$, *** $p < 0.001$.

of border settlement – compared to cases where conflict management does not occur.[45]

[45] Critics might argue that a border cannot settle without *a* conflict management attempt. For them, the more appropriate baseline might therefore be the first conflict management attempt, rather than none. Were we to adopt this baseline instead, we would obtain the same general result. The only difference is that the significant increase would be delayed until the sixth conflict management effort, after which it would again remain significantly higher than this new baseline throughout further iterations of conflict management.

Model 5 (Table 4.5) disaggregates this finding. It splits all conflict management into *negotiations* (which lack third-party assistance) and *any third-party* assistance (which accounts for mediation, arbitration, adjudication, and postwar conferences). In so doing, it indicates that third-party assistance drives our aggregate conflict management finding. Iterated negotiations do not increase the likelihood of border settlement significantly, contrary to Hypothesis 3.5. The coefficient on third-party efforts, in contrast, is positive and statistically significant, suggesting that iterated third-party conflict management significantly increases the odds that border settlement occurs.

Both of the conflict management variables in Model 5 produce substantive results that follow a similar pattern. Successive iterations of conflict management consistently increase the probability of border settlement. At the first negotiation, for example, the probability of border settlement is 0.028. By the fifth and tenth negotiations, this probability rises to 0.040 and 0.061, respectively. Likewise, the probability of border settlement at the first third-party effort is 0.033, while at the fifth effort, it is 0.085. Nonetheless, none of these increases is statistically significant. Fewer dyads experience each successive round of conflict management, causing the confidence intervals to widen further at each round. These widened intervals overlap with the confidence intervals of the original estimates. In short, even though we observe that successive rounds of conflict management generally increase the likelihood of border settlement, the greater uncertainty introduced at each successive round – a result of less data, or fewer dyads that experience that level of conflict management – makes us less confident that this trend is statistically meaningful (for a visual depiction of this property in a related model, see panels b and c of Figure 4.8).

Model 6 (Table 4.5) unpacks this result still further: into *negotiations*, *mediation*, and *legal* approaches. In so doing, it suggests that legal approaches in particular are responsible for the results we observe in Models 4 and 5. Negotiations once again exert no statistically significant effect on the likelihood of border settlement. The coefficient on this variable is positive (as expected), but statistically insignificant. And the substantive results associated with the negotiation variable mirror those for Model 5 discussed above: a statistically *in*significant upward trend line (see panel b of Figure 4.8).[46] Hypothesis 3.5 therefore receives no support across either Model 5 or Model 6.

Mediation, likewise, does not significantly alter the probability of border settlement. In fact, the coefficient's sign suggests the relationship might run in the opposite direction to our hypothesis's prediction – in other words, repeated mediation may *lower* the likelihood of border settlement (see panel c of Figure 4.8). For example, at the first mediation, the probability of border settlement is 0.027. By the fifth mediation, however, this probability falls to 0.018. We cannot make much of this trend; neither the statistical results (see

[46] The predicted probability values are similar to Model 5, so we do not discuss them in detail here.

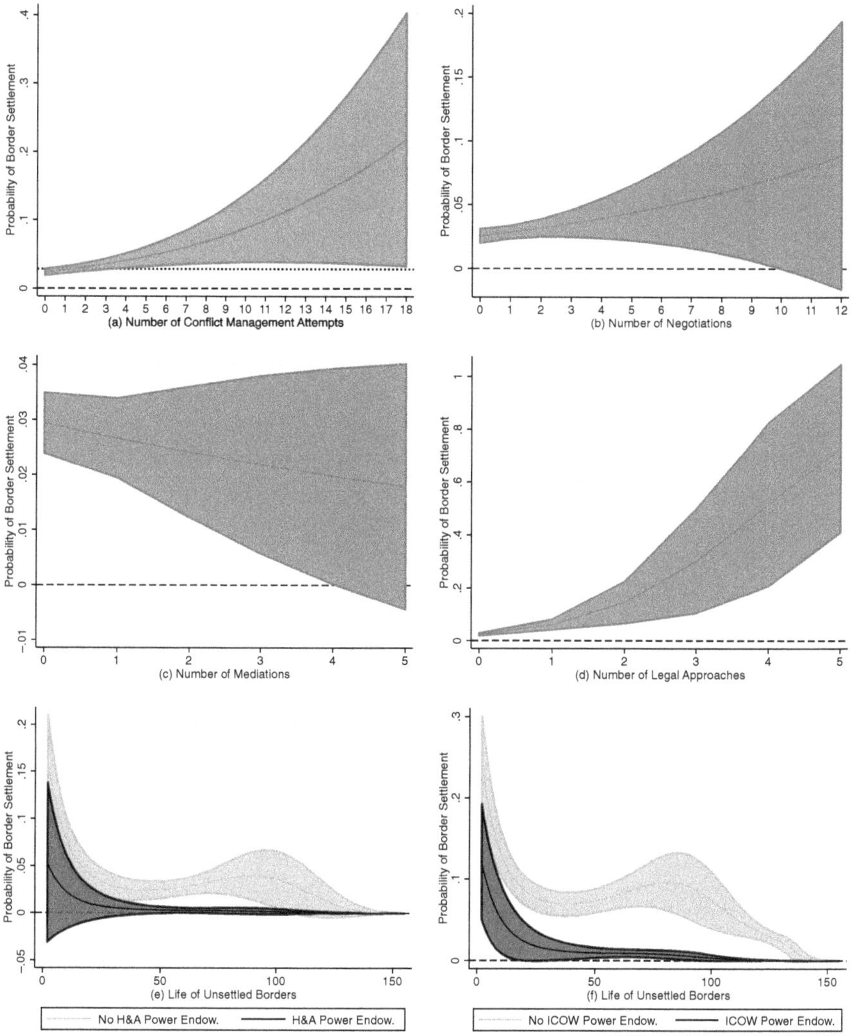

FIGURE 4.8. Conflict management and border settlement, 1816–2001

Notes: Derived from the results in Tables 4.5 and 4.6. Panel (a), Model 4; panels (b–d), Model 6; panels (e–f), a variant of Models 7–8 (not shown), in which we interact power endowments with the length of time that a border remained unsettled. Y-axes differ to best illustrate results.

Model 6) nor the substantive results (see Figure 4.8) are statistically significant. Nonetheless, we can conclude that these results do not support Hypothesis 3.6.

Legal approaches, on the other hand, *do* significantly increase the odds that border settlement will occur. The positive, statistically significant coefficient on the *legal* variable indicates as much, but the substantive results provide a clearer illustration of legal approaches' effect. Panel (d) of Figure 4.8 graphs these substantive results. When neighboring states do not use legal approaches, the probability that they reach border settlement is 0.023. Introducing a single legal approach increases this probability to 0.061 – a 162%, statistically significant increase. By the third legal approach, the probability rises further to 0.302; this represents a statistically significant increase over both previous values. Finally, the probability of border settlement hits 0.728 at the fifth legal approach. These results cumulatively provide rather strong evidence in support of Hypothesis 3.7; the iterated use of legal approaches significantly improves the odds that a contiguous dyad settles its borders in a given dyad-year.[47]

We have reason to suspect, however, that power endowments might alter the relationships identified thus far between conflict management approaches and border settlement. Table 4.6 – along with Figures 4.8 and 4.9, which each graph results from the table – consider this possibility. We begin with the *power endowment* variable itself. In Models 7–8, the coefficients on this variable are both negative and statistically significant. When border territory contains a power endowment, the likelihood that a contiguous dyad settles its border in a given year is significantly lower than if the territory lacked such an endowment.

Panels (e) and (f) of Figure 4.8 demonstrate that the substantive effect underlying this result varies over time. In these panels, we graph the predicted probability of border settlement – including the mean predicted value (solid line) and the 95% confidence interval around this value (shaded area around the line) for each year that a dyad's borders remain unsettled – given the presence (darker trend line) and absence (lighter trend line) of power endowments in the territory. Panel (e) uses the Huth and Allee territorial claims data to do this, while panel (f) relies on the ICOW territorial claims data. Nevertheless, the trends that the different datasets produce mirror one another. Regardless

47 We discuss control variables across Tables 4.4–4.6 earlier and, therefore, do not repeat that discussion here.

The effect of domestic legal preferences may also affect how states bargain during the border settlement process, including which conflict management strategies they select. In particular, states that share a domestic legal tradition (whether Islamic, common, or civil law) approach international law differently (Mitchell and Powell 2011). We run versions of the models in Table 4.5 that account for this possibility, and the results (available from the authors) show that dyad members who share a domestic legal tradition select conflict management strategies differently than other dyads. For example, dyads whose members share an Islamic law domestic system rely significantly more on negotiation than dyads whose members have different domestic legal systems. We do not include these variables in the models we present here because theory does not indicate how domestic legal systems affect either border settlement or bargaining over power endowments, making it unlikely that domestic legal systems confound our analysis. Including them would therefore not change our results, while also introducing additional complexity into the discussion. Future work might develop the relationship between domestic legal systems, border settlement, and power endowments further. For more information on how domestic preferences interact with international bargaining, see Cohen (1991), Simmons (2009), Simmons and Danner (2010), Mitchell and Powell (2011), Powell and Wiegand (2014), and Zartner (2014), among others.

TABLE 4.6. *Power endowments, conflict management, and border settlement, 1816–2001*

Hypotheses	Model 7 3.8–3.10 Huth & Allee Claims	Model 8 3.8–3.10 ICOW Claims
Power endowment	−2.018***	−0.965***
	(0.414)	(0.263)
Negotiation	0.197***	0.893***
	(0.052)	(0.118)
*Powerendowment*negotiation*	−0.275	−0.879***
	(0.155)	(0.129)
Mediation	0.375	0.899***
	(0.197)	(0.253)
*Powerendowment*mediation*	−0.657	−1.233**
	(0.585)	(0.404)
Legal	0.655*	−0.052
	(0.260)	(0.279)
*Powerendowment*legal*	0.733	1.569***
	(0.466)	(0.389)
Ethnic value	−1.244**	−0.726
	(0.399)	(0.382)
Joint democracy	1.723***	1.761***
	(0.432)	(0.466)
Allied	0.924***	0.297
	(0.248)	(0.239)
Major power	0.244	0.295
	(0.262)	(0.264)
Capability ratio (ln)	−0.065	−0.181*
	(0.079)	(0.081)
Dyad life	−0.156***	−0.173***
	(0.024)	(0.026)
Dyad life^2	0.003***	0.003***
	(0.000)	(0.001)
Dyad life^3	−0.000***	−0.000***
	(0.000)	(0.000)
Constant	−1.966***	−1.671***
	(0.275)	(0.288)
N	3,701	3,821

Notes: Standard errors in parentheses; * $p < 0.05$, ** $p < 0.01$, *** $p < 0.001$.

of how long an unsettled border exists, the likelihood of border settlement remains consistently lower if territory contains power endowments than if it does not (i.e., the darker trend line generally sits below the lighter one). Moreover, the two types of territory – endowed and not – produce dynamic trends over time that coincide with our theoretical argument (see Chapter 3). We propose that territory without power endowments primarily produces information problems, a bargaining obstacle that interferes with disputants' ability to convey their intentions, capabilities, and resolve to one another credibly. As bargaining begins ($x = 0$ in the panels), this problem initially impedes settlement, causing the likelihood of border settlement to fall. Yet after a history of interactions (including iterated bargaining; Hypotheses 3.5–3.7), sufficient information changes hands. This increases the likelihood of settlement once again, or at least stabilizes it for a while. In contrast, a greater flow of information cannot solve a commitment problem, which encourages disputants to avoid a settlement altogether. When a commitment problem manifests (i.e., when border territory contains a power endowment), we therefore expect that the likelihood of settlement falls quickly and does not rebound, even if repeated conflict management efforts take place (Hypotheses 3.8–3.10). Each of these trends appears in both panels (e) and (f).

Although revealing about the effects of power endowments generally, the discussion so far says nothing about how (if at all) power endowments alter the effects of conflict management efforts on the border settlement process. The interactions in Table 4.6, however, supply this information. To read these interaction effects, it helps to know two things (Braumoeller 2004). First, lower order terms (e.g., *negotiation*) indicate a given variable's effect on border settlement when power endowments are absent (*power endowments* = 0). The higher order terms (e.g., *power endowment*negotiation*), in contrast, denote any change in the variable's effect (over the lower order term) in the presence of power endowments (*power endowments* = 1). Second, the interaction term coefficients cannot be directly interpreted. The higher order terms reveal whether or not an effect differs significantly from that associated with the lower order term(s). In order to understand what that means substantively, one must return to predicted probabilities. Figure 4.9 graphs the main probabilities of interest. The left and right columns use the Huth and Allee (H&A) and ICOW territorial claims data, respectively. Each row examines a different conflict management strategy: negotiation (row 1), mediation (row 2), and legal approaches (row 3). Finally, within each panel in the figure, we separately chart the effect of conflict management on border settlement in both the presence (darker area) and absence (lighter area) of power endowments. These areas pull away from each other when a statistically significant, substantive difference between them exists and overlap when it does not.

The interactive effects produce three major findings. First, iterated negotiations increase the likelihood of border settlement, but only when border territory lacks power endowments. The coefficient on the lower order *negotia-*

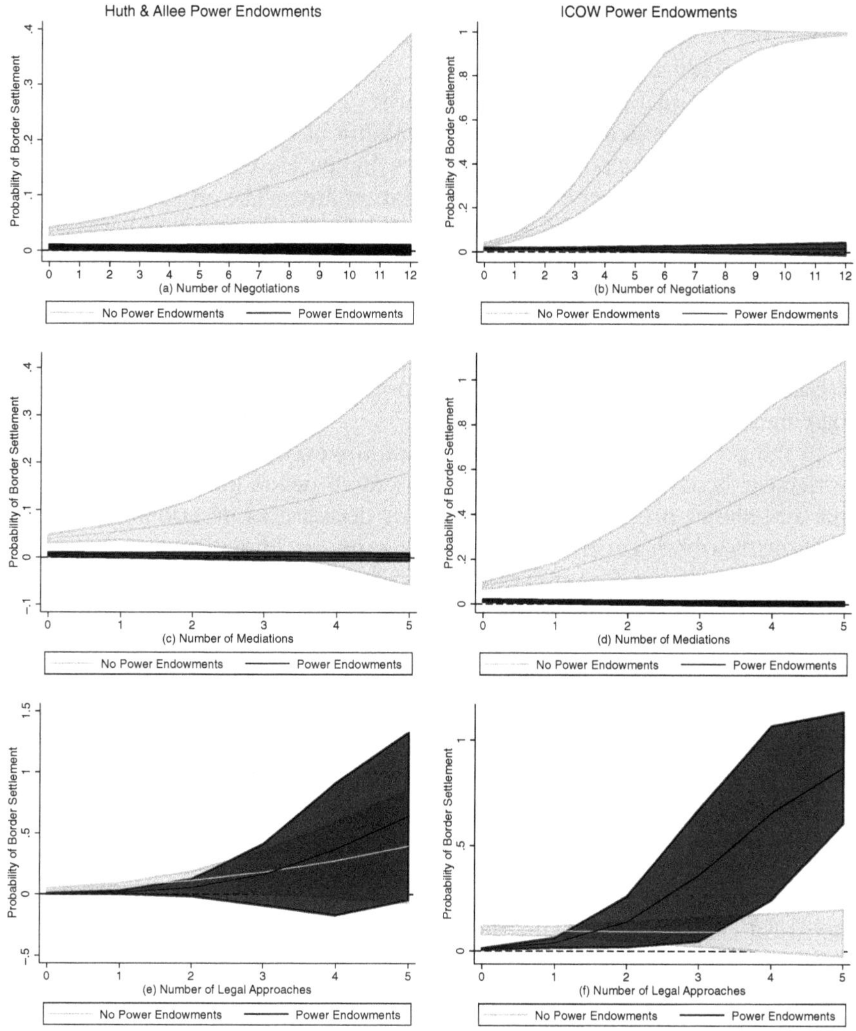

FIGURE 4.9. Power endowments, conflict management, and border settlement, 1816–2001

Notes: Derived from the results in Models 7–8, Table 4.6. Y-axes vary to best illustrate results.

tions term in both Models 7 and 8 is positive and statistically significant. This offers some support to Hypothesis 3.5, for negotiations conditionally increase the odds of border settlement – namely, when the border does not involve power endowments. In addition, the higher order, interactive term is negative (*power endowment*negotiation*), and in Model 8, also statistically significant;

this means that when we change from territory lacking power endowments to territory containing them, the positive effect of negotiations (i.e., the lower order term finding) goes away.

Panels (a) and (b) of Figure 4.9 illustrate these coefficients' substantive effects. At the first negotiation, the probability of border settlement is around 0.05 if territory lacks power endowments (lighter area), but 0.01 (or below) if territory possesses power endowments (darker area). The probability of border settlement then rises through successive rounds of negotiation in the absence of power endowments (lighter area) – with the magnitude of this effect depending on the territorial claims data used (see panel a versus panel b). We argue that these borders primarily involve information problems, and that the exchange of information that accompanies repeated negotiation will help disputants overcome this problem. The results support such an argument, as well as the logic underlying Hypothesis 3.5.

In the presence of power endowments, however, the probability of border settlement behaves differently through iterated negotiations. It hugs the zero line and shows no substantial increase or decrease as iterations occur ($pr \leq 0.016$ across both panels a and b). This supports Hypothesis 3.8, as well as our larger argument. Power endowments often trigger a commitment problem, which interferes with the border settlement process. Repeated negotiations do not directly address the commitment problem's logic, though; they neither prevent a power shift nor guarantee that any settlement reached will not be revised. Consequently, when the commitment problem exists (i.e., border territory contains power endowments), iterated negotiations do not increase the likelihood that border settlement occurs.

The second finding is that repeated mediation facilitates border settlement; as with negotiations, however, it only does so in the absence of power endowments. The coefficient patterns associated with the lower and higher order *mediation* variables mirror those of the *negotiation* variables – although statistical significance obtains only when using the ICOW territorial claims data (see Table 4.6). The substantive effects also look similar to those of the negotiation variables (see panels c and d of Figure 4.9). Mediation is more likely to facilitate border settlement when border territory lacks power endowments (i.e., the lighter area sits distinct from and above the darker area in each panel).

Repeated mediations may also increase this effect. Panel (c) shows that, with no power endowments involved, the average effect of mediation on border settlement increases over successive rounds of mediation (see solid line within the lighter area). The widening confidence intervals as one moves from left to the right across panel (c) suggest that this trend may be superficial. Yet panel (d) shows a similar, more dramatic effect. Using the ICOW data, the probability of border settlement at the first mediation in panel (d) is 0.143, if no power endowments are involved. This probability rises to 0.379 at the third mediation and 0.702 at the fifth mediation. Once again, it seems that when information problems dominate the bargaining process – that is, when power endowments do not afflict bargaining – conflict management strategies that can facilitate the credible exchange of information (e.g., mediation) increase the likelihood that border settlement occurs. The cumulative weight of this evidence supports Hypothesis 3.6; we qualify, however, that the support remains weak, since statistical and substantive significance depends on the territorial claims data used (Huth & Allee versus ICOW).

At the same time, the presence of power endowments undermines the boost to border settlement that mediation provides, as Hypothesis 3.9 predicts. The higher order interaction terms on the mediation variable in Table 4.6 are negative and, when using the ICOW data (Model 8), statistically significant; this suggests that the presence of power endowments erodes the positive effect of mediation on border settlement that was discussed earlier. Panels (c) and (d) of Figure 4.9 confirm this substantively. As with negotiations, the probability of border settlement remains low at the first mediation – around 0.004–0.011 (using the Huth & Allee and ICOW data, respectively). At the third mediation, this probability remains low – at 0.003–0.006 – as it does at the fifth mediation (0.002–0.003). Moreover, the confidence intervals around these estimates suggest that the probability of border settlement in the presence of power endowments may actually be zero over successive mediations; that is, the confidence intervals frequently cross the zero threshold (i.e., the dotted horizontal line in each panel), particularly for higher rounds of mediation.

This finding lends still further support to our larger theoretical story. Mediation is well-positioned to help disputants overcome an information problem. If, therefore, disputants' bargaining stalls because of such a problem – which we argue primarily occurs when border territory lacks power endowments – then repeated mediation facilitates the credible exchange of information, moves disputants over their primary bargaining obstacle, and promotes border settlement. Greater information exchange, however, cannot overcome the commitment problem, leaving mediation less equipped to assist with this obstacle.[48] Indeed, when border territory contains power endowments, one mediation – let alone three or five – fails to increase the probability of border settlement at all. Absent a mechanism to prevent a power shift or a revision of the settlement terms from occurring during the settlement's implementation phase, the commitment problem cannot be overcome.

We posit that legal approaches may provide such a mechanism, which leads us to the third main finding derived from Table 4.6 and Figure 4.9. Legal rulings constitute part of international law, which carries two defining characteristics. First, a single disputant cannot unilaterally change a legal ruling; to suggest otherwise undermines the function of law itself. Second, interest

[48] As noted earlier, third-party mediators who guarantee agreement terms will be implemented as signed may help overcome commitment problems (Walter 1997, 2002). Our narratives suggest that this rarely occurs; the most notable case captured by our narratives involves Argentina, Brazil, Chile, and the United States underwriting the 1942 Rio Protocol between Ecuador and Peru.

in the respect for international law transcends the disputants involved in any particular disagreement. The wider international community wants to see international law protected, and so they sanction violators of legal rulings – both reputationally (e.g., reducing cooperation with violators) and materially (e.g., reducing aid or other direct benefits to violators). These characteristics will not prevent a power shift when territory containing power endowments changes hands; yet they will interfere with the renegotiation of legal rulings' terms. This, we argue, gives legal approaches a greater ability to overcome commitment problem, relative to negotiations and mediation.

The patterns in the data are generally consistent with our argument. We first consider the management of territory that lacks power endowments. In these instances, the statistical results indicate that iterated legal approaches may promote border settlement, but only if we use the Huth and Allee data (see coefficients on the *legal* variables in Models 7–8, Table 4.6). The ICOW data shows no such effect. Nonetheless, the substantive effects behave similarly for both datasets. These effects – graphed in the lightly shaded areas of panels (e) and (f) of Table 4.9 – show that the probability of border settlement at the time of the first legal approach ($x = 1$) is 0.065–0.096 (for the Huth and Allee & ICOW data, respectively). The Huth and Allee data then reveal a slight upward trend in this probability as legal approaches repeat. At the fifth legal approach, for example, the probability of border settlement is 0.397; yet the confidence interval associated with this latter estimate overlaps that of the earlier estimate, suggesting that the trend may not exist at all (i.e., the two values may be identical). The ICOW data, meanwhile, directly report no trend at all; at the fifth legal approach, the odds of border settlement change only 0.010 over the original estimate – dropping the probability to 0.086. More noteworthy, however, is that calculations using both datasets show that by the fourth legal approach, the probability of border settlement may actually be zero (i.e., the 95% confidence intervals cross the horizontal, dotted zero line in both panels). We therefore cannot conclude that repeated rounds of legal approaches increase the probability of border settlement when states bargain over territory that lacks power endowments. This contradicts Hypothesis 3.7.

A different story emerges when power endowments are present, although a discrepancy exists across the two territorial claims datasets. The Huth and Allee dataset reports no statistical or substantive effect. The coefficient on the higher order *power endowment*legal* variable is positive (as expected), but not statistically significant. We would consequently expect it to predict that the effect of legal approaches on border settlement does not differ across the power-endowed and nonpower-endowed territorial contexts, which is what happens. At the first legal approach, the probability of border settlement is 0.015 (see darker shaded area of panel e in Figure 4.9). The model predicts that this probability rises to 0.640 at the fifth legal approach, but the confidence interval associated with this estimate overlaps that of the earlier one. Once again, what looks to be an upward trend may, in fact, be no trend at all; this contradicts the prediction of Hypothesis 3.10.

The ICOW data, in contrast, report a significant upward trend. The coefficient attached to the higher order *power endowment*legal* variable in Model 8 is positive and statistically significant. This suggests that iterated legal approaches increase the odds of border settlement when neighboring states bargain over power-endowed territory. The substantive results support this conclusion. At the first legal approach, the probability of border settlement sits at 0.039. By the third, fourth, and fifth legal approach, however, the probability climbs to 0.359, 0.655, and 0.871, respectively – with the latter two estimates representing significant increases over the original estimate (i.e., the compared confidence intervals do not overlap; see darker shaded area of panel f in Figure 4.9). This lends significant support to Hypothesis 3.10.

In the end, power endowments interfere with the relationship between conflict management efforts and border settlement.[49] The most striking confirmation of this emerges when we compare how the lightly shaded and darkly shaded regions behave in panels (a–d) of Figure 4.6, as opposed to panels (e–f). In panels (a–d), iterated negotiation and mediation promote border settlement, but only when the bargaining does not involve power-endowed territory. In the presence of power endowments, negotiation and mediation do not alter the odds that border settlement will occur. Panels (e–f) illustrate the converse. Iterated legal approaches do not increase border settlement in the absence of power endowments, but may do so in the presence of power endowments.

Our theoretical story largely explains why this occurs. Disputants bargaining over territory without power endowments primarily face an information problem. Iterated negotiations and mediations help disputants surmount this obstacle. Legal approaches, however, have limited value here. This may occur because (i) disputants do not trade sufficient information in the shadow of the legal process; (ii) the discovery process associated with legal approaches provides disputants with only limited information; or (iii) disputants only send their border disagreements to the legal process if negotiation and mediation cannot overcome the information problem (i.e., a selection effect exists). Regardless of the reason, rounds of legal approaches do not promote border settlement when territory lacks power endowments, while rounds of negotiation and mediation do.

Disputants bargaining over power-endowed territory, however, face a different obstacle: the commitment problem. Repeated negotiations and mediations fail to interfere with the commitment problem logic – that is, to either prevent a power shift or enforce settlement terms during the settlement's implementation phase. As a result, they exert little pull on the probability of border settlement when power endowments are present. Legal approaches, however, complicate disputants' ability to renegotiate settlement terms unilaterally. This offers

[49] We discuss control variables across Tables 4.4–4.6 earlier and, therefore, do not repeat that discussion here.

disputants a greater chance of overcoming the commitment problem and, in so doing, reaching border settlement. Iterated legal approaches therefore promote border settlement when power endowments are at stake.

4.4 CONCLUSION

This chapter sets out to understand the border settlement process better – with particular attention to the conditions that foster or impede it. Toward this end, a battery of empirical models are used to assess the generality of the ten hypotheses we laid out in Chapter 3 and produce a number of significant insights. Table 4.7 summarizes these insights. It lists each hypothesis, how strongly the evidence we present throughout this chapter supports it, and the main substantive conclusions we draw about it. The details underlying each conclusion appear throughout the chapter.

Importantly, the conclusions listed in Table 4.7 are consistent, in aggregate, with our theoretical story. Border settlement – as a bargaining context – requires states to find the range of mutually acceptable solutions and to determine which particular solution within that range to adopt. Myriad incentives, however, pull and push leaders toward and away from border settlement. Numerous benefits, for example, accrue to states once borders settle (e.g., increased security and economic); yet leaders will not accept *any* settlement. They want to receive the most favorable set of terms possible and avoid making themselves more vulnerable to adversaries. Moreover, they know that any settlement will likely persist indefinitely (unless mutually renegotiated). As a result, the border settlement process fosters an incentive to misrepresent the state's interests, intentions, capabilities, and resolve in order to secure better settlement terms; domestic demands not to "give away the state" or sell out compatriots; fear that territorial concessions might set a precedent for other potential claimants (e.g., see Walter 2006), and worries that any concessions to a neighbor will strengthen the neighbor and subsequently yield demands for further concessions.

The border settlement process consequently proves challenging, but not impossible. Border settlement does occur. How it does so depends on the territory at stake. When the disputed territory lacks power endowments – that is, the territory gives its possessor neither a militarily strategic advantage nor access to highly desirable economic resources – disputants primarily face an information problem. They struggle to convey credible information to one another about their respective intentions, positions, capabilities, and resolve. Repeated rounds of negotiation and mediation assist with this. Each process encourages the exchange of information, and over time, disputants learn enough to reach a border settlement more successfully.

When the disputed territory contains power endowments, however, the disputants encounter a different obstacle: a commitment problem. Negotiation

TABLE 4.7. *Hypotheses and conclusions about border settlement*

Hypothesis	Evidence	Conclusion
3.1	Strongly supported	Democratic dyads are more likely than nondemocratic dyads to reach border settlement. The strength of this conclusion depends on the extent to which democratic characteristics themselves facilitate border settlement, something recent research questions.
3.2	Not supported	Dyad members closer to power parity are generally no more or less likely to settle their borders. On the few occasions where power parity significantly alters the probability of border settlement, it does so in the opposite direction as that predicted by the hypothesis; greater power parity increases the odds of border settlement, while greater power asymmetry reduces it.
3.3	Weakly supported	Alliances increase the likelihood of border settlement, but only in a minority of models. The remaining models suggest alliances exert no effect on border settlement.
3.4	Strongly supported	Unsettled border territory containing power endowments is significantly less likely to settle than similar territory lacking these endowments. This result holds across all models and using two different measures of power endowments. Moreover, the relationship between power endowments and border settlement produces dynamic patterns that our theoretical argument expects. Nonpower-endowed territory behaves as if an information problem drives it, while power-endowed territory behaves as if a commitment problem underlies it.
3.5	Moderately supported	Iterated negotiations increase the likelihood of border settlement, but only when the border territory over which states bargain does *not* contain power endowments. If one does not control for power endowments, it will appear that negotiation has no effect on border settlement.
3.6	Weakly supported	Repeated mediations increase the likelihood of border settlement, but only when the border territory over which states bargain does *not* contain power endowments. This result, however, depends on the territorial claims data used. If one does not control for power endowments, it will also appear that mediation has no effect on border settlement.

(*continued*)

TABLE 4.7. *(continued)*

Hypothesis	Evidence	Conclusion
3.7	Moderately supported	Repeated legal approaches increase the likelihood of border settlement. This result appears more consistently than that associated with any other conflict management approach. It does not, however, hold across all models.
3.8	Strongly supported	Rounds of negotiation increase the probability of border settlement, but only when the territory under dispute lacks power endowments. If states bargain over power-endowed territory, negotiations do not affect the odds that border settlement will occur.
3.9	Moderately supported	Rounds of mediation increase the probability of border settlement, but only when the territory under dispute lacks power endowments. If states bargain over power-endowed territory, mediations do not affect the odds that border settlement will occur. The strength of this finding varies according to the territorial claims data we use.
3.10	Moderately supported	Repeated legal approaches increase the probability of border settlement, but only when the territory under dispute possesses power endowments. If states bargain over nonpower-endowed territory, iterated legal approaches do not affect the odds that border settlement will occur. The strength of this finding varies according to the territorial claims data we use.

and mediation prove futile in this context because they do not interfere with the commitment problem mechanism; that is, negotiation and mediation are ill-equipped, on average, to prevent either a power shift from occurring or a renegotiation of a settlement's terms during the settlement's implementation phase. Legal approaches also cannot prevent a power shift, but they hinder a disputant's ability to renegotiate a settlement's terms unilaterally. Because legal rulings constitute international law, those who violate legal rulings face sanctions from the wider international community – both reputational and material. This does not preclude the renegotiation of settlements altogether, but it does reduce the likelihood that these renegotiations occur. In so doing, it offers disputants a way to overcome the commitment problem. Legal approaches therefore promote border settlement when neighboring states dispute power-endowed territory.

Our conclusions risk painting legal approaches as a silver bullet for managing commitment problems. Yet states prefer *not* to use these approaches because they lose significant control when doing so (see Table 4.2). Many disputes over power-endowed territory therefore remain outside the reach of legal approaches. If negotiation and mediation cannot push these disputes toward settlement, what happens to them? What happens, in other words, when states struggle to settle their borders and conflict management generally proves to be of little use? These are the questions that motivate the next chapter.

4.5 APPENDIX

Strong theoretical and empirical considerations suggest the wisdom of excluding noncontiguous dyads from our study. In this section, we offer a brief analysis that further supports this decision. It focuses on rivalry onset, rather than border settlement (the main topic of this chapter) for a couple of reasons. First and foremost, our theoretical argument predicts that border disagreements over territory with power endowments will create commitment problems that foster interstate rivalry (see Chapter 5). We propose that this causal pathway is unique to contiguous dyads. So the appropriate general question to ask is: does evidence indicate that contiguous and noncontiguous dyads generally follow separate causal pathways to rivalry onset? If so, then a decision to separate these two groups seems well-founded, for a single explanation is unlikely to cover both groups. Second, the decision to restrict the scope of the study affects the entire study and is therefore difficult to postpone for later chapters. We consequently elect to address the matter here, but as an appendage to the chapter.

The research design underlying Table 4.8 largely repeats information contained earlier in this chapter (e.g., independent and control variables) and in Chapter 6 (e.g., rivalry and shock variables). We employ logistic regression models that control for temporal interdependence among observations. Readers interested in the exact measurement of the included variables can visit the research design sections of Chapters 4 and 6. To capture differences between contiguous and noncontiguous dyads, we interact a dichotomous *(land) contiguity* variable with each other variable in the model. Contiguity takes a value of 1 if a dyad's members share an inland or river boundary – the closest level of contiguity in the Correlates of War data, and the one to which our border argument applies (Stinnett et al. 2002). Lower order terms therefore reveal a variable's effect in noncontiguous dyads (i.e., when contiguity is 0), while the interactions indicate whether this effect changes significantly when the focus shifts to contiguous dyads instead (i.e., when contiguity is 1; Braumoeller 2004).

The results in Table 4.8 strongly suggest different causal pathways to rivalry in contiguous versus noncontiguous dyads. The interaction terms (i.e., those marked **contiguity*) obtain statistical significance frequently. Moreover, these terms often have signs opposite to their lower order terms, thereby indicating

TABLE 4.8. *Logistic regression of rivalry onset, all dyads, 1816–2001*

Rivalry Type	Model (1) Klein et al. (2006)	Model (2) Enduring Rivalry	Model (3) Strategic Rivalry
(Land) contiguity	4.866***	4.792***	4.540***
	(0.345)	(0.667)	(0.613)
Joint democracy	−1.750***	−12.800***	−14.450***
	(0.457)	(0.567)	(0.747)
Joint democracy*contiguity	0.132	11.190***	12.910***
	(0.698)	(1.159)	(1.257)
Major state	3.117***	3.365***	3.169***
	(0.222)	(0.519)	(0.500)
Major state*contiguity	−2.624***	−2.814***	−2.995***
	(0.318)	(0.652)	(0.736)
Alliance	1.058***	1.607***	1.729***
	(0.195)	(0.400)	(0.426)
Alliance*contiguity	−1.128***	−1.850***	−1.783***
	(0.269)	(0.521)	(0.542)
Relative capabilities (ln)	−0.344***	−0.402***	−0.895***
	(0.057)	(0.154)	(0.215)
Relative capabilities (ln)*contiguity	0.169*	0.191	0.333
	(0.087)	(0.191)	(0.263)
Independence (shock)	0.224	−0.432	−0.310
	(0.236)	(0.494)	(0.508)
Independence (shock)*contiguity	0.350	1.151**	0.246
	(0.279)	(0.577)	(0.581)
World war (shock)	1.177***	1.972***	0.700
	(0.271)	(0.449)	(0.506)
World war (shock)*contiguity	−1.219***	−1.441**	0.227
	(0.421)	(0.686)	(0.720)
Cold war (shock)	0.937***	–	−13.840***
	(0.246)		(0.582)
Cold war (shock)*contiguity	−0.197	–	14.130***
	(0.351)		(0.775)
Power distribution change (shock)	1.485***	2.343***	1.195*
	(0.305)	(0.520)	(0.646)
Power dist. change (shock)*contiguity	−1.430***	−1.531**	−0.666
	(0.451)	(0.701)	(0.909)
Civil war (shock)	0.853***	0.763**	0.685*
	(0.153)	(0.363)	(0.358)
Civil war (shock)*contiguity	−0.130	−0.524	0.533
	(0.231)	(0.481)	(0.497)
Territorial change (shock)	0.706***	0.810*	0.245
	(0.236)	(0.434)	(0.430)

Rivalry Type	Model (1) Klein et al. (2006)	Model (2) Enduring Rivalry	Model (3) Strategic Rivalry
Territorial change (shock)*contiguity	−0.581*	−0.115	0.044
	(0.326)	(0.579)	(0.596)
Time (until onset)	−0.051***	–	–
	(0.017)		
Time (until onset)*contiguity	−0.009**	–	–
	(0.004)		
Time (until onset)^2	0.001***	–	–
	(0.000265)		
Time (until onset)^3	−0.000***	–	–
	(1.19e−06)		
Time (until onset)	–	−0.097***	–
		(0.032)	
Time (until onset)*contiguity	–	0.004	–
		(0.007)	
Time (until onset)^2	–	0.002***	–
		(0.000)	
Time (until onset)^3	–	−0.000***	–
		(0.000)	
Time (until onset)	–	–	−0.070**
			(0.032)
Time (until onset)*contiguity	–	–	−0.018**
			(0.008)
Time (until onset)^2	–	–	0.001***
			(0.000)
Time (until onset)^3	–	–	−0.000***
			(0.000)
Constant	−9.205***	−10.190***	−8.932***
	(0.344)	(0.682)	(0.681)
Observations	647,699	650,282	611,855

Notes: Robust standard errors in parentheses; * $p < 0.10$, ** $p < 0.05$, *** $p < 0.01$.

that variables behave differently across the two groups. As an illustration, consider the effect of joint democracy. A noncontiguous dyad composed of two democratic states is less likely to develop a rivalry, as democratic peace research predicts (see joint democracy variable; Russett and Oneal 2001). Consistent with recent research (Park and James 2015), however, this pacific effect erodes significantly in contiguous, democratic dyads (see *joint democracy*contiguity* variable). Alliances, in contrast, increase the probability of rivalry onset in noncontiguous dyads, but this effect lessens when we consider contiguous dyads instead. Overall, there is sufficient variation across contiguous and noncontiguous dyads to suggest that the two groups require distinct causal arguments. It seems unlikely, in other words, that a causal argument applicable to one group transports easily to the other. We therefore restrict the scope of our argument to contiguous dyads in this book and save theorizing about the mechanisms that produce rivalry among noncontiguous states for future work.

A full treatment of rivalry onset demands an extensive discussion. We explore this topic in more detail in Chapters 5 and 6. Moreover, if the mechanism we propose operates, then how rivals settle their borders also deserves a detailed treatment. Chapters 7 and 8 pursue this topic.

PART II

THE EFFECTS OF UNSETTLED BORDERS ON INTERSTATE RELATIONSHIPS

5

A Theory of Borders and Rivalry Initiation

> When one is being attacked and has to think about the safety of one's own country, one cannot go in for calculations about what is prudent. ... As for these neighbours ... trying to spread their domination ... we must simply fight it out to the last.
>
> Thucydides

5.1 INTRODUCTION

States consistently work toward border settlement, and most eventually reach it. Yet this does not imply that the settlement process proceeds smoothly. In fact, many unsettled borders persist for large periods of time as a result of three interrelated factors. First, borders – once delimited – persist indefinitely under international law, unless altered via mutual renegotiation (see Chapter 2). Because states know this, they bargain hard over the placement of interstate borders, often preferring no agreement to one that they believe will either suboptimally meet their needs or not be implemented as planned. Second, incentives to misrepresent interests, capabilities, resolve, and intentions lead states to miss the bargaining range within which settlement terms lay – or to fail to reach agreement about which terms to accept (Fearon 1995). Finally, states may find agreement terms, but lack confidence in those terms' stability (i.e., a commitment problem). Neighboring states that bargain over valuable territory fear that a (re)distribution of that territory will favor one of them at the expense of the other. In particular, giving an opponent more of the valuable territory threatens to shift the relative power between neighboring states, thereby incentivizing the newly strengthened state to renege on the agreement and renegotiate its terms from a place of newfound strength. Foreseeing this possibility, the to-be-weakened state eschews reaching any settlement in the first place.

Failure to reach a border settlement, however, reduces neither the salience of the disputed border territory nor the incentive for pursuing a settlement. Neighboring states therefore rack up a history of bargaining failures – both in the formal (e.g., failed negotiations) and informal sense (e.g., general inability to settle the matter). What happens as states want to settle their borders, but fail? The current chapter pursues an answer to this broad question, arguing that these failures encourage the formation of an interstate rivalry – that is, mutual feelings of threat, enmity, and competition, accompanied by an increased likelihood of militarized conflict.

As we note in Chapter 3, states face two primary obstacles when bargaining over border territory: an information problem and a commitment problem. Information asymmetry (i.e., problems) among bargaining states impedes settlement progress, but (iterated) conflict management efforts – by design – clarify bargainers' interests, intentions, capabilities, and resolve. Any conflict that such asymmetries produce will also be relatively short-lived (or isolated), since bargainers will reach a settlement as soon as their information about one another converges. Commitment problems, however, present a different scenario – and the one that we propose leads to interstate rivalry. States facing a commitment problem have the information needed to reach a settlement, but fear enacting that settlement. Unless conflict management efforts directly address the logic underlying the commitment problem – that is, prevent a future power shift or preclude the to-be-strengthened state from reneging and renegotiating the settlement – they prove ineffective. This is almost always the case. Unsettled borders then persist, despite conflict management efforts, because the stakes are high (i.e., there exists a salient issue, as well as the threat that one state will be made more vulnerable by a settlement) and states see no way to escape their disagreement through a negotiated settlement.

Traditional research argues that states use war to resolve a commitment problem. We propose, however, that forming a rivalry offers states another policy pathway. Like war, rivalries are costly and inefficient; states should therefore prefer to settle their disagreement, rather than engage in a rivalry. They choose a rivalry because they cannot resolve the commitment problem via (most) conflict management efforts, and they choose a rivalry over war for numerous reasons. War often aims to destroy the source of power – to prevent the power shift that states fear. When, however, border territory contains power endowments – that is, a militarily strategic position or economically valuable resources – states do not want that territory destroyed; rather, they want to obtain those endowments for themselves. A war of destruction does not help them achieve such a goal. War of conquest then serves as an alternative, but international law precludes that – both in the narrow (i.e., taking a piece of territory) and broad sense (i.e., conquering an entire neighboring state). Conquest is also very costly, with a favorable outcome quite uncertain. The bargaining states consequently need another means by which to compete over the disputed good – to either prepare for the war they might want to fight or operate within the domestic and international constraints. Rivalry offers them suck a means. In this way, unsettled borders – in particular, those that contain power endowments that trigger a commitment problem – foster interstate rivalry.

We outline our argument in the pages that follow. If it is correct, then the rivalries we theorize will pass through three phases.[1] First, unsettled borders remain so because of a commitment problem that neighboring states cannot overcome in the short-term. The dyad is then at increased risk of *rivalry formation*. Second, rivals (eventually) *overcome the commitment problem*. This stage begins when the rivalry forms and ends when the rivals sign an international border agreement that delimits their mutual border(s). Rivals therefore negotiate over their border's delimitation during this phase, but these negotiations need not occur during every moment of this phase. In fact, it is entirely possible that rivals actually prefer conflict to peace at some times during this phase of the conflict because of continued fear of future exploitation (i.e., the commitment problem). Therefore, as relations ebb and flow, this phase can vary in duration. Finally, the signing of a border agreement signifies that the commitment problem has been cleared, thereby permitting rivals to change their perception of one another and *terminate the rivalry*. It is during this phase that the rivals move from being enemies to being more amicable with one another.

We explore the first of the three rivalry phases in this chapter, and the remaining two phases in Chapter 7. The sections that follow consequently link unsettled borders, via the commitment problem mechanism, to rivalry onset. We begin with a brief overview of what scholars know about how rivalries form. This discussion identifies a series of theoretical frameworks, but each lacks a causal mechanism by which neighboring states move from an initial disagreement to a rivalry relationship. It also highlights a series of disparate factors that correlate with rivalry onset and might serve as the foundation – or, at least, key components – of such a mechanism. We then briefly reintroduce the border settlement bargaining process that we outlined in Chapter 3, and build on it to explain how bargaining over power-endowed territory leads to a commitment problem, repeated bargaining failures, and eventually, rivalry onset. Our work not only integrates the various common correlates associated with interstate rivalry, but also generates a series of novel hypotheses. Finally, we entertain a series of alternative arguments that might account for the relationship we hypothesize between unsettled borders and interstate rivalries.

5.2 HOW RIVALRIES FORM

Interstate relationships lie along a continuum, from highly hostile relationships to highly cooperative ones (Goertz, Diehl, and Balas 2016). Rivalries – that is,

[1] We reiterate that our theory does not (and cannot) explain *all* interstate rivalries. The mechanism we propose will be a prominent, but not the only, path to rivalry.

dyadic interstate relationships defined by mutual perceptions of threat, enmity, and competition, as well as a heightened likelihood of militarized conflict – occupy the hostile end of this continuum. Although few interstate relationships qualify as an interstate rivalry, the (small) subset of dyads that do account for a disproportionate percentage of all militarized conflict, including both MIDs[2] and war (Goertz and Diehl 1993, 148).[3] The rivalry concept has therefore received considerable attention, as scholars seek to understand why certain pairs of states are particularly conflict-prone. This attention, however, has yet to produce a rigorous theory of rivalry formation for two reasons. First, researchers often use rivalry as a case selection device, rather than an outcome (e.g., see Greig 2001; Hensel, Goertz, and Diehl 2000; Vasquez 1996). Lacking the subset of states that do not become rivals, studies of this type are unable to consider rivalry onset, even if they had wanted to do so.[4] Second, those interested in the "causes" of rivalry (i.e., rivalry formation) typically focus on creating a conceptual framework, rather than specifying a causal mechanism by which rivalry forms. Given that multiple causal paths to rivalry likely exist, such an approach has merit – for it sidesteps the need to elaborate an unknown number of causal paths and, thereby, offers greater generalizability. Indeed, existing frameworks provide a strong foundation that informs our thinking about the rivalry process for exactly these reasons. Nevertheless – and by design – conceptual frameworks lack a satisfactory, underlying causal mechanism that explains exactly why and how rivalries begin.

5.2.1 Understanding Rivalry Dynamics

Existing frameworks of the rivalry process take three primary forms: process-oriented, punctuated equilibrium, and (statistical) correlates. Vasquez (2009) and Hensel (1999) typify the process framework. Both characterize rivalry development as a long-term, or "evolutionary," process, wherein two states with a status quo disagreement use coercive or bellicose rhetoric, in conjunction with military means (e.g., military mobilization, alliance seeking, and arms races), as their primary bargaining tools. The repeated use of coercion incrementally builds and reinforces feelings of threat, enmity, and competition. Eventually, such feelings come to dominate each states' foreign policy apparatus, as the

[2] A MID occurs when one state threatens, displays, or uses force against another state in the international system (Ghosn, Palmer, and Bremer 2004; Palmer et al. 2015).

[3] Diehl and Goertz (2000, 62), for example, report that 82% of all interstate wars and 74% of all MIDs during the period 1816–1992 occur within some type of rivalry relationship. Similarly, Colaresi, Rasler, and Thompson (2007) note that 67% of interstate crises in the period 1918–1994 occur within the context of rivalry. The consistency of this pattern is stark, especially given the very different conceptual and operational definitions of rivalry that scholars employ (see Colaresi, Rasler, and Thompson 2007).

[4] Using rivalry as a case selection device may be appropriate, depending on the research question under investigation.

involved states expect to confront one another militarily for the foreseeable future. They also entrench within domestic politics, binding the hands of leaders who might wish to reverse course and pursue less hostile means of managing the dispute (Colaresi 2004). The enemy image, in other words, "locks-in" (see also McGinnis and Williams 2001; Vasquez 2009).

Although informative and a descriptively accurate picture of the rivalry dynamic, the process approach does not explain why the first negative interaction occurs or why it festers – rather than remaining an isolated event, as many disputes do. Similar to war (Fearon 1995) and arms races (Kydd 2000; Rider 2009), rivalry is a costly and inefficient means of achieving one's preferred distribution of a disputed good. We would therefore expect rational states to settle their disagreements without resorting to a protracted, costly, and inefficient competition if at all possible. The question therefore remains: why don't they?

As an alternative to the process framework, Goertz and Diehl (1995) view shifts between peaceful (nonrivalry) and conflictual (rivalry) interactions as abrupt, rather than gradual. Their punctuated equilibrium model of rivalry proposes that "political shocks" act as a necessary – but not sufficient – condition for rivalry onset and termination. A political shock is "a dramatic change in the international system or its subsystem that fundamentally alters the processes, relationships, and expectations that drive nation-state interactions" (Goertz and Diehl 1995, 31). Numerous potential shocks exist – both exogenous (systemic) and endogenous (state-level) – and each of these might jolt interstate relationships dramatically (e.g., the end of the Cold War, or a state's independence).[5] Nevertheless, empirical analysis lends limited support to such a proposition. Stinnett and Diehl (2001), for example, conclude that shocks increase the likelihood of a first dispute, but do not subsequently affect rivalry formation.[6] In other words, the punctuated equilibrium framework predicts disputes but does not explain why those disputes would fester or the conditions under which they would subsequently produce a rivalry.

Finally, Colaresi, Rasler, and Thompson (2007) offer a framework that rests on the statistical correlates of rivalry. They start with Bremer's (1992) canonical study of "dangerous dyads," in which Bremer ranks six variables according to the magnitude of their positive or negative statistical association with war-prone pairs of states: contiguity, alliances, economic development, democracy, distribution of power, and major power status. Using this variable list, Colaresi, Rasler, and Thompson (2007) then explore the onset of two different types

[5] For a full list of shocks, see the research design section of Chapters 6 or 8.

[6] Bennett (1998) reaches a similar conclusion regarding the effects of shocks on rivalry termination. In his study, these effects are inconsistent and weak. First, whether they exist depends upon how one measures the variables. Changing the ten-year window that Goertz and Diehl (1995) advocate (to fifteen or twenty years) dramatically alters the results. Second, he finds evidence that rivalries display positive duration-dependence – that is, they are more likely to end as time drags on. This necessarily weakens the role that shocks might play in ending rivalries.

of rivalry – positional (i.e., struggles over status or influence) and spatial (i.e., struggles over territory). They find, as with the other frameworks, that Bremer's propositions poorly inform our understanding of the causes of rivalry (Colaresi, Rasler, and Thompson 2007, 190). Nevertheless, one important implication arises from their work: there are different types of rivalries – for example, spatial and positional – and the factors affecting rivalry onset seem to vary by rivalry type. This suggests the need to theorize (at least) two potentially different causal processes – one for each type of rivalry. Indeed, the empirical analysis presented in the appendix to Chapter 4 underscores this point. It demonstrates that rivalries between contiguous states – often dominated by spatial considerations – and those between noncontiguous states – often dominated by nonspatial (e.g., positional or ideological) considerations – differ markedly in the statistical correlates that drive them. Rivalries between contiguous and noncontiguous states, in other words, seemingly follow different causal processes. The paths to rivalry therefore need greater theorization.

Each of the three frameworks discussed earlier is useful; yet each also fails to specify the causal mechanism(s) that produces and sustains interstate rivalries. In particular, none of the frameworks provide an answer to the inefficiency puzzle: given that rivalry is costly and states would be better off settling their disagreements without paying these costs, why do rivalries form? The inability of existing rivalry frameworks to answer this puzzle suggests the need for additional theoretical development. To identify the starting point for developing such a theory, we turn next to the empirical research on recurrent conflict, which strongly hints at one prominent, underlying causal mechanism that generates rivalries.

5.2.2 Empirical Referents of Recurrent Conflict

If repeated militarized conflicts – or their threat – lie at the heart of rivalry relationships, then understanding the factors responsible for producing recurrent conflict will be helpful for understanding rivalry formation – for these factors should be similar, if not identical, in both cases. Indeed, our survey of the research on recurrent conflict suggests numerous variables that likely affect rivalry onset as well. First, MIDs over territory are more likely to be followed by another MID (Hensel 1996). Subsequent disputes also occur faster if the initial dispute involves territorial, as opposed to nonterritorial, issues (Quackenbush 2010). And territorial disputes are more likely than nonterritorial disputes to be followed by another dispute over that *same* (territorial) issue (Hensel 2001). It therefore seems that unresolved territorial issues fester, which leads to subsequent conflict.

How a dispute ends also significantly affects whether another will occur. According to Hensel (2001), MIDs that end with a stalemate outcome (i.e., one that favors neither disputant) lead to a subsequent dispute more quickly than those that end either decisively (i.e., with an outcome that produces a clear winner via battlefield victory or concession) or with a compromise (i.e., an outcome that yields a mutually satisfying agreement).[7] These outcomes also interact with the presence of territorial issues; although territorial disputes generally recur more quickly than nonterritorial disputes, this is not true if the territorial dispute ends with a compromise agreement. A longer period of peace follows when states resolve a territorial dispute through a compromise agreement, than when they resolve a nonterritorial dispute via stalemate or compromise. This latter point is important to highlight, for it indicates that if two states could find an agreement that resolves their territorial dispute, these states would delay their next military encounter (*over any issue*) significantly (Hensel 2001, 291). Territory seems to be the main danger to dispute recurrence, even though how a dispute ends will matter as well.

Third, Quackenbush (2010) finds that, as both states in a dyad become more democratic, the time until their next MID increases.[8] Given the empirical strength of the democratic peace, this result may be expected (see Russett and Oneal 2001). Recent research, however, argues that the democratic peace may fall within a larger, territorial peace (Gibler 2007), a point to which we return subsequently. Finally, both contiguity and the number of previous MIDs hasten the next MID, although the effects of both seem to diminish over time. The former indicates that neighboring states fight one another more quickly than non-neighbors, while the latter suggests that a history of conflict hastens future conflict. Neither is particularly surprising, especially given that contiguity remains one of the most important predictors of interstate conflict (see Bremer 1992) and MID frequency often features prominently in the operational–definitional component of the rivalry concept (i.e., rival dyads possess a history of conflict that begets more conflict; see Diehl and Goertz 2000).

After surveying the factors associated with recurrent disputes, two things stand out. First, every study finds a strong empirical connection between territorial disputes and rivalry, a pattern noted elsewhere as well. Tir and Diehl (2002), for example, find that (i) the vast majority of enduring rivalries contain some territorial component, (ii) both contiguity and territorial disputes encourage the development of rivalry, and (iii) contiguous rivals are more severe than noncontiguous ones.[9] This suggests a large role for territory within the rivalry

[7] See Quackenbush (2010) for a (perhaps) contrary perspective. He finds that decisive outcomes hasten the next dispute; yet, because he does not disaggregate compromises and stalemates, it is unclear whether this finding supports or contradicts Hensel (2001). Similarly, Quackenbush (2010) finds that imposed settlements delay the next dispute; however, because he does not disaggregate cases of negotiated and no settlement, the finding provides us no additional information here.

[8] This effect increases over time, which systemic democratic peace studies might predict (see Mitchell 2012).

[9] Tir and Diehl (2002) also attempt to examine the interaction between territory and contiguity, but they omit the lower order terms from the model containing the interaction term. It is therefore not clear what the interaction effect actually is (Braumoeller 2004). For evidence that the importance of territory and contiguity exercise independent effects on conflict, see Hensel (2000).

process – a role that only amplifies if contiguity largely captures territorial conflict, as opposed to a general opportunity for conflict through increased interaction (on this point, see Hensel 2000; Vasquez 1995). Nonetheless, Tir and Diehl explicitly note that their purpose is to provide a prima facie case that geography matters for rivalry formation, rather than "to develop a full and coherent explanation of the connection" (270).[10] In short, they thoroughly document that a connection between territory and rivalry exists, but set aside why that might be.

Senese and Vasquez (2008), in contrast, provide a possible explanation for the relationship between territorial disputes and rivalry; although their steps-to-war theory does not directly examine how rivalries form, the authors nevertheless articulate an implied, underlying causal explanation for it. According to the steps-to-war argument, states learn that it is acceptable (and perhaps, prudent) to handle territorial disputes through power politics practices – that is, resorting to the use of force, building alliances, and engaging in arms races. This leads territorial disputes to recur more frequently than nonterritorial disputes, as the (territorial) issue is both highly salient to each disputant and each believes that the use of force will best resolve that issue (Senese and Vasquez 2008, 12). Dispute recurrence, in turn, necessarily produces repeated coercive threats, competitions, and militarized encounters, ultimately fostering perceptions that the adversary is a long-term enemy. In short, territorial disputes fuel rivalry.

The second conclusion we draw from research on recurrent conflict is that the seemingly disparate list of variables discussed throughout this section can be unified without much difficulty. Gibler (2007), for example, theoretically ties territorial disputes, contiguity, and democracy together. He argues that unstable borders – that is, territorial disputes among only contiguous states – produce a salient threat, and states centralize executive power and militarize to confront that threat strongly and efficiently (i.e., they move farther from democratic, and more toward nondemocratic, institutions; see also Gibler 2012). Owsiak (2012) confirms this relationship in his study of border settlement and also accounts for national independence – a shock variable – in the process (see also Owsiak 2013). Finally, combining these works with research on credible commitments (Powell 2006) potentially offers a way to incorporate stalemate outcomes as well. Were one to lean on and successfully integrate these various works, as well as the steps-to-war thesis, the result would be a theoretical explanation for how and why interstate rivalries form – one that accounts for what existing research believes contributes to interstate rivalries.

Senese and Vasquez (2008, chapter 4) find something similar, including a complex interaction effect. According to their findings, territorial disputes have a larger affect on the probability of MID occurrence than contiguity. Since we are concerned primarily with rivalry formation (as opposed to individual MID onset), we do not discuss their findings in detail here.

10 See also Vasquez and Leskiw (2001), who find a strong relationship between territorial disputes and rivalry formation, but only when states are of relatively equal power.

In the end, existing research offers us a solid foundation for making sense of rivalry dynamics generally. Yet it leaves us with a basic, unanswered puzzle: why do states pursue an inefficient, costly rivalry, rather than settle their contentious issues? Empirical studies of recurrent conflict – a precursor to rivalry – point toward the importance of territorial disputes in any potential answer. This work, however, is merely suggestive of a relationship and does not offer a fully developed theoretical account of how and why interstate rivalries form from or in the presence of territorial disputes. We fill this gap in the sections that follow. In particular, we elucidate a theory of bargaining failure between contiguous (i.e., neighboring) states, who dispute territory along their mutual border. The logic of this theory builds directly on the logic of border settlement (or more appropriately, failed settlement) presented in previous chapters. In so doing, it offers one path to rivalry – a path that, although not accounting for all rivalries, proves prominent.

5.3 THEORETICAL FOUNDATIONS

We argue that rivalry onset – a term used to signify the beginning, or initiation, of an interstate rivalry – is the product of a contiguous dyad's repeated, failed attempts to settle its mutual border(s). Rivalry and the border settlement bargaining process are therefore intimately linked – meaning that to understand why rivalry occurs in our model, one must first understand the border settlement process. We outline this process's assumptions, logic, and theory in Chapter 3 (see Section 3.3). Rather than repeat the earlier discussion in detail here, we abridge it, presenting only the most relevant points for understanding how the border settlement process yields interstate rivalry. Those interested in the details of the settlement process itself might refer to our earlier discussion (see Chapters 3 and 4).

For the sake of simplicity, we once again assume two neighboring state actors exist: State A and State B. Each state individually holds sovereign rights over a distinct territorial space of a certain size; yet they also dispute the limits of their respective jurisdictional control (i.e., they lack a clearly delimited, mutually shared, jurisdictional border). Because they find the border territory to be a highly salient issue, understand that the dispute threatens violent conflict and impedes joint cooperation, and realize that they cannot escape the issue entirely (i.e., the neighbors cannot simply avoid one another or move), they would like to agree upon the exact location of a mutual border between their territories – one that would define the legal jurisdiction of their respective governments. As they work in good faith toward this goal – through multiple, potential rounds of bargaining – we make a few assumptions about how they behave. First, we assume the leaders of the involved states are rational – to the extent that they have preferences over the border's placement, can identify their most and least preferred outcomes, and will act in a manner consistent with those preferences. Second, we assume leaders care about the distribution of the good being disputed – in our case, the territory to be divided. More specifically, they want as much of the territory as they can get (Fearon 1995; Hopmann 1996; Schelling 1960), making them self-interested actors. Note that because there exist only two states and a border must be drawn somewhere, any gains in territory distributed to State A will necessarily reduce the area available for distribution to State B (and vice versa). This gives the involved states competing preferences, and the possible outcomes can consequently be conceptualized as a continuum (running from 0 to 1, or equivalently, 0% to 100%), with any given point along the continuum denoting the fraction of the disputed good going to State A (x) and State B ($1 - x$) if a settlement were reached at that point (x).

Subject to the above assumptions, States A and B might pursue myriad paths toward a settlement of their border disagreement. When, however, both realize that neither of them can unilaterally obtain their goal (i.e., that they are truly interdependent – unable to force their will on the other), they enter a three-stage bargaining process. In the first stage, the states search for the bargaining range – that is, the set of all settlement terms that both actors prefer to having no settlement at all. They next work to select specific settlement terms from among the various acceptable terms falling within that bargaining range. And finally, they implement the agreed-upon settlement terms. These three stages, although conceptually distinct, are theoretically and practically interrelated. Concerns at one stage affect progress at other stages – as, for example, when the suspicion that implementation will not follow a settlement undermines the bargaining states' willingness to agree to a settlement in the first place (Fearon 1998).

We see interrelationships among the bargaining stages most clearly when we consider the two common obstacles that arise during the border settlement process: Incomplete information and commitment problems. Incomplete information exists when actors bargain without full, accurate information about one another's interests, capabilities, intentions, and resolve. It necessarily arises when rational states bargain with one another. Because the amount of a disputed good each state receives depends on its relative strength – and each bargainer knows this – states have incentives to misrepresent what they want, how strong they are (i.e., capabilities), and what costs they will pay to pursue the disputed good (i.e., resolve). If the adversary believes them, these misrepresentations promise a bigger payoff. Yet a problem also emerges. Bargainers reject settlement terms that they would mutually find acceptable because they lack an accurate assessment of one another's relative strength or resolve. In short, incomplete information complicates the states' ability to find the bargaining range and to agree upon settlement terms that lie within it.

Commitment problems present a different obstacle. Here, states have the information they need to strike a bargain successfully, but still do not. The explanation for this phenomenon lies with how they expect the post-settlement period (i.e., implementation) to unfold. Some settlements alter the relative power between bargainers. For example, when states bargain over a good –

like border territory – that affords its holder certain power (e.g., a militarily strategic or economically valuable resource, or what we generally call "power endowments"), a redistribution of that good necessarily redistributes power between the states. In such scenarios, a state that the settlement makes stronger cannot credibly promise not to sign a settlement today, allow the power to redistribute tomorrow, and then renege and renegotiate the settlement terms from its position of newfound strength. A state that the settlement weakens, in contrast, knows such an incentive exists for its adversary, so it prefers not to sign a settlement at all. From its perspective, the settlement will not only be unstable, but also increases its vulnerability. And it may even prefer to fight over the good today, rather than settle, redistribute the good, and fight from a less advantageous (i.e., weaker) position in the (near) future.

The general process described earlier applies to interstate bargaining over any issue. When states bargain specifically over border territory, however, a few additional characteristics enter the process. First, states are motivated to settle their borders as soon as possible, but will not make just *any* concession necessary to reach one. States find the delimitation of their borders to be a highly salient issue – one of the most important issue that appears on their policy agenda. Land, and therefore borders, constitute a central characteristic of the modern state. Indeed, loss of territory might be the end of the state itself; yet even if not that extreme, land matters for the history and identity of the state's population. Any changes in territorial borders therefore carry great implications for the people involved. In addition, a lack of jurisdictional clarity impedes trade, tourism, travel, and agriculture (e.g., livestock grazing, which often crosses borders). These considerations give states a strong incentive to negotiate the placement of their borders – and sooner, rather than later – even if these negotiations repeatedly fail.

Although this promises to push states significantly forward in the settlement process, a second characteristic pulls them back: states recognize that, once borders are settled, there will be limited (if any) opportunity to reopen negotiations over them. A settlement locks in a border's placement under international law; the border cannot (legally) be subsequently abrogated or changed unilaterally. States, in other words, surrender the ability to further challenge the territorial status quo upon settlement (i.e., with respect to the settled border). Given these long-term implications, states want to ensure that they receive the best deal possible. They therefore bargain hard over border delimitation, perhaps delaying settlements that they believe do not fully meet their needs or will likely be unstable. This will make border settlements difficult to achieve. Nevertheless, once settled, these delimitations will endure.

Finally, not all borders are created equal. Some borders have characteristics that make them easier or harder to settle. Borders, for example, that run through relatively valueless territory – where moving the line a few miles in either direction is inconsequential – or those with prominent geographic features (e.g., a river) may be uncontroversial. In those cases, the natural feature, precedent, or another focal point makes disputing the border unnecessary or futile (Schelling 1960).[11] In other cases, however, the border territory possesses characteristics – or "endowments" – that make settlement more difficult. These endowments include a population, which may be desirable to obtain a larger tax base or to (re)unite ethnic brethren; natural resources, which translate into significant economic wealth (e.g., oil); or a specific location or feature, which grants the state's military an advantage over adversaries. A couple of these endowments – notably, those that afford the territory's holder significant economic wealth or a militarily strategic, advantageous position – translate more readily into state power than the remainder, and we therefore refer to them as "power endowments." When states try to settle power-endowed border territory, they face an acute dilemma. Any settlement necessarily (re)distributes power-endowed territory among the bargainers, thereby (re)distributing power between them too. As we will argue subsequently, it is this territory specifically that triggers a commitment problem and, consequently, promotes the onset of protracted, interstate rivalries.

5.4 BORDERS, COMMITMENT PROBLEMS, AND RIVALRY INITIATION

Border settlement typically follows one of two general, divergent paths. In the first, the involved states follow a largely peaceful process and reach a relatively durable agreement. In the second, the involved states experience repeated, failed bargaining; persistent disagreement; mounting hostility; and enduring conflict. What explains these two paths? To answer this question, we follow two hypothetical, contiguous pairs of states (i.e., dyads): A–B and C–D. Each dyad bargains over the placement of its respective, mutual border(s); yet each also experiences a bargaining process dominated by a distinct, primary obstacle. Dyad A–B, the more peaceful dyad, primarily faces an information problem, while C–D primarily experiences a commitment problem (for more details on these two obstacles, see Chapter 3). The management of these bargaining obstacles moves states down the different settlement paths we observe. Before elaborating the details of this argument, however, we underscore at the outset that the hypothetical dyads we sketch are purposively stylized, theoretical examples. We use them to be parsimonious and to simplify the discussion that follows. Although this may introduce constraints (e.g., the inability to speak to a given dyad's idiosyncratic circumstances), the two dyads illustrate well the commonly observed, divergent paths to settlement that many dyads walk.

Both hypothetical dyads begin from the foundations noted earlier; each state is rational, demands a share of border territory based on its preferred placement

[11] This, again, is a generalization. Neighboring states often agree that a river serves as their mutual border, but subsequently disagree over whether the exact border should be placed on either bank, the river's median, or the river's thalweg.

of the border, and understands that multiple rounds of bargaining will potentially occur. At this point, however, the paths diverge. The first dyad contains States A and B, who begin bargaining in earnest over the placement of their mutual border. Through a series of bilateral negotiations, the states attempt to clarify one another's preferences, intentions, capabilities, and resolve. Incentives to misrepresent these various factors exist, but each successive negotiation allows the involved states to explore and erode information asymmetries, as well as to build the amount of credible information they hold about the other. The states therefore inch ever closer to border settlement. If, however, they get stuck and are unable to come to agreement on their own, an interested third-party actor may join the fray. This third party – whether a mediator, arbiter, or international court – facilitates the exchange of (credible) information. Eventually, the various bilateral and third-party conflict management efforts reduce – or eliminate – the information problem that pervades the bargaining process sufficiently, which then allows States A and B to sign and (if necessary) ratify a treaty that delimits the entirety of their mutual border(s).

The earlier description admittedly risks trivializing the border settlement process. In reality, States A and B may travel a long and arduous journey to settlement. For our purposes, however, the key is that these states reach a mutually acceptable border delimitation without – or with only isolated, transient – violence. We propose that such a process captures how most neighboring states establish their borders (e.g., see Bolivia–Brazil, China–Afghanistan, India–Bhutan, or Libya–Egypt). Most interstate borders, in other words, result from a bargaining process dominated by peaceful conflict management techniques, with violence (or its threat) playing a relatively smaller role. Strong incentives to cooperate for mutual gain, as well as to avoid costly violence, facilitate this outcome. Yet, there exist a significant subset of dyads that follow a noticeably different path, even in the face of similar incentives. What explains this divergent path?

The answer lies with the second hypothetical dyad, which contains States C and D. Its bargaining process begins identically to that of the A–B dyad. The involved states attempt to establish their mutual border through negotiations or with third-party assistance. But try as they may, States C and D struggle to reach an agreement, even after repeated rounds of bargaining. This failure, we propose, occurs not because the states fail to ascertain preferences, capabilities, or resolve accurately; the repeated conflict management attempts they experience theoretically assist with this (for empirical evidence supporting this supposition, see Chapter 4). Rather, the involved states struggle because they foresee that any potential settlement will be short-lived.

Commitment problems explain why states would reach such a conclusion. A commitment problem exists when an actor cannot credibly agree to honor tomorrow an agreement made today. Most often, this incentive derives from the expectation that a large, rapid change in the bargainers' relative power will alter their preferences for implementing the agreed-upon settlement as planned (Powell 2006). Any anticipated, large shift in future power threatens to trigger the commitment problem; we focus, however, on a particular situation, in which actors bargain over a good (e.g., border territory) whose redistribution contributes to the shift in power that would undermine their agreement's terms. To see how this works and might alter interstate bargaining, imagine that States C and D control x and $1-x$ proportion of a given border territory, respectively. State C prefers the status quo and therefore wants the distribution of territory to remain as it is. State D, the revisionist state, wishes to increase its share of the territory (i.e., increase the quantity $1 - x$), which necessarily means decreasing State C's share (i.e., to increase the quantity $1 - x$, the value of x – or State C's share of the territory – must fall). Now assume further that the territory contains a source of power uniformly distributed over it (i.e., the source of power appears equally in all parts of the disputed territory).[12] In this scenario, redistributing the territory according to State D's proposal will alter the relative power between States C and D. State C, the status quo state, will be made weaker by transferring territory to State D; it loses the power (or resources) contained within the territory it transfers. In contrast, State D will be made stronger because it gains not only territory, but also the power that territory contains.

Through redistributing the territory, State D has enhanced its power, and it then has an incentive to demand a revision to the original agreement – one that grants it an even larger share of the disputed territory and the resources that territory contains. State C – having been made weaker through the redistribution – finds itself at a bargaining disadvantage when State D's new redistribution demand comes; it can try to refuse that demand, but State D's relatively stronger position makes it more difficult for State C to resist. In fact, depending on the extent of territory (and power) redistributed, States C may not be able to stop State D from simply reasserting a redistribution. Mindful of this possibility, State C prefers to forego settlement with State D altogether, rather than settle today and renegotiate with a stronger State D in the near future. Herein lies the dilemma. The states could agree upon border settlement terms today, but the threat of a power shift during the settlement's implementation phase (i.e., in the near future) leads them to eschew such a settlement. The bargaining process consequently breaks down, and the border remains unsettled.

In sum, anticipated, substantial, future shifts in relative power create incentives that undermine negotiation. A state whose power would increase as a result of a proposed settlement – because the settlement alters the distribution of power in her favor – will be motivated to renege on the settlement in the (near) future. Doing so allows her to renegotiate the settlement after gaining power, thereby securing even better terms for herself. A state made weaker by that same settlement, however, understands the to-be-strengthened state's interests.

[12] This simplifies the discussion greatly.

Holding the expectation that its counterpart has an incentive to void any settlement they reach, the to-be-weakened state withholds concessions (which may create an unstable settlement if the other side agrees) or refuses to conclude any settlement at all. Furthermore, if the to-be-weakened state believes its counterpart may grow in power, it may prefer a military confrontation to negotiation – before a power shift puts it at a disadvantage; such a confrontation allows it to consolidate the best possible settlement terms for itself (Werner 1999a). Either way, the disputing states postpone a final settlement of their disagreement. Conflict persists, then, not because of incomplete information about one another's preferences, capabilities, and resolve, but because the involved states cannot escape the conflict via a credible, negotiated settlement – that is, because of a commitment problem.

Scholars typically posit that commitment problem-driven bargaining failures most likely result in war; with negotiation avenues closed off, states turn to violence as the only means of resolving their disagreement (Fearon 1995; Powell 2006). We propose, however, that war need not be the only outcome that commitment problems produce. Indeed, the commitment problem may also explain why states engage in long-term, inefficient competitions (i.e., rivalry). Why would this be the case? In particular, why would states prefer a long-term military competition – for example, rivalry – to fighting a war? We identify four reasons. First and foremost, war may not be a practical means of resolving the type of commitment problem that the states face. On the one hand, conventional logic suggests that states fight commitment problem-driven wars to destroy the source of the potential power shift they fear. Powell (2006), for example, traces this logic in preventive war scenarios – as when one state tries to impede another's ability to acquire nuclear weapons (e.g., see Israel's behavior toward Syria, Iraq, and Iran). Yet if the states are bargaining over an object that is a source of power (e.g., an economically valuable or militarily strategic piece of border territory), then destroying that object may not be an outcome they desire. Both actors want the powerful object; they do not want it destroyed. On the other hand, states might – rather than seek to destroy the object of dispute – next consider a war to take that object in its entirety. Numerous factors encourage them not to do so, however, especially when (border) territory is at stake. War is a gamble, with a highly uncertainly outcome. Unless they eliminate the neighboring state entirely – a rare event in modern international politics – they will border that neighbor for the foreseeable future. Any territorial grab today will therefore transform into a source of prolonged contention going forward. The neighbor, in other words, will look for ways to take the territory back (e.g., see Syria and the Golan Heights). In addition, the international community discourages wars of territorial conquest – and increasingly so over time (Hathaway and Shapiro 2017; Zacher 2001). Were a state to wrest border territory from its neighbor successfully, the international community would likely not recognize that outcome as legitimate, at least not under international law (see Shaw 2014). Thus, although logically possible, war may not be states' preferred means of trying to resolve a (border) territorially based commitment problem.

Second, if war is not a practical solution to their bargaining failures, settlement agreements seem incredible, and states do not want to concede the issue, then states will need to find some other means by which to compete over the issue at hand. Rivalry offers them one such means. Third, even if actors seek war as their preferred means to seize and hold the valuable, disputed territory, they may need time to prepare for that war. Rivalry gives them not only a way to compete over the disputed good while preparing for war, but also an avenue through which to build support and resources for war. In particular, it re-orients foreign and domestic policy, signaling the salience of both the (rivalry) relationship and the disputed issues that fall within it. Resources and support then flow into confronting the rival over the contested issues. Finally, states often face internal (e.g., domestic veto players) or external (e.g., punishment by major powers or international institutions) constraints to launching a war that might resolve the commitment problem. Rivalry allows them to circumvent these constraints – that is, to compete over the disputed issues using a tool that proves more acceptable than war.

Given that states might initiate a rivalry in response to a commitment problem, the next step in our argument requires that we connect bargaining over border territory explicitly to commitment problems themselves. To do this, we return to a key feature of commitment problem logic – namely, that one prominent source of commitment problems is when actors compete over a good that itself contains a source of power (see also the earlier discussion, as well as Chapter 3). Some – but not all – border territory possesses this characteristic, with potential power derived from three particular sources. First, border territory may possess strategic value (e.g., the Golan Heights or the Sinai Peninsula to Israel); this allows the territory's occupier to extract (further) concessions from an opponent by increasing the probability that it will win future military battles. Second, border territory may contain a population that its holder can employ in economic production, draft into military service, or tax to generate additional revenue (e.g., well-populated sections of Kashmir).[13] Each raises the likelihood that the state holding the territory will obtain greater military resources (e.g., more industrial production, a larger standing army, or greater military funding, respectively). Third, border territory may contain the economic resources needed to fulfill the basic human needs of a state's population or to produce revenue for the government through trade. These resources include, inter alia, access to fresh water (e.g., the Burkina Faso–Mali border), navigation rights (e.g., Iran–Iraq), or oil (e.g., Argentina–Uruguay). And once again, each resource allows the holding state an advantage in future

[13] Ethnic claims might also be listed here, since the goal of such claims is to retain a certain group of people within the state. In many cases, however, only one side justifies its position on the basis of ethnic claims (e.g., see Burkina Faso–Mali).

confrontations – for example, the ability to field forces, to survive a competition of attrition, or to fund military activities generally.[14]

When border territory contains a potential source of power – what we refer to as power-endowed, as opposed to nonpower-endowed, territory – neighboring states carefully consider how acquiring or losing portions of that territory will affect the future distribution of relative power (i.e., capabilities) between them. In particular, concerns about how a territory's (re)distribution might alter relative power affects the likelihood that the involved states reach a settlement via negotiation. A state potentially made stronger by a settlement cannot credibly promise not to exploit its better bargaining position in the future to renegotiate any agreement reached. A state potentially weakened by an agreement may choose not to offer concessions for fear that they lead to further, future concessions. The highly salient border disagreement therefore festers, and border settlement eludes the states. Furthermore, because losing territory threatens state security (by definition), leaders rely more heavily on power politics practices to defend themselves and the land they claim to be theirs (Vasquez 2009). These two factors combine to create perceptions of threat, enmity, and competition, as well as repeated military encounters among neighboring states – the conceptual foundations of rivalry. They also suggest that neighboring state's repeated short-term preferences not to sign a border agreement have the long-term consequence of increasingly souring their relations. Through such a process, border territory triggers rivalries – a trigger overlooked by existing frameworks of rivalry formation.

Based on this logic, we expect that:

***Hypothesis* 5.1.** A rivalry is more likely to form (*ceteris paribus*) when contiguous states have unsettled, as opposed to settled, borders.

Although our argument leads to the general prediction discussed earlier, it makes a more specific one as well. Because of the opportunity costs associated with unsettled borders (i.e., lost trade, decreased cross-border movement, and a higher likelihood of militarized conflict), states hold strong incentives to settle them. Indeed, leaders regularly convey this sentiment. To reach a settlement, however, leaders need settlement terms. These terms derive largely from the distribution of power in effect at the time the states are bargaining (this assumption follows prominent research; see Fearon 1995; Werner 1999a); yet states also look ahead (Fearon 1998). If they do not foresee that the distribution will change in the (near) future, then they expect any settlement they reach

14 Existing research suggests that states might fight over land simply because it has economic value. One might therefore argue that a correlation between border territory endowed with economic resources (on the one hand) and rivalry (on the other hand) would be consistent with other theories as well. Nevertheless, such an argument seems incomplete. Even if states fight over economically endowed territory *simply because of* the value, that does not explain why those states could not – given the cost of war – reach an agreement that avoids protracted conflict (Fearon 1995). Our argument provides such an explanation: the commitment problem.

today to endure – that is, to be implemented as planned, with no incentives to renege. Such a scenario occurs when states bargain over territory that lacks power endowments (i.e., a militarily strategic location or valuable economic resources). (Re)distributing this type of territory does not threaten to shift power between the disputants and, therefore, does not lead to expectations that settlement terms will be unstable. As a result, states more willingly make concessions, thereby moving the dyad toward border settlement and, relatedly, the realization of the cooperative joint gains that follow.

A different scenario arises, though, when states dispute power-endowed border territory. The presence of power endowments necessarily means that a (re)distribution of the disputed territory threatens to shift the relative power between the disputants. Because the settlement terms derive from their relative power, the involved states realize that there will exist a strong incentive for one of them – the one made stronger by the settlement – to renege on the agreement in the (near) future and try to renegotiate the settlement's terms from a place of newfound strength. The to-be-weakened state therefore digs in its heels, refusing to sign an agreement that will ultimately hurt their bargaining power. Bargaining breaks down, and settlement stalls. The dispute also festers. Each state finds the disputed territory worth pursuing (i.e., they will not renounce their claim), perceives the other states' claim and behavior to be threatening, and sees no way to resolve the disagreement. In this way, power-endowed border territory will be more likely than nonpower-endowed border territory to remain unsettled and lead to both the perceptions (threat, enmity, and competition) and behavior (militarized conflict and aggressive foreign policies) that constitute an interstate rivalry.

In short, if the theoretical logic underlying our general argument is correct, then we would expect only *certain types* of border territory to drive the commitment problem logic and, thus, rivalry development. The commitment problem operates between neighboring states when they bargain over border territory that itself contains a source of bargaining power. Border territory endowed with these sources of power – such as a militarily strategic location or valuable economic resources (i.e., power-endowed territory) – will therefore be more likely to generate a commitment problem than territory lacking such endowments (i.e., nonpower-endowed territory). And if the commitment problem leads to rivalry, then rivals will form disproportionately more often when power-endowed, as opposed to nonpower-endowed, territory is at stake.[15] In other words, we predict that:

***Hypothesis* 5.2.** Neighboring states' borders are more likely to be unsettled, as opposed to settled, when they dispute territory that contains a source of future bargaining power (i.e., a power endowment).

[15] We do not claim that reaching a border settlement will be easy under either condition. It will, however, be *comparatively easier* when border territory lacks the power endowments that might alter the involved states' relative power.

***Hypothesis* 5.3.** A rivalry is more likely to form (*ceteris paribus*) when contiguous states dispute territory that contains a source of future bargaining power (i.e., a power endowment), compared to when they dispute territory without such a source (i.e., lacking a power endowment).

5.5 ALTERNATIVE EXPLANATIONS

We believe the previously discussed theory represents a plausible explanation for why some neighboring states develop rivalry relationships; yet we do not claim that this is the only possible explanation for interstate rivalries. Complex social phenomena are likely multicausal. Moreover, it is always possible that our hypothesized relationship might be spurious – that is, that factors theoretically and causally linked to both the likelihood of border settlement (our key explanatory variable) and rivalry (our key outcome variable) account for any relationship we might observe between the two. What might these factors be? Chapter 3 supplies an answer. In that chapter, we identify various factors that alter the level of uncertainty between bargaining states, thereby also changing the likelihood that the states reach a border settlement. Those same factors, however, are also causally related to the probability of conflict and, by extension, to the emergence of interstate rivalry. Rigor therefore demands that we present these alternative factors again in this chapter, for they not only might theoretically connect unsettled borders with rivalry onset, but also might erase any relationship we observe between these two variables of interest.

We briefly present the logic by which these myriad factors relate to uncertainty, bargaining failure, and conflict throughout this section. Readers interested in a more detailed discussion will find it in Chapter 3.

States must transmit credible information to one another if they are to reach a mutually acceptable (border) settlement. Yet they also each hold incentives to misrepresent how strong they are (i.e., capabilities) and what costs they will pay to win a disputed good (i.e., resolve). This incentive derives directly from bargaining theory. Since the settlement terms a state can demand depend on the power it holds relative to its adversary, successfully signaling either greater power or resolve translates into a more favorable outcome for the state – ideally short of war (i.e., a more powerful state can demand, and should receive, more than a weaker one). Each side knows this, however, so both engage in this behavior. Moreover, mindful of such an incentive, states question one another's credibility. They doubt and scrutinize the information they provide to one another about capabilities and resolve, thereby increasing the risk that they miss the bargaining range, forego mutually acceptable settlement terms (i.e., reject acceptable offers and counteroffers), and, as bargaining fails, find themselves in a violent confrontation.

Under such a model, any factors that alter the level of uncertainty between states will necessarily change the bargaining dynamics. As uncertainty about one another's capabilities and resolve rises, states find it more difficult to determine credible information about their adversary. Greater room for error exists, as more states pretend – plausibly – to be strong. As uncertainty falls, however, states fall victim less frequently to the information problem – that is, they more successfully locate the bargaining range, select mutually acceptable settlement terms short of war, and consequently, avoid unnecessary conflict.

Numerous factors might alter uncertainty between bargaining states. We focus, however, on four factors that appear prominently in studies of interstate conflict: democratic pairs of states (i.e., joint democracy), (a)symmetric relative power, alliance relationships, and the presence of ethnic co-nationals in the disputed border territory. First, democratic pairs of states (i.e., dyads) theoretically bargain in an environment with lower uncertainty than other pairs of states (e.g., dyads containing one or more nondemocracies). The lower uncertainty derives from four noteworthy sources. The first concerns audience costs (Fearon 1994b). A leader invokes audience costs by publicly stating demands or threatening escalatory actions, thereby making these known to both an opponent and the leader's own domestic constituency (i.e., supporters). If the leader fails to follow through on these demands or threats, then domestic publics may choose to punish the leader for damaging the state's honor, obligations, or diplomatic reputation, or for being imprudent or incompetent in executing policy (Schelling 1966). From the opponent's perspective, this threat of punishment gives the leader's statements greater veracity. Fewer leaders would falsely issue demands or threats under such conditions, since they – if not intending to follow through on those demands or threats – would eventually need to back down and, therefore, face an increased likelihood of paying the audience costs. Statements backed by audience costs therefore carry less uncertainty about whether a state intends to follow through.

A second source of reduced bargaining uncertainty in democratic dyads involves opposition parties (Schultz 1998). Because opposition parties in a democracy typically contest the incumbent party's power, they criticize the incumbent party heavily. When, however, the opposition party agrees with the incumbent party – for example, about escalating a conflict – opponents receive a more credible message about whether a state will likely follow through on its threats. The state speaks with one voice, as opposed to many, even though there exist strong incentives for democratic parties to disagree with one another. Thus, the credibility of its statements rise. Both this and the audience costs discussed earlier operate in a single democracy; yet when two democracies bargain with each other, these forces operate in both states, giving democratic dyads an advantage over other dyads. Because they can each observe audience costs and opposition parties within the other, the likelihood of bluffing falls on both sides, and the states (theoretically) inch closer to settlement, as opposed to war.

The remaining two sources – institutional features and democratic norms – alter bargaining in a slightly different way: they reduce uncertainty about whether a state will execute the "outside option" to go to war. Stated differently, each of these factors increases the costs of war, which widens the bargaining range and, therefore, makes it relatively easier for states to find the bargaining range. Institutional features accomplish this through checking the executive's power to escalate disputes quickly in a democratic state (e.g., obtaining legislative approval or generating public support for military conflict (Bueno de Mesquita et al. 1999).[16] Democratic norms achieve this by activating the "norm of bounded competition" (Dixon 1994). Democracies, in other words, expect political disputes to be managed via peaceful (i.e., nonviolent) conflict management. When such constraints or norms exist on both sides, escalation slows, buying the bargaining states more time to find a nonviolent settlement to their dispute.[17]

Given that democratic pairs of states bargain with less uncertainty than other dyads, two neighboring, democratic states will be better able to resolve disagreements – here, settle their borders – and to do so short of protracted conflict (i.e., rivalry). Rivalry, in other words, will be less likely in democratic, contiguous dyads.

***Hypothesis* 5.4.** Democratic, neighboring states are less likely to experience rivalry onset than other contiguous dyads.

The relative power between bargaining states constitutes a second factor that affects levels of uncertainty. According to the bargaining model of war (Fearon 1995), bargaining breaks down, inter alia, when states lack accurate information about one another's capabilities. States always hold an incentive to misrepresent their capabilities, in order to secure better settlement terms for themselves. Yet this strategy will not be equally effective in all circumstances. When, for example, one state's power far outpaces the other (i.e., dyad members have asymmetric power), there will be less uncertainty about who would win a potential military conflict. Misrepresenting may move settlement terms under such conditions, but only marginally so; the involved states know with greater certainty who is stronger and, therefore, who should receive better settlement terms. In contrast, when dyad members' power approaches parity (i.e., dyad members have relatively more symmetric power, or approach equality in their relative power), the marginal movement that misrepresentation brings can have larger effects. It is less clear which state is objectively stronger militarily and deserves better settlement terms; either state *could* win a confrontation. In these circumstances, states consequently rely more on their assessment of the adversary's resolve, the quality of commanders, battlefield strategy, and the willingness of domestic populations to endure the costs of conflict. These factors are harder to assess than pure military capabilities, creating greater uncertainty about what would happen if the involved states fight militarily and,

[16] For a critique of this idea, however, see Rosato (2003).

[17] Democracies abandon the norm of bounded competition when facing a nondemocratic state. See Chapter 3.

therefore, increasing the risk that they mistakenly turn to militarized conflict – that is, forego settlement – and end up in a protracted conflict (i.e., rivalry).

***Hypothesis* 5.5.** Neighboring states closer to, as opposed to farther from, relative power parity are more likely to experience rivalry onset.

A third, prominent factor that affects bargaining uncertainty involves alliance relationships. Scholars and policy-makers traditionally conceive of alliances as instruments of deterrence. According to this logic, states form alliances to convey credible information about the (aggregate) capabilities an adversary will likely face should it choose to start a conflict (Smith 1995). If the adversary is rational and expects alliance partners to fulfill their commitments, then building alliances reduces the likelihood of conflict. It makes conflict, on average, more costly, thereby encouraging the adversary to pursue a nonviolent bargaining strategy instead.

Alliances, however, also alter bargaining *between* alliance partners. Members of an alliance, by definition, coordinate security policy more closely than non-allies. Joint training, military planning, command structures, and equipment procurement provide allies with an inside look at their partner's military capabilities and operations. This complicates alliance partners' ability to exaggerate their capabilities to one another; their hopes of receiving better settlement terms (i.e., a larger share of any disputed good) through misrepresenting their strength are dashed. Moreover, a breakdown in bargaining – and relatedly, the outbreak of conflict – between alliance partners threatens to diminish the deterrent function for which they designed the alliance. A third-party adversary will question alliance partners' willingness to assist one another if the partners themselves are engaged in intra-alliance conflict. If alliance reliability falls, then the costs to an adversary of attacking fall as well. Intra-alliance disputes consequently make the alliance partners more vulnerable to outside challengers. Partners, then, only make demands of or threaten one another when they are highly resolute; in other words, they risk escalation only when willing to trade their alliance's integrity to win the good at hand. Demands and threats between alliance partners therefore hold greater credibility (i.e., less uncertainty) than those between nonallies.[18] This, in turn, allows allies to more successfully conclude settlements and, relatedly, to avoid protracted conflict – something the alliance commitments themselves would encourage them to avoid explicitly as well.

***Hypothesis* 5.6.** Neighboring states that are allied, as opposed to nonallied, to one another are less likely to experience rivalry onset.

A final factor that affects bargaining uncertainty is the presence of ethnic kin in a disputed border territory. States seek sovereignty over (border) territory

[18] See Gartzke, Li, and Boehmer (2001) for a similar argument regarding trade, information, and conflict.

for a variety of reasons. Two of these – militarily strategic advantages or economically valuable resources – fall within the main theory we advance in this book. An additional reason, however, is that ethnic kin live in the disputed territory. In such circumstances, the state tries to reincorporate the ethnic kin into the "homeland," arguing that this is what the population wants or needs (e.g., to protect them from alleged human rights atrocities).

Demands involving ethnic kin produce two noteworthy effects. First, they reduce uncertainty about a state's resolve. Although a bargaining state can threaten to escalate a dispute for many reasons, some of these prove more credible than others. The demand to (re)incorporate ethnic kin into the state falls onto the more credible side of the spectrum. States issuing such a demand often contain a sizable population of the ethnic group on which the demand is based – a requirement for the demand's credibility and legitimacy. Promising to (re)incorporate a minority from that same group – that is, a minority residing in the disputed territory – and then subsequently conceding the territory in which that minority lives to a neighboring state will likely be viewed as unforgivable by the domestic population of the same ethnic group. To the extent that all leaders are beholden to (some set of) domestic supporters (Bueno de Mesquita et al. 2003), and that the ethnic group in question comprises a significant portion of the state's population, issuing such a demand and subsequently backing down from it brings great risk for the leader. The domestic group may directly or indirectly punish the leader for abandoning its ethnic brethren.

Second, and relatedly, room for concessions in bargaining falls. If the goal becomes about incorporating ethnic kin into the homeland state, then few compromises exist. Splitting the territory makes little sense if it leaves some ethnic kin outside the state. Moreover, forced population transfers violate human decency – not to mention humanitarian international law. States therefore treat the territory as indivisible.[19] Importantly, they do so at the same time that their resolve for escalation increases. The result is impasse and conflict. In other words, the probability of reaching border settlement falls, while the likelihood that a protracted conflict – one fueled by the desire to protect ethnic kin and the inability to settle the border territory's status – rises.

***Hypothesis* 5.7.** Neighboring states whose ethnic kin reside in a disputed (border) territory are more likely to experience rivalry onset than neighboring states whose ethnic kin do not live in the disputed territory.

The hypotheses outlined in this section capture four factors that may affect the onset of interstate rivalry. Although admittedly not the only factors that

[19] Some scholars view indivisibility as an unlikely bargaining issue; they propose that side payments will almost always exist, which then avoids a bargaining impasse (Fearon 1995). Rather than weigh in on this theoretical discussion, we simply note that bargaining states will treat the territory as indivisible. If they do so, the outcome we discuss here will be obtained, regardless of whether there exists a theoretical side payment that might move their settlement progress forward.

might do so, we focus on these with purpose. Scholars commonly advance them as sources of (protracted) interstate conflict. More importantly, however, each also potentially affects the likelihood that states reach a border settlement. As a result, they offer true alternative explanations for any hypothesized – or observed – relationship between border settlement and rivalry onset. Accounting for them allows us to ensure that, if we find a relationship between our two variables of interest, that relationship obtains because of the theoretical, causal path we propose, rather than an alternative.

5.6 CONCLUSION

Myriad incentives push states toward border settlement; at the same time, various considerations and obstacles pull them away from it as well. The settlement process therefore stalls and fails repeatedly. What effect does this have on interstate politics? More specifically, how (if at all) do repeated, failed settlement attempts affect the relationship between neighboring states? This chapter offers an answer to these questions, and it does so via what is – to our knowledge – one of few explicitly causal arguments of how interstate rivalries form.

Our theory conceptualizes border settlement as a straightforward bargaining process (for greater detail, see Chapter 3). As states navigate this process, two common obstacles arise: information problems and commitment problems. Repeated conflict management (e.g., negotiations and mediations) directly aims to address information asymmetries, thereby helping states inch incrementally closer toward a settlement. When the primary bargaining obstacle is not informational, however – that is, when states experience a commitment problem, in which they fear a rapid, future power shift that will leave a settlement unstable and one of them more vulnerable to future demands of the other – conflict management proves less helpful. Unless equipped to prevent power from shifting in the future or to preclude the to-be-strengthened state from reneging and renegotiating the settlement (e.g., see the discussion of legal approaches in Chapter 3), it fails to address the operating, underlying mechanism. The commitment problem then persists, despite conflict management efforts to foster a settlement.

In order to resolve a commitment problem, common wisdom suggests that states turn to war. Yet rivalry offers states an alternative policy through which to address the commitment problem – one that states may prefer to war, particularly when bargaining over power-endowed territory. War typically resolves the commitment problem by destroying the source of a future power shift. Neighboring states, however, do not want to destroy the territory's source of power, but rather seek to obtain it for themselves. War cannot assist with such a goal unless one state can conquer the territory in question or the entirety of the adversarial state, the latter of which is a rare and costly outcome. Unfortunately, international law precludes territorial gains through conquest. States therefore turn to rivalry as a way to pursue their competition, perhaps prepare for a future war, and operate within the domestic and international constraints they face. In this way, unsettled borders – particularly those containing the power endowments that trigger a commitment problem – lead states from an initial disagreement over the placement of their mutual border to the formation of a costly, inefficient, interstate rivalry.

The next chapter develops an empirical strategy for evaluating how well the data patterns are consistent with the predictions we derive from our argument. As we expect, unsettled borders feature prominently in the formation of interstate rivalries. Importantly, they also do so via the causal mechanism we advance – power endowments – while simultaneously ruling out the theoretical alternative possibilities. We therefore reach two conclusions. First, when unsettled borders involve power-endowed territory, they trigger a commitment problem that neighboring states struggle to overcome. Second, the commitment problem leads to feelings of threat, enmity, and competition, along with an increased likelihood of militarized conflict (i.e., rivalry). In this way, unsettled borders – under carefully specified conditions – lead interstate rivalries to form.

6

An Empirical Evaluation of Borders and Rivalry Initiation

> The government in power on either side [of a border dispute] will push its claims to the utmost, to gain domestic support, and diplomatic correspondence, strategy, and maneuvers will postpone as long as possible facing the critical choice between an expensive appeal to force and the public-pride-wounding resort to arbitration [i.e., concessions to resolve the dispute].
>
> G. Ireland

6.1 INTRODUCTION

What happens when neighboring dyads cannot settle their borders? Or relatedly, what happens to a neighboring dyad when bargaining obstacles leave persistent, unsettled borders? The current chapter addresses these general questions – focusing specifically on the hypotheses presented in the previous chapter. The first part of the chapter outlines the research design we use to evaluate these hypotheses. This research design will look somewhat familiar. It employs many of the variables we discuss and use in Chapter 4. To reduce repetition, we consequently abridge the research design discussion that follows and refer those seeking greater detail to our earlier discussion (see Chapter 4). The second part of the chapter implements the research design, presenting the evidence that allows us to evaluate the argument we advance in Chapter 5 thoroughly. We then end the chapter with a synthesis of our main findings. In brief, we find that unsettled borders – particularly those containing power endowments – promote the formation of interstate rivalries. These long-term, hostile, institutionalized relationships, however, then raise yet another question for the remaining chapters to pursue: how do rivals settle their borders, and what happens to their relationship when they do?

6.2 DESIGNING THE EMPIRICAL STUDY

Evaluating a causal mechanism proves challenging in most instances – including ours. We argue that certain territorial endowments trigger commitment problems that leave borders unsettled and promotes the onset of rivalry. Direct evidence of this, however, can be difficult to obtain. To know whether a potential power shift creates a commitment problem, Powell (2006) suggests that one compare the difference between a state's power today (i.e., pre-border settlement) and that state's future power (i.e., post-border settlement; focusing on the weakening state, since the territorial redistribution will harm it) against the costs of a possible war. If the power shift outweighs the cost of war, then war is the preferable option, and a commitment problem exists. The critical factor, then, becomes whether the power shift that border settlement produces will exceed the expected cost of a potential war (i.e., the worse case scenario if borders remain unsettled and must be managed through military force).

To know whether a given power shift crosses this threshold, we require three measurements: (a) the potential cost of war, (b) the value of the territory's power endowment, and (c) the power shift generated by the (potential) border settlement. Herein lies the challenge. We cannot accurately measure the cost of an unobserved war between the involved states (point a). Moreover, obtaining a precise value for a given territory's power endowment(s) eludes us (point b). For example, although we may know that a mountain pass or high ground (e.g., the Golan Heights) gives the possessing state a strategic advantage, what numeric value (e.g., dollar value) corresponds with this possession? Finally, without knowing part (b), it is impossible to quantify the power shift that a border settlement produces (point c). In short, we lack the means to measure the various components needed to directly assess the mechanism Powell proposes. We therefore cannot directly calculate whether the power endowments that lie within the (border) territory under dispute are capable of generating a sufficiently large power shift and, thus, a commitment problem.

This limitation is not ideal, but it is also not crippling. We can instead focus on the observable implications of our argument, rather than the precise mechanism. If the theory is correct, the observable implications are as follows: (a) the failure to settle borders will be associated with protracted conflict (i.e., rivalry; Hypothesis 5.1), (b) unsettled borders will disproportionately involve disputed territory that contains a power endowment (Hypothesis 5.2), and (c) the presence of power endowments in disputed territory increases the likelihood of protracted conflict (Hypothesis 5.3). Each expectation pursues distinct evidence consistent with our causal story. Moreover, each proves essential to that story. The first shows the connection between unsettled borders and rivalry; the second links those unsettled borders to the power endowments that lie at the heart of the commitment problem logic; and the third demonstrates that these power endowments drive the protracted conflict that we initially associate with unsettled borders. We therefore design our study to shed light on these three components. Ultimately, we simply want to establish that there are general patterns in the data consistent with the expectations of the model.

The results we present in this chapter rely, once again, on quantitative analysis, which allows us to maximize the generalizability of our findings. To evaluate the effects of unsettled borders (and the power endowments they contain), we must observe the behavior of neighboring states – those both with and without settled borders. Our strategy for doing this follows the general research design outlined in Chapter 4. We use EUGene to create one observation for each year that a unique pair of states (hereinafter, a dyad) exists as members of the international system (Bennett and Stam 2000). Next, we employ the Correlates of War (COW) Project's Direct Contiguity Data to identify all the dyad-years (from EUGene) in which the members share a land contiguous border (Stinnett et al. 2002). Only contiguous (i.e., land adjacent, neighboring) states share land borders, so only dyads composed of land contiguous members can theoretically settle their borders (for further, detailed discussion on this point, see Chapter 4). We consequently restrict our analyses to land contiguous dyads, making our unit of analysis the contiguous dyad-year. The territorial claims data needed to investigate the role of power endowments then limit the temporal range of our analyses to the period 1816–2001.

6.2.1 Dependent Variable: Rivalry Onset (or Initiation)

Our hypotheses concern rivalry onset, necessitating the identification of a rivalry population. There are two widely used rivalry datasets: Klein, Goertz, and Diehl (2006) and Colaresi, Rasler, and Thompson (2007). The Klein, Goertz, and Diehl (2006) data builds on the work of Diehl and Goertz (2000).[1] It defines a rivalry as a dyadic, interstate relationship in which the two states confront one another repeatedly in a series of related MIDs (as defined earlier; see Palmer et al. 2015). Two key aspects of this definition stand out. First, rivalries require multiple, related MIDs. The issues under dispute determine whether MIDs relate to one another, and MIDs that fall within a rivalry consequently occur over a similar (set of) issue(s). Second, MIDs are behavioral manifestations of rivalry, but are not the rivalry itself. The states' disputed issues create, sustain, and terminate the rivalry. A rivalry can therefore begin (or end) slightly before (or after) the first (or last) MID in the rivalry series, which "means there are no precise beginning or termination dates for each rivalry" in these data (Klein, Goertz, and Diehl 2006, 338). Nonetheless, consistent with Klein, Goertz, and Diehl (2006), we classify a rivalry as beginning when a dyad experiences the first MID in its series of related MIDs; a rivalry ends when a rival dyad lives ten to fifteen years without experiencing a MID over the issue(s) that motivate the rivalry and tie its disputes together. We refer to these rivalries throughout the analysis as *Klein et al. rivalries*.

[1] See also Goertz, Diehl, and Balas (2016).

A second rivalry measure, *enduring rivalries*, is a subset of the Klein et al. data. Rivalries vary substantially from one to the next. Research therefore distinguishes the most intense interstate competitions, enduring rivalries, from less intense ones (e.g., "proto-rivalries" or "lesser rivalries"; for a review of this research, see Diehl and Goertz 2000; Goertz, Diehl, and Balas 2016).[2] Enduring rivals experience a minimum of six MIDs over at least twenty years. Because Klein, Goertz, and Diehl (2006) identify the enduring rivalries in their dataset – using the criteria that Diehl and Goertz (2000) establish – they provide the data source for enduring rivalries as well.

Finally, in contrast to the rivalry measures presented so far, the Colaresi, Rasler, and Thompson (2007) data conceptualize and measure *strategic rivals*, building on the earlier work of Thompson (1995).[3] Strategic rivalries form between states that perceive one another as competitors, threats, and enemies. Each of these components serves a necessary purpose in rivalry (see Colaresi, Rasler, and Thompson 2007, 23–28). The competitor dimension ensures that rivals see one another as contesting an important issue that they might lose. An adversary with too much strength gives a state no hope of competing for the issue at stake, while an adversary with too little strength turns the competition into more of an inconvenience. The threat dimension increases the likelihood that the competition becomes militarized and focuses the state's attention on the rival as the source of the threat. Finally, as states repeatedly compete in a high-threat environment, they see one another as enemies as well. The foreign policy apparatus institutionalizes the rivalry; it develops plans to confront the rival for the foreseeable future. Meanwhile, domestic constituents begin viewing the rival as a salient threat to the state, encouraging their leaders to confront that threat, and restricting their leaders' ability to pursue more accommodating policies with the rival. Identifying strategic rivalry under this conceptualization therefore depends on an interpretation of historical narratives; strategic rivalries exist when all three perceptions – competitor, threat, and enemy – are present and end when at least one of the three perceptions disappears.

Our dependent variables are three dichotomous indicators of *interstate rivalry onset*: one each for the Klein et al., enduring, and strategic rivalry populations. These indicators each adopt a value of 1 in the first year of a dyadic rivalry (however measured) and a value of 0 otherwise.

6.2.2 Key Theoretical Variables

We require three groups of independent variables in order to assess whether the various hypotheses outlined in Chapter 5 generalize to the data. The first

[2] Klein, Goertz, and Diehl (2006) note that the distinction between enduring and proto-rivalries is artificial. Yet Goertz, Diehl, and Balas (2016) reintroduce a related distinction – between "severe" and "lesser" rivalries. Given its rich research tradition (for a review, see Diehl and Goertz 2000) and the value such a distinction holds for identifying the most conflict-prone rivalries, we elect to include enduring rivalry as a separate rivalry indicator.

[3] For narratives of these rivalries, see Thompson and Dreyer (2012).

two – settled borders and power endowments – focus on our main theoretical argument, while the third group accounts for alternative explanations. This section identifies and operationalizes each group of variables.

Border Settlement

We propose that unsettled borders underlie many hostile relationships among neighboring states; conversely, *settled borders* reduce the likelihood that these hostile relationships form. We consider a border settled (a value of 1) beginning in the dyad-year after which neighboring states sign an international agreement that delimits the entirety of their mutual border; before this, we classify the dyad members' border as unsettled (a value of 0; see Owsiak, Cuttner, and Buck 2018). Those interested in the coding decisions underlying this variable – for example, how we handle borders that settle in parts – will find more details in Chapter 4.

Power Endowments

The commitment problem logic connects unsettled borders to interstate rivalry. That logic, in turn, depends on the presence of *power endowments* within the disputed territory. Power endowments exist (a value of 1) when disputed territory contains either militarily strategic or economically valuable land (or both); if it instead lacks both of these characteristics, then the disputed territory is without power endowments (a value of 0). We create two distinct versions of this variable: one derived from the Huth and Allee (2002) territorial claims data (covering 1919–1995) and the other from the Issue Correlates of War (ICOW) Project's territorial claims data (covering 1816–2001; Frederick, Hensel, and Macaulay 2017).[4] These two, distinct datasets allow us to check the robustness of our findings.

A lengthier discussion of the details underlying these variables, as well as their appropriateness for measuring the power endowment concept, appears in Chapter 4. We note here, however, that, even though we lack the ability to follow Powell's (2006) plan to quantify the power shift responsible for a commitment problem, a straightforward measure of whether the disputed border territory contains power endowments at all offers a reasonable approximation. Powell argues that territory with power endowments has a higher probability of generating a power shift than territory that lacks these endowments (see also Fearon 1995). Our variable captures this expectation; it permits a comparison of territory with power endowments to territory without them. We therefore think the variable offers the best way to evaluate the implications of our argument empirically, given data limitations.

4 On the conceptual and operational differences between (un)settled borders and territorial claims, see Owsiak, Cuttner, and Buck (2018).

Alternative Explanations

The variables presented so far relate to our main argument. Chapter 5, however, also outlines four alternative factors thought to be associated with both our key theoretical variable (settlement) and the formation of interstate rivalry. First, dyads composed of two democratic states generally behave more peacefully than those containing at least one nondemocratic state. Rivalry should therefore form less often in democratic than nondemocratic dyads (Hypothesis 5.4). A dichotomous variable – *joint democracy* – entertains this possibility. It takes on a value of (1) when both a dyad's member states score +6 or higher on the Polity IV Project's Democracy-Autocracy Index (what Polity calls the Polity2 variable; see Marshall and Jaggers 2009); otherwise, it receives a value of (0). This accords with how scholars in the field typically measure democratic dyads.

Second, relative power affects rivalry onset. As power distributes more evenly, a dyad's members cannot easily determine which of them is stronger (or perhaps, more resolved). Each state believes that it has a significant chance of winning any militarized conflict that ensues. And each state also has a greater incentive to misrepresent their capabilities and resolve. Bluffing about such things affects bargaining only marginally in highly asymmetric dyads. As states approach power parity, however, the plausibility of a bluff increases, allowing it to sway the bargaining process significantly in one's favor should the adversary believe it. The challenges of determining the likely winner of militarized conflict ex ante – along with the encouragement to misrepresent – leaves dyads at power parity at greater risk of conflict. Moreover, because these conflicts are unlikely to produce an absolute winner, they will also stalemate and recur – some of the defining features of rivalry (Hypothesis 5.5). To address these dynamics, we construct a continuous variable that measures the ratio of the stronger to the weaker state's capabilities (using the Composite Index of National Capabilities score for each state; see Singer, Bremer, and Stuckey 1972). Movement toward 1 along the *capability ratio* indicates that the involved states are approaching perfect parity; as values of the ratio increasingly exceed 1, the stronger state gains asymmetrically greater power. To account for diminishing effects near the extreme values of this variable, we use the natural log (ln) of the raw capabilities ratio.

A third factor stresses alliance relationships. Although alliances vary greatly in the commitments members make to one another, all alliances require the coordination of security policy in some capacity. It seems theoretically unlikely for a state to coordinate security policy with a threat, enemy, and competitor. Moreover, the alliance relationship provides allied states with a foundation for managing disputes that short-circuits the development of an entrenched, hostile relationship. Allies should therefore be less likely to form rivalries with one another (Hypothesis 5.6). A dichotomous variable allows us to examine this argument. It indicates whether a contiguous dyad's members have any alliance obligations with one another during each year of their existence (Leeds, Ritter, and Mitchell 2002). The variable accepts a value of (1) in the presence of one or more such obligations, and (0) otherwise.

Finally, ethnic conflict features prominently in international relations research (for an overview, see Tang 2018). Most rivalry scholars do not entertain ethnic differences as a cause of interstate rivalry. Nevertheless, it is reasonable to argue that the inability to reunite ethnic brethren within the state, along with the possible mistreatment of these brethren at the hands of a neighboring state, fosters the development of interstate rivalry among neighbors (Hypothesis 5.7). If these factors also explain why borders remain unsettled, then adding ethnic concerns to our statistical models gains methodological import as well; not doing so would bias the results we observe for the relationship between unsettled borders and rivalry onset (our main argument). We consequently create an *ethnic value* variable that takes a value of (1) when at least one of the dyad members has ethnic co-nationals that live in the disputed border territory; otherwise, the variable takes a value of (0). Two versions of this variable exist: one using the Huth and Allee (2002) territorial claims data and another using the ICOW (Frederick, Hensel, and Macaulay 2017) territorial claims data. This allows us to align the source of our ethnic value variable with that of the power endowment variable in our models.

6.2.3 Control Variables

In addition to the variables noted so far, we also include prominent control variables thought to influence rivalry onset. The first of these accounts for differences between major and minor states. Major powers, by definition, hold interests all over the world. These expanded interests bring major powers into conflict more frequently with other states and, therefore, could lead to the formation of significantly more rivalries. A dichotomous variable tracks whether at least one of a dyad's members qualifies as a *major power* during each year of the dyad's existence. We use the Correlates of War Project's (2008) State System Membership List to identify which states are major powers and when.

The remaining control variables consist of a series of "shocks." Goertz and Diehl (1995) argue that key political events – in both the domestic and international arenas – can cause rapid and dramatic changes in dyadic, interstate relationships. Domestic shocks include *civil wars* and the *independence* of new states, while international shocks consist of the *world wars*, the end of the *cold war*, and a *power (re)distribution* between major states.[5] All of the shock indicators are distinct dichotomous variables, which we code (1) if the given

5 Power (re)distribution among major states only occurs around the time of German and Italian state unification (1859–1877; see Goertz and Diehl 1995). Given that the analysis in Table 6.4 covers the period 1919–1995, we necessarily exclude the power (re)distribution shock and end of the cold war shock from the models presented in that table.

shock occurred in that year (or within the prior ten years) and a (0) otherwise. This ten-year window adheres to the argument and operationalization that Goertz and Diehl (1995) advance.

6.2.4 Modeling

Our modeling decisions in this chapter closely follow those we outline in Chapter 4 (for a lengthier discussion of the choices that follow, see Chapter 4). We use conditional logistic regression throughout the chapter. Our dichotomous dependent variable (i.e., rivalry onset) makes this an appropriate technique to use. It is "conditional" in the sense that each model includes only the contiguous dyad-year observations for which the involved dyad members were nonrivals in the previous dyad-year. Dyads already involved in a rivalry cannot form a rivalry with one another; our analysis sets these observations aside.

We control for temporal interdependence through the use of time polynomials, labeled *dyad life*, *dyad life*^{2}, and *dyad life*^{3} (Carter and Signorino 2010). These polynomials measure the life of our nonrival dyads (see the "conditional" component of the regression discussed earlier). The inclusion of linear, square, and cubic terms allows the effect of time to vary nonlinearly over the nonrival dyad's life.

Finally, the temporal domains differ across our various models. Our general models predict rivalry onset in contiguous dyads during the period 1816–2001. When we incorporate the Huth and Allee (2002) data on power endowments and ethnic linkages, however, the analysis restricts to the period 1919–1995. This restriction derives directly from the Huth and Allee (2002) data. We overcome this limitation with the Issue Correlates of War (ICOW) data, which offers an alternative method for measuring the power endowment and ethnic value variables. ICOW covers the entire 1816–2001 period (Frederick, Hensel, and Macaulay 2017). We nevertheless retain the Huth and Allee (2002) data to evaluate the robustness of our results.

6.3 EMPIRICAL FINDINGS

Empirical regularities consistent with our argument will involve two related components. To begin, we should find a positive association between unsettled borders that produce rivalry onset. Such a pattern in the data provides some confidence in the veracity of our theoretical story; yet it alone proves insufficient, for it will not indicate the *reason* that unsettled borders foster interstate rivalries – if they do. We propose that this reason stems from commitment problems that arise when neighboring states dispute border territory that contains power endowments. Thus, the second component investigates whether the presence of power endowments in disputed border territory links to unsettled borders and promotes rivalry onset. It aims to pinpoint the exact mechanism that we propose operates, thereby piercing to the argument's core logic.

6.3.1 The Role of Unsettled Borders in Rivalry Onset

Do unsettled borders encourage the formation of interstate rivalries? We begin answering this question by examining the bivariate relationship between border settlement and interstate rivalry. Table 6.1 presents this bivariate relationship for each of the three distinct rivalry indicators we use – Klein et al. rivalries (upper panel), enduring rivalries (middle panel), and strategic rivalries (lower panel). The panels of this table reveal two main findings. First, border settlement and rivalry are negatively related, regardless of how we measure rivalry. Focusing on Klein et al. rivalries, for example, Table 6.1 shows that rivalry appears in 36.60% of contiguous dyad-years in which borders are unsettled ($n = 1,410$ of $3,852$; first row, second column). In contrast, only 12.55% ($n = 1,700$ of $13,545$) of contiguous dyad-years with settled borders possess a rivalry. The remaining rivalry indicators produce a similar finding, although the exact prevalence of rivalry varies with the indicator employed. Enduring rivalry exists in 30.22% of contiguous dyad-years with unsettled borders but only 12.54% of contiguous dyad-years with settled borders. Likewise, strategic rivalry features in 56.37% of contiguous dyad-years in which borders remain unsettled, but only 13.78% of contiguous dyad-years that contain settled borders instead. In short, we consistently find that interstate rivalry appears less often when borders are settled and more often when they are not.

The second finding from Table 6.1 confirms that this negative bivariate relationship is statistically meaningful. The chi-squared (χ^2) statistic indicates the likelihood that the two variables under consideration have no relationship to one another (i.e., are independent of one another), given the frequency distribution observed in the data (i.e., how the observations are distributed across the cells of each panel). The null hypothesis is that the variables are not related, while the alternative hypothesis is that they are. As the chi-squared statistic climbs, we reject the null hypothesis with greater certainty. Thus, the large chi-squared statistics in Table 6.1 suggest that it is unlikely that rivalry and border settlement are unrelated. If, for example, these two variables had no relationship to one another, then the probability of obtaining the frequency distributions in each of the various panels of Table 6.1 is less than 0.000.[6]

In addition, the gamma (γ) statistic measures the strength of the bivariate relationship. A value of 0 indicates no relationship, while -1 and 1 signify a perfect negative and positive relationship respectively (for more details, see Blalock 1979). Each panel of Table 6.1 reports a negative, moderate-to-strong relationship between border settlement and rivalry; the gamma statistic ranges from -0.602 in the top panel to -0.780 in the lower panel. We can therefore

[6] This is derived from a Fisher's exact test. See Blalock (1979).

TABLE 6.1. *Settled borders and interstate rivalry, 1816–2001*

	Klein et al. Rivalry		
	No (row percentage)	Yes (row percentage)	Total
Unsettled borders	2,442 (63.40%)	1,410 (36.60%)	3,852
Settled borders	11,845 (87.45%)	1,700 (12.55%)	13,545
Total	14,287 (82.12%)	3,110 (17.88%)	17,397

$\chi^2 = 1,200$ ($p < 0.000$)
$\gamma = -0.602$ (adjusted standard error = 0.013)

	Enduring Rivalry		
	No (row percentage)	Yes (row percentage)	Total
Unsettled borders	2,688 (69.78%)	1,164 (30.22%)	3,852
Settled borders	12,527 (92.48%)	1,018 (7.52%)	13,545
Total	15,215 (87.46%)	2,182 (12.54%)	17,397

$\chi^2 = 1,400$ ($p < 0.000$)
$\gamma = -0.684$ (adjusted standard error = 0.013)

	Strategic Rivalry		
	No (row percentage)	Yes (row percentage)	Total
Unsettled borders	1,664 (43.63%)	2,150 (56.37%)	3,814
Settled borders	11,248 (86.22%)	1,797 (13.78%)	13,045
Total	12,912 (76.59%)	3,947 (23.41%)	16,859

$\chi^2 = 3,000$ ($p < 0.000$)
$\gamma = -0.780$ (adjusted standard error = 0.008)

Note: Contiguous dyad-years only.

conclude that, if interstate rivalry occurs within a contiguous dyad, it largely does so when borders remain unsettled.

Despite evidence of a bivariate relationship between border settlement and rivalry, two legitimate criticisms of the analysis presented so far remain. The first is that the relationship in Table 6.1 captures rivalry generally, but not rivalry *onset* specifically. Mindful of this, we repeat the analysis contained in Table 6.1, focusing on rivalry onset instead (results table not shown). This reanalysis yields identical results. It demonstrates that rivalry onset occurs more frequently in contiguous dyad-years that contain unsettled borders, as opposed to settled ones. As before, this bivariate relationship is statistically significant and moderate-to-strong ($-0.411 < \gamma < -0.755$); moreover, the probability that we observe such a finding if the two variables are truly independent of one another is less than 0.000 – for each of the rivalry indicators. We therefore conclude strongly that border settlement and rivalry onset are related, with rivalry being more likely (and specifically, more likely to *begin*) if a contiguous dyad has unsettled borders.

The second criticism concerns meaningfulness of the association. Border settlement and rivalry might be related, but does the status of a contiguous dyad's borders (i.e., settled or unsettled) affect the likelihood with which a rivalry forms? Even though we cannot establish causality we can use theory and statistical tools to generate greater confidence that the relationship is not spurious? Table 6.2 considers this concern directly. It measures the onset of Klein et al., enduring, and strategic rivalries in Models 1, 2, and 3, respectively. The three models otherwise contain identical specifications, accounting for a series of factors thought to promote interstate rivalry.

The results presented in Table 6.2 are consistent with our main argument (see Hypothesis 5.1). Settled borders significantly impede rivalry onset; or conversely, unsettled borders significantly promote rivalry onset.[7] This conclusion derives from the negative, statistically significant coefficients on the *settled borders* variable across all three models. As we note earlier, however, these coefficients cannot be interpreted directly (see Chapter 4). We therefore turn to predicted probabilities.

Figure 6.1 graphs the likelihood of rivalry onset within contiguous dyads for each of the three rivalry indicators, holding all other variables at their mean values. The lighter gray line in each panel (on the left) illustrates the mean predicted probability of rivalry onset when borders are unsettled (dot), along with the 95% confidence interval around this estimate (line). The darker line shows the same information (on the right), but for cases in which neighboring states have settled borders instead. Our argument anticipates that the unsettled border line will sit noticeably higher than the settled border line – that is, that rivalry onset is significantly more likely when borders remain unsettled. To better illustrate whether this is true, we consequently insert a horizontal

7 Because the *settled borders* variable is dichotomous, these two statements are identical.

TABLE 6.2. *Border settlement and rivalry onset, 1816–2001*

	Model 1	Model 2	Model 3
Hypothesis	5.1, 5.4–5.6		
Rivalry Data	Klein et al.	Enduring	Strategic
Settled borders	−0.805***	−1.320***	−1.718***
	(0.208)	(0.359)	(0.356)
Joint democracy	−1.474**	−1.064	−1.207
	(0.533)	(1.026)	(1.036)
Capability ratio (ln)	−0.205**	−0.278*	−0.604***
	(0.073)	(0.127)	(0.152)
Allied	0.066	−0.028	−0.093
	(0.194)	(0.348)	(0.349)
Major power	0.523*	0.989*	−0.077
	(0.262)	(0.415)	(0.603)
Civil War	0.608**	0.174	1.021**
	(0.192)	(0.332)	(0.346)
Independence	0.896***	0.941*	0.496
	(0.200)	(0.367)	(0.335)
World wars	−0.206	0.025	0.611
	(0.293)	(0.450)	(0.442)
Cold War	0.638*	0.000	0.404
	(0.250)	(.)	(0.436)
Power distribution	−0.302	−0.003	0.179
	(0.381)	(0.493)	(0.627)
Dyad life	−0.003	−0.084	−0.042
	(0.017)	(0.054)	(0.072)
Dyad life^2	−0.000	0.003	0.001
	(0.000)	(0.002)	(0.003)
Dyad life^3	−0.000	−0.000	−0.000
	(0.000)	(0.000)	(0.000)
Constant	−4.291***	−4.493***	−3.706***
	(0.325)	(0.546)	(0.616)
N	13,968	12,086	12,597

Notes: Standard errors in parentheses; * $p < 0.05$, ** $p < 0.01$, *** $p < 0.001$.

(short-dashed) reference line at the low end of the 95% confidence interval associated with the unsettled border estimate of rivalry onset. If the dark line (on the right) falls fully below this reference line, then rivalry onset is

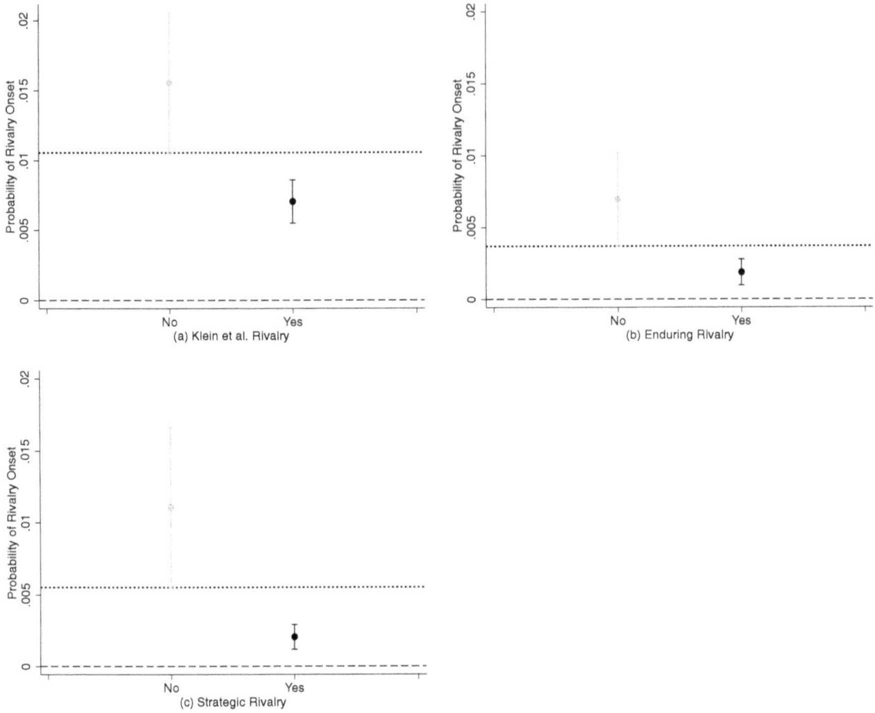

FIGURE 6.1. Unsettled borders and rivalry onset, 1816–2001

Notes: Derived from the results in Models 1–3, Table 6.2.

significantly lower in the presence of settled, as opposed to unsettled, borders – as our argument predicts (i.e., the 95% confidence intervals associated with the unsettled and settled border estimates do not overlap).

The results presented in Figure 6.1 strongly support our larger argument, and Hypothesis 5.1 in particular. The probability of rivalry onset – *ceteris paribus* – sits significantly higher when borders are unsettled, as opposed to when they are settled. For example, the likelihood that a Klein et al. rivalry forms in a contiguous dyad-year that contains unsettled borders is about 0.016. If the contiguous dyad-year has settled borders instead, this probability falls to 0.007 – a 55%, statistically significant decline over the unsettled borders value (i.e., the dark line in panel (a) sits below the horizontal short-dashed reference line). Similarly, the odds that an enduring rivalry will begin in a contiguous dyad-year is 0.007 if borders are unsettled, but 0.002 if borders are settled; the latter represents a 73%, statistically significant decrease over the unsettled border value (panel b). And the probability that a strategic rivalry starts in a given contiguous dyad-year sits around 0.011 when borders are unsettled and 0.002 when they are settled; this, too, constitutes an 82%, statistically

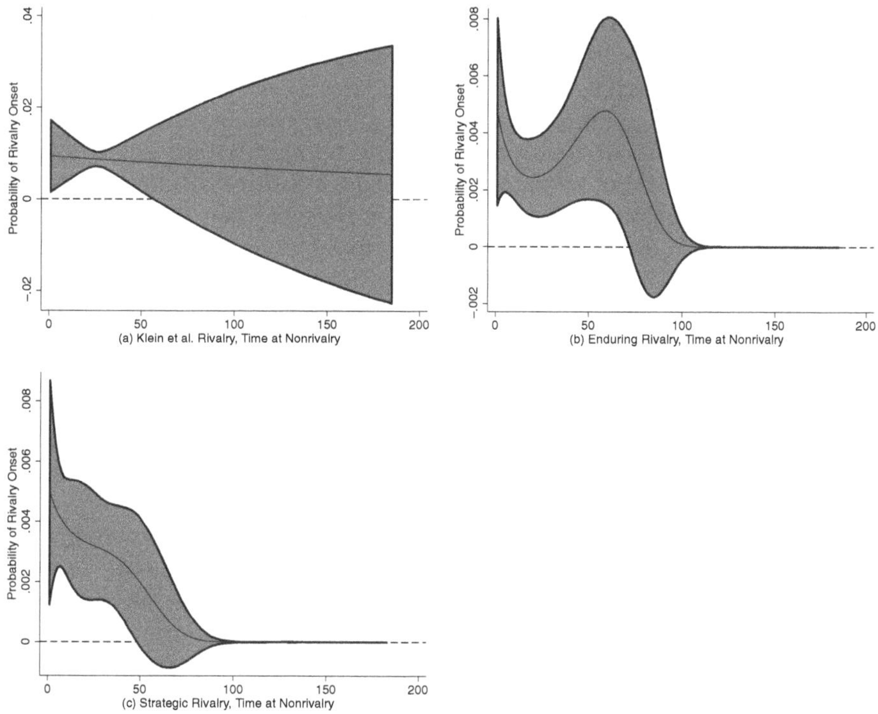

FIGURE 6.2. The dynamic probability of rivalry onset
Notes: Derived from the results in Models 1–3, Table 6.2. *Y*-axes vary to best illustrate results.

significant decrease over the unsettled border value (panel c). Regardless of how we measure rivalry, then, the likelihood that a contiguous dyad develops a rivalry is significantly higher in the presence of unsettled, as opposed to settled, borders.

One might ask how this probability changes over the life of unsettled borders. The time trend (i.e., *dyad life*) variables in Table 6.2 allow us to answer this question. The coefficients on these time trend variables are not statistically significant in Models 1–3. Nonetheless, the triple interaction term (i.e., linear, quadratic, and cubic terms) complicate the ability to understand their cumulative, substantive interpretation. We therefore chart the predicted probability of rivalry onset across the nonrival dyad's life in Figure 6.2. Restricting our attention to the nonrival dyad's life derives from theory and research design. In our analysis, we condition the logistic regression (Table 6.2) to observations in which members of a contiguous dyad were nonrivals in the previous year. Only these dyads potentially form rivalries; in the remaining dyad-year observations, the dyads are already involved in rivalries, making the onset of rivalry a moot point. Panels (a–c) of Figure 6.2 report predictions for

Klein et al, enduring, and strategic rivalries, respectively. The line tracks the mean likelihood of rivalry onset as a nonrival dyad ages, while the shaded area captures the 95% confidence interval around this mean estimate.

Figure 6.2 leads to three main findings. First, the likelihood of rivalry onset *seemingly* falls as nonrival dyad ages. As neighboring states develop a nonrivalrous working relationship – that is, a history of interactions not dominated by high levels of hostility – it is plausible that the likelihood of their relationship turning drastically more hostile declines. This trend, in theory, would continue over time; repeated, benign interactions build and reinforce a nonrivalry relationship history, making it more difficult for any particular episode to push the dyad into a rivalry. This appears, at first glance, to be shown in each of the panels of the figure. Second, the strength of the first finding varies across rivalry indicators and may be no trend at all. In their first year as nonrivals, for example, the likelihood that a contiguous dyad develops a Klein et al. rivalry is 0.009. This falls to 0.008 by year 50, 0.007 by year 75, and 0.006 by year 100; yet the confidence intervals associated with each of these estimates overlaps, suggesting the trend may be superficial. The formation of an enduring rivalry in a nonrival, contiguous dyad's first year is similarly low – at 0.005. This number fluctuates between 0.001 and 0.005 as the nonrival dyad ages, but slips below the confidence interval associated with the initial year-one estimate only in year 95 of the nonrival dyad's history. In other words, the intermediate fluctuations lack meaning; they may be identical values. After year 95, however, we are confident that the odds of a nonrival, contiguous dyad developing an enduring rivalry falls below the odds it experiences in its first year. Strategic rivalries behave similarly to enduring rivalries – both in the predicted probability values and their visual trends (compare panels b and c of Figure 6.2). Third, for both enduring and strategic rivalries, the probability of rivalry onset converges on zero after a nonrival dyad reaches the age of about 100. Not only do the mean values approach zero, but the confidence intervals also tighten around and remain at zero. In the end, a nonrival dyad's age appears to affect rivalry onset only minimally. Yet a nonrival dyad that lives long enough seemingly cements its nonrivalry relationship.

Despite the weak relationship (if any) between dyad age and rivalry onset, one might still ask whether the relationship between border settlement and rivalry onset varies over time. Figure 6.3 provides an answer to this question. For each of the three rivalry indicators, it illustrates the probability of rivalry onset over the course of a nonrival dyad's life under two conditions – when the dyad has unsettled (lighter area) and settled (darker area) borders. Evidence in support of Hypothesis 5.1 will produce two patterns in these panels. First, the hypothesis predicts that the odds of rivalry onset are higher if a dyad has unsettled borders than if it has settled borders. If true, then the darker region should sit (vertically) lower than the lighter region in each panel. Second, the hypothesis implies that the relationship between (un)settled borders and rivalry onset is meaningful; thus, we ideally will see white space between the lighter and

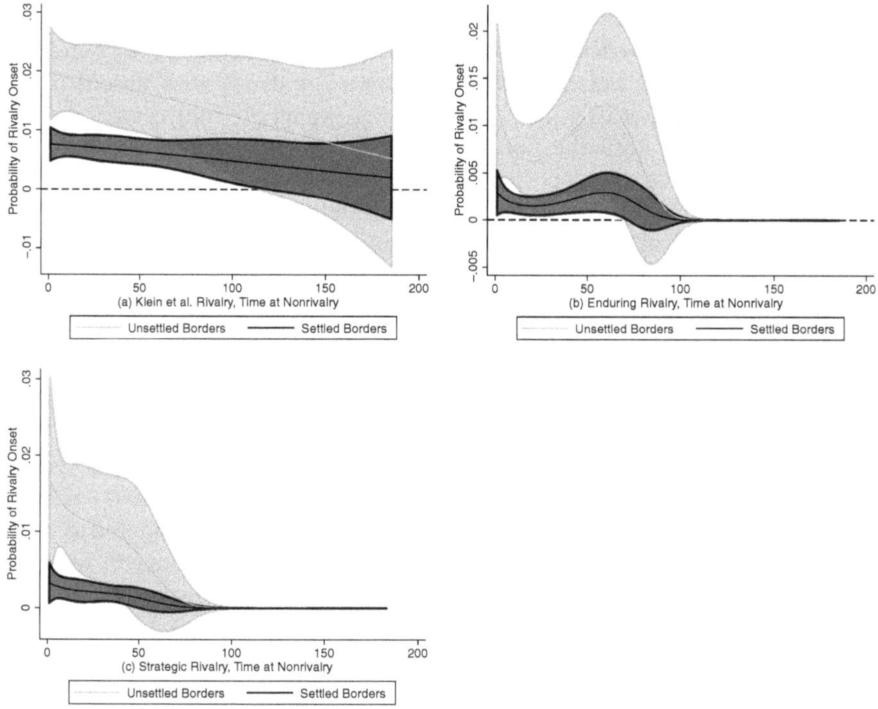

FIGURE 6.3. The dynamic effect of border settlement on rivalry onset
Notes: Derived from the results in Models 1–3, Table 6.2. *Y*-axes vary to best illustrate results.

darker regions, which indicates that the confidence intervals associated with the unsettled and settled border estimates do not overlap (i.e., the two estimates can be discerned from one another). The more often the white space appears, the greater the evidence in support of the hypothesis.

Both patterns consistent with Hypothesis 5.1 appear in every panel in Figure 6.3. For example, in its first year of existence, the probability of Klein et al. rivalry onset for a nonrival, contiguous dyad that has unsettled borders is 0.020 (holding all other variables at their mean estimates). By the nonrival dyad's twentieth, fortieth, and sixtieth year, this probability slides successively downward to 0.018, 0.017, and 0.016, respectively (see lighter line running through lighter shaded area). In contrast, the odds that a Klein et al. rivalry forms in a nonrival, contiguous dyad with settled borders is 0.008 in the dyad's first year; this probability declines to 0.007 by the dyad's sixtieth year, but during this time, always remains well below the values for a comparable dyad with unsettled borders (see darker line running through darker shaded area). A similar trend appears in the panels pertaining to enduring (panel b) and strategic (panel c) rivalry onset as well.

We can also frequently distinguish the unsettled and settled border estimates from one another. For Klein et al. rivalries, for example, the 95% confidence intervals around the estimates of rivalry onset for dyads with unsettled and settled borders do not overlap in young dyads (panel a). They remain distinct from one another until the nonrival dyad reaches the age of 64, at which point they begin to overlap (see white space between the shaded regions). Similar, discernible differences also appear in the enduring rivalry panel when contiguous, nonrival dyads lie between the ages of 3 and 18, and in the strategic rivalry panel when contiguous, nonrival dyads lie between the ages of 3 and 32. In fairness, the mean estimate of rivalry onset (i.e., the line running through the shaded regions) for dyads with unsettled borders almost always lies above that for dyads with settled borders. It is, however, only during times when the white space appears that we can confidently conclude that these estimates differ meaningfully from one another.

The cumulative weight of the evidence we present throughout this section strongly supports Hypothesis 5.1. Rivalry onset – however measured – is more likely when neighboring states have not settled their borders, compared to when they have. What exactly about unsettled borders provides the impetus for these interstate rivalries? We argue that the answer lies with power endowments. Disputed territory that contains power endowments leads to a commitment problem. States have incentives to try to overcome the commitment problem, but they will generally struggle to do so. Indeed, traditional conflict management tools prove unhelpful (see Chapter 4). This leaves a highly salient issue unresolved (i.e., the borders unsettled) and, since nonviolent conflict management fails, encourages the involved states to use violence. As a result, feelings of threat, enmity, and competition develop and become entrenched.

6.3.2 The Role of Power Endowments in Rivalry Onset

The previous section demonstrates a positive association in the data between unsettled borders and interstate rivalry. In this section, we first connect these unsettled borders to power endowments. Then, we show that power endowments are associated with rivalry onset. These steps allow us to conclude that power endowments link unsettled borders and rivalry. They also represent evidence consistent with our causal story for why unsettled borders often produce rivalries.

The first step requires that we connect unsettled borders to power endowments. We therefore begin with a bivariate analysis of this relationship. Table 6.3 presents the analysis and leads to the conclusion that power endowments appear more often alongside unsettled, as opposed to settled, borders. Using the Huth and Allee territorial claims data (upper panel), power endowments feature in 30% of the contiguous dyad-years in which borders are unsettled (n = 1,121 of 3,734; first row, second column), but only 4% of the contiguous dyad-years in which borders are settled (n = 540 of 12,049; second row, second column).

TABLE 6.3. *Power endowments and settled borders, 1816–2001*

Hypothesis	5.2		
	Huth & Allee Territorial Claims		
	No Power Endowments (row percentage)	Power Endowments (row percentage)	Total
Unsettled borders	2,613 (69.98%)	1,121 (30.02%)	3,734
Settled borders	11,509 (95.52%)	540 (4.48%)	12,049
Total	14,122 (89.48%)	1,661 (10.52%)	15,783

$\chi^2 = 2,000$ ($p < 0.000$)
$\gamma = -0.803$ (*a.s.e.* = 0.010)

	Issue Correlates of War Territorial Claims		
	No Power Endowments (row percentage)	Power Endowments (row percentage)	Total
Unsettled borders	1,539 (39.95%)	2,313 (60.05%)	3,852
Settled borders	11,895 (87.82%)	1,650 (12.18%)	13,545
Total	13,434 (77.22%)	3,963 (22.78%)	17,397

$\chi^2 = 3,900$ ($p < 0.000$)
$\gamma = -0.831$ (*a.s.e.* = 0.007)

Conversely, when contiguous dyads have unsettled borders, nearly 70% of the dyad-year observations contain no power endowments ($n = 2,613$ of 3,734; first column, first row). This value jumps to nearly 96% of similar dyad-year observations if borders have been settled ($n = 11,509$ of 12,049). Territory that possesses power endowments is therefore more common in contiguous dyad-years that have unsettled borders, while territory lacking these endowments is more common in contiguous dyad-years with settled borders. This relationship is statistically significant ($\chi^2 = 2,000$; $p < 0.000$) and strongly negative ($\gamma = -0.803$), offering strong support to Hypothesis 5.2.

Further support for Hypothesis 5.2 derives from the second panel of Table 6.3, which employs the ICOW territorial claims data instead of the Huth and Allee data. Despite using different data, the results remain the same. Power endowments appear in 60% of the contiguous dyad-years in which borders are settled ($n = 2,313$ of 3,852; first row, second column); in contrast, a mere 12% of the contiguous dyad-years with settled borders contain power endowments ($n = 1,650$ of 13,545; second row, second column). To take the converse perspective, nearly 40% of the contiguous dyad-years with unsettled borders lack power endowments ($n = 1,539$ of 3,852; first row, first column), while almost 89% of contiguous dyad-years with settled borders lack power endowments ($n = 11,895$ of 13,545; second row, first column). This relationship is statistically significant ($\chi^2 = 3,900, p < 0.000$), strongly negative ($\gamma = -0.831$), and therefore, consistent with Hypothesis 5.2.

Critics may question whether the relationship we observe in Table 6.3 is artificial – a consequence of how we code our data. Most contiguous dyad-years do not involve a territorial claim and will therefore necessarily lack power endowments as well. Mindful of this possibility, we repeated the analysis, restricting it to active territorial claim-dyad-years only. The strength of the relationship weakens as the critics expect (i.e., the γ statistic falls; see subsequent discussion), but it does not disappear. For both the Huth and Allee and ICOW territorial claim populations, we still find a statistically significant ($\chi^2 = 8.435, p < 0.004$ and $\chi^2 = 70.692, p < 0.000$, respectively) and negative relationship ($\gamma = -0.131, a.s.e. = 0.045$ and $\gamma = -0.258, a.s.e. = 0.029$, respectively). We therefore conclude that the evidence robustly supports Hypothesis 5.2. Dyad-years in which neighboring states' borders are unsettled see disproportionately more power endowments at stake than those dyad-years during which borders are settled.

Even though power endowments and unsettled borders frequently appear together, are power endowments responsible for interstate rivalry? Tables 6.4 and 6.5 explore this question and supply an affirmative answer. Table 6.4 examines the onset of Klein et al. (Model 4), enduring (Model 5), and strategic (Model 6) rivalries using the Huth and Allee territorial claims data. Table 6.5 presents similar models (Models 7–9) using the ICOW territorial claims data instead. These models cumulatively confirm that the likelihood of rivalry increases significantly when contiguous states dispute territory that contains power endowments – exactly as Hypothesis 5.3 predicts. The coefficient on the *power endowment* variable is always positive. Moreover, it obtains statistical significance at the $p < 0.05$ level in five out of six models (Model 6 being the exception).

Figure 6.4 illustrates the substantive interpretation of this relationship. The left column in the figure presents calculations that use the Huth and Allee (2002) data (see Table 6.4), while the right column's calculations use the ICOW data (see Table 6.5). The first, second, and third rows focus on Klein et al. (Models 4 and 7), enduring (Models 5 and 8), and strategic (Models 6 and 9) rivalries, respectively. Within each panel, we offer two estimates of the probability of rivalry onset (however measured): one under the condition that the hypothetical, contiguous dyad disputes territory that lacks a power endowment in a given year (the lighter line) and one for when the disputed territory contains

TABLE 6.4. *Rivalry onset and Huth & Allee power endowments, 1816–2001*

	Model 4	Model 5	Model 6
Hypothesis: 5.3, 5.4–5.7			
Rivalry Data	Klein et.al	Enduring	Strategic
Power endowment	1.250***	2.307***	1.189
	(0.378)	(0.531)	(1.031)
Joint democracy	−1.539**	−1.550	Perfect predictor
	(0.583)	(1.001)	(no rivalry)
Capability ration (ln)	−0.118	−0.202	−0.618***
	(0.082)	(0.123)	(0.179)
Allied	−0.163	−0.590	−0.326
	(0.233)	(0.402)	(0.379)
Ethnic value	0.293	−0.250	1.119
	(0.415)	(0.606)	(1.003)
Major power	0.611	0.886	0.167
	(0.347)	(0.496)	(0.814)
Civil War	0.773***	−0.081	1.137**
	(0.205)	(0.401)	(0.389)
Independence	0.703**	1.110**	0.493
	(0.227)	(0.415)	(0.354)
World war	−1.035**	−0.354	−0.255
	(0.351)	(0.507)	(0.654)
Dyad life	−0.044	−0.119	0.021
	(0.047)	(0.070)	(0.104)
Dyad life^2	0.001	0.005	−0.001
	(0.002)	(0.003)	(0.004)
Dyad life^3	−0.000	−0.000*	0.000
	(0.000)	(0.000)	(0.000)
Constant	−4.607***	−5.703***	−5.479***
	(0.400)	(0.588)	(0.773)
N	9,794	10,421	7,927

Notes: Standard errors in parentheses; * $p < 0.05$, ** $p < 0.01$, *** $p < 0.001$.

a power endowment (the darker line). The dot represents the mean of this estimate, and the vertical line around it indicates the 95% confidence interval around that mean. Finally, because we expect the probability of rivalry onset to be significantly higher when disputed territory contains power endowments, we place a short-dashed horizontal line at the high end of the confidence interval

TABLE 6.5. *Rivalry onset and ICOW power endowments, 1816–2001*

	Model 7	Model 8	Model 9
Hypothesis: 5.3, 5.4–5.7			
Rivalry Data	Klein et al.	Enduring	Strategic
Power endowment	0.619*	1.697***	1.179*
	(0.258)	(0.437)	(0.465)
Joint democracy	−1.513**	−1.149	−1.404
	(0.523)	(1.039)	(1.007)
Capability ratio (ln)	−0.181**	−0.178	−0.579***
	(0.065)	(0.119)	(0.145)
Allied	−0.015	0.010	−0.129
	(0.188)	(0.337)	(0.340)
Ethnic value	1.042***	0.482	0.614
	(0.289)	(0.451)	(0.530)
Major power	0.442	0.668	0.173
	(0.232)	(0.429)	(0.522)
Civil War	0.694***	0.165	1.133***
	(0.175)	(0.324)	(0.335)
Independence	0.937***	1.150**	0.437
	(0.199)	(0.396)	(0.345)
World war	−0.425	−0.407	0.409
	(0.289)	(0.464)	(0.443)
Cold War	0.539*	Perfect predictor	0.002
	(0.222)	(no rivalry)	(0.414)
Power distribution	−0.197	−0.184	0.248
	(0.337)	(0.520)	(0.658)
Dyad life	−0.008	−0.094	−0.037
	(0.018)	(0.056)	(0.055)
Dyad life^2	0.000	0.003	0.001
	(0.000)	(0.002)	(0.002)
Dyad life^3	−0.000	−0.000	−0.000
	(0.000)	(0.000)	(0.000)
Constant	−5.292***	−6.154***	−5.257***
	(0.288)	(0.606)	(0.556)
N	16,062	13,988	14,410

Notes: Standard errors in parentheses; * $p < 0.05$, ** $p < 0.01$, *** $p < 0.001$.

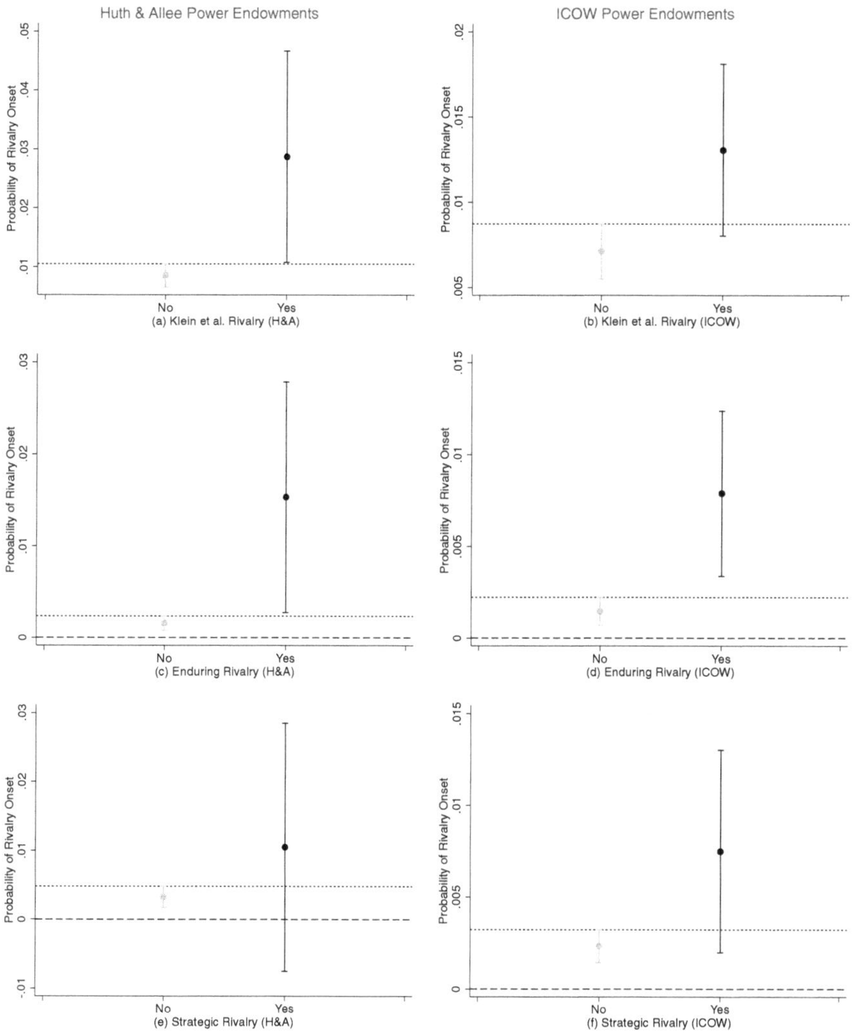

FIGURE 6.4. Power endowments and rivalry onset, 1816–2001

Notes: Derived from the results in Models 4–6, Table 6.4 and Models 7–9, Table 6.5. *Y*-axes vary to best illustrate results.

associated with the *non*power-endowment estimate (lighter line). If the 95% confidence interval around the power-endowment estimate (darker line) sits entirely above this dotted reference line, then we can confidently conclude that both (a) the nonpower-endowment and power-endowment efforts differ from one another and (b) rivalry onset is significantly more likely when dyads dispute territory that possesses power endowments, as opposed to when they dispute territory lacking such endowments.

The patterns depicted in the various panels of Figure 6.4 are generally consistent with Hypothesis 5.3. We find – in all six panels – that the likelihood of rivalry onset is greater in the presence than in the absence of power endowments. Nonetheless, there are some notable caveats. First, each panel's pair of estimates does not always differ meaningfully from one another. The strongest evidence consistent with the hypothesis obtains when the confidence intervals in each panel's estimates do not overlap; were we, for example, to draw a horizontal line anywhere in a given panel, would that line hit both the lighter and darker vertical lines? If so, then the panel's estimates may be identical, and we cannot confidently conclude that the estimates differ from one another. If not, then we would reach the opposite conclusion: the estimates differ meaningfully.

Strong evidence in support of Hypothesis 5.3 appears within three panels (panels a, c, and d). For example, the probability that a contiguous dyad forms a Klein et al. rivalry in a given year is 0.009 when the dyad disputes territory lacking a power endowment (according to the Huth and Allee data; lighter line, panel a); the 95% confidence interval places this estimate as low as 0.007 and as high as 0.010. If a similar dyad disputes territory containing a power endowment instead, this probability rises to 0.029 (a 237% increase), although it likely falls within the range 0.011–0.047. Since the confidence intervals around these two estimates do not overlap, we can conclude not only that the probability of Klein et al. rivalry onset is higher when power endowments are present, but also, importantly, that we are able to distinguish these two estimates from one another (i.e., they differ significantly). We observe a similar effect for enduring rivalry in panels (c) and (d). The likelihood that an enduring rivalry will form among contiguous states disputing territory without power endowments in these panels is 0.002 and 0.001, respectively; in contrast, the introduction of power endowments into the disputed territory raises the odds to 0.015 and 0.008, respectively – a significant increase of 878% and 439% (respectively) over the nonpower-endowment estimates (i.e., the 95% confidence intervals do not overlap). We therefore conclude decisively from these panels that the odds that a contiguous dyad develops a rivalry in a given year is significantly higher if the dyad members dispute territory containing power endowments than if they do not.

The remaining panels yield a less certain conclusion. The probability of strategic rivalry onset in a contiguous dyad-year, for example, is 0.002 or 0.003 when a dyad disputes territory that lacks a power endowment, depending on whether we use the ICOW (panel f) or Huth and Allee (panel e) data, respectively. If territory containing a power endowment is under dispute, however, this probability rises to 0.007 and 0.011, respectively – an increase of about 220% in both cases. This aligns with what Hypothesis 5.3 expects. Yet the confidence intervals associated with the nonpower-endowed and power-endowed estimates in each panel overlap, suggesting that these estimates may be identical (i.e., the short-dashed, horizontal reference line crosses the darker vertical line in each panel). A similar effect appears in panel (b). Thus, although we observe a higher mean estimate of rivalry onset in these panels when dyads dispute power-endowed territory – as expected – there is a good chance that this difference is illusory.

A second caveat to the strength of evidence supporting Hypothesis 5.3 concerns its distribution. A robust (i.e., strong) finding will produce similar results using different, but similar, measures. This motivated not only our use of both the Huth and Allee and ICOW territorial claims data, but also our desire to predict Klein et al., enduring, and strategic rivalries. As we look across these indicators, two patterns emerge. First, the power endowment finding remains weak when predicting strategic rivalry onset (Models 6 and 9, Tables 6.4 and 6.5; the 95% confidence intervals overlap in panels e and f, Figure 6.4). Second, evidence using the ICOW data (second column, Figure 6.4) proves weaker than that using the Huth and Allee data (first column, Figure 6.4). Although it is not clear why this occurs, it nevertheless limits the robustness of our conclusion somewhat.

We also consider whether the general results presented so far vary over a nonrival dyad's life. Figure 6.5 displays the results of this analysis. Its panel layout follows that of Figure 6.4. The panels themselves, however, differ in two notable ways. First, the x-axis tracks how long the hypothetical dyad's members have been nonrivals (holding all other variables at their mean values unless otherwise specified in the discussion). Second, the probability estimates appear as lines (i.e., mean estimates) within broadly shaded regions (i.e., 95% confidence intervals) – an artifact of the change in the x-axis. The lighter shaded region once again corresponds to dyads disputing nonpower-endowed territory, while the darker region represents dyadic disputes over power-endowed territory. Where the two regions overlap, the probability estimates cannot be distinguished from one another with great confidence.

Evidence consistent with Hypothesis 5.3 would produce two general patterns throughout the panels in Figure 6.5. The first of these patterns would be a darker region that sits (vertically) higher than the lighter region. This indicates that dyadic disputes over power-endowed territory are more likely to produce interstate rivalry than dyadic disputes over nonpower-endowed territory. The second pattern would be white space between the darker and lighter regions. This white space signifies that the 95% confidence intervals associated with the nonpower-endowed and power-endowed estimates do not overlap – that is, that the estimates differ from one another meaningfully.

Of note, we see both patterns appear in each of the panels of Figure 6.5, even those whose corresponding panels in Figure 6.4 suggest no aggregate, significant, substantive finding. For example, consider panel (b). In Figure 6.4, we conclude that panel (b) offers limited support to Hypothesis 5.3; even though the mean estimate of (Klein et al.) rivalry onset increases when territory

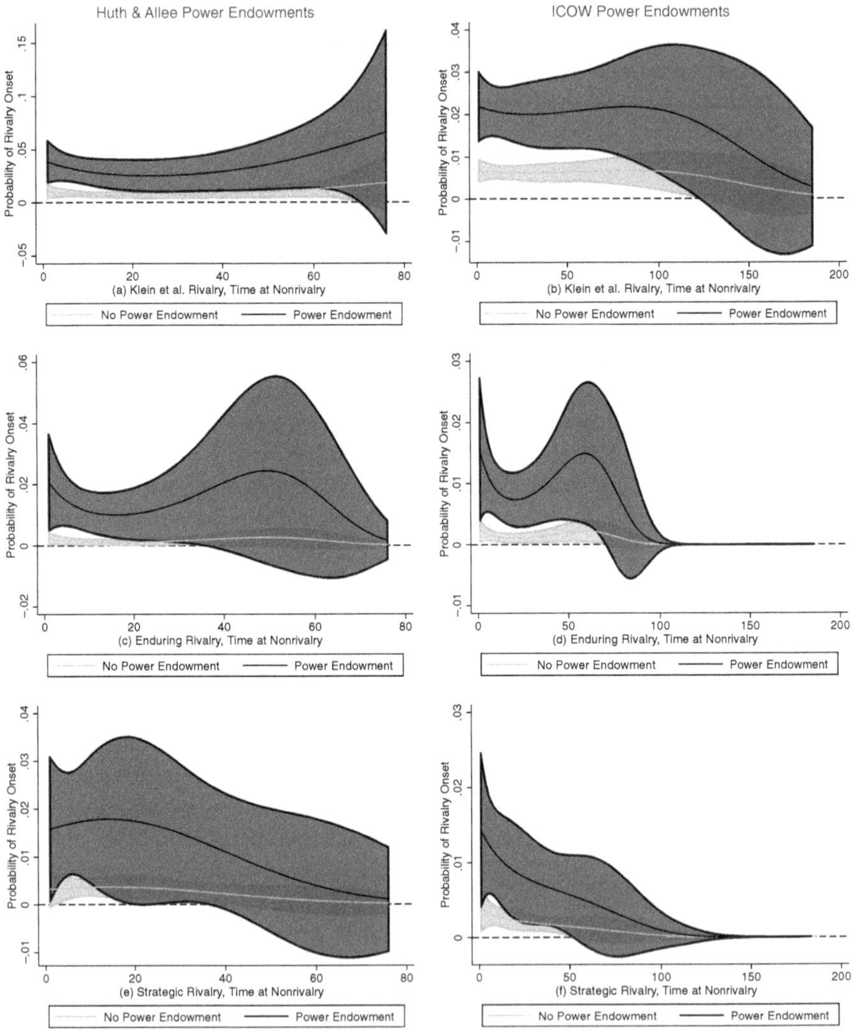

FIGURE 6.5. The Dynamic effects of power endowments on rivalry onset

Notes: Derived from the results in Models 4–6, Table 6.4 and Models 7–9, Table 6.5. *Y*-axes vary to best illustrate results.

contains power endowments – as compared to when it does not – the overlap in the 95% confidence intervals leaves us uncertain about whether this difference is meaningful. In Figure 6.5, we learn that this aggregate result misleads. Panel (b) shows a significant, lasting difference between the estimates in younger, nonrival dyads (i.e., the white space between the lighter and darker shaded regions). For example, in its first year as nonrivals, the probability that a contiguous dyad forms a Klein et al. rivalry when disputing nonpower-endowed territory is 0.007; if a contiguous dyad disputes power-endowed territory instead, that probability is 0.022 – 223% higher (and meaningfully different) than the nonpower-endowed value. The probability of Klein et al. rivalry onset remains significantly higher for a dyad disputing territory that contains power endowments than for a dyad disputing territory without power endowments at all ages of the nonrival dyad (i.e., setting the shaded regions aside, the dark [mean estimate] line within the figure lies above the lighter [mean estimate] line); this difference only becomes indistinguishable when the dyad reaches the age of 80 (i.e., the point at which the confidence intervals – or shaded regions – overlap). In other words, the aggregate finding in Figure 6.4 obscures substantial evidence in support of Hypothesis 5.3 – evidence we only uncover if we unpack the aggregate result.

Similar effects appear in the other panels of Figure 6.5. The strategic rivalry panels admittedly produce the weakest evidence in support of Hypothesis 5.3 (panels e and f), but even there, supportive evidence can be had. The likelihood that a strategic rivalry develops in a given year is generally greater for a dyad disputing territory with power endowments than for a dyad disputing territory without such endowments. Moreover, these differences can be discerned from one another – albeit for short bursts of time. This discernible period appears for a nonrival dyad whose age lies between five and eight years in panel (e) and between four and nine years in panel (f). Unpacking the aggregate findings from Figure 6.4 once again supplies evidence consistent with our argument.

In the end, we find evidence consistent with the expectation that power endowments increase the likelihood of rivalry onset. Our statistical models confirm that the presence of power endowments pushes the probability of rivalry onset upward. This finding holds across three measures of rivalry and using two distinct territorial claims datasets. Examining the substantive effects that the statistical models produce subsequently supplies our argument with additional support. They consistently predict a higher probability of rivalry onset in the presence, as opposed to the absence, of power endowments. Yet the predictions do not always allow us to distinguish the estimates of rivalry onset for dyads with nonpower-endowed and power-endowed territorial disputes from one another – at least not in the aggregate. When we unpack the aggregate finding to look at trends over the life of nonrival dyads, we then discover that the aggregate finding masks further support for our argument. Across all three rivalry measures and when using two distinct territorial claims datasets, the probability of rivalry onset is higher when contiguous dyads dispute territory containing power endowments than when they dispute territory lacking such endowments – especially when the dyads in question are young.

6.3.3 Alternative Explanations

The results tables that appear throughout this chapter allow us to evaluate the alternative explanations of rivalry onset that we outline in Chapter 5 as well (Hypotheses 5.4–5.7). First, some scholars propose that pairs of democratic states will be more likely to avoid a rivalry, given their shared norms of resolving political disputes peacefully (Dixon 1994), the institutions that complicate democracies' ability to take hostile action against other democracies (see Russett and Oneal 2001), and therefore, their ability to engage more effectively in diplomatic conflict management efforts. We find some, albeit limited, support for this argument. The coefficients on the *joint democracy* variable are negative across all nine models we present in this chapter, as Hypothesis 5.4 predicts (see Tables 6.2, 6.4, and 6.5). Only the coefficients associated with the Klein et al. rivalries, however, are statistically significant (Models 1, 4, and 7). To these latter, supportive results, we might add those of Model 6, which reveal that joint democracy is a perfect predictor of no strategic rivalry; in other words, nonrival, joint democracies with an active Huth and Allee territorial claim never develop a strategic rivalry.

In substantive terms, the probability that a nonrival, nondemocratic, contiguous dyad develops a Klein et al. rivalry in a given year is about 0.010 (Model 1; holding all other variables at their mean values). A similar, but democratic, dyad experiences a significantly lower probability of Klein et al. rivalry onset: 0.002 (77% lower than the nondemocratic value). Similar, significant differences of 77–78% derive from Models 4 and 7. The other rivalry indicators produce a similar trend, but the 95% confidence intervals associated with the nondemocratic and democratic estimates overlap. For example, the odds that a nonrival, nondemocratic, contiguous dyad develops an enduring rivalry in a given year is 0.003. A similar, democratic dyad, though, faces a probability of 0.001 instead – a 65% decline over the nondemocratic value (Model 2). This difference increases in Models 5 and 8 (to 79% and 68%, respectively), but the 95% confidence intervals associated with these predictions always overlap, suggesting a chance that the difference may, in effect, be zero (i.e., that democracy does not inhibit enduring rivalry onset at all). Similarly, the likelihood that a nonrival, nondemocratic, contiguous dyad develops a strategic rivalry in a given year is 0.004 (Model 3). In contrast, a similar, but democratic, dyad sees this probability fall to 0.001 – a 70% decrease over the nondemocratic value. The other strategic rivalry models yield a similar effect; Model 9 reveals a 75% reduction in the odds of strategic rivalry onset across the nondemocratic and democratic dyads, while Model 6 sees the probability of strategic rivalry onset drop from 0.004 to 0.000 (i.e., joint democracy is a perfect predictor of no strategic rivalry onset in this model). Once again, however, these differences may be nonexistent; because the 95% confidence intervals associated with the nondemocratic and democratic states' probability estimates overlap (in each case), we cannot conclude that joint democracy significantly impedes the formation of strategic rivalries.

These various results weakly support Hypothesis 5.4. We observe consistent, negative effects across all nine empirical models. Moreover, the substantive results illustrate that joint democracy reduces the likelihood of rivalry onset –

however measured – by roughly 65–80% in each of the models we estimate. The challenge, however, is that many of these effects (e.g., coefficients or probability differences) cannot be confidently distinguished from zero. We therefore must exercise caution with this finding. It seems that joint democracy reduces the likelihood of Klein et al. rivalries significantly, but perhaps does not forestall the onset of either enduring or strategic rivalries.

A second explanation of rivalry onset stresses the relative capabilities of the involved states. As dyad members' capabilities approach parity, their ability to both distinguish who will win a military contest between them and defeat one another soundly declines. Three effects follow. First, both states compete earnestly for the disputed good, since each stands a decent chance of obtaining it. The final result of their competition is not a foregone conclusion. Second, the likelihood of a militarized conflict rises (Fearon 1995). Whereas a substantially weaker state often lacks the ability to convince a substantially stronger one that it will win a military contest they have, states with more equal capabilities can mislead one another more easily. Misrepresentations about capabilities or resolve consequently offer the promise of significant, marginal gains. This incentive to misrepresent the state's position, however, decreases the probability that the involved states avoid military conflict. Finally, given their relative parity, any militarized dispute will likely end in a stalemate, rather than a victory for one side or the other. The dispute therefore festers, recurs, and sours the interstate relationship. In this way, the probability of rivalry onset rises as dyad members' capabilities approach parity and falls as these capabilities become more asymmetric (Hypothesis 5.5).

Our analysis produces moderate support for this hypothesis. In six out of nine models, the coefficient on the *capability ratio* variable is negative and statistically significant. This coincides with Hypothesis 5.5, for it indicates that the likelihood of rivalry onset in a given year falls (or alternatively, rises) as a dyad members' capabilities distribute more asymmetrically (or alternatively, symmetrically). To see what this means substantively, consider the most supportive results – those for strategic rivalries (Models 3, 6, and 9; on the other substantive results, see subsequent discussion). When a nonrival, contiguous dyad has a stronger member whose capabilities are 0.18 times that of the weaker member, the probability that the dyad develops a strategic rivalry in a given year is about 0.008 (holding all other variables at their mean values). Increasing the stronger member's capabilities to 2.16, 5.61, 17.49, and 98.87 times that of the weaker member causes this probability to fall to 0.006, 0.003, 0.002, and 0.001, respectively. The hypothesis predicts this trend. Nonetheless, we must pay particular attention to the confidence intervals around these estimates, which tell us whether any two estimates can be distinguished from one another. These confidence intervals often overlap, suggesting many of the estimates may be identical to one another. A significant difference, however, appears when moving from the 5th (or alternatively, the 25th) to the 75th percentile – cases in which the stronger member's capabilities are 0.18 (or alternatively, 2.16) times those of the weaker member to cases where they are 17.49 times stronger.

At first glance, it may seem strange that we conclude that the evidence supports Hypothesis 5.5 only moderately, especially in light of the above discussion. There are, however, strong reasons to do so. The first involves the strategic rivalry concept. States classified as strategic rivals must perceive one another as competitors – that is, "capable of 'playing' in the same league" (Colaresi, Rasler, and Thompson 2007, 25). In practice, this generally requires that capabilities distribute more symmetrically than asymmetrically across rival states.[8] We would therefore expect strategic rivalry to be more likely among states closer to power parity; indeed, the concept is designed this way. If we set the strategic rivalry findings aside (Models 3, 6, and 9), then only three of six models support Hypothesis 5.5 (rather than six of nine). Second, the substantive results derived from the nonstrategic rivalry models undercut the strength of these models' statistical findings. Some models with a statistically significant coefficient (e.g., Model 2) predict no substantively significant decline in the probability of rivalry onset – even when we make predictions under the most extreme conditions (e.g., comparing a hypothetical dyad whose stronger member is 0.18 times stronger than the weaker member [5th percentile] to one whose stronger member is 75.18 times stronger than the weaker member [95th percentile]). At other times (Models 1 and 7), we observe a significant decrease in the probability of (Klein et al.) rivalry onset, but *only* under extreme circumstances. For example, imagine a nonrival, contiguous dyad with unsettled borders whose stronger member is about 0.18 times stronger than the weaker member (the 5th percentile in the data; holding all other variables at their mean values). The likelihood that this hypothetical dyad forms a Klein et al. rivalry in a given year is 0.012. As we give the stronger state 1.97, 4.48, 14.17, and 82.70 times more capabilities than the weaker state, the probability of Klein et al. rivalry onset steadily drops to 0.011, 0.009, 0.007, and 0.005, respectively. It is, however, only the last value (0.005) that significantly differs from the first (0.012; i.e., the 95% confidence intervals associated with the first four estimates overlap somewhat). In other words, we can confidently say only that the likelihood of rivalry onset is significantly higher for a dyad closer to parity than for one whose stronger member possess 83 times more capabilities than its weaker member (both Models 1 and 7 produce similar results and interpretations). These are unusual situations. As a result of the considerations raised here, we therefore conclude that the empirical support for Hypothesis 5.5 may not be as strong as it initially appears.

The third alternative explanation of rivalry onset focuses on alliance partners (Hypothesis 5.6). Because alliance partners must coordinate their security policy in some respect, it would be counterproductive for them to develop

[8] As Colaresi, Rasler, and Thompson (2007, 25) argue, "Capability asymmetry does not preclude rivalry but it does make it somewhat less probable."

a rivalrous relationship capable of undermining that coordination. Alliance partners should therefore be less likely to develop rivalries with one another. Although plausible, we uncover no support for this hypothesis. The coefficients on the *allied* variable are most often in the direction that the hypothesis specifies (i.e., negative; except for Models 1 and 8). Under no circumstances, however, are they statistically significant; we therefore cannot conclude that the effect of alliances on rivalry onset differs from zero. Substantive results reinforce this conclusion. Compared to a nonallied, nonrival, contiguous dyad (and holding all other variables at their mean values), allies are 1–15% less likely to experience the onset of a Klein et al. rivalry in a given year (Models 1, 4, and 7), 1–44% less likely to face the onset of an enduring rivalry (Models 2, 5, and 8), and 9–27% less likely to form a strategic rivalry (Models 3, 6, and 9). Nonetheless, these differences are never statistically significant, suggesting once again that they may be illusory. We therefore conclude that this alternative argument – and Hypothesis 5.5 in particular – lacks any empirical support. Allies are no less (or more) likely to form rivalries in a given year than nonrival dyads.

The final alternative explanation for rivalry onset invokes ethnic concerns. States contest border territory that contains myriad characteristics, one of which involves the residence of ethnic kin. Where ethnic groups live does not neatly align with interstate borders, especially if colonial parents drew the borders in question. Ethnic groups therefore span interstate borders frequently, and the desire to see these kin reunited with their brethren can motivate territorial claims, discourage border settlement, and perhaps foster interstate rivalry. If the opposing, neighboring state mistreats ethnic kin, then the impetus for interstate rivalry grows further.[9]

Our analysis generates weak support for this argument. In Models 4–9, the coefficient on the *ethnic value* variable possesses the correct directional sign most of the time (i.e., positive; except for Model 5). It only obtains statistical significance, however, in a single model: a prediction of Klein et al. rivalries using the Issue Correlates of War territorial claims data (Model 7). From this model's results, we predict the probability of rivalry onset in two hypothetical dyads. Both are nonrival, contiguous dyads with an active ICOW territorial claim (holding all other variables at their mean values). They differ over whether the territorial claim lacks or possesses ethnic concerns. In the absence of the ethnic concern, the probability that the dyad forms a Klein et al. rivalry in a given year is 0.007. Introducing ethnic concerns into the territorial claim raises the probability of rivalry onset to 0.019 – a 177%, statistically significant increase over the nonethnic concern value.

[9] We find some evidence that ethnic concerns impede border settlement, but only when using the Huth and Allee territorial claims data (see Chapter 4). The ICOW data produce no similar finding. Given that the territorial claims datasets are at odds with one another (as they are here; see discussion), this evidence supports the ethnic concerns argument only moderately.

Such a finding offers some support to Hypothesis 5.7, for as the hypothesis predicts, the presence of ethnic concerns raises the likelihood that a rivalry forms. Nonetheless, the remaining models erode the strength of this conclusion. In all other models, neither the regression model results (Tables 6.4 and 6.5) nor the substantive predictions detect an effect of ethnic concerns on rivalry onset that differs from zero. This gives us pause. The significant results remain confined to one rivalry indicator (i.e., Klein et al.) and one territorial claims dataset (i.e., ICOW). The weight of the evidence therefore runs counter to the hypothesis's claim, although we cannot ignore what little support it receives.

In the end, the various alternative explanations perform poorly relative to our main theoretical story. A contiguous dyad faces a significantly higher rate of rivalry onset when it possesses unsettled – as opposed to settled – borders. This, importantly, derives from the effects of power endowments. Not only are unsettled borders disproportionately likely to involve territory with power endowments, but a contiguous dyad disputing border territory that contains a power endowment also experiences a significantly higher risk of rivalry onset than a similar dyad disputing territory that lacks these power endowments. The commitment problem explains why; fearing that border settlement will weaken it and increase its vulnerability, a state chooses to forego border settlement when power endowments are at stake and might shift to its adversary. This leaves unsettled borders – a highly salient issue to the involves states – to fester, ultimately causing the involved states to perceive one another as threats, enemies, and competitors for a good that each earnestly wants to possess.

6.4 CONCLUSION

This chapter investigates the consequences of leaving interstate borders unsettled. We argue that, under certain conditions (see subsequent discussion), unsettled borders promote interstate rivalries between neighboring states. The chapter therefore focuses on rivalry onset, giving significant attention both to our main theoretical argument and to a series of alternative arguments about why rivalries occur. Table 6.6 summarizes the hypotheses derived from these various arguments (as presented in Chapter 5), how strongly the chapter's evidence supports each hypothesis (individually), and the substantive conclusions we can draw from our study. Those interested in the details underlying each conclusion will find them throughout the chapter's discussion.

The conclusions listed in Table 6.6 integrate to support our larger theoretical story. The consequences of leaving borders unsettled depends on the characteristics of the border territory under dispute. States generally find border territory to be a salient issue; thus, they attempt to gain control of it through both nonviolent (e.g., negotiation or mediation) and violent (e.g., the use of force) conflict management strategies (Hensel et al. 2008). In cases where incomplete information impedes the bargaining process, nonviolent conflict

TABLE 6.6. *Hypotheses and conclusions about rivalry initiation*

Hypothesis	Evidence	Conclusion
5.1	Strongly supported	A bivariate analysis reveals a negative, statistically significant relationship between border settlement and rivalry onset. In addition, statistical models of rivalry onset suggest that border settlement significantly impedes rivalry formation (or conversely, that unsettled borders significantly promote the formation of rivalry). This finding holds across all measures of interstate rivalry.
5.2	Strongly supported	Power endowments feature disproportionately more often in contiguous dyad-years with unsettled, as opposed to settled, borders. This finding obtains regardless of which territorial claims dataset we use.
5.3	Strongly supported	A contiguous dyad is more likely to form a rivalry in a given year when it is disputing territory that contains power endowments, compared to when it is disputing territory that lacks power endowments. This is especially true for younger, nonrival dyads. Although not robust to every measure of rivalry or territorial claims, it holds across the majority of these measures.
5.4	Weakly supported	Joint democracy reduces the likelihood of rivalry onset by about 65–80% (depending on the model). Nonetheless, this effect is significant (i.e., distinguishable from zero) only for Klein et al. rivalries (three of nine models), which indicates that this finding is not robust.
5.5	Moderately supported	Our statistical models show that symmetric, contiguous dyads are more likely than asymmetric, contiguous dyads to begin an interstate rivalry in a given year. This finding, however, may be limited in scope; it relates definitionally to the measure of strategic rivalry (three of the significant findings) and only generates significant substantive results for other measures of rivalry under extreme conditions.
5.6	Not supported	Allied dyad members are never significantly more or less likely than nonallied dyads to form an interstate rivalry in a given year.
5.7	Not/weakly supported	Concerns about the residence and well-being of ethnic kin living in disputed border territory generally do not alter the likelihood of rivalry onset – either positively (as expected) or negatively. Only one model in nine reveals a statistically significant effect.

management efforts clarify states' capabilities and resolve, thereby leading to border settlement (see Chapter 4). Rivalry can form in these cases, especially if the information problem cannot be overcome. Nonetheless, this will be relatively rare.

In contrast, when neighboring states dispute border territory that contains a source of power – that is, strategically or economically valuable land – a commitment problem emerges and impedes successful bargaining. Redistributing the disputed territory necessarily redistributes power among the involved states, and the state strengthened by the redistribution cannot credibly promise not to use its newfound power to press the weakened state for more favorable terms in the future (e.g., a further allocation of valuable land). The state weakened by the redistribution knows this, though, and chooses to forego border settlement. Although this choice deprives the state of the benefits that accompany border settlement (e.g., jurisdictional certainty, greater economic activity, and a more secure state), it also prevents a territorial redistribution, a power redistribution, and therefore, a situation where it is more vulnerable to its counterpart's future demands. The neighboring states' borders consequently remain unsettled.

Myriad factors converge to promote rivalry onset when commitment problems exist. First, nonviolent conflict management fails to settle the border, despite repeated efforts to do so (see Chapter 4). This reduces the promise of future, nonviolent conflict management in the eyes of the involved states; indeed, the commitment problem logic encourages the state to be weakened by territorial redistribution to abandon the settlement process altogether. Second, without nonviolent options, the involved states turn increasingly to violence; yet even here, a decisive victor does not emerge, causing the dispute to fester and militarized actions to recur (e.g., see Ecuador–Peru). Finally, the fear that the adversary will obtain the power-endowed territory and exploit the state – along with the repeated, hostile, military encounters states experience with each other – encourages each state to conceive of the other as a threat, enemy, and competitor. They even institutionalize these perceptions, as each expects to compete over the disputed territory for the foreseeable future.

Despite this pessimistic story, borders settle and rivalries end, including when power-endowed territory is at stake. Dyads such as the United States–Mexico, Ecuador–Peru, Bolivia–Paraguay, Austria-Hungary–Turkey, Mali–Burkina Faso, Jordan–Israel, and China–Myanmar all achieved this feat – to name but a few. How did they do so? More generally, how do rivals settle their borders? And what happens to their relationship when they do? These questions motivate the next set of chapters.

PART III

BORDERS AND RIVALRY TERMINATION

7

A Theory of Borders and Rivalry Termination

> The material purposes on which one's work had been centered, every process of thought on which one had lived, crumbled into nothing. The whole vast business of supply, the growing outputs, the careful hoards, the secret future plans – but yesterday the whole duty of life – all at a stroke vanished like a nightmare dream, leaving a void behind.
>
> W. Churchill

7.1 INTRODUCTION

We argued earlier that rivalries pass through three phases. First, unsettled borders remain so because of a commitment problem that neighboring states find it difficult to overcome in the short-term. This places them at increased risk of rivalry formation. Second, rivals work to – and eventually – overcome the commitment problem. This phase begins when the rivalry forms and ends when the rivals sign a border settlement that delimits the entirety of their mutual border(s). Based on the conflict management tools they employ, as well as the effectiveness of these tools at addressing the rivals' bargaining obstacles, this phase varies in duration. Finally, the signing of a border settlement agreement signifies that the commitment problem has been cleared (and policy preferences have shifted), thereby permitting rivals to change their perception of one another and terminate the rivalry. It is during this phase that the rivals move from being enemies to being more amicable with one another.

This chapter deals with the latter two rivalry phases, and it does so in two noteworthy ways. First and foremost, it applies the bargaining framework used in earlier chapters to the rivalry context. The result is not only what is – to our knowledge – one of few explicitly causal arguments about how interstate rivalries end, but also a unified model of the rivalry process – that is, a theoretical argument that uses a single mechanism to explain why rivalries form, persist, and end. We believe this constitutes a significant advancement in existing rivalry research. And although our mechanism cannot explain *all* rivalries, it does cover many of them, including some of the most well-known. In addition, this chapter integrates the book's multiple, earlier arguments. It revisits and extends the bargaining framework, the theory of how border settlement occurs (in rivalry phase two; see Chapter 3 for more detail on this theory), and our territorial theory of rivalry (in rivalry phase three; see Chapter 5 for more detail on this theory).

Our theoretical argument in this chapter begins with the second rivalry phase: how do rivals reach border settlement? We argue that rivals face three main bargaining obstacles: mistrust, incomplete information, and commitment problems. All rivals contain mistrust, and to a lesser extent, confront incomplete information. Negotiation and mediation, especially when iterated, help address these obstacles; yet they are ill-equipped to handle the commitment problem because they fail to interfere with its logic. When rivals dispute power-endowed territory – that is, when the commitment problem arises – negotiation and mediation therefore prove futile, even if attempted repeatedly. Legal approaches (i.e., arbitration and adjudication) supply a potential solution to this dilemma, succeeding more often where these other conflict management tools fail. By design, legal approaches necessarily produce legal awards, which states find more costly to violate than bilateral agreements – in both reputational and material terms. Raising the costs of reneging and renegotiating then allows legal approaches to decrease the likelihood that a state engages in such behavior, even if the settlement makes it stronger. In this way, legal approaches foster border settlement in the presence and absence of commitment problems.

With this foundation in place, we next ask: what happens to rivals in the aftermath of border settlement. Our argument relies on a straightforward logical claim. Many rivalries form because of a commitment problem that results when neighboring states dispute power-endowed territory. These rivalries likely persist for the same reason, but even if they do not, states find territorial issues highly salient and handle them more aggressively than other, nonterritorial issues (Vasquez 2009). If, therefore, rivals have settled their borders – and necessarily overcome any commitment problem present – then either the rivalry's raison d'être disappears or the rivals have cleared a conflict-prone issue from their agenda. This will place rivalries at increased risk of termination. Of note, though, even if rivalries persist in the wake of border settlement, the settlement itself removes a significant source of hostility from the relationship, meaning that the rivals no longer have as strong of an incentive to treat one another with the same level of hostility. We would consequently also expect hostility levels to fall within rivalries after border settlement occurs. For these reasons, border settlement constitutes a watershed moment in contiguous rivals' relationship; after border settlement, rivals transition from a highly hostile relationship to a less hostile (or more benign) one.

The sections that follow examine how rivals reach border settlement, as well as the consequences that occur when they do. We begin with a brief overview of what scholars know about how rivalries end. This discussion identifies a series of theoretical frameworks, but each lacks a causal mechanism by which neighboring states move from their locked-in, institutionalized, mutual hostility to a more benign relationship. We then explore the importance that border territory likely plays in any general theory of how rivalries end; indeed, this discussion gives us greater confidence in the value of the theory we offer. Next, we briefly reintroduce the border settlement process that we outlined in Chapter 3, explain how rivals might navigate this process, and theorize about the effects that reaching a border settlement will have on the rivals' relationship. Finally, we entertain a series of alternative arguments that might account for the relationships we hypothesize between power-endowed territory, border settlement, and interstate rivalries.

7.2 WHY RIVALRIES END

An interstate rivalry is an intense, hostile relationship between a pair of states that possesses three key characteristics: disagreement over a (set of) specific issue(s) for an extended period of time; a perception within each state that the opposing state is a competitor, threat, and enemy; and an increased likelihood of the display, threat, or use of force to confront the "enemy" over the disputed issue(s) (Colaresi, Rasler, and Thompson 2007; Diehl and Goertz 2000). Although few interstate relationships qualify as an interstate rivalry, the (small) subset of dyads that do account for a disproportionate percentage of all militarized conflict, including both MID[1] and war (Goertz and Diehl 1993, 148). The rivalry concept has therefore received considerable attention, as scholars seek to understand why certain pairs of states are particularly conflict-prone. This attention, however, has yet to produce a rigorous theory of rivalry termination for two main reasons. First, many scholars do not study rivalry as an outcome. They instead employ rivalry data as a case selection device (i.e., to identify a unique population of states; for example, see Greig 2001; Hensel, Goertz, and Diehl 2000; Vasquez 1996), demonstrate that the rivalry and nonrivalry contexts differ substantially from one another (e.g., see Colaresi and Thompson 2002; Mitchell and Prins 2004), or control for rivalry in their study of other phenomena (i.e., to assure proper model specification or ensure the robustness of results; see Braithwaite and Lemke 2011; Horowitz, Poast, and Stam 2017). These may be appropriate decisions, depending on the research question being investigated; nevertheless, they do not allow one to study *why* rivalry begins, persists, or ends. Second, those explicitly interested in rivalry itself typically focus on rivalry *initiation*, rather

[1] A MID occurs when one state threatens, displays, or uses force against another state in the international system (Ghosn, Palmer, and Bremer 2004; Palmer et al. 2015).

than termination. The canonical works on rivalry by Diehl and Goertz (2000) and Colaresi, Rasler, and Thompson (2007), for example, contain extremely detailed empirical analysis on the formation and escalation of rivalries, but much less analysis of the factors associated with rivalry termination (see also Maoz and Mor 2002a).[2] Why states end up in rivalrous relationships garners more investigation than how states escape them.

Despite these general trends, a handful of studies directly consider the question of how rivalries end. Their explanations fall into two general frameworks: punctuated equilibrium and issue resolution. The punctuated equilibrium framework emerges from the work of Goertz and Diehl (1995), who assert that shifts between conflictual (rivalry) and relatively peaceful (nonrivalry) dyadic interactions occur abruptly, rather than gradually. Their framework proposes that "political shocks" act as a necessary – but not sufficient – condition for rivalry onset and termination. A political shock is "a dramatic change in the international system or its subsystem that fundamentally alters the processes, relationships, and expectations that drive nation-state interactions" (Goertz and Diehl 1995, 31). Numerous potential shocks exist – both exogenous (systemic) and endogenous (state-level) – and each of these might jolt interstate relationships dramatically (e.g., the end of the Cold War, or a state's independence).[3] Nevertheless, because these shocks are necessary, but not sufficient, for rivalry termination, many shocks will not change rivals' relations. Political shocks therefore overpredict rivalry termination, and we have no method by which to ascertain ex ante which shocks announce a change in rivals' behavior (on this point, see also Morey 2011, 264). This may explain why empirical analyses repeatedly reveal no consistent, significant relationship between political shocks and rivalry termination (Bennett 1998; Diehl and Goertz 2000; Goertz and Diehl 1995).

Similarly, although he does not use the term "political shocks" to describe the process, Cox (2010) argues that foreign and domestic policy failures drive rivalry termination. He seems to believe that rivalries form when states' bargaining spaces do not overlap. Policy failures then expand bargaining spaces, through leadership turnover or shifting preferences, and pressure leaders to abandon the rivalry.[4] Although a reasonable start, this argument possesses three weaknesses that we believe our approach can remedy. First, it does not adequately address the strategic nature of rivalry (i.e., it takes two states to end a rivalry, not merely failures within a single, rival state). Second, it seems to assume that policy failures will always result in policy moderation, not escalation, toward the rival state. Third, as Diehl and Goertz (2012, 101)

[2] Klein, Goertz, and Diehl (2006) note that rivalry termination dates are imprecise. They *assume* that the rivalry ends within ten to fifteen years of the last known military confrontation between the rivals. We want to know why and whether this might be true.

[3] For a full list of shocks, see the research design section of Chapters 6 or 8.

[4] See also Morey (2011), who makes a similar point. He claims that intense conflict (i.e., many fatalities in a short period of time) erode public support for continuing a rivalry.

succinctly argue,"self-declared measurement problems and the likelihood of many false positives (economic downturns and foreign policy failures are common) raise concerns about the robustness of his [Cox's] results."

A second framework for rivalry termination stresses that rivalries end when the involved states settle their outstanding differences. Bennett's (1997) work, for example, maintains that a rivalry ends when the rival states both (a) formally agree that the contested issue has been resolved and (b) refrain from further militarized disputes with one another for a period of ten years.[5] We agree with Bennett (1997) that issue resolution matters for rivalry termination. Yet, from our perspective, Bennett's conceptualization and operationalization contain a shortcoming – namely, he *assumes* that the presence of an international agreement (e.g., a border settlement in our case) equates to rivalry termination. It therefore becomes impossible to ask whether the agreements (or settlements) actually influence or signal rivalry termination – as we propose – or whether there is some other process at work.

Gibler (1997) implicitly recognizes this limitation. His study examines the role that certain alliance agreements (i.e., those that contain territorial settlements) play in reducing violence within rivalries. He finds that after rivals sign alliance agreements that resolve (some, but not necessarily all) outstanding territorial issues, they experience significantly fewer disputes – especially territorial disputes. Such findings hint that international agreements may affect rivals' relationship.[6] If this is true, what kind(s) of agreements should one investigate? To address this question, we turn to conflict research more broadly, which we believe suggests an answer.

7.3 TERRITORIAL ISSUES IN INTERSTATE RIVALRIES

Research examining the issues over which states fight produces findings that converge heavily on two conclusions. First, states handle territorial disputes differently than disputes over other issues; in particular, states are more likely to militarize territorial disputes and to escalate the disputes that become militarized (for a review, see Vasquez 2009). Second, absent resolution, territorial disputes are more likely to fester and, therefore, to recur (Hensel 2001). Because repeated militarized conflicts – or their threat – lie at the heart of rivalry (Colaresi, Rasler, and Thompson 2007; Diehl and Goertz 2000), many rivalries should contain disagreements over territory. Indeed, this appears to be the case

[5] See Cornwell and Colaresi (2002) for confirmation of Bennett's expectations (see also Prins and Daxecker 2008).

[6] Critics will argue that agreements (or settlements) appear when a rivalry enters its termination phase. The agreement, in other words, is a manifestation – but not a cause – of the rivalry termination process. The argument we outline subsequently is consistent with such a position. We do not propose that a border settlement *causes* the rivalry to end. Rather, a border settlement behaviorally signifies that rivals have surmounted their bargaining obstacle(s) and, therefore, that their rivalry is more likely to end. It is, in this sense, a harbinger of changed relations.

(although it need not imply that rivalries are *primarily* about territory alone; see Dreyer 2010; Tir and Diehl 2002).

Unpacking the concept of territory further, however, reveals that an important subset of territorial disputes concerns border territory. Both Holsti (1991) and Huth (1996), for example, find that many territorial disputes involve disagreement over the delimitation of interstate borders. According to Vasquez (2009), this occurs largely as a result of territoriality – that is, the human tendency to divide the world into units and to defend those units with force. If true, then territoriality produces two observable effects. First, many neighboring states will fight one another over the delimitation of their respective territorial domains. Second, relations among neighboring states will become substantially less conflictual after they agree upon the placement of their mutual border; after all, once they clearly divide this territory, fewer disputes exist in which it is necessary, desirable, or acceptable for neighbors to use violence (i.e., territoriality declines). This prediction receives strong empirical support. States that have signed international border agreements are substantially less likely to experience militarized disputes or war – over any issues that might arise (Kocs 1995; Owsiak 2012).

Although the preceding discussion derives largely from general work on international conflict, the importance of territorial disputes applies specifically to rivalry as well. From a theoretical and conceptual perspective, if territorial disputes become militarized and escalate to war more often than nonterritorial disputes and a large proportion of militarized disputes and wars occur within rivalries (Diehl and Goertz 2000), then territorial disputes will feature prominently in interstate rivalries. Indeed, this seems to be true. Depending on the operationalization of rivalry one uses, 52–79% of all rivalries contain some territorial element (Bennett 1996; Dreyer 2010; Tir and Diehl 2002).

Importantly, empirical work reveals a relationship not just between rivalry and territorial disputes, but between rivalry and border disagreements in particular. Bennett (1996), for example, finds that 79% of his rivalries involve contestation over the control of border territory. These border conflicts not only produce rivalries, but also prolong them (Bennett 1998). Furthermore, empirical evidence strongly suggests that the resolution of border disputes may end rivalry. This derives implicitly from the work of Owsiak (2012), who finds a negative relationship between border agreements and dyadic conflict generally. Yet Gibler (1997) identifies a more direct connection; the likelihood of future militarized disputes between rivals declines significantly when rivals sign an alliance that settles some outstanding territorial dispute between them (which is sometimes a border dispute). Although Gibler does not track full border settlement and his work does not indicate whether the rivalry actually terminated, it nevertheless hints that territorial settlements may significantly affect rivalry termination.

We argue in previous chapters that border disputes facilitate the development of rivalrous relations between neighbors – an argument that is consistent with descriptive inferences drawn from the research on territory and rivalry (see previous discussion). If it is the case that unsettled borders contribute to many contentious, rivalrous relationships, then it is likely that the settlement of borders among these same rivals will contribute to their rivalry's termination. In other words, although issue resolution may generally affect rivalry termination (Bennett 1996), the process of settling international borders, in particular, holds great promise for explaining why a large proportion of interstate rivalries among contiguous states end. Once rivalries are entrenched, however, resolving disagreement may become increasingly difficult. Any theory of issue resolution within rivalry must therefore account for not only how rivals overcome the initial bargaining problem that led to the onset of their rivalry (in our case, the commitment problem), but also how the rivals achieved a settlement in spite of their mutual perception that the other constitutes a threat, enemy, and competitor – a factor that would significantly complicate, if not undercut, any settlement attempts.

Research on how rivals manage their conflict(s) can be voluminous (e.g., see Bercovitch and Diehl 1997; Blum 2007; Diehl and Goertz 2000; Feste 1991; Greig 2001, 2005; Kupchan 2010). Yet because our theory stresses the role of unsettled borders as a cause of rivalry – and subsequently, as an influencer of rivalry termination – we need not examine *all* conflict management efforts between rivals. The management of border territorial issues will be of primary import, while the management of nonborder issues will play a lesser role. Cooperation, or even agreements, about nonborder issues may certainly contribute to border settlement, but more likely than not, it will *follow*, as opposed to precede, border settlement. States should be hesitant to sign nonborder, functional agreements (e.g., over trade or the environment) when significant security issues (e.g., border disagreements) remain outstanding (Goertz and Diehl 2002). Functional agreements may therefore only affect rivalry termination marginally.

Regardless of the exact role that nonborder issues play in the process by which rivals transition from rivals to nonrivals (or what others may label "conflict resolution" in rivalries), we propose that examining the border settlement process will be key, especially in the many contiguous rivalries formed because of disputed border territory. As we argue throughout the book, unsettled borders represent an external threat to state sovereignty and, by extension, to both state survival and identity as well. The most credible border threats originate from neighboring states, who can not only threaten a state's sovereignty, but also offer a simple alternative to that sovereignty – namely, that the neighbor absorb the border area into its state instead. Thus, leaders find border disputes with neighboring states extremely salient (Hensel 2001). The heightened threat and salience, in turn, then easily lead to competition, threat perception, and feelings of enmity (i.e., rivalry; see Chapters 5 and 6). Conflict resolution within rivalries among contiguous states – or rivalry termination – therefore requires addressing and settling the issue that produces and sustains this threat: unsettled borders. We turn now to that process and its effects on the rivalry relationship.[7]

7.4 A TERRITORIAL THEORY OF RIVALRY TERMINATION

Our theory of rivalry termination builds upon the arguments laid out in earlier chapters. In this section, we briefly reiterate the theoretical foundations on which the general argument rests. Then, we advance a more specific argument to explain how rivals move toward border settlement, and how their relationship changes in the aftermath of such a settlement. Finally, we entertain a series of alternative explanations to ensure that any results we uncover during the empirical analysis (Chapter 8) were obtained because of our causal mechanism, rather than a viable alternative one. As we account for and rule out these alternatives, we gain greater confidence that our argument has merit.

7.4.1 Theoretical Foundations

Our theory of rivalry termination builds upon territorial explanations of conflict (for an overview, see Vasquez 2009), recent work on the territorial peace (Gibler 2012), and rational explanations of war (e.g., Fearon 1995; Powell 2006). It begins from the vast body of research that connects territorial disputes to the increased likelihood of conflict, including rivalries (see above). Much of this work hints at a strong connection between undelimited interstate borders and conflict. We propose, however, that the connection is both direct and causal: undelimited borders contribute significantly to the development of rivalries between states. If true, then it is reasonable to expect that the settlement (i.e., delimitation) of international borders will play a significant role in how rivalries end. Additionally, if territorial or border disagreements are fundamentally more salient than other issues, and rivals are likely to handle border issues more aggressively than other issues (see Vasquez 2009), then the settlement of border issues should fundamentally alter future interstate interactions, even if the rivalry does not end.

Although the above argument sounds simple, it is admittedly not. States hold strong incentives to settle their borders; yet numerous obstacles to settlement exist. We believe that the same bargaining framework used to explain border settlement (or failed settlement; Chapters 3 and 4) and rivalry initiation (Chapters 5 and 6) accounts for these obstacles within the rivalry context too – as rival states work toward border settlement and their rivalry's termination. The framework begins from the same premises outlined earlier: a simple,

[7] Our conceptualization of settled borders is not tautological so long as we do not define settled borders as the absence of conflict (and we do not; see Chapter 2). Furthermore, empirical evidence suggests that states can and do dispute territory after border settlement occurs (e.g., Ecuador and Peru).

multiround bargaining model, in which two states dispute the placement of their mutual border. This model makes two broad assumptions. First, it assumes that the leaders of the involved states are rational – to the extent that they have preferences over the border's placement, can identify their most and least preferred outcomes over the border's placement, and will act in a manner consistent with those preferences. Second, it assumes that leaders care about the distribution of the good being disputed – in our case, the territory to be divided. More specifically, they want as much of the territory as they can get (Fearon 1995; Hopmann 1996; Schelling 1960), which makes them self-interested actors.

As rival states bargain within this framework, they encounter three obstacles. The first two are now familiar: incomplete information and commitment problems. Incomplete information exists when actors bargain without full, accurate information about one another's interests, capabilities, intentions, and resolve. It arises naturally when rational actors bargain. Because the amount of a disputed good each bargainer receives depends on its relative strength (Fearon 1995), bargainers misrepresent their strength in order to secure better settlement terms. This complicates the bargainers' ability to find the bargaining range and select specific settlement terms that lie within that range. Commitment problems, in contrast, arise from a different logic: one bargainer cannot credibly agree to honor tomorrow a settlement they sign today. An expected, rapid, future power shift produces this obstacle (Powell 2006). When a settlement threatens to shift the power balance between bargainers, one state gains power, while the other loses it. The to-be-strengthened state may forego a settlement today, preferring to wait until the power shifts so that it can bargain from a stronger position and, therefore, gain better settlement terms. If the settlement itself *causes* the shift, it may sign a settlement, allow power to shift in its favor, and then renege and renegotiate the settlement from a position of newfound strength. The to-be-weakened state, however, understands these incentives; indeed, it appreciates that signing a settlement will render it vulnerable to the adversary's future demands. In response, it either refuses to sign a settlement that it expects will be voided shortly or instigates conflict (e.g., war) to consolidate the best possible terms for itself (i.e., it fights before it weakens; see Werner 1999a).

To resolve a commitment problem, one must interfere with its logic – that is, prevent the power shift from occurring, or inhibit the to-be-strengthened state's ability to renege and renegotiate any settlement it signs. War can serve this purpose (Powell 2006), but states may be unready or unwilling to go to war. The latter, for example, might occur if states bargain over an object that is a direct source of power. Rather than destroy that particular power source, states may prefer to engage in a long-term competition over it (i.e., a rivalry; see Chapters 5 and 6). The competition protects their claim to the disputed object, concedes nothing, and leaves the power source available for capture in the future – when conditions might offer them better settlement terms. In this way, commitment problems increase the likelihood of interstate rivalries (see Chapter 5 for further elaboration of the logic here).

Using rivalry to address a commitment problem depends on a key characteristic: the disputing states must compete over an object that itself serves as a source of bargaining power. Some – but not all – border territory possesses this characteristic, with potential power derived from three particular sources. First, border territory may possess strategic value (e.g., the Golan Heights or the Sinai Peninsula to Israel); this allows the territory's occupier to extract (further) concessions from an opponent by increasing the probability that it will win future military battles. Second, border territory may contain a population that its holder can employ in economic production, draft into military service, or tax to generate additional revenue (e.g., well-populated sections of Kashmir). Each raises the likelihood that the state holding the territory will obtain greater military resources (e.g., more industrial production, a larger standing army, or greater military funding, respectively). Third, border territory may contain the economic resources needed to fulfill the basic human needs of a state's population or to produce revenue for the government through trade. These resources include, inter alia, access to fresh water (e.g., the Burkina Faso–Mali border), navigation rights (e.g., Iran–Iraq), or oil (e.g., Argentina–Uruguay).[8] And once again, each resource allows the holding state an advantage in future confrontations – for example, the ability to field forces, to survive a competition of attrition, or to fund military activities generally. We refer to these characteristics – that is, a military strategic position or economically valuable resources – collectively as "power endowments." The presence of these endowments puts states – via the commitment problem logic – at an increased risk of both bargaining failure (i.e., not settling their borders; see also Chapters 3 and 4) and developing an interstate rivalry (Chapters 5 and 6).

If unsettled, power-endowed border territories fuel interstate rivalries, then rivalries theoretically pass through three phases. The first phase deals with *rivalry formation*. All neighboring states compete over border territory. The presence of power endowments in the disputed border territory, however, raises the likelihood of a commitment problem, which states struggle to overcome in the short-term. This places the states at increased risk of rivalry formation. The second phase involves rivals navigating and moving beyond the commitment problem to reach *border settlement*. Once the rivalry forms, states must find a way to overcome the commitment problem. This phase begins when the rivalry forms and ends when the rivals sign an international border agreement that delimits the entirety of their mutual border(s). Rivals therefore negotiate over their border's delimitation during this phase, but the negotiations need not occur during every moment of this phase. In fact, it is entirely possible that rivals actually prefer conflict to peace at various times because they fear future

[8] See also Gleditsch et al. (2006), who find that access to river water often serves as a source of conflict.

exploitation (i.e, the commitment problem operates). Relations therefore ebb and flow, causing the second phase to vary in duration. Finally, the third phase concerns *rivalry termination*. The signing of a border agreement signals that the disputed border has been settled (i.e., the commitment problem has been cleared). This permits rivals to begin updating their perceptions of one another and terminating the rivalry – that is, shifting away from the entrenched threat, enemy, and competitor images.

This chapter focuses on the second and third phases: reaching border settlement and terminating the rivalry. Addressing these phases requires that we theorize about issue management (i.e., border delimitation) and conflict resolution (i.e., rivalry termination) within the rivalry context. We achieve this through integrating the bargaining framework, theories of conflict management, and characteristics unique to the rivalry relationship. The last of these presents the third bargaining obstacle that rivals face: mistrust.

7.4.2 (Mis)Trust in Rivals' Bargaining

It is useful to think in terms of "settleability" when theorizing about how actors resolve disagreements. Settleability refers to how easy or difficult it is for actors to find a mutually acceptable solution to their disagreement – a characteristic that varies by both issue and actor type. The book's main argument concerns the issue type dimension. When disputed territory contains power endowments, a commitment problem emerges, making borders more challenging to settle short of protracted competitions (i.e., rivalry) and violence. Through this mechanism, power endowments negatively affect settleability.

A further problem arises when we introduce the actor type dimension. When states bargain with one another, they often try to discern the adversary's "type." A type informs expectations about how bargaining will unfold. Is the state dealing with an adversary that will bargain in good faith, make reasonable concessions, implement a settlement as planned, and rely primarily on nonviolent bargaining tools? Or is it instead interacting with an adversary that will bargain in bad faith, make excessive demands, renege on a settlement, and resort to threats and coercion?

States screen for and signal various types.[9] As an illustration, two common types in interstate bargaining are "resolved" and "not resolved" (or bluffing). A resolved-type state possesses high resolve; because it is willing to incur more costs in pursuit of the disputed good (i.e., has greater resolve), it is more likely to escalate a conflict and therefore deserves better settlement terms – assuming, that is, that relative capabilities and resolve determine the pre- and post-conflict bargaining terms that states should strike (see Fearon 1995).

[9] Signaling occurs when a state tries to convey its type to an adversary. Screening occurs when a state tries to get the adversary to reveal its type. Screening and signaling are therefore two sides of the same coin, following similar logic. See Morrow (1999).

A not-resolved-type state possesses low resolve. It has a low tolerance for costs and prefers not to escalate a conflict; yet it often mimics a resolved-type state to try to obtain better (pre-conflict) settlement terms for itself. Which type of adversary the state faces determines how it should bargain. The state should offer better (pre-conflict) settlement terms to the resolved-type adversary than the not-resolved-type one; after all, it could offer less to the latter without fear of escalation. The challenge, of course, is that it must first determine which adversary type it faces.

A second illustration derives from the normative variant of the democratic peace argument, which relies on a type-identification mechanism when explaining why democracies do not fight each other, but do fight nondemocratic regimes. According to this argument, if a democratic state observes that its adversary is also a democratic state (i.e., type), then it anticipates that the adversary will externalize the norm of managing political disagreements nonviolently (Dixon 1994; Maoz and Russett 1993). If it observes a nondemocratic state instead (i.e., type), it anticipates no similar norm externalization, and fighting ensues. Through type identification, then, democratic states sort adversaries into boxes: democratic or nondemocratic. The adversary type, in turn, determines the bargaining strategy that the democratic state pursues.

Friend and foe are two additional adversary types. A foe is an actor that the state believes to hold (an) incompatible goal(s), hostile intentions, and the willingness and capability to confront it with coercion. A friend, in contrast, is a not-foe – an actor that holds (a) compatible goal(s), benign (at worst) or beneficial (at best) intent, and no willingness to confront the state with force.[10] Which of these two boxes an adversary falls in will inform how a state bargains; more specifically, the boxes are lenses through which the state interprets the behavior and intentions of its bargaining adversaries. The act of increasing armaments, for example, may be labeled innocuous if a friend does it (e.g., the United States' interpretation of the United Kingdom's behavior); slide the foe lens in place, however, and the same actions become potentially threatening (e.g., the United States' interpretation of North Korean behavior).

Moving an adversary from friend (or not-foe) to foe (e.g., rival) alters how the state bargains. Such a move happens frequently during the border settlement process (see Chapters 5 and 6). As borders remain unsettled – particularly when power endowments are at stake – perceptions of threat, enmity, and competition grow. Once these rivalrous characteristics lock-in, a rivalry relationship then becomes an institutionalized cornerstone of each state's foreign policy – a lens through which they view the rival adversary in all bargaining scenarios.

[10] Type conceptualization is purest – and therefore, most accurate – when categorization follows an "A"/"not A" (A/~A) format. Thus, we use resolved/not-resolved, democratic/not-democratic, and foe/not-foe. One type has a clear label, while the other is the negation of that label. Giving the negation a separate label (e.g., democracy/autocracy) potentially introduces conceptual confusion (e.g., are all not-foes considered friends, etc.; for evidence that various categories of "not-foes" exist, see Goertz, Diehl, and Balas 2016).

This enmity image erodes settleability; it breaks down trust between the bargainers, thereby making it more difficult for them to overcome any bargaining obstacles.

To see why this would be the case, we need only consider what trust is and what role it plays in the bargaining process. Kydd (2007, 6) defines trust as "a belief that the other side prefers mutual cooperation to exploiting one's own cooperation, while mistrust is a belief that the other side prefers exploiting one's cooperation to returning it." Rivalry relations, because of the perceptions that necessarily accompany them, are often characterized by mistrust. Both sides believe the adversary state has a preference for defecting (and exploiting) rather than cooperating. Indeed, domestic actors often incentivize such a preference, preferring to punish a leader for (mistakenly) cooperating with an enemy when they expect her to defect instead (Colaresi 2004). The source of the preference aside, however, mistrust presents yet another obstacle that rivals must overcome to settle their border and terminate their rivalrous relationship. A difficult issue will present settlement challenges; yet these challenges will be easier to navigate if those involved trust one another. In contrast, when states fear that an adversary will use the bargaining process to prepare for further conflict (i.e., bargain in bad faith; Richmond 1998), might use bargaining to harm or exploit it, or plans to abandon any settlement terms during the implementation phase, the likelihood falls that it enters conflict management with the adversary – or that any conflict management it enters will succeed.

Once neighboring states move from friend (i.e., nonrivalry) to foe (i.e., rivalry), they therefore encounter a new bargaining obstacle. We propose that many such rivals – particularly those disputing power-endowed border territory – face a commitment problem. To this issue-driven obstacle, we now add a second, actor-type one: mistrust. Rivals must circumvent the "foe lens" that colors their interactions – a lens that negatively affects settleability through raising the level of mistrust that permeates their bargaining.

7.4.3 How Rivals Reach Border Settlement

As we note earlier, rivals face three bargaining obstacles: information problems, commitment problems, and mistrust. We detail how conflict management tools address the information and commitment problem in Chapter 3 (see also Chapter 4). Mistrust underlies both of these obstacles generally (e.g., incentives to misrepresent one's strength or welch on a settlement), but is exacerbated further and takes on special meaning within a rivalry relationship. Rivalry locks in and institutionalizes images of threat, enmity, and competition. This necessarily sows the seeds of mistrust.

When significant trust is present between bargainers, a state has greater confidence that its bargaining adversary will not betray its interests, even when that adversary holds the opportunity (i.e., power or potential interest) to do so (Hoffman 2002). Trusting that another actor will behave as agreed constitutes a form of risk taking. Friends engage in such risk taking too, but also perceive the actual risk involved to be relatively low; they do not anticipate the friend to betray them often (if at all). In contrast, when foes interact – including within some of the most bitter of rivalries (e.g., India–Pakistan or Syria–Israel) – trust may be low or nonexistent, and the risk of being exploited or betrayed will therefore be high. If, for example, trust is a "willingness to place the fate of one's interests under the control of another" (Hoffman 2002, 376), then trusting an enemy often proves unwise (at best) or a bridge too far (at worst). The problem is further exacerbated in the presence of commitment problems, where without some mechanism to prevent the feared power shift or inhibit a state's ability to exploit it (i.e., to renege and renegotiate), credible commitments elude the bargaining states.

Conflict management tools are frequently effective at helping states navigate and overcome mistrust. In fact, the lack (or absence) of trust motivates disputing states to bring third parties into the process in the first place – either as credible conduits of information or as monitors that create and support strong, binding agreements (Hoffman 2002, 378). Rivals are no different in this regard. Once rivals lock-in their threat, enemy, and competitor images of each other, they neither stop attempting to resolve their various disagreements nor militarize all of their interactions. Peaceful conflict management tools frequently prove necessary, as a way to manage or resolve both their relationship and the disputed issues it contains.

Some may see this behavior as odd. Why cooperate with an enemy at all? There are three general reasons. First and foremost, cooperating in some capacity is a more stable policy than always not cooperating (Bendor and Swistak 1997). States cannot always "defect" (i.e., not cooperate), especially when they reside next to each other and must interact on everything from trade to tourism to immigration to the environment. Activity in a border region – and across neighboring states – does not halt altogether simply because those states have not delimited their mutual border. Cooperation on some (cross-) border issues (e.g., transitional crime) will therefore be prudent (Blum 2007), and once introduced, this cooperative behavior often expands (Axelrod 1984). Second, cooperation does not preclude the continuation of the rivalry – that is, the threat, enemy, and competitor images. It is, in other words, not a trade-off between rivalry and cooperation; the two are different dimensions – one a *relationship type* that lies along the rivalry–security community continuum (Goertz, Diehl, and Balas 2016), the other a *behavior* along the continuum from conflict to cooperation that takes place within any relationship (including a rivalry). Finally, there exist material benefits to cooperation. As Bendor, Kramer, and Stout (1991) show, for example, actors that cooperate more than their counterparts fare better than those counterparts. This does not imply that cooperation *easily* emerges; the desire to cooperate will be mitigated by expectations about a partner's behavior, assumptions about a partner's intentions, and one's own motivation (see Maoz and Mor 2002b). In other words, rivals may be reluctant to cooperate, though they have incentives not to hold out on all issues or indefinitely. This may explain why previous research finds that rivalries display positive duration dependence (i.e., the likelihood of rivalry termination rises as the rivalry ages Bennett 1998). Based on these considerations, we would expect frequent conflict management efforts of all types within rivalries and, over time, that these attempts may increase the likelihood of issue resolution (e.g., border settlement).

The appearance of conflict management efforts and those efforts' *effectiveness*, however, are two different matters (Greig, Owsiak, and Diehl 2019). We expect rivals to employ conflict management tools regularly during the course of their rivalry. Yet the effectiveness of any given conflict management tool likely varies by both the type of tool and the primary type of bargaining problem that the disputing states face. We therefore need to theorize more explicitly about how effective our three specific tools – (bilateral) negotiations, mediation, and legal approaches (i.e., arbitration and adjudication) – prove in the border settlement process that unfolds among rivals (for additional information on these tools, see Chapters 3 and 4).

The first conflict management tool – (bilateral) negotiations – serves as a mechanism for confidence building and information revelation. In negotiations, disputants sit together, without the assistance of a third party, to find common ground. This process unfurls as an exchange of offers and counteroffers between the disputants, as they search together for the bargaining range (i.e., the set of all possible settlement terms that they each prefer to no settlement at all) and select a mutually agreeable set of specific settlement terms that reside within that range. Because bargainers expect to receive settlement terms commensurate with their relative power (i.e., stronger bargainers get better terms; see Chapter 3), they have incentives to lie about their intentions, interests, capabilities, and resolve (Fearon 1995). This increases mistrust, beyond the levels already present within the rivalry (see earlier discussion). Nevertheless, the process of making and rejecting offers credibly reveals information and builds confidence among the disputants, which inches them closer to a settlement (Slantchev 2003).

The negotiating process described earlier addresses two of the rivals' bargaining obstacles: mistrust and the information problem. It does not, however, adequately address the commitment problem because it fails to interfere with that problem's logic – namely, to prevent a feared power shift from occurring or to block the strengthened state's ability to renege and renegotiate the settlement. Thus, negotiations, even repeated rounds of them, will be ineffective when rivals dispute the power-endowed border territory – that is, territory that possesses either a militarily strategic position or economically valuable resources – that we argue produces a commitment problem. The obstacle in such cases is not informational, but rather whether a settlement will hold during the settlement's implementation phase, given incentives for the to-be-strengthened state to abandon the settlement and take advantage of its vulnerable, to-be-weakened counterpart. Negotiations are not equipped to overcome these fears and incentives, leading us to expect that:

***Hypothesis* 7.1.** (Repeated) Bilateral negotiations will be less likely to facilitate border settlement between rival states when power endowments are present than when they are not present.

The second conflict management tool – mediation – brings a third party into the process. Mediation is a nonbinding, voluntary process, in which a third party offers various services to disputants to help them settle their disagreement. Within this broad definition, three characteristics stand out. First, the process is voluntary, meaning that the participants – that is, each disputant and the third party – can walk away at any time, thereby terminating the conflict management effort. Second, the process itself is nonbinding. A third-party mediator assists the disputants, but the disputants ultimately take responsibility for accepting and implementing any settlement. Stated differently, the third-party mediator cannot "force" a settlement on unwilling disputants, although she might offer rewards or impose costs to encourage the disputants to find settlement worth their while. She also cannot force a recalcitrant disputant to implement a settlement that it initially signs but later finds unpalatable. Finally, the third-party mediator might offer one or more of a combination of services, which include hosting and coordinating negotiation logistics (i.e., providing good offices), facilitating communication between the disputants, gathering and verifying information pertinent to the dispute and its settlement (i.e., conducting fact-finding), making suggestions about the substantive settlement terms the disputants should select (i.e., performing conciliation), or encouraging settlement itself through a system of rewards and punishments (Frazier and Dixon 2006).

Once again, such a process typically addresses two bargaining obstacles that rivals encounter: mistrust and information problems. A mediator typically enters the fray because the disputants struggle to communicate with one another. The mediator opens communication channels – that is, increases the exchange of information – and enhances the communication's credibility (Crescenzi et al. 2011; Kydd 2003). When a mediator conducts fact-finding, for example, it gathers information independently of the disputants and verifies the veracity of disputant positions (e.g., issue positions, or the strength of capabilities or resolve). Similarly, when it serves as a simple conduit of information, the mediator can sift through misinformation via "information pooling" (Princen 1992, 41–42). Disputants may fear sharing their exact positions with one another (e.g., in negotiations), lest they get a suboptimal settlement; they therefore accept the risk that they miss the bargaining range altogether. With the mediator, though, disputants can be more honest, for the mediator can pool information from its private conversations with the disputants, integrate it, and then report back on where the bargaining range is (i.e., not reveal the exact position of the disputants) – leaving the disputants to discuss what precise terms to adopt that lie within the bargaining range. In an environment characterized by mistrust and incentives to mislead one another, such as a rivalry, these activities provide a more credible, independent source of information that facilitates effective bargaining.

Third parties may also "soften-up disputants" through an iterative process that accompanies mediating difficult disputes (Greig and Diehl 2006). Through iteration, disputants gain familiarity with the mediator, the mediator's role, how the process will work, and each other. Iteration also gives disputants greater information about the true positions and motivations of their adversary – through an exchange of offers and counteroffers (see earlier discussion), facilitated by the mediator. All of this moves the disputants closer to a settlement.

The benefits of mediation, including iterated mediation, hit a limit when rivals face a commitment problem. As with negotiation, mediation is typically not equipped to address the commitment problem logic. Indeed, none of the mediator activities listed earlier – bar one[11] – interfere with the commitment problem logic. We therefore expect that mediation will be effective at addressing border settlement within only some rivalries: those that do not dispute power-endowed territory. When, however, a power endowment is present in the disputed territory, the commitment problem emerges, and mediators' ability to reduce mistrust, enhance the flow of credible information, and soften-up disputants will prove far less effective. In short:

***Hypothesis* 7.2.** (Repeated) Third-party mediation will be less likely to facilitate border settlement between rival states when power endowments are present than when they are not present.

The third conflict management tool – legal approaches – comes in two broad forms: arbitration and adjudication. We group these forms together because both are binding, legalized processes (Greig, Owsiak, and Diehl 2019). "Binding" means that, once they agree to participate in a legal process,[12] the disputants necessarily agree not to abandon the process or avoid implementation of the settlement terms that the process recommends; they are "bound" to both, which essentially transfers control of the dispute's management and outcome from the disputing states to the third party. For example, both arbitration and adjudication operate according to pre-established procedures (e.g., see the 1899 Hague Convention on the Pacific Settlement of Disputes, which deals with the Permanent Court of Arbitration, or the court statutes that

11 The exception is the use of rewards and punishments to encourage settlement, which alters the disputants' decision calculus to make nonsettlement more costly. Most mediations of border delimitation disputes do not raise the costs of nonsettlement high enough to prevent reneging and renegotiating. We therefore believe that they will be, on balance, ineffective at addressing commitment problems.

12 Agreement to the process occurs either ex ante, as when a state recognizes the general jurisdiction of an international court, or via a special agreement (or *compromise*) that submits the dispute to an arbiter or legal body.

accompany standing bodies like the ICJ). A disputant's case necessarily follows these procedures, even if the disputant objects (e.g., see China's behavior in the 2016 China–Philippines arbitration over the South China Sea). In addition, the legal process allows the third party to decide the substantive settlement terms that resolve the issue at hand, and disputants agree at the outset to accept, implement, and abide by these terms, even if the terms fall short of the ideal terms (a) disputant(s) would like.

Legal approaches share some benefits of mediation, particularly the ability to generate and transmit credible information. During the legal process, for example, the disputing states produce detailed legal arguments – both in writing and orally – that lay out and substantiate a bargaining position. The third party may supplement these with expert testimony or independent fact-finding. All of this enhances the exchange of more credible information, and indirectly addresses mistrust. Yet legal approaches offer disputants other benefits that mediation cannot. First, legal approaches theoretically offer domestic political cover to the disputants (Huth and Allee 2002), thereby allowing them to compromise over highly salient issues (Gent and Shannon 2011). It affords disputing leaders, in other words, an opportunity to overcome the hard-line domestic consensus (including mistrust) often created when a rivalry forms (Vasquez 2009). Second, legal approaches may create a focal point (Schelling 1960) based on past legal precedent, around which decisions may converge. After the Spanish arbitration within the Colombia–Venezuela dispute, for example, the disputants (and other third parties) frequently referred to the Spanish award as the foundation upon which their position was based, until everyone finally accepted the terms of this agreement (Ireland 1938). As this case demonstrates, it may take awhile for the disputants to accept the focal point as their agreement, but having something off of which to work may greatly facilitate the border settlement process. Third, and relatedly, a legal approach theoretically promises to resolve the substantive dispute (i.e., delimits the border with finality).

Finally, legal approaches settle border delimitations via legal rulings, which states find harder to repudiate. Herein lies legal approaches' unique ability to address the commitment problem logic, for they make a to-be-strengthened state less likely to renege and renegotiate a settlement in the future (see Chapter 3 for more detail). Once a third party issues a legal award, states' cost–benefit calculations change in two primary ways. On the one hand, violating a legal award carries reputation costs. Guzman (2002), for example, argues that failing to abide by one's international commitments can cost a state future deals (to varying degrees, depending on numerous factors; see also Goemans 2000); other states will cooperate less with a known cheater than with an honest counterpart (for limitations to this argument, see Brewster 2009; Downs and Jones 2002). On the other hand, violating a legal award threatens more immediate, material costs as well. The international system rests on expectations that states abide by their commitment to one another (i.e., *pacta sunt servanda*; Shaw 2014, 66–69). Unilaterally repudiating and renegotiating a legal award therefore prompts interest from a wider community of states – beyond the disputants or even key third parties. Such behavior, in other words, introduces international audience costs, and states can – and do – sanction one another in a variety of ways for violating international law (Guzman 2002).

None of these various costs will guarantee that a to-be-strengthened state will not renegotiation a legal award's terms after gaining power through the redistribution of territory that the award offers. Indeed, sanctions for violating international law – whether reputational or material – are rarely optimal, which undermines states' incentives to comply perfectly (Guzman 2002). Nevertheless, such costs will alter a rational, self-interested state's willingness to renegotiate a legal award's terms; higher costs decrease the attractiveness, and therefore likelihood, of a renegotiation. This interferes directly with the commitment problem logic and allows legal approaches to facilitate border settlement, even when the border territory under dispute contains power endowments. We consequently expect:

***Hypothesis* 7.3.** (Repeated) Legal approaches will facilitate border settlement between rival states both when power endowments are present and when they are not present.

7.4.4 Border Settlement and Rivalry Termination

Many rivalries begin because neighboring states dispute power-endowed territory and, consequently, face a commitment problem that they struggle to overcome in the short-term. This argument yields a logical implication: once rivals achieve border settlement, they necessarily have overcome any bargaining obstacle that impeded such a settlement, including the commitment problem. If the commitment problem produces and sustains these rivalries, then removing the commitment problem should increase the likelihood that the rivalries end. Much as a fire peters out when deprived of fuel, a rivalry likely winds down when its raison d'être disappears.

Two observations are necessary about the process by which rivals reconcile and terminate their hostile relationship. First, ending a rivalry does not imply that states become close allies or great friends. Rather, they demilitarize their relationship, relax hostile tensions, redeploy resources formerly directed at confronting the rival, and focus on other foreign policy priorities. Friendship might follow, but more than likely, the rivals transition to a relationship defined by negative peace – a more benign relationship, in which the use of military force to address any disagreement still remains possible (Goertz, Diehl, and Balas 2016). Second, reconciliation and rivalry termination may not occur quickly. States institutionalize rivalries within their policy-making apparatus – to direct resources into it. Moreover, rivals often link together or accumulate many issues (Dreyer 2010; Vasquez 2009). De-institutionalizing the rivalry or disentangling various issues requires time. Border settlement may provide the impetus for those processes to occur, but it does not mean that those processes will *always* occur, or that they will proceed quickly when they do.[13]

In our argument, treaties – or border settlement agreements – feature prominently (see Chapter 2). Through these specific treaties, states dispatch with their main issue of contention (i.e., the border territory under dispute), decide the settlement terms that will delimit the entirety of their mutual border, and lay the foundation for a better relationship. Yet we wish to be clear: we do not argue that treaties (i.e., border settlement agreements) have an explicit mechanism that itself resolves the commitment problem, thereby rendering the treaty durable and terminating the rivalry. A robust debate entertains these two competing positions – examining the exact role that treaties play in the durability of peace. Fortna (2003), for example, argues that the terms of a treaty are important for peace durability because states can design treaties to include provisions that make them more difficult to violate (e.g., monitoring provisions, which raise the costs of violating a treaty). Others, such as Werner and Yuen (2005), believe the substantive settlement terms – who gets what, or in our case, the exact division of border territory – matter more than any nonsubstantive treaty provisions (e.g., monitoring provisions). They argue that treaties will be most durable if the substantive settlement terms coincide with actors' beliefs about the potential gains they would receive from (continued) fighting. For our purposes, it does not matter whether rivalry termination follows border treaties because of the substantive settlement or nonsubstantive terms they contain. Indeed, we are agnostic on this point. In our argument, treaties (i.e., border settlement agreements) simply function as a symptom; they indicate that rivals have solved their underlying commitment problem.

Using border agreements as a symptom produces a simple argument. The commitment problem creates and sustains many contiguous rivalries, and leaves these rivals' borders unsettled. If, therefore, we observe that rivals sign a border settlement agreement (i.e., rivals delimit the entirety of their mutual border), then they must have cleared the commitment problem. Because the commitment problem was the rivalry's raison d'être, the settling of the mutual border not only serves as the culminating step in the resolution of a highly salient issue, but also removes fuel from the rivalry fire. Feelings of threat, enmity, and competition should therefore dissipate in the wake of border settlement, giving way to a more amicable, dyadic relationship. In short, the rivalry will be at increased risk of ending. In other words, we expect that:

***Hypothesis* 7.4.** A rivalry is more likely to end (*ceteris paribus*) once contiguous states have settled their mutual border(s).

To get more directly at the commitment problem logic, rather than the border settlement symptom alone, we derive a second predication from our argument

[13] Our argument is therefore probabilistic, not deterministic.

that focuses more specifically on power endowments – that is, territory with a militarily strategic position or economically valuable resources. We propose that power endowments set the commitment problem logic in motion. Their presence in disputed border territory therefore makes settlement more difficult (Chapters 3 and 4) and rivalry more likely (Chapters 5 and 6). If true, then rivals who dispute power-endowed border territory will be less likely to terminate their rivalry; in such cases, the raison d'être for the rivalry persists, providing the rivalry with the fuel to sustain it. More formally, we predict that:

***Hypothesis* 7.5.** A rivalry is less likely to terminate (*ceteris paribus*) if the border contains, as opposed to lacks, power endowments.

7.4.5 Rivalry after Border Settlement

Even though border settlement plays a significant role in the onset and termination of rivalry, this does not imply that border – or territorial issues more broadly – are the only disagreements that rivals experience. Indeed, many rivalries are multidimensional, meaning a nontrivial proportion of all rivalries experience disagreements over more than one issue during the life of the rivalry. According to data on strategic rivalries, for example, Dreyer (2010, 786, table 1) finds that almost half (approximately 46%) of strategic rivals have at least two issues on the table at some point during their rivalry. Vasquez (2009) explains why this likely occurs. Once a rivalry locks-in and institutionalizes, each rivals' policy becomes about the *relationship* – that is, confronting and causing harm to its adversary. Any disputed issues that arise in the relationship therefore link together into a larger, overarching issue: harming its counterpart.

If rivalries involve multiple issues, institutionalize their relationship, and shift attention from individual issues to the rivalrous relationship, it is theoretically possible for rivals to settle one issue – for example, border settlement – but for other disputed issues, or the rivalry itself, to persist. The rivalry would subsequently end after the involved states satisfactorily resolved all remaining, disputed issues. Nonetheless, there are two reasons to suspect that the interaction between such rivals may fundamentally change after they delimit their mutual border(s). First, border (territorial) issues are the most salient and conflict-prone issues over which states disagree. Because territorial disagreements most often prompt aggressive foreign policies (Vasquez 2009), rivals who resolve these issues should experience fewer and less violent conflict episodes (including both crises and MIDs). Second, recent research suggests that having more issues under dispute increases the likelihood of violent clashes (Dreyer 2010). As rivals resolve (any) issues (in this case, border territory ones), it stands to reason that the rivalry should then become less conflict-prone, particularly if the resolved issues also happen to be the most salient ones. We therefore propose that rival dyads will experience less frequent conflict episodes after border settlement, and that any episodes that do occur will be both of shorter duration and less severe than those occurring before border settlement. Consistent with this argument, we anticipate that:

***Hypothesis* 7.6.** Rivals will experience fewer conflict episodes after border settlement, as opposed to before it.

***Hypothesis* 7.7.** Rivals will experience shorter conflict episodes after border settlement, as opposed to before it.

***Hypothesis* 7.8.** Rivals will experience less severe conflict episodes after border settlement, as opposed to before it.

7.4.6 Alternative Explanations

As we note in Chapter 5, complex social phenomena are likely multicausal. Moreover, it is possible that our main hypothesized relationships – that is, the link between border settlement, via commitment problems, to rivalry termination – might be spurious, particularly if there exist factors that theoretically and causally link to the likelihood of (successful) conflict management (a key independent variable), border settlement (a key independent and outcome variable), and rivalry termination (a key outcome variable). We identify four such factors in Chapters 3 and 5: whether both members of a rival dyad are joint democracies, have a relatively greater (a)symmetric power balance, or are allied to one another, as well as whether one or more of the dyad members have ethnic kin living in the disputed border territory. These factors each alter uncertainty between bargaining states, thereby theoretically changing the odds that the states engage in conflict management, succeed at conflict management, reach a border settlement, and consequently, escape a rivalrous relationship.

We present the logic by which each factor reduces bargaining uncertainty in Chapter 5 (see also Chapter 3). To reduce repetition, we present the hypotheses here, but refer readers to the earlier chapter for a detailed discussion of the logic underlying the hypotheses.[14] Based on that earlier discussion, we expect that:

***Hypothesis* 7.9.** Democratic, neighboring states are more likely to terminate their rivalry than other contiguous dyads.

***Hypothesis* 7.10.** Neighboring states closer to, as opposed to farther from, relative power parity are less likely to terminate their rivalry.

***Hypothesis* 7.11.** Neighboring states that are allied, as opposed to nonallied, to one another are more likely to terminate their rivalry.

[14] Rivalry termination is the inverse of rivalry continuance (i.e., a rivalry that does not end will continue). This directly connects the hypotheses that follow to Chapter 5, which focuses on why rivalries form and persist. Indeed, the hypotheses presented in this section are the inverse of those presented in Chapter 5 for exactly this reason; the underlying theoretical logic is identical.

***Hypothesis* 7.12.** Neighboring states whose ethnic kin reside in a disputed (border) territory are less likely to terminate their rivalry than neighboring states whose ethnic kin do not live in the disputed territory.

These four factors are admittedly not the only ones that might alter the likelihood of rivalry termination; yet we focus on them with purpose. Scholars commonly advance them as sources of (protracted) interstate conflict. More importantly, however, each also potentially affects the likelihood that states engage in conflict management, succeed at conflict management, and reach a border settlement. As a result, they offer true alternative explanations for any hypothesized – or observed – relationship between border settlement and rivalry termination. Accounting for them allows us greater confidence that any observed relationships are likely a product of the theoretical story we advance, rather than a viable alternative.

7.5 CONCLUSION

When neighboring states dispute power-endowed border territory, they face a commitment problem, which places them at increased risk of developing a rivalry. What happens after that rivalry begins? How do rivals overcome the commitment problem to reach a border settlement? And what happens to their relationship if they achieve such a milestone? This chapter supplies an answer to these questions, and it does so via what is – to our knowledge – one of few explicitly causal arguments of how interstate rivalries end. By using the same framework that we develop in earlier chapters, it also produces a unique argument – one that unifies the rivalry onset, persistence, and termination processes under a single causal mechanism.

Our theory conceptualizes border settlement within rivalries as a straightforward bargaining process (for greater detail, see Chapter 3). As states navigate this process, two common obstacles arise: information problems and commitment problems. States struggle with both problems, but the commitment problem proves particularly troubling and increases the odds that neighboring states develop a rivalry (for greater detail, see Chapter 5). Once a rivalry forms, the involved states then confront both of these obstacles in their border settlement process, as well as a third: mistrust.

Rivals resort to conflict management regularly – to manage their relationship and their disputed issues, along with the bargaining obstacles that underlie both. Yet, if many contiguous rivalries form because of unsettled borders (see Chapters 5 and 6), then the border settlement process will prove particularly important in their relationship. We therefore first explore how rivals reach border settlement, extending the arguments elaborated at length in Chapter 3 to the rivalry context. In general, (repeated) negotiations and mediation induce border settlement when rivals primarily face mistrust and an information problem (i.e., no power-endowed territory is at stake). These same tools, however, prove less useful when rivals dispute power-endowed territory. Negotiation and mediation are ill-equipped to interfere with the commitment problem logic that power-endowed territory introduces; more specifically, these tools neither prevent a feared power shift from taking place or alter a to-be-strengthened state's incentive to renege and renegotiate a settlement after the settlement transfers power in its favor. Repeatedly using these tools to address a commitment problem will therefore prove futile.

Legal approaches, in contrast, prove better equipped to confront the commitment problem logic. These approaches necessarily produce legal awards (or rulings). Violating such awards carries both reputational and material costs, especially as the wider international community has an incentive to protect the efficacy and integrity of the international legal system. To be clear, this neither prevents a power shift nor *entirely* precludes a powerful state from reneging on a settlement; yet it does raise the costs associated with reneging or renegotiating a settlement and, in that sense, makes such behavior less likely among rational, self-interested states. Based on this logic, we argue that legal approaches foster border settlement among rivals, even when they dispute power-endowed border territory.

If many rivalries form because of commitment problems, then two broad predictions follow. First, the presence of a commitment problem (i.e., power-endowed territory) will make it more difficult for rivalries to end. Essentially, the same logic that produces rivalries in the first place likely sustains them too. Second, rivals' relationship transforms fundamentally if they obtain border settlement. If rivals reach border settlement, then they must have overcome the commitment problem (or any other bargaining obstacles in operation). And if many rivalries form because of the commitment problem, then clearing this obstacle removes the rivalry's raison d'être and should, therefore, fundamentally transform the rivals relationship – increasing the possibility that the rivalry ends and reducing hostility significantly if the rivalry continues.

The next chapter offers an empirical strategy to determine if model's predictions generalize to the data. As we expect, commitment problems – measured through the presence of power endowments within disputed border territory – impede rivals' ability to both settle their borders and terminate their rivalry. Legal approaches, but not negotiation or mediation, help the rivals move significantly toward border settlement when these commitment problems are present, and if they achieve a border settlement, the rivals' relationship changes fundamentally. On the one hand, border settlement increases the likelihood that the rivalry itself ends – turning a hostile interstate relationship into a more benign one. On the other hand, even where the rivalry persists, we find that rivals treat one another with significantly less hostility after settlement occurs. Such empirical patterns are consistent with our expectations that unsettled borders – via the commitment problem logic – create and sustain many rivalries between neighboring states, for when we remove that impetus (or fuel), the dyadic relationship transforms.

8

An Empirical Evaluation of Borders and Rivalry Termination

> To make a peace durable, what may give occasion for future wars should if practicable be removed.
>
> B. Franklin

8.1 INTRODUCTION

How do rivals reach border settlement? That is, how might rivals overcome the commitment problem that we identify as a primary bargaining obstacle they face? And when they reach border settlement, as many rivals eventually do, how might their relationship change (if at all)? This chapter identifies and evaluates the empirical patterns needed to answer such questions – focusing specifically on the hypotheses advanced in the previous chapter. We begin by sketching the research design underlying the chapter's analyses. This research design will once again look familiar. It employs many of the variables we use and discuss in both Chapters 4 and 6. To reduce repetition, we abridge the research design discussion subsequently and refer those seeking additional details to the earlier chapters of the book. The second section then implements our research design. It investigates (i) the factors that alter the likelihood of border settlement, including the presence of power endowments, various conflict management efforts, and the interactions between the two; (ii) the role border settlement plays in terminating rivalries; and (iii) whether rivals' dispute behavior (e.g., frequency, duration, and severity) differs markedly across the pre- and post-border settlement phases of their relationship. The final section then synthesizes our findings, which cumulatively lend strong support to our argument. Not only do power endowments impede border settlement among rivals – however, measured – but border settlement itself transforms the rivalrous relationship, both increasing the likelihood that rivalry terminates and decreasing the duration and severity of disputes within the rivalries that persist after border settlement.

8.2 DESIGNING THE EMPIRICAL STUDY

In order to explore the intersection of border settlement, power endowments, and interstate rivalry – and draw generalizable conclusions about the relationships involved – we turn again to quantitative analysis. This chapter, however, studies the contiguous-rivalry-dyad-year, which is both a theoretically informed and appropriate unit-of-analysis for us. The focus on rivalry stems from our desire to understand how rivals manage their unsettled borders. Chapters 5 and 6 find that power-endowed territory fosters interstate rivalry – that is, a hostile, dyadic interstate relationship; yet if this occurs because of the commitment problem logic, as we argue, how do rivals escape that trap? An answer requires that we study *interstate rivalries* specifically. Consistent with the previous chapters, we rely on various datasets to identify three distinct populations of interstate rivalries: Klein, Goertz, and Diehl (2006) rivalries, enduring rivalries (Diehl and Goertz 2000), and strategic rivalries (Colaresi, Rasler, and Thompson 2007). A more detailed definition of each rivalry population appears in the next subsection. Note that because we study interstate rivals, dyads outside of a rivalry relationship will not appear in our analysis.

A second scope limitation concerns contiguity. Only contiguous rivals have borders to settle, making noncontiguous rivals theoretically inappropriate to include in our models. We identify contiguous rivals by cross-referencing each rivalry population against the Correlates of War (COW) Project's Direct Contiguity data (Stinnett et al. 2002). For our purposes, contiguous states include only those neighboring states whose homelands share an inland or river boundary – the closest level of contiguity in the COW data. Any dyad whose members are separated by either gulfs or seas, regardless of how narrow or wide, is considered noncontiguous; their land borders are determined by the water separating them, thereby obviating the need for them to sign an international (land) boundary agreement. There are 3,308 contiguous Klein et al., 2,250 contiguous enduring, and 4,362 contiguous strategic rivalry dyad-years during the period 1816–2001 (as defined in the next section).[1]

8.2.1 Dependent Variables

The outcomes of interest in this chapter are *border settlement* and *rivalry termination*. A detailed operationalization of our dichotomous border settlement variable appears in Chapter 4. In brief, a border is "settled" (a value of 1) beginning in the dyad-year after which neighboring states have signed an international agreement that delimits the entirety of their mutual border (Owsiak, Cuttner, and Buck 2018); before this, it is considered "unsettled" (a value of 0). Those wishing to understand how we handle particular circumstances – for

[1] As noted in Chapter 4, we create the initial dyad-year observations with EUGene (Bennett and Stam 2000) and then merge all other variables into the dataset from their original sources (unless otherwise noted).

example, borders that settle in parts or the independence of colonial states – will find this information in Chapter 4.

To address rivalry termination, we rely upon the three populations of interstate rivalry that appear in our analysis of rivalry onset: Klein et al., enduring, and strategic rivalries (see Chapter 6). Klein, Goertz, and Diehl (2006) define a rivalry as a dyadic, interstate relationship in which the two states confront one another repeatedly in a series of related MIDs (which occur when one state threatens, displays or uses force against another state; see Palmer et al. 2015). Because a similar set of issues connect these MIDs to one another in the Klein et al. conceptualization of rivalries, resolving these issues should, in theory, terminate the rivalry (see also Bennett 1997). It is, however, difficult to know when actors have resolved an issue with finality (see Chapter 2). Klein et al. therefore use MIDs – behavioral manifestations of the rivalry – to track the rivalry itself. A rivalry begins when a dyad experiences the first MID in its series of related MIDs; it ends when a rival dyad lives ten to fifteen years without experiencing a MID over the issue(s) that motivate the rivalry and, relatedly, tie its disputes together. We refer to these as *Klein et al. rivalries* throughout the chapter.

The second rivalry population, *enduring rivalries*, is a subset of Klein et al. rivalries – namely, the most protracted. Enduring rivals experience a minimum of six MIDs over at least twenty years. Their initiation and termination dates follow the same coding scheme as the Klein et al. rivalries (see earlier discussion). Klein, Goertz, and Diehl (2006) identify the enduring rivalries in their dataset, using the criteria that Diehl and Goertz (2000) establish in earlier work; thus, Klein et al. provide the data source for our enduring rivalry population as well.

Finally, *strategic rivalries* form between states that perceive one another as competitors, threats, and enemies (Colaresi, Rasler, and Thompson 2007). A strategic rivalry begins when all three perceptions – competitor, threat, and enemy – are present and ends when at least one of the three perceptions disappears. Identification of these perceptions requires an interpretation of historical narratives. These narratives appear in Thompson and Dreyer (2012), but also generate the data presented in Colaresi, Rasler, and Thompson (2007); the latter serves as our data source.

Our dependent variables of *rivalry termination*, then, are three dichotomous indicators – one each for the Klein et al., enduring, and strategic rivalry populations. These indicators receive a value of 1 in the year that a dyadic rivalry ends (however measured) and a value of 0 otherwise.[2]

[2] The statistical models are conditional logistic regressions (see Section 8.2.4). Only rivalries can end; therefore, only rivalries appear in the analyses of rivalry termination. Once a rivalry ends, it effectively exits the data.

8.2.2 Key Independent Variables

Determining whether hypotheses outlined in Chapter 7 generally hold in the data requires four groups of independent variables. The first two groups – settled borders and power endowments – stress components of our main theoretical argument. The third group contains a series of conflict management variables to help us understand the border settlement process better, while the final group then accounts for alternatives to our argument. We identify and operationalize each of these sets of variables in turn.

Border Settlement

In addition to investigating how border settlement occurs within rivalries, we also examine the effect that border settlement has on rivalry relationships. The former uses border settlement as a dependent variable (see earlier discussion), while the latter uses it as an independent variable (in separate analyses). Nonetheless, the operationalization remains the same in both cases. *Border settlement* exists (a value of 1) beginning in the dyad-year after which neighboring states sign an international agreement that delimits the entirety of their border. Prior to this, we consider the border to be unsettled (a value of 0). More details about the coding decisions that underlie this variable appear in Chapter 2.

Power Endowments

Unsettled borders foster interstate rivalry because they generate a commitment problem that neighboring states find difficult to overcome. Yet, not all unsettled borders will logically produce this effect; only unsettled borders with *power endowments* do so, since the power endowments threaten to shift power between neighboring states significantly when border settlement occurs. Border settlement therefore proves difficult in the presence of power endowments. This failure to settle – combined with the highly salient border territory at stake – then facilitates not only the formation of interstate rivalries (see Chapter 6), but also increases the likelihood that interstate rivalries persist, In other words, power endowments not only encourage rivalries to form, but also undermine rivalry termination.

A power endowment exists empirically within a disputed territory (a value of 1) when that territory contains either militarily strategic or economically valuable land. If, in contrast, the disputed territory lacks both of these characteristics, we consider power endowments to be absent from it (a value of 0). Separate data from Huth and Allee (2002) and the Issue Correlates of War Project (ICOW; Frederick, Hensel, and Macaulay 2017) produce our two (separate) dichotomous indicators of power endowments. We discuss the details underlying these variables – as well as their being an appropriate measure of the power endowment concept – in Chapter 4.

Conflict Management

To investigate how border settlement unfolds in rivalries, we need – once again – to incorporate the tools that states use in the settlement process into our analysis. We identify, define, and describe these tools in Chapter 4. That discussion collapses the myriad tools available into three variables: (bilateral) *negotiations*, *mediation*, and *legal approaches* (i.e., arbitration, adjudication, and post-war conferences). Combined, these categories then constitute a fourth variable: *all conflict management efforts*.

Each of these four variables consists of a running sum of the number of conflict management attempts that occurred in the rival dyad's border delimitation process prior to the dyad-year in question. A running sum best captures the logic underlying many theories of conflict management, which propose that the effects of conflict management efforts accumulate. No single conflict management attempt, in other words, proves decisive; rather, the cumulative effort changes the probability that disputants resolve their disagreement (see Chapter 4; Greig and Diehl 2006). Anecdotal evidence within dyadic border settlement processes offers prima facie support for this logic (e.g., see Blum 2007; Ireland 1938). We therefore create four running sum variables: all conflict management, negotiations (only), mediation (only), and legal approaches (only).

Our argument also proposes that the effects of individual conflict management tools will vary in the presence and absence of power endowments. Investigating this expectation requires the use of interaction terms (Braumoeller 2004). The negotiation, mediation, and legal approaches variables discussed earlier constitute the lower-order interaction terms; when they appear in models with the higher-order terms, they capture the effects of the given conflict management tool in the absence of power endowments. Three higher-order variables – *power endowment*negotiation*, *power endowment*mediation*, and *power endowment*legal* – then denote whether the effect of each conflict management tool varies in the presence of power endowments. Because interaction terms are notoriously difficult to interpret directly, we graph the results involving interaction terms throughout the chapter.

Alternative Explanations

The variables presented so far relate to our main argument; yet, Chapter 7 also outlines four factors that might promote either border settlement or rivalry termination via distinct, alternative routes. First, dyads composed of two democratic states generally behave more peacefully than those containing at least one nondemocratic state. This characteristic might enhance the prospects for border settlement (see Dixon 1994; but see also Gibler and Owsiak 2019). Moreover, although it likely leads democratic states to form fewer rivalries with one another in the first place (see Chapter 6), it may also help any democratic rivalries that form to end (Hypothesis 7.9). A dichotomous variable – *joint democracy* – considers this possibility, capturing whether (1) or not (0) a dyad's members both score +6 or higher on the Polity IV Project's

Democracy–Autocracy Index (what Polity calls the Polity2 variable; see Marshall and Jaggers 2009). This operationalization, including the threshold used, corresponds with how scholars in the international conflict subfield typically measure democratic dyads.

Second, relative power alters bargaining dynamics significantly – with respect to both the management of territorial claims (including border settlement; see Hensel et al. 2008; Zawahri and Mitchell 2011) and international conflict (including rivalries; see Colaresi, Rasler, and Thompson 2007; Fearon 1995). Dyads in which power splits asymmetrically among members face less uncertainty during bargaining. They expect the stronger state to get more, thereby obviating the need for militarized conflict and reducing the need for prolonged, repeated, peaceful conflict management. Since their members' expectations about how to distribute a disputed good converge more easily, one might anticipate that these dyads will reach border settlement faster. Similarly, asymmetrically powerful states do not often become rivals. As power asymmetry grows among a dyad's members, the likelihood that its members see one another as "competitors" – a hallmark characteristic of an interstate rivalry – declines. These dyads, then, are less likely to become rivals, and if the asymmetry develops or deepens during a rivalry, logic suggests that the rivalry is more likely to end (Hypothesis 7.10).

A continuous variable addresses these theoretical predictions. It measures the ratio of the stronger to the weaker state's capabilities within the dyad-year in question (using the Composite Index of National Capabilities score for each state; see Singer, Bremer, and Stuckey 1972). In the resulting *capability ratio*, movement toward a value of (1) indicates that the dyad members are approaching power parity, while values that increasingly exceed (1) demonstrate that the stronger state is gaining asymmetrically greater power relative to the weaker state. To account for diminishing effects near the extreme values of this variable, we use the natural log (ln) of the raw capabilities ratio within our models.

A third, alternative factor highlights alliance relationships. Alliances vary greatly in the commitments that members make to one another; yet all alliances require their members to coordinate security policy on some level. It seems theoretically unlikely for such coordination to take place while highly contentious issues remain unsettled (e.g., borders) or while feelings of threat, enmity, and competition persist (i.e., during rivalries). We expect that border settlement and rivalry termination therefore typically precede alliance formation. If, however, alliances form much earlier than we expect, then it seems plausible that alliance relationships might facilitate border settlement and rivalry termination (Hypothesis 7.11). A dichotomous variable investigates this possibility. It indicates whether a contiguous rival dyad's members have any alliance obligations with one another during each year of their rivalry's existence (Leeds, Ritter, and Mitchell 2002). The variable accepts a value of (1) in the presence of one or more such obligations, and (0) otherwise.

Finally, ethnic considerations feature prominently in decisions about the placement and contestation of many borders, and ethnic tensions often serve as a potential source of hostility within and between states. More specifically, ethnic considerations raise the salience of a border's placement. This potentially complicates – and undermines – settlement attempts. Theorizing about why this might occur yields two pathways by which ethnic considerations might connect to interstate rivalries as well. On the one hand, given high salience in and repeated settlement failures over the border, feelings of threat, enmity, and competition – that is, an interstate rivalry – may form and persist. On the other hand, neighboring states will especially worry about ethnic brethren falling into another state if that other state (threatens to) mistreat(s) the brethren. The mistreatment of ethnic kin, along with the desire to protect them, then generates feelings of threat, enmity, and competition (Hypothesis 7.12).

Regardless of the exact mechanism(s) at work, this line of argument maintains that ethnic considerations inhibit border settlement and rivalry termination. We account for this possibility with an *ethnic value* variable that takes a value of (1) when at least one of the dyad members has ethnic co-nationals living in the disputed border territory; if this condition is not met, the variable takes a value of (0). Two versions of this variable exist: one using the Huth and Allee (2002) territorial claims data and another using the ICOW (Frederick, Hensel, and Macaulay 2017) territorial claims data. This allows us to align the source of our ethnic value variable with that of the power endowment variable in each of the models.

8.2.3 Control Variables

In addition to the variables noted so far, we include other, prominent variables thought to influence either border settlement or rivalry termination. The first of these accounts for differences between major and minor states. Major powers, by definition, hold interests throughout the world. This potentially embroils them in more territorial disputes and rivalries. Depending on their carrying capacity and the ebb and flow of their strategic interests, they may end some disputes or rivalries in order to focus on others of greater importance. Their great power status, in other words, will necessarily influence how they approach the settlement of borders and the sustenance of interstate rivalries – an influence that minor powers do not experience. Mindful of this, a dichotomous variable tracks whether at least one of a dyad's members qualifies as a *major power* during each year of the rival dyad's existence. We use the Correlates of War Project's 2008 State System Membership List to identify which states are major powers and when.

The remaining control variables consist of a series of "shocks." Goertz and Diehl (1995) argue that key political events – in both the domestic and international arenas – can cause rapid and dramatic changes in dyadic, interstate relationships (e.g., causing a rivalry to end). Domestic shocks include *civil wars* and the *independence* of new states, while international shocks consist of the *world wars*, the end of the *cold war*, and a *power (re)distribution* between the major states.[3] All of the shock indicators receive a disparate dichotomous indicator, which receives a value of (1) if the given shock occurred within the rival dyad's last ten years of existence, and a (0) otherwise. This ten-year window adheres to the argument and operationalization presented in Goertz and Diehl (1995).

8.2.4 Modeling

The modeling decisions we adopt in this chapter closely follow those we outline in Chapters 4 and 6 (for a lengthier discussion of the choices that follow, see Chapter 4). We use conditional logistic regression throughout the chapter. Our dichotomous dependent variables – whether border settlement or rivalry termination – make this an appropriate technique to use. It is "conditional" in the sense that the observations included in the analysis depend on the lagged value of the (respective) dependent variables. When studying border settlement, for example, we include only the observations in which contiguous rivals possessed unsettled borders in their previous dyad-year. This ensures that the rivals have a border to settle (i.e., that the dependent variable can theoretically take a value of 1). Our analysis therefore omits contiguous rival dyad-years if and when rivals settle(d) their borders. Similarly, the models of rivalry termination require that a rivalry exist (i.e., dyads that are not rivals cannot logically terminate a rivalry between them). We therefore include only contiguous *rival* dyad-years in the analyses of rivalry termination. Nonrivals do not enter the analyses.

We control for temporal interdependence through the use of time polynomials, labeled *dyad life*, *dyad life*^{2}, and *dyad life*^{3} (Carter and Signorino 2010). In our border settlement models, these polynomials track the length of time a dyad has persisted with unsettled borders, while in the rivalry termination models, they indicate the rivals' age (see the "conditional" component of the regression discussed earlier). The inclusion of linear, square, and cubic terms allows the effect of time to vary nonlinearly.

Finally, the temporal domains differ across our various models. Our tables generally report models of border settlement and rivalry termination that cover the period 1816–2001. When we incorporate the Huth and Allee (2002) data on power endowments and ethnic value, however, the analysis restricts to the period 1919–1995. This is an artifact of the Huth and Allee data, which gathers data on territorial claims within the period 1919–1995. We overcome

[3] Power (re)distribution among major states only occurs around the time of German and Italian state unification (1859–1877; see Goertz and Diehl 1995). This, as well as time restrictions imposed by the other shock variables (e.g., the end of the cold war), explain why individual shocks occasionally drop from the models we present throughout the chapter.

the limitation that this temporal restriction creates by using the Issue Correlates of War (ICOW) data on territorial claims as well; these data offer an alternative method of measuring power endowments and ethnic value and cover the entire 1816–2001 period (Frederick, Hensel, and Macaulay 2017). We nevertheless retain the Huth and Allee (2002) data to gain insight into the robustness of our results.

8.2.5 Dispute-Level Characteristics

We anticipate that border settlement raises the likelihood that neighboring states end their rivalry (Hypothesis 7.4). This probabilistic prediction, however, does not imply that the rivalry *immediately* ends after borders settle. Because rivalries are long-term competitions with high levels of threat and hostility, states institutionalize these rivalries within their policy-making apparatus; that is, they incorporate their rivalries into their policy planning for the extended future. Ending a rivalry therefore requires reorienting the policy apparatus – from perceiving the other state as a threat, enemy, and competitor to viewing it in more benign terms. Such a reorientation requires time.

Nonetheless, if unsettled borders fuel the hostility that produces rivalry – as we claim – then border settlement will fundamentally change how rivals behave toward one another, even though the rivalry might take additional time to unwind (Hypotheses 7.6–7.8). After presenting our models of border settlement and rivalry termination, an analysis of rivals' dispute-level behavior considers this possibility. In particular, we examine the disputes that take place within rivalries, track these disputes' characteristics, and compare the disputes that fall within rivals' pre-border settlement period with those that happen after border settlement. Tables 8.1 and 8.2 list these characteristics for international crises (Brecher et al. 2017; Brecher and Wilkenfeld 2000) and MIDs (Palmer et al. 2015) respectively. Within the tables, we identify each dispute-level characteristic (i.e., as labeled in later tables), describe the information that the characteristic (variable) captures, and provide the minimum and maximum values along the variable's scale. The latter helps interpret the results that appear later in the chapter. As an illustration, the *Gravity of Value Threat* characteristic measures the most salient threat perceived by any of the actors in a given international crisis. The scale (from minimum to maximum salience) includes economic threat (a value of 0), limited military damage, political threat, territorial threat, threat to influence, threat of great damage, and threat to existence (a value of 6, as well as an "other" category; for details, see Brecher et al. 2017).

Similar information for the remaining characteristics appears throughout Tables 8.1 and 8.2. In the aggregate, these characteristics measure dispute frequency (Hypothesis 7.5), duration (Hypothesis 7.6), and severity (Hypothesis 7.7) from numerous – and often, unexpected – angles. How a dispute ends, for example, offers an indicator of whether it will recur (i.e., frequency; Hensel

TABLE 8.1. *Characteristics of international crises*

Characteristic	Description	Minimum (value)	Maximum (value)
Crisis onset	Probability of crisis onset in dyad-year	Never (0)	Always (1)
Overall duration	Days that disputants were involved in crisis (first in/last out)	Days	
Crisis duration for Disputant A (or B)	Days Disputant A (or B) in crisis	Days	
Trigger	The event that begins the crisis	Verbal act (1)	Violent act (9)
Gravity of value threat	Gravity of threat driving the crisis (most salient)	Economic (0)	Threat to Existence (6) / Other (7)
Crisis management technique	Primary technique used to manage the crisis	Negotiation (1)	Violence (8)
Centrality of violence	Relative importance that leaders attach to the use of violence for managing the crisis	No violence used (1)	Violence preeminent (4)
Severity of violence	The most intense use of violence by any crisis actor	No violence used (1)	Full-scale war (4)
Extent of violence	Extent of violence throughout the crisis	No violence used (1)	Full-scale war (4)
Number of involved actors	Number of states involved in the crisis	Number	
Who approaches global organization	The actor that approaches either the League of Nations or United Nations during the crisis	No global organization in existence (0) or involvement (1)	Multiple actors (7)
Global organization actions	What the global organization does in response to crisis	No global organization in existence (0)/involvement (1)	Emergency military forces (12)/ Other (13)

Characteristic	Description	Minimum (value)	Maximum (value)
Ambiguous/ definitive outcome	Whether actors perceive crisis outcome as definitive or ambiguous	Ambiguous (1)	Definitive (2)
Form of outcome	How the crisis ends	Formal agreement (1)	Crisis fades (7)
Disputant satisfaction with outcome	How satisfied disputants are with the crisis outcome	All satisfied (1)	Single-actor case (6)/No adversarial actor (7)
Outcome effect on tensions	How crisis outcome affected tensions among the states involved	Tension escalation (1)	Undetermined (3)
Whether mediation occurs	Whether a third party mediated the crisis	No (1)	Yes (4)
Number of mediators	How many mediators assisted	Number	

Source: Brecher et al. (2017).

1994; Quackenbush 2010). In contrast, the involvement of mediators, as well as global organizations, proxies severity, since third-party conflict managers select into the more difficult interstate disputes (Gilligan and Stedman 2003; Greig 2005). These atypical indicators, when combined with the more typical ones (e.g., direct measures of duration and violence), allow us to triangulate the effects of border settlement on rivals' dispute behavior best.

8.3 EMPIRICAL FINDINGS

The empirical analysis pursues three distinct, albeit related, avenues of inquiry. The first considers how border settlement unfolds within rivalries. It shows that rivals competing over border territory characterized by power endowments suffer from commitment problems that plague the settlement process. The second line of inquiry demonstrates that if rivals can achieve border settlement, their rivalry is more likely to end. Such a finding suggests the large role that unsettled borders play in creating and sustaining rivalries. Finally, the third line of inquiry entertains what happens to rivals' relationship if border settlement happens but the rivalry continues anyway. We find that, in such cases, the rivals treat each other much more peacefully in the post-border settlement, as opposed to pre-border settlement, phase of their relationship. This, once again,

TABLE 8.2. *Characteristics of militarized interstate disputes (MIDs)*

Characteristic	Description	Minimum (value)	Maximum (value)
MID onset	Probability of MID onset in dyad-year	Never (0)	Always (1)
Maximum/ minimum Duration	Days that disputants were involved in MID (first in/last out; max/min estimated where exact days unknown)	Days	
Maximum duration for Disputant A (or B)	Days Disputant A (or B) were involved in MID (maximum estimated where exact days unknown)	Days	
Reciprocated dispute	Whether the target reciprocated the initiator's behavior	No (0)	Yes (1)
Fatality level	Number of fatalities (ordinal scale)	None (0)	> 999 battle deaths (6)
Highest action	The highest militarized action taken by any state involved in the dispute	No militarized action (0)	Begin (20)/ Join (21) interstate war
Hostility level	Highest hostility level reached during the dispute	No militarized action (0)	War (5)
Severity (Diehl/Goertz measure)	Total hostility displayed within dispute (includes consideration of battle deaths)	Least severe (0)	Most severe (200)
Dispute outcome	How the dispute ended	Victory for Disputant A (1)	Unclear (8)/ Joins ongoing war (9)
Settlement type	How the dispute reached its end	Negotiated (1)	None (e.g., fades; 3)/ Unclear (4)

Source: Diehl and Goertz (2000); Palmer et al. (2015).

underscores the role that unsettled borders play in fostering interstate rivalry. The sections that follow elaborate on these lines of inquiry, with the last section then investigating the alternatives to our argument.

8.3.1 Border Settlement in Rivalries

How does border settlement proceed in rivalries? What factors either encourage or hinder it? Tables 8.3, 8.4, and 8.5 offer insight into these questions, modeling

TABLE 8.3. *Border settlement in Klein et al. rivalry, 1816–2001*

	Model 1	Model 2	Model 3	Model 4
Hypothesis 7.1–7.3 Territorial Claims Data	Huth & Allee		ICOW	
Any conflict management	−0.130 (0.118)	–	0.072 (0.078)	–
Power endowment	−3.415** (1.057)	−3.241** (1.099)	−1.850** (0.639)	0.362 (0.877)
Negotiation	–	−0.263 (0.160)	–	2.815*** (0.615)
Powerendowment negotiation*	–	0.883** (0.328)	–	−2.971*** (0.596)
Mediation	–	−0.114 (0.426)	–	3.630** (1.150)
Powerendowment mediation*	–	Perfect failure (no settlement)	–	−4.129** (1.488)
Legal	–	3.381*** (1.026)	–	6.101*** (1.295)
*Powerendowment*legal*	–	Perfect failure (no settlement)	–	−3.311* (1.304)
Joint democracy	1.532 (1.120)	0.381 (1.127)	0.690 (1.380)	1.655* (0.809)
Allied	0.721 (0.727)	0.348 (0.641)	0.086 (0.633)	−0.450 (0.685)
Capability ratio (ln)	−0.386 (0.422)	−0.172 (0.406)	−0.466 (0.392)	−0.176 (0.342)
Ethnic value	−1.548 (0.829)	−1.215 (0.865)	−0.646 (0.607)	−0.451 (0.700)
Major power	0.266 (0.948)	1.306 (1.014)	−0.506 (1.023)	0.775 (0.931)
Dyad life	−0.362* (0.164)	−0.310 (0.162)	−0.232* (0.115)	−0.371* (0.153)
Dyad life^2	0.015* (0.007)	0.011 (0.007)	0.009* (0.005)	0.010 (0.006)
Dyad life^3	−0.000* (0.000)	−0.000 (0.000)	−0.000 (0.000)	−0.000 (0.000)
Constant	−0.622 (0.891)	−1.121 (0.907)	−1.021 (0.875)	−2.485 (1.378)
N	867	697	1,371	1,371

Notes: Standard errors in parentheses; * $p < 0.05$, ** $p < 0.01$, *** $p < 0.001$.

TABLE 8.4. *Border settlement in enduring rivalry, 1816–2001*

	Model 5	Model 6	Model 7	Model 8
Hypothesis 7.1–7.3 Territorial Claims Data	Huth & Allee		ICOW	
Any conflict management	−0.139 (0.128)	–	−0.012 (0.091)	–
Power endowment	−3.599** (1.135)	−3.420** (1.112)	−2.770*** (0.772)	−0.475 (1.106)
Negotiations	–	−0.182 (0.159)	–	2.779** (0.859)
Powerendowment negotiation*	–	0.798** (0.282)	–	−3.021*** (0.724)
Mediation	–	−0.086 (0.414)	–	3.488* (1.501)
Powerendowment mediation*	–	Perfect failure (no settlement)	–	−3.613* (1.767)
Legal	–	2.827* (1.147)	–	5.619*** (1.471)
Powerendowment legal*	–	Perfect failure (no settlement)	–	−2.798* (1.220)
Joint democracy	1.357 (1.036)	0.358 (1.181)	1.469 (1.318)	2.167* (0.982)
Allied	0.942 (0.940)	0.337 (0.861)	−0.514 (0.672)	−0.972 (0.715)
Capability ratio (ln)	−0.918* (0.438)	−0.871* (0.442)	−0.473 (0.414)	−0.233 (0.426)
Ethnic value	−1.934 (1.107)	−1.513 (1.064)	−1.843* (0.897)	−1.236 (1.113)
Major power	−0.717 (1.147)	0.010 (1.240)	−2.508* (1.144)	−0.836 (1.234)
Dyad life	−0.346 (0.179)	−0.316 (0.166)	−0.290* (0.147)	−0.552* (0.279)
Dyad life^2	0.013 (0.007)	0.011 (0.007)	0.012* (0.006)	0.016 (0.011)
Dyad life^3	−0.000 (0.000)	−0.000 (0.000)	−0.000 (0.000)	−0.000 (0.000)
Constant	0.179 (0.865)	0.179 (0.829)	0.127 (0.968)	−0.439 (1.557)
N	751	584	1,144	1,144

Notes: Standard errors in parentheses; * $p < 0.05$, ** $p < 0.01$, *** $p < 0.001$.

TABLE 8.5. *Border settlement in strategic rivalry, 1816–2001*

	Model 9	Model 10	Model 11	Model 12
Hypothesis 7.1–7.3 *Territorial Claims Data*	Huth & Allee		ICOW	
Any conflict management	0.141	–	0.186**	–
	(0.082)		(0.057)	
Power endowment	−2.972***	−2.296**	−1.907***	−1.085*
	(0.758)	(0.752)	(0.439)	(0.453)
Negotiation	–	−0.058	–	1.465***
		(0.157)		(0.439)
*Powerendowment*negotiation*	–	−0.045	–	−1.445***
		(0.439)		(0.378)
Mediation	–	−0.262	–	0.441
		(0.296)		(0.581)
*Powerendowment*mediation*	–	0.163	–	−0.888
		(0.548)		(0.766)
Legal	–	2.821***	–	0.021
		(0.648)		(0.860)
*Powerendowment*legal*	–	−0.705	–	1.834
		(0.522)		(0.956)
Joint democracy	2.317	2.418	1.396	1.555
	(1.301)	(1.566)	(0.843)	(0.844)
Allied	−0.259	−0.349	0.037	0.043
	(0.526)	(0.564)	(0.453)	(0.450)
Capability ratio (ln)	−0.139	0.038	−0.460	−0.493
	(0.293)	(0.286)	(0.276)	(0.286)
Ethnic value	−2.083***	−3.102**	0.248	0.253
	(0.620)	(1.048)	(0.341)	(0.365)
Major power	−0.815	−0.308	−0.141	0.053
	(0.927)	(0.917)	(0.557)	(0.586)
Dyad life	−0.105	−0.018	−0.151**	−0.142**
	(0.055)	(0.056)	(0.052)	(0.045)
Dyad life^2	0.002	−0.001	0.003**	0.003**
	(0.001)	(0.001)	(0.001)	(0.001)
Dyad life^3	−0.000	0.000	−0.000*	−0.000***
	(0.000)	(0.000)	(0.000)	(0.000)
Constant	−1.083	−1.933***	−1.534**	−2.193***
	(0.609)	(0.576)	(0.498)	(0.666)
N	1,099	1,099	2,112	2,112

Notes: Standard errors in parentheses; * $p < 0.05$, ** $p < 0.01$, *** $p < 0.001$.

the border settlement process in Klein et al., enduring, and strategic rivalries, respectively. Within each table (i.e., for each rivalry population), we present four models: two that use the Huth and Allee (2002) territorial claims data and two that use the ICOW territorial claims data (Frederick, Hensel, and Macaulay 2017). These pairs of models contain one specification that lacks and one that contains the interactive effects that accompany our main argument – namely, that power endowments alter the ability of conflict management approaches to produce border settlement (Hypotheses 7.1–7.3).

The models across Tables 8.3–8.5 yield four main conclusions. First, conflict management in general does not promote border settlement among rivals. If it did, we would see a positive and statistically significant coefficient on the *any conflict management* variable. Yet in five of six models (Models 1, 3, 5, 7, and 9), these coefficients obtain the wrong directional sign and fail to achieve statistical significance at the $p < 0.05$ level.[4] The exception seemingly occurs with strategic rivalries (Model 11), but even here, the effect proves illusory. In the absence of any conflict management, the likelihood that a strategic rival dyad settles its borders in a given year is 0.013 (95% confidence interval: 0.009–0.018) – holding all other variables at their mean values. The probability of border settlement rises with repeated conflict management, as we might expect; after the first, fifth, and tenth conflict management effort, for example, the probability of border settlement reaches 0.016 (95% confidence interval: 0.011–0.021), 0.031 (95% confidence interval: 0.015–0.047), and 0.070 (95% confidence interval: 0.011–0.129), respectively. Confidence intervals around each of these mean estimates all overlap – both with each other and with the estimate of border settlement for the cases in which conflict management does not occur. The various probability estimates therefore cannot be confidently distinguished from one another; in other words, there is a decent chance that the estimates are similar and the increasing trend does not exist. We consequently conclude that conflict management, in general, does not help rivals increase the odds of border settlement.

Second, Tables 8.3 – 8.5 demonstrate decisively that power endowments consistently impede border settlement among rival states (see also Chapter 4 on nonrival dyads). Our focus here lies on the *power endowment* variable, and it must be interpreted two ways. In the odd numbered models (i.e., those without the interaction terms), the negative, statistically significant coefficients mean that the likelihood of border settlement falls significantly when rivals dispute territory that contains power endowments, compared to when they dispute territory without power endowments. We obtain this result in every odd numbered model, making it one of the most robust results in our analysis. Its exact substantive interpretation depends on the model. The likelihood that

[4] The coefficient on the *any conflict management* variable is statistically significant in Model 9 at the $p < 0.10$ level. This underscores that the strategic rivalry population behaves differently than the Klein et al. and enduring rivalry populations.

a Klein et al. rivalry settles its border in a given year, for example, is 0.049 when the rivals dispute territory without a Huth and Allee power endowment, but 0.002 when they dispute territory with a power endowment – a 96%, statistically significant decrease (i.e., the 95% confidence intervals associated with the two estimates do not overlap; all other variables held at their mean values; see Model 1, Table 8.3). A similar effect appears in the remaining models; the likelihood of border settlement among rival states – however we measure rivalry – is 83–97% lower in the presence, as opposed to the absence, of power endowments (Models 3, 5, 7, 9, and 11).

The even numbered models (i.e., those with the interaction terms) require a slightly different interpretation of the *power endowment* variable. In these models, the variable denotes the effect of power endowments on border settlement when no conflict management has taken place (Braumoeller 2004). This will, generally speaking, be a rare event; borders need conflict management of some type to settle, whether these efforts occur directly among the neighboring states (e.g., negotiations), with the involvement of third parties (e.g., mediation) or colonial parents (e.g., administrative efforts), or through major powers (e.g., post-war conferences; see Chapter 4; Owsiak, Cuttner, and Buck 2018). Who, then, are these dyads? The conflict management variables themselves are a running sum of neighboring states' efforts to settle their border through a variety of conflict management tools (see Section 8.2 for research design). Two types of dyads will receive a score of zero on these variables: (i) dyads within which conflict management of a given type has yet to occur but will (i.e., the running sum will climb over the dyad's history, but has not done so before the dyad-year in question) and (ii) dyads whose conflict management efforts pre-date the dyad members' existence, leaving them with no conflict management among themselves (e.g., borders that colonial parents largely settle before the dyad members become independent states). Regardless of the restricted dyads that fall into the "no conflict management" camp, we note that four of six models produce results consistent with the theoretical story we present throughout this book. When conflict management efforts have yet to occur, rival, neighbor states who dispute border territory that contains power endowments are significantly less likely to settle their borders in a given year than similar dyads who are disputing nonendowed territory (Models 2, 6, 10, and 12). Exceptions arise for some Klein et al. and enduring rivals models, but only when using the ICOW territorial claims data to measure the power endowments (Models 4 and 8). The cumulative weight of the evidence therefore supports our central argument; power endowments complicate the border settlement process, reducing the likelihood that it will occur.

A third conclusion from Tables 8.3–8.5 concerns the interaction of conflict management with power endowments (Hypotheses 7.1–7.3; see even models in the tables). We find that, in general, conflict management significantly promotes border settlement when rival, neighboring states dispute territory that *lacks* power endowments. This conclusion receives consistent support, most notably from the often positive, statistically significant coefficients on the lower-order conflict management variables – that is, *negotiation*, *mediation*, and *legal* approaches. As an illustration, consider Model 4, which looks at border settlement within Klein et al. rivalries using the ICOW territorial claims data. Repeated conflict management, of all kinds (i.e., negotiation, mediation, and legal approaches), significantly increases the likelihood of border settlement within these rivalries when the involved states contest nonpower-endowed territory (holding all other variables at their mean values; see the lower-order conflict management variables). In such dyads, the probability of border settlement is 0.020 if no negotiations occur. After the first negotiation, this probability climbs to 0.126 (a 522%, statistically significant increase); after the second and third negotiation, it rises further still to 0.498 and 0.884 respectively – both successively, statistically significant increases. Mediation shows a similar pattern. Absent mediation, the likelihood of border settlement is 0.048 in Klein et al. rivalries when nonpower-endowed territory is at stake. The first mediation pushes this likelihood up to 0.337 (a 673%, statistically significant increase). The second and third mediations increase it further – to 0.840 and 0.988, respectively (the last being statistically significant over the "first mediation" value). Finally, legal approaches follow suit. The odds that Klein et al. rivals achieve border settlement without legal approaches is 0.040 when disputing nonpower-endowed territory. At the first legal approach, these odds jump to 0.714, while after the second legal approach, they hit 0.996 (both statistically significant increases over the "no legal approaches" estimate). In short, no matter what conflict management approach rival dyads use, the probability that they achieve border settlement climbs if that they use the same approach repeatedly (i.e., see aggregate conflict management findings above) and do not contest power-endowed territory.

The latter qualification is key and yields a fourth main finding: introducing power endowments erodes the settlement-promoting effects of conflict management. Two specific findings illustrate this well. First, many of the higher-order interaction terms – that is, *power endowment*negotiation*, *power endowment*mediation*, and *power endowment*legal* – carry negative and statistically significant coefficients (e.g., see Model 4 or 8). Whereas conflict management in the absence of power endowments generally promotes border settlement (i.e., the positive, statistically significant coefficients on the lower-order terms; see earlier discussion), these same conflict management strategies exert a smaller effect on border settlement when power endowments are present (i.e., the positive effects found with the lower-order terms erode when we introduce power endowments; see the higher-order interaction terms; on the interpretation of interaction terms, see also Braumoeller 2004). Second, and relatedly, the higher-order terms for mediation and legal approaches predict "no border settlement" perfectly in Klein et al. and enduring rivalries when we use the Huth and Allee data (see cells labeled "Perfect failure (no settlement)" in Models 2 and 6). A perfect predictor exists when a factor of interest does not vary with the outcome of interest (e.g., dogs never fly). In our case, when Klein et al. and enduring rivals dispute territory that contains a power endowment *and* they use mediation or legal approaches (separately) in pursuit of border settlement, their borders never settle. This constitutes an extreme form of the first finding. The likelihood of border settlement does not merely decline when Klein et al. and enduring rivals use mediation and legal approaches in the presence of power endowments; it is effectively zero.

Figures 8.1–8.3 graph the substantive results derived from the models discussed so far. We set up these figures – and the others throughout this chapter – similar to those we present in previous chapters. Each figure investigates border settlement within a distinct rivalry type – Klein et al. (Figure 8.1), enduring (Figure 8.2), or strategic rivalries (Figure 8.3). Within each figure, the rows present the effects of a different conflict management tool on border settlement, including negotiation (first row), mediation (second row), and legal approaches (third row). The columns use different territorial claims datasets to measure power endowments: Huth and Allee (first column) and ICOW (second column). Finally, the panels within each figure chart the probability that a rival dyad reaches border settlement in a given year, contingent on the number and type of conflict management attempts (x-axis), as well as whether the dyad disputes territory that lacks (lighter shaded region) or contains (darker shaded region) power endowments.

Evidence consistent with Hypotheses 7.1–7.3 will manifest in these figures in two ways. On the one hand, we anticipate that border settlement will be more likely when rivals dispute territory that lacks, as opposed to contains, power endowments. Visually, this means that the lighter region (i.e., no power endowments at stake) will climb faster as one moves left to right across each panel and will sit vertically higher than the darker region (i.e., power endowments at stake). On the other hand, our argument implies that estimates of the probability of border settlement for disputes with and without power endowments will be distinguishable from one another. This presents as a gap – however minuscule – between the lighter and darker shaded regions. These shaded regions each contain both a line, which represents the mean probability estimate of border settlement, and a shaded area around that line, which constitutes the 95% confidence intervals around the mean estimate. A gap between the shaded regions therefore indicates that the confidence intervals associated with the estimate of border settlement for the nonpower-endowment and power-endowment disputes do not overlap. Such a gap allows us to conclude that the estimates of border settlement under these two distinct conditions differ meaningfully from one another. In tandem, these two pieces of evidence would lend strong support to the general argument.

The vast majority of the panels in the figures display both trends and, therefore, support our argument. The starkest illustrations appear in the behavior of Klein et al. and enduring rivalries, when using the ICOW data to measure power endowments (see the second column of Figures 8.1 and 8.2).

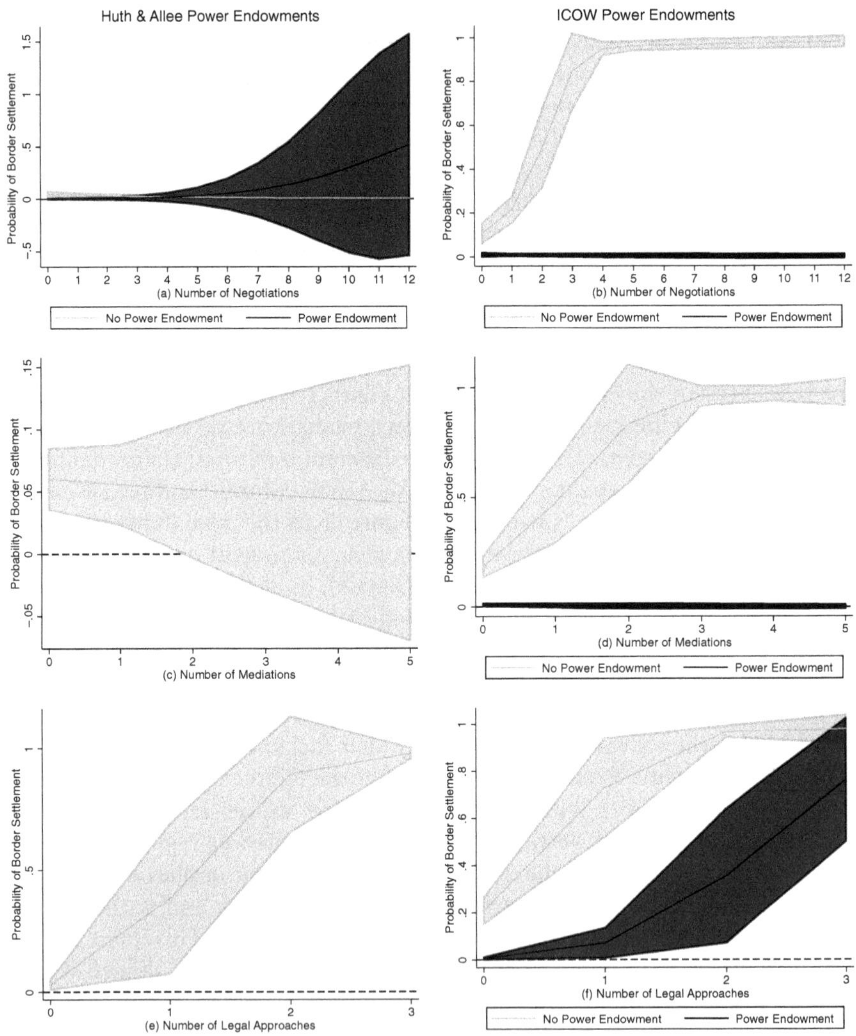

FIGURE 8.1. Power endowments, conflict management, and border settlement in Klein et al. rivalries, 1816–2001

Notes: Results derived from Models 11 and 13 (Table 8.3). *Y*-axes vary to best illustrate results. All nongraphed variables held at their mean values.

Consider, for example, panel (b) of Figure 8.1. This tracks the probability that Klein et al. rivals settle their borders as multiple rounds of negotiation unfold. When (ICOW) power endowments are not at stake and no negotiations have yet occurred, the probability that Klein et al. rivals settle their borders in a given year is low – around 0.020. The first negotiation increases this probability to

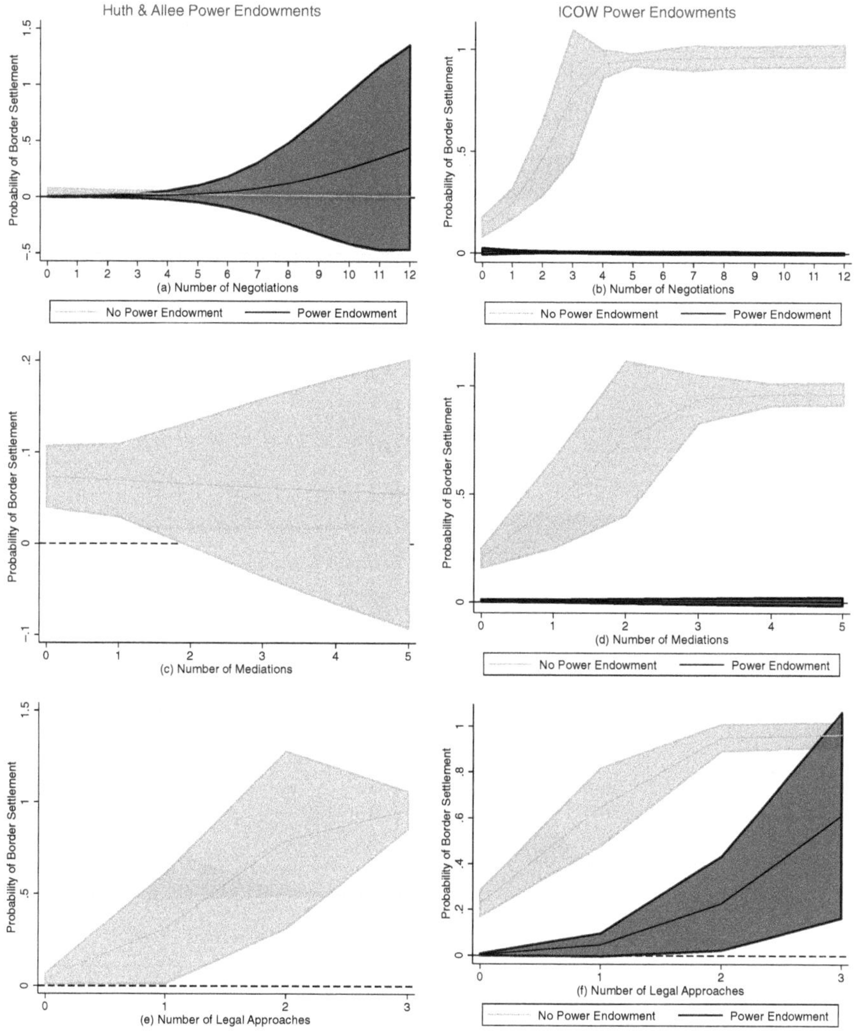

FIGURE 8.2. Power endowments, conflict management, and border settlement in enduring rivalries, 1816–2001

Notes: Results derived from Models 15 and 17 (Table 8.4). *Y*-axes vary to best illustrate results. All nongraphed variables held at their mean values.

0.126, while the second, third, and fourth negotiations raise it to 0.498, 0.884, and 0.968, respectively. Introducing power endowments causes this upward trend to flatline, however. Absent negotiations, the likelihood that Klein et al. rivals settle their borders in a given year is only 0.009 when they are disputing power-endowed territory. Repeated rounds of negotiation fail to raise this

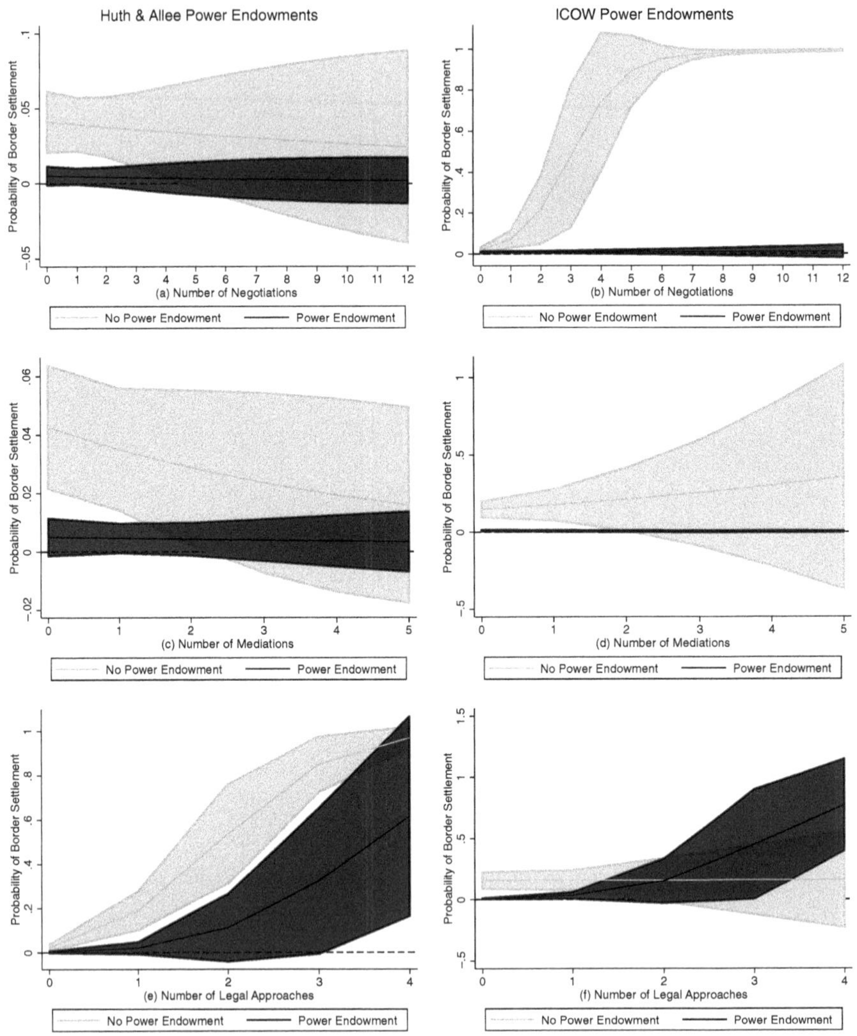

FIGURE 8.3. Power endowments, conflict management, and border settlement in strategic rivalries, 1816–2001

Notes: Results derived from Models 19 and 21 (Table 8.5). *Y*-axes vary to best illustrate results). All nongraphed variables held at their mean values.

probability at all. After the first, fifth, and tenth negotiations, the probability slides successively *downward* to 0.008, 0.005, and 0.002, respectively. The presence of power endowments, it seems, impedes conflict management's ability to promote border settlement. Various other panels in Figures 8.1–8.3 tell a similar story.

This general pattern accords with our theoretical argument. Two different bargaining obstacles seem to afflict the rivals who contest nonpower-endowed and power-endowed territory. The nonpower-endowed territory evokes an information problem, in which rivals struggle both to find the bargaining range and, once found, to agree upon a distribution of the territory that lies within that range. The promise of obtaining better terms incentivizes each rival to misrepresent its capabilities and resolve. Yet, repeated conflict management helps the rivals to sift through this misleading and incomplete information. It clarifies intentions, capabilities, and resolve, and in so doing, increases the likelihood that border settlement can be had.

Power endowments generate a different bargaining obstacle: the commitment problem. This obstacle arises when states bargain over a source of power. Border settlement redistributes disputed goods (i.e., territory), which necessarily redistributes power and strengthens one state at the expense of the other. The to-be strengthened state then cannot credibly promise not to revise the original settlement terms in its favor in the future (from a newfound place of strength), and the to-be weakened state consequently decides to forego settlement altogether. Conflict management generally does not overcome this obstacle because the redistribution of the disputed territory constitutes the sticking point, not the quality and completeness of the information with which rivals bargain.

There are exceptions to this overarching trend, however. As we argue in Chapter 4, legal approaches may be better suited than negotiation and mediation for addressing the commitment problem. Legal approaches lock-in a border settlement under international law, making it more difficult for a state (e.g., a to-be strengthened one) to change settlement terms unilaterally – at least, not without incurring significant costs (e.g., in the form of reputation costs and material sanctions). This explains why the flatlined conflict management trends that we observe for rivals disputing power-endowed territories in panels (b) and (d) of each figure (i.e., darker regions) show an upward trend in the final rows of each figure (panels e and f) – that is, the cases in which rivals employ legal approaches as they work toward border settlement. When Klein et al. rivals dispute (ICOW) power-endowed territory, for example, the probability of border settlement is 0.005 in a given year before legal approaches occur. After the first, second, and third legal approach, this probability rises to 0.060, 0.321, and 0.732, respectively (see panel f, Figure 8.1). Similarly, absent legal approaches, the odds that strategic rivals settle their borders in a given year when disputing (Huth & Allee) power-endowed territory is 0.005. The first legal approach raises these odds to 0.031, while the second, third, and fourth legal approach increase it further still – to 0.147, 0.437, and 0.762, respectively (see panel e, Figure 8.3). Legal approaches therefore increase the chances that rivals disputing power-endowed territory obtain a border settlement – something neither negotiation nor mediation seem able to do.

In addition to the empirical patterns discussed so far, Figures 8.1–8.3 offer two additional pieces of evidence consistent with our hypotheses. First, as noted earlier, mediation and legal approaches *never* help Klein et al. and enduring rivals settle border disputes involving Huth and Allee power endowments (see Models 2 and 6). Panels (c) and (e) of Figures 8.1 and 8.2 display this finding visually. In these panels, there is no estimate for border settlement in the presence of power endowments (i.e., no darker shaded region) because border settlement never occurs when these rival types use mediation (panels c) or legal approaches (panels e) to address power-endowed territory. The probability of border settlement under these conditions is, in effect, zero. We consider this to be a special case of the first general finding discussed earlier. In the presence of power endowments, the effect of conflict management on border settlement flatlines. Other panels estimate this probability close to zero (e.g., see panels b and d in Figures 8.1 and 8.2); here, it is zero.

Second, estimates of border settlement among rivals are often significantly higher in the absence (i.e., lighter regions), compared to the presence (i.e., darker regions), of power endowments. Figure 8.3 illustrates this well. The likelihood of border settlement sits higher when strategic rivals dispute nonpower-endowed, as opposed to power-endowed, territory – that is, the lighter line almost always appears vertically above the darker line in the various panels.[5] There is also frequently a discernible difference between the confidence interval estimates of border settlement that we obtain under these two conditions (i.e., the differently shaded regions do not always overlap). This discernible difference does not necessarily persist throughout the entire panel examined. In panel (a), for example, the regions remain separate in the range 0–3 negotiations, after which they begin to overlap. We therefore cannot be confident that the estimates differ meaningfully from one another after the third negotiation. Nonetheless, (i) there exists a discernible, meaningful difference between the effect that conflict management has on nonpower-endowed and power-endowed territorial border disputes; (ii) this statistical difference, when it exists, always accords with our hypotheses – conflict management efforts increase the odds of border settlement when rivals do not dispute power-endowed territory (not the other way around); and (iii) these general patterns exist across almost all panels in Figures 8.1, 8.2, and 8.3.[6]

These myriad findings are consistent with the expectations of Hypotheses 7.1 (on negotiations), 7.2 (on mediation), and 7.3 (on legal approaches), each of which argues that power endowments undermine the ability of conflict management to foster border settlement. Yet there are a couple caveats worth mentioning. The first is that the Huth and Allee territorial claims data produces results that are less consistent with our argument than the ICOW data (e.g., compare Models 2 and 6 to Models 4 and 8, respectively). The negotiation

[5] The exception is panel (f). The earlier discussion of legal approaches' ability to address disputed, power-endowed territory more successfully explains why.

[6] There are possible exceptions in panel (a) of both Figures 8.1 and 8.2. See the discussion that follows.

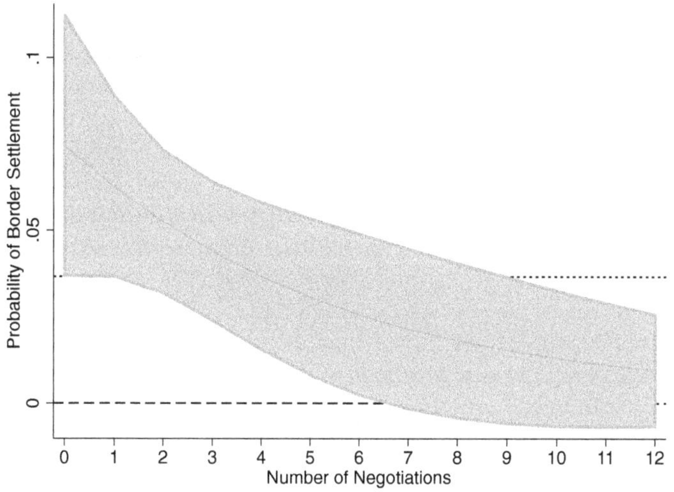

FIGURE 8.4. Negotiation and border settlement in Klein et al. rivalries that lack power endowments

Notes: Results derived from Model 2 (Table 8.3). All nongraphed variables held at their mean values.

variable offers the starkest example. As a general rule, repeated conflict management should increase border settlement in the absence of power endowments (see Chapter 4). Analysis using the Huth and Allee data, however, suggests that repeated negotiations *decrease* the likelihood of border settlement in the absence of power endowments, but *increase* it when power endowments are present – the opposite of what we might expect to happen (see Models 2, 6, and 10).[7] Substantive results reveal a similar conclusion. Panel (a) in Figure 8.1, for example, shows such a trend within Klein et al. rivalries (see also panel a in Figure 8.2). As one moves left to right across the panel, the mean estimate of border settlement declines slightly over successive rounds of negotiation if power endowments are not present (see lighter line), but increases if they are (see darker line).

To illustrate this oddity in greater detail, we reproduced panel (a) of Figure 8.1, removing the power-endowed estimates that distort the *y*-axis scale significantly. The revised graphic appears as Figure 8.4, and it demonstrates vividly that, in the absence of power endowments, the likelihood of border settlement within Klein et al. rivals falls over successive rounds of negotiation. Moreover, this decrease is statistically significant over time; by the ninth negotiation, the upper bound of the 95% confidence interval drops below the lower bound of the confidence interval estimate of border settlement when no negotiations have occurred (see horizontal dotted reference line in Figure 8.4).

[7] The lower-order coefficient in Model 2 is statistically significant at $p < 0.102$.

More than likely, this trend results from the rivalry context itself. Chapter 4 analyzes the effect of conflict management in general, bracketing the rivalry context, and it uncovers no such trend. We find there that iterated negotiations increase the likelihood of border settlement when states dispute territory lacking power endowments (Hypothesis 3.5; see also Hypothesis 3.6). Here, we obtain a seemingly opposite finding. Why? Our analysis in this chapter considers *only* rivals – that is, states who perceive one another as threats, competitors, and enemies. These rivals face pressure to settle their borders, so they try to do so (e.g., through negotiations). Yet, as the rivalry matures and institutionalizes, the perceptions driving the rivalry increasingly undermine conflict management efforts. Rivals lock themselves into a hostile competition that they expect to continue for the foreseeable future. Under those conditions, neither rival can easily convey credible information to its counterpart – the information necessary to overcome the information problem that dominates bargaining over nonpower-endowed territory. Moreover, rivals may not even *want* to overcome this obstacle. Once the rivalry forms, the goal becomes to win the competition – that is, to get a better deal for oneself at the expense of the other. Misinformation, if accepted by the other, promises to supply better agreement terms. This incentive promotes incomplete information, which in turn lowers the probability that repeated negotiations solve the information problem.[8]

Such a finding seems inconsistent with Hypothesis 7.1, but not necessarily. The critical aspect of Hypotheses 7.1–7.3 is the interaction – how conflict management affects the settlement of nonpower-endowed and power-endowed border disputes relative to one another. On this score, the evidence – even of negotiations in rivalry – supports our argument partially. Within the range 0–3 negotiations, the likelihood of border settlement in Klein et al. rivalries is significantly higher when the rivals dispute nonpower-endowed territory than when they dispute power-endowed territory (based on Model 2, Table 8.3, which is graphed in panel a of Figure 8.1; see also Figure 8.4). The confidence intervals *then* overlap, indicating that the nonpower-endowed and power-endowed estimates can no longer be distinguished from one another beginning with the fourth negotiation. The evidence therefore supports Hypothesis 7.1 for at least a portion of the data's empirical range. Moreover, it is worth noting that the reverse is *never* true. The likelihood of border settlement is never significantly higher when rivals dispute power-endowed territory, as opposed to nonpower-endowed territory; in visual terms, the darker shaded region in each figure panel never sits higher than the lighter shaded region without overlapping it. At best, then, our hypotheses receive partial (or moderate) support from

[8] Third-party mediation may not be sufficient to overcome this informational challenge either. Panel (b) in Figures 8.1–8.3, which also relies on the Huth and Allee data, shows a similar downward trend; the likelihood of settlement falls slightly over repeated rounds of mediation when rivals dispute nonpower-endowed territory. The confidence intervals around these estimates, however, suggest the trend may not exist (i.e., they overlap).

these panels, especially during early conflict management attempts. At worst, the results are inconsistent, eroding as conflict management iterates. They never, however, uncover a relationship that runs entirely opposite to our proposed hypotheses.

A second caveat about our findings is that strategic rivals seem to behave differently than the Klein et al. and enduring rivals. In particular, the conflict management variables receive less statistical support from the strategic rivalry models (see Models 10 and 12) than the Klein et al. and enduring rivalry models (see Models 2, 4, 6, and 8). This is particularly true for the mediation and legal variables (see panels d and f of Figure 8.3). Nonetheless, we note that the general patterns remain supportive of our argument. As Figure 8.3 demonstrates, although estimates of border settlement for nonpower-endowed and power-endowed border territory overlap at times – meaning that the estimates cannot be distinguished meaningfully from one another – they frequently do not. Moreover, when this occurs, the nonpower-endowed territory generates a higher probability of border settlement than the power-endowed territory. These patterns persist across all three conflict management strategies (negotiation, mediation, and legal approaches), mimic those found in the other panels, and are therefore consistent with the argument underlying Hypotheses 7.1–7.3.

Despite any caveats, the results presented in this section demonstrate that – as we argue – different bargaining obstacles exist when rivals dispute nonpower-endowed territory, as opposed to power-endowed territory. In the absence of power endowments, rivals primarily face an information problem, in which they try to overcome the incentives to misrepresent their capabilities, intentions, and resolve. When power endowments are present, however, a different obstacle afflicts the rivals: a commitment problem. These rivals expect that redistributing territory after border settlement will alter their mutual incentives to respect any settlement reached. The expectation of an unstable agreement, in turn, undermines rivals' willingness to settle borders in the first place.

Different bargaining obstacles alter the likelihood with which rivals settle their mutual border. The information problem proves easier to overcome than the commitment problem. Thus, the likelihood of border settlement is often significantly higher when rivals dispute nonpower-endowed, rather than power-endowed, territory (Hypotheses 7.1–7.3). Conflict management frequently raises the likelihood of border settlement for these rivals because it helps them sift through incomplete and misleading information. Nonetheless, they will not find conflict management to be a panacea; rivalry dynamics, perhaps combined with the experience of failed conflict management efforts, cause the positive effect of conflict management on border settlement to erode as rivals use the same conflict management tool repeatedly (in contrast to nonrivals' experience; see Chapter 4).

In contrast, (iterated) conflict management is not well positioned to help rivals overcome the commitment problem. Repeated negotiations and (most) mediation activities do not address the factors that make an agreement unstable – namely, the transfer of territory or rivals' post-agreement incentives. Legal approaches offer a potential exception. Because legal approaches threaten reputation costs and material sanctions if a rival unilaterally tries to alter a settlement's terms after signing it (i.e., break international law), they change rivals' post-agreement decision calculus. This does not mean that legal approaches lock a rival into an agreement's terms altogether; they simply raise the cost to a rival of unilaterally changing an agreement. Legal approaches therefore *can* assuage fears and permit border settlement to proceed, although they are an incomplete means of thoroughly addressing the commitment problem.

8.3.2 Rivalry Termination

Disputes over power-endowed border territory drive many rivalries among neighboring states (see Chapters 5 and 6). If this is true, then border settlement should increase the likelihood that rivalry ends; removing the main issue of contention theoretically allows the hostile relationship to turn more benign.[9] Although logical, this prediction need not necessarily be true. Rivalries link many issues together, making it unclear whether solving one issue – even if a *key* source of hostility – will increase the likelihood of rivalry termination (Dreyer 2010; Vasquez 2009). Nonetheless, it is worth asking: if rivals can reach a border settlement, which happens empirically, does the likelihood of rivalry termination increase?[10]

Tables 8.6, 8.7, and 8.8 address this question directly, modeling rivalry termination within Klein et al., enduring, and strategic rivalry populations respectively. Each table presents three models. The first examines the effect of border settlement on the likelihood that a rivalry ends (Hypothesis 7.4). The latter two then unpack this finding to investigate whether the patterns in the data are consistent with the causal mechanism underlying our argument. In particular, they consider whether the presence of power endowments – as operationalized by either Huth and Allee (2002) or ICOW (Frederick, Hensel, and Macaulay 2017) – alter the odds of rivalry termination (Hypothesis 7.5). Various additional variables then also assess the value of the alternative explanations across each of the models (Hypotheses 7.9–7.12; see Section 8.3.4 later in the chapter).

9 An immediate shift to "friendly" terms seems unlikely. Most hostile relationships travel first through a benign, or apathetic, phase (i.e., a relationship at negative peace) before then transferring on to a more friendly phase. See Goertz, Diehl, and Balas (2016) and Kupchan (2010).

10 Elsewhere, we present a bivariate analysis of settled borders and interstate rivalry (see Table 6.1), as well as settled borders and power endowments (separately; see Table 6.3). We do not repeat those analyses here. Because they offer foundational evidence for the discussion that follows, however, readers may wish to revisit them.

TABLE 8.6. *Klein et al. rivalry termination, 1816–2001*

	Model 1	Model 2	Model 3
Hypothesis: 7.4, 7.5, 7.9–7.12 ***Territorial Claims Data***	N/A	Huth & Allee	ICOW
Settlement	0.855*** (0.233)	–	–
Power endowment	–	−0.886** (0.286)	−0.537* (0.246)
Joint democracy	−1.258* (0.540)	−2.054* (1.042)	−1.232* (0.547)
Capability ratio (ln)	0.167 (0.097)	0.242 (0.127)	0.141 (0.085)
Allied	0.321 (0.211)	0.252 (0.240)	0.258 (0.195)
Ethnic value	–	0.660* (0.299)	0.060 (0.256)
Major power	−0.385 (0.327)	−0.506 (0.474)	−0.155 (0.290)
Civil War	−0.119 (0.225)	0.209 (0.272)	−0.141 (0.209)
Independence	0.187 (0.297)	−0.187 (0.363)	0.169 (0.265)
World war	0.643* (0.277)	0.849** (0.289)	0.668** (0.259)
Cold War	1.054*** (0.238)	0.347 (0.333)	1.186*** (0.226)
Power distribution	0.336 (0.457)	Omitted	0.292 (0.422)
Dyad life	0.020 (0.025)	0.019 (0.032)	0.013 (0.024)
Dyad life^2	−0.001 (0.001)	−0.000 (0.001)	−0.000 (0.001)
Dyad life^3	0.000 (0.000)	0.000 (0.000)	0.000 (0.000)
Constant	−4.464*** (0.387)	−3.990*** (0.489)	−3.594*** (0.336)
N	2,959	2,190	3,135

Notes: Standard errors in parentheses; * $p < 0.05$, ** $p < 0.01$, *** $p < 0.001$.

TABLE 8.7. *Enduring rivalry termination, 1816–2001*

	Model 4	Model 5	Model 6
Hypothesis: 7.4, 7.5, 7.9–7.12 *Territorial Claims Data*	N/A	Huth & Allee	ICOW
Settlement	0.920* (0.398)	–	–
Power endowment	–	−0.719 (0.560)	−0.322 (0.473)
Joint democracy	−0.296 (0.867)	−0.785 (1.162)	−0.367 (0.805)
Capability ratio (ln)	0.077 (0.229)	0.063 (0.281)	0.073 (0.194)
Allied	0.170 (0.371)	0.289 (0.429)	0.074 (0.346)
Ethnic value	–	1.238* (0.601)	−0.380 (0.445)
Major power	−0.690 (0.718)	−0.140 (0.869)	−0.447 (0.709)
Civil War	−0.246 (0.408)	0.114 (0.433)	−0.349 (0.371)
Independence	0.016 (0.915)	0.094 (0.759)	0.099 (0.706)
World wars	0.807 (0.538)	1.114* (0.532)	0.894 (0.462)
Cold War	0.887* (0.430)	0.001 (0.549)	1.027* (0.437)
Power distribution	Omitted	Omitted	Omitted
Dyad life	0.264*** (0.077)	0.267** (0.089)	0.205** (0.069)
Dyad life^2	−0.004** (0.002)	−0.004** (0.002)	−0.003* (0.001)
Dyad life^3	0.000** (0.000)	0.000* (0.000)	0.000* (0.000)
Constant	−8.960*** (1.076)	−8.711*** (1.420)	−7.209*** (1.015)
N	1,989	1,608	2,053

Notes: Standard errors in parentheses; * $p < 0.05$, ** $p < 0.01$, *** $p < 0.001$.

TABLE 8.8. *Strategic rivalry termination, 1816–2001*

	Model 7	Model 8	Model 9
***Hypothesis*: 7.4, 7.5, 7.9–7.12**			
Territorial Claims Data	N/A	Huth & Allee	ICOW
Settlement	0.490	–	–
	(0.273)		
Power endowment	–	−0.464	−0.999**
	–	(0.278)	(0.321)
Joint democracy	−0.449	−0.197	−0.362
	(0.756)	(0.612)	(0.767)
Capability ratio (ln)	0.164	0.095	0.199
	(0.171)	(0.195)	(0.155)
Allied	0.243	0.136	0.191
	(0.262)	(0.276)	(0.264)
Ethnic value		0.200	0.795*
		(0.299)	(0.329)
Major power	−0.344	0.068	−0.533
	(0.357)	(0.414)	(0.347)
Civil War	0.040	0.069	−0.045
	(0.250)	(0.281)	(0.244)
Independence	−0.838*	−0.772	−1.052*
	(0.411)	(0.410)	(0.432)
World wars	0.752*	0.553	0.958**
	(0.322)	(0.322)	(0.326)
Cold War	1.092**	1.121**	1.292***
	(0.353)	(0.342)	(0.348)
Power distribution	−0.525	Omitted	−0.437
	(0.535)		(0.533)
Dyad life	−0.004	0.018	−0.000
	(0.026)	(0.028)	(0.026)
Dyad life^2	−0.000	−0.000	−0.000
	(0.000)	(0.000)	(0.000)
Dyad life^3	0.000	0.000	0.000
	(0.000)	(0.000)	(0.000)
Constant	−4.206***	−3.836***	−3.961***
	(0.556)	(0.569)	(0.527)
N	3,833	2,452	4,232

Notes: Standard errors in parentheses; * $p < 0.05$, ** $p < 0.01$, *** $p < 0.001$.

The results presented in Tables 8.6–8.8 reveal two broad patterns. First, border settlement consistently encourages rivalry termination – a finding that holds across all measures of rivalry. The coefficient on the border *settlement* variable is always positive (Models 1, 4, and 7; note that we reset the model numbering in this section, since the dependent variable changes). Moreover, it obtains statistical significance for Klein et al. and enduring rivalries (Models 1 and 4), indicating that border settlement meaningfully alters rivalry termination in these populations. This, of course, suggests an insignificant effect for strategic rivalries, and by conventional standards (i.e., $p < 0.05$), this is true. Nevertheless, we note that the coefficient on the border settlement variable in Model 7 is statistically significant at the $p < 0.10$ level. It therefore not only has the directional sign that our argument predicts, but also approaches the meaningful effect the argument expects.

The second broad result confirms the logic of our argument: power endowments within disputed territory hinder rivalry termination. Whether we measure power endowments with the Huth and Allee or ICOW data, the coefficient on the *power endowment* variable always carries a negative sign. The significance of the effect, however, varies by rivalry type. It is strongest for Klein et al. and strategic rivalries (Models 2–3 and 8–9), but weaker for enduring rivalries (Models 5–6).[11] On some level, this makes theoretical sense. Enduring rivals constitute a subset of Klein et al. rivalries that includes the most hostile, longest-lasting rivalries in the international system. One would expect these rivals to institutionalize their relationship more deeply and experience more entrenched hostility than "lesser rivalries."[12] If true, then the resolution of one issue – even an important one like border settlement – might not dislodge the relationship from its historic, well-worn, hostile path (Dreyer 2010; Vasquez 2009).

To understand what the above results mean substantively, Figure 8.5 estimates the effect of border settlement on the probability of rivalry termination. We begin with the aggregate point predictions, which appear in the first column of the figure. Each panel in this column presents the probability of rivalry termination under two possible conditions: when rivals have either unsettled borders (the left, lighter line in the panels) or settled borders (the right, darker line in the panels). These probability estimates contain both a mean prediction (the dot) and a 95% confidence interval around that mean (the line). Finally, because our argument anticipates that rivalry termination is significantly higher when rivals' borders are settled – as opposed to when they are not – we insert a dotted, horizontal reference line at the top end of the 95% confidence interval associated with the unsettled borders condition. If the "settled border" estimate,

[11] The coefficient on the *power endowment* variable is statistically significant at the $p < 0.10$ level in Model 8.

[12] This is the term that Goertz, Diehl, and Balas (2016) use.

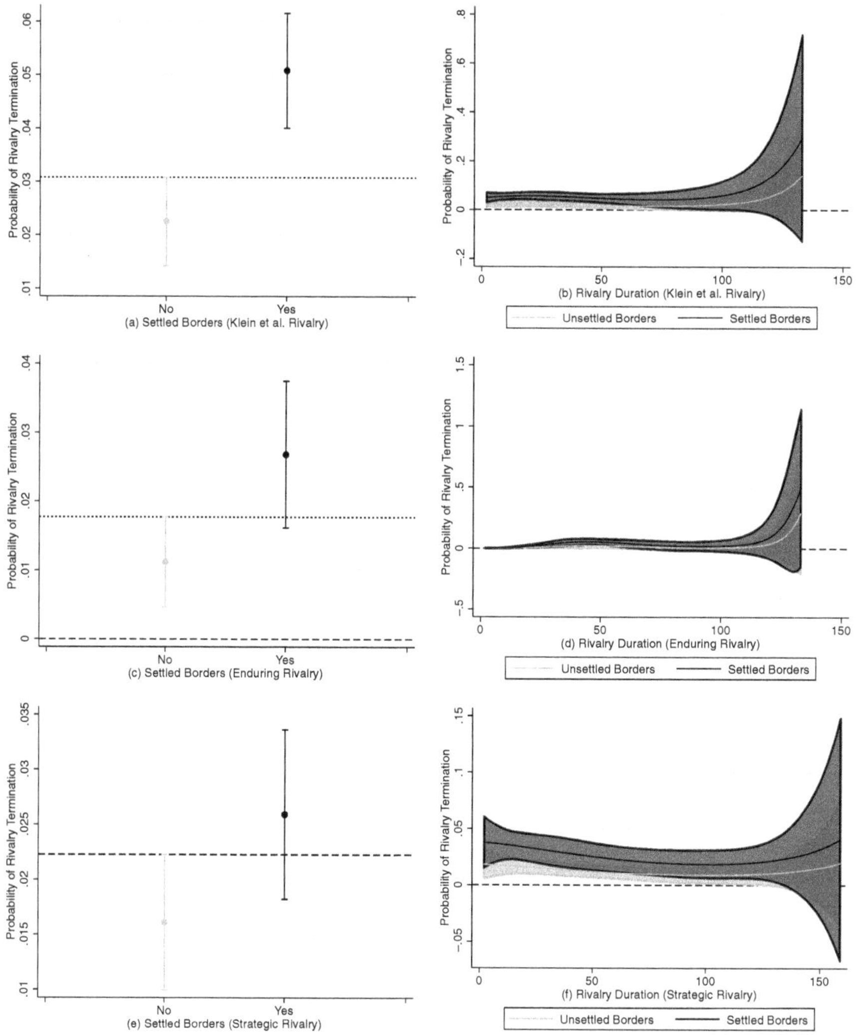

FIGURE 8.5. Settled borders and rivalry termination, 1816–2001

Notes: Results derived from Models 1 (Table 8.6), 4 (Table 8.7), and 7 (Table 8.8). *Y*-axes vary to best illustrate results. All nongraphed variables held at their mean values.

including the entirety of its confidence interval, lies above this reference line in a given panel, the evidence for that panel strongly supports our argument.

The first column of Figure 8.5 offers moderate support for our argument (Hypothesis 7.4). The probability that a Klein et al. rivalry ends in a given dyad-year is 0.023 if the rivals have unsettled borders (panel a); that probability, however, increases to 0.051 if the rivals possess settled borders instead – a

126%, statistically significant increase. A similar effect occurs for enduring and strategic rivalries as well (panels c and e respectively). Enduring rivalries are 139% more likely to end when they have settled borders – as opposed to when they do not – while strategic rivals are 61% more likely to end under the same conditions. Neither of these two effects, however, is statistically significant (i.e., the 95% confidence interval crosses the horizontal reference line, indicating an overlap between the unsettled and settled border estimates). The direction of the effect for these latter two rivalry types, in other words, coincides with our argument, but its magnitude leaves us less confident that the effect we observe is meaningful.[13] Such results, in the aggregate, lend moderate support to Hypothesis 7.4. Rivals that have settled their borders are generally more likely than those with unsettled borders to end their rivalry relationship; this effect is strongest and most meaningful for Klein et al. rivalries, less so for enduring rivalries, and weakest for strategic rivals.

In Chapter 6, we demonstrate that unsettled borders promote rivalry onset, but that this effect also varies over the life of a contiguous dyad (see Figure 6.4). One may therefore wonder whether the effects of border settlement on rivalry termination vary over time too – here, over the life of a contiguous rival dyad's lifespan. The time trend (i.e., *dyad life*) variables in Tables 8.6–8.8 allow us to investigate this question. The coefficients on these time trend variables are often not statistically significant (for an exception, see Table 8.7). Nevertheless, the use of a linear, quadratic, and cubic term complicate the ability to understand the variables' cumulative, substantive effect. We therefore chart the predicted probability of rivalry termination across rivals' lifespan. Figure 8.6 examines the baseline probability of rivalry termination over time – that is, without introducing the settled status of borders – as a way to understand any general, underlying temporal trends. Panels (a), (b), and (c) of the figure report predictions that Klein et al., enduring, and strategic rivalries, respectively, will end. As elsewhere, the line in each panel tracks the mean probability estimate of rivalry termination at any given point in an average rival's life, while the shaded area around that line captures the 95% confidence interval associated with the mean estimate.

Figure 8.6 suggests two main patterns. First, the mean likelihood of rivalry termination does shift over time, although the exact pattern depends on the rivalry population under investigation. Termination in the Klein et al. and enduring rivalries follows a cubic function. In their first years, the likelihood that Klein et al. and enduring rivalries will end is 0.0357 and 0.0005 respectively (panels a and b). It then climbs until reaching a peak in each rivalry's mid-life. For Klein et al. rivalries, the peak appears in year 18 of the rivalry

[13] The confidence interval overlap associated with the enduring rivalry estimates is 0.0015481 (i.e., the upper bound of the unsettled border estimate is 0.0177290, while the lower bound of the settled border estimate is 0.0161809). This explains why we lean optimistic, rather than pessimistic, in our assessment here.

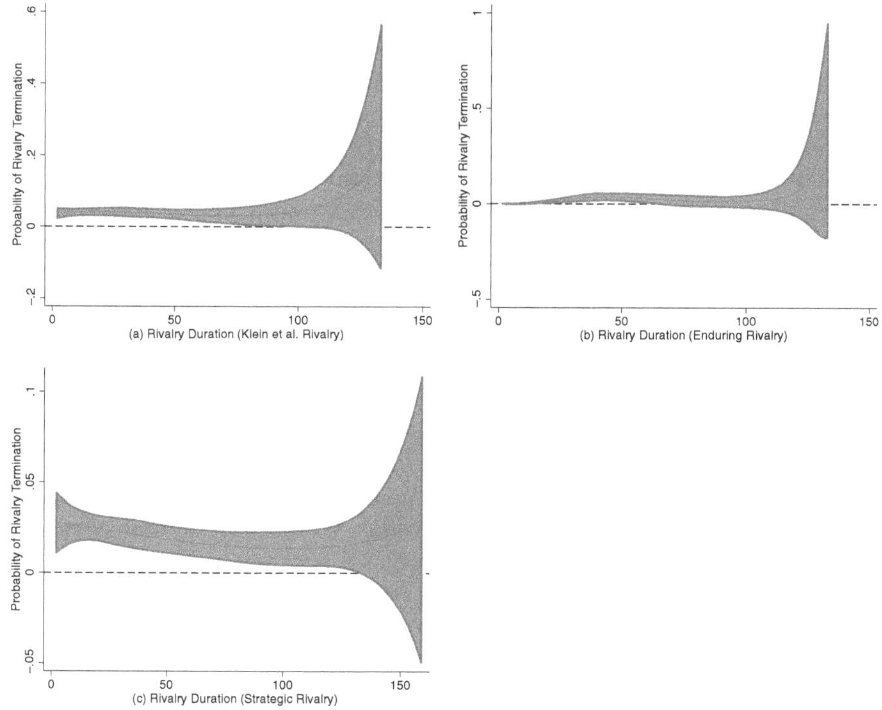

FIGURE 8.6. Rivalry termination over a rival dyad's life, 1816–2001

Notes: Results derived from Models 1 (Table 8.6), 4 (Table 8.7), and 7 (Table 8.8). *Y*-axes vary to best illustrate results. All nongraphed variables held at their mean values.

(a value of 0.041; a statistically insignificant increase over the year-one value), while for enduring rivalries, it occurs in year 43 (a value of 0.039; a statistically significant increase over the year-one value). The likelihood next falls, hitting a low point of 0.030 in year 70 of Klein et al. rivalries and 0.013 in year 91 of enduring rivalries (both a statistically insignificant change over the year-one and high values just noted). Finally, after this, the probability of rivalry termination rises again; before the oldest Klein et al. and enduring rivalry leaves our dataset, the model estimates the likelihood of rivalry termination at 0.225 and 0.388, respectively (both statistically insignificant changes over the previous values noted).

Strategic rivalries, in contrast, follow a quadratic function (panel c). In their first year, the likelihood that a strategic rivalry ends is 0.027. It then falls until it hits a low of 0.013 in year 99 of the strategic rivalry, before climbing again to 0.030 when the oldest strategic rivalry exits our data. None of these values differs in a statistically meaningful way from each other (i.e., the 95% confidence intervals all overlap).

It is unwise to make too much of these patterns. As noted, the confidence intervals associated with the various probability estimates nearly always overlap (within rivalry population types). This suggests that the cubic or quadratic trends we observe in the mean probability estimates may be nonexistent (for an exception, see enduring rivalries), and two explanations exist for such a "nonfinding." On the one hand, it may result from insufficient data. The figure demonstrates that the model struggles to estimate the likelihood of rivalry termination accurately as rivalries age. After year 100, for example, the confidence intervals expand quickly outward – a function of the fact that few rivalries survive to such ages. Additional data might permit more accurate estimates (i.e., smaller confidence intervals), which would then reveal (or not) any underlying trends with greater confidence. On the other hand, it is possible that no cubic or quadratic trends actually exist. This seems the likelier conclusion, particularly for the younger rivalries on which more data can be had.

What then *can* be concluded from Figure 8.6 with confidence? In short, a second, simpler conclusion: *ceteris paribus*, rivalries are almost always at some risk of ending. Each panel of Figure 8.6 contains a dotted, horizontal reference line at zero. If the entire shaded region (i.e., 95% confidence interval) sits above this line at any given rivalry age (i.e., value of the x-axis), then we can confidently conclude that the rivalry's risk of ending is greater than zero for rivals of that age. This happens for large sections of the panels in the figure. Klein et al. rivalries, for example, experience a positive likelihood of rivalry termination at ages 1–104. Enduring and strategic rivalries face a similar positive likelihood during ages 8–65 and 1–132, respectively. Such a finding should not be surprising. Rivalries are expensive to maintain, since they demand significant resource investment; as a result, rivals will look for opportunities to terminate their hostile relationship and redirect resources if they can.

The next question to ask is: do the above baseline results differ according to the settled status of rivals' borders? The second column of Figure 8.5 answers this question. It presents the probability that Klein et al. (panel b), enduring (panel d), and strategic rivalries (panel e) end subject to two conditions. The first is the age of the rivalry (i.e., the x-axis). The second is the status of the rival dyad's borders, either unsettled (lighter shaded) or settled (darker shaded). As in previous figures, the mean probability estimate of rivalry termination under each condition appears as a line, while the area around that line represents the 95% confidence interval. (Because the confidence intervals associated with the settled and unsettled border estimates overlap in each panel, the lighter, unsettled border region often disappears somewhat behind the darker, settled border region.)

Our argument proposes that the probability of rivalry termination is higher when rivals have settled – as opposed to unsettled – borders (Hypothesis 7.4). The strongest evidence in support of this argument will manifest visually in the second column of Figure 8.5 in two ways: a darker line that sits above a lighter line, and a darker region that sits entirely above the lighter region (ideally, with a sizable gap between the two). One panel – the Klein et al. rivalries (panel b) – provides exactly this evidence. Throughout the entire panel, the probability that a Klein et al. rivalry ends is higher when the rivals' borders are settled, compared to when they are not. In the first year of the rivalry, for example, the likelihood that the rivalry ends is 0.019 if borders are unsettled, but 0.050 if they are (i.e., 158% higher). This difference persists throughout rivals' lifespan. Klein et al. rivals with unsettled borders face a 0.022 chance that their rivalry ends in their 25th year of existence – a probability that clocks in at 0.018, 0.016, and 0.024 in the rivals' 50th, 75th, and 100th year, respectively. In contrast, the probability that a Klein et al. rivalry with settled borders ends is 0.056, 0.047, 0.042, and 0.061 in rivals' 25th, 50th, 75th, and 100th year, respectively. These latter estimates consistently sit 155–160% higher than the unsettled border estimates. Moreover, the differences between the unsettled and settled border estimates are often statistically meaningful. That is, the 95% confidence intervals around the two sets of estimates do not overlap one another if the rivals are less than fifty-two years old (see the gap between the shaded regions in panel b of Figure 8.5). We can therefore confidently conclude that Klein et al. rivals with settled borders are more likely to end their rivalry than similar rivals without settled borders – provided they are less than fifty-two years old. After that age, the confidence intervals expand rapidly (see earlier discussion on why this occurs); this erodes our confidence in such a conclusion, even though we note that the mean probability estimates always correspond with our argument's expectation (i.e., the mean probability estimate associated with settled borders always is higher than that associated with unsettled borders).

The remaining rivalry types show weaker evidence consistent with Hypothesis 7.4. Enduring rivals with settled borders experience a 137–146% higher likelihood of rivalry termination than their counterparts with unsettled borders (panel d, Figure 8.5).[14] This effect, although consistent with our hypothesis's prediction, is never statistically meaningful; the confidence intervals associated with the unsettled and settled border estimates overlap one another significantly, regardless of the enduring rivals' age. Similar results obtain for strategic rivals (panel f, Figure 8.5). When it has settled – as opposed to unsettled borders – the likelihood that a strategic rivalry ends is roughly 107–109% higher. This effect, once again, coincides with Hypothesis 7.4; yet it too is never statistically meaningful, although acute observers will see that it comes close to being so briefly in strategic rivals' teenage years (e.g., there is only an overlap of 0.0005172 at age 18). In the end, settled borders exert the effect on enduring and strategic rivalry termination that Hypothesis 7.4 predicts, but not strongly. Moreover, the overlap in the confidence intervals suggests a chance that the difference between the estimates associated with settled and unsettled borders

[14] The range results because the exact difference varies slightly over the course of the rivalry's lifespan.

in these two rivalry types may be zero. We are therefore less confident that such an effect exists within enduring and strategic rivalries.

Why does border settlement exert this effect? To investigate this question further, we next turn our attention to power endowments. According to our theoretical argument, border settlement alters rivalry onset and termination through commitment problems, which arise most concretely when the border territory under dispute contains power endowments (i.e., strategic or economic value whose (re)distribution threatens to destabilize dyad members' relative power if border settlement occurs). In earlier chapters, we show that settled borders and rivalry (generally) go hand-in-hand (see Table 6.1); in fact, unsettled borders place a dyad at greater risk of forming a rivalry (however measured; see Table 6.2). This is consistent with the commitment problem logic we advance. Unsettled borders disproportionately contain power endowments (see Table 6.3). Moreover, power endowments impede border settlement and foster rivalry formation (see Table 4.6, as well as Tables 6.4 and 6.5) – a pattern in the data that is consistent with the causal mechanism linking border settlement on the one hand and rivalries on the other.

The current chapter searches for still further evidence of such a link. We begin with a bivariate analysis of the relationship between power endowments and rivalry, which appears in Tables 8.9–8.10. The first of these tables uses the Huth and Allee power endowment data, while the second uses ICOW power endowment data instead. Within both tables, we present the bivariate relationship between power endowments (however measured) and rivalry for each of the three distinct rivalry indicators – Klein et al. rivalries (upper panel), enduring rivalries (middle panel), and strategic rivalries (lower panel).

The various panels of these tables produce two main associations. First, power endowments and rivalry are positively related, regardless of how we measure either power endowments or rivalry. Within dyads whose members do not dispute power-endowed territory, for example, Klein et al. rivalries appear in only 9.98% (n = 1,554 of 15,568; first row, second column of Table 8.10) to 13.20% (n = 2,142 of 16,230; first row, second column of Table 8.9) of contiguous dyad-years, depending on the power endowment data used. These percentages jump markedly, however, if dyads dispute power-endowed territory. When valuable territory is at stake, Klein et al. rivalries instead appear in 41.67% (n = 1,754 of 4,209; second row, second column of Table 8.10) to 52.06% (n = 897 of 1,723; second row, second column of Table 8.9) of contiguous dyad-years – a 294–318% change. The remaining rivalry types produce a similar finding. Enduring rivals exist in 5.45–8.34% of contiguous dyad-years when no power-endowed territory is under dispute, but 33.29–44.92% of contiguous dyad-years when it is (a 439–511% change). Likewise, strategic rivalry features in 12.37–19.82% of contiguous dyad-years when no power-endowed territory is under dispute, but 59.78–60.71% of contiguous

TABLE 8.9. *Huth & Allee power endowments and interstate rivalry, 1816–2001*

	Klein et al. Rivalry		
	No (row percentage)	Yes (row percentage)	Total
No power endowment	14,088 (86.80%)	2,142 (13.20%)	16,230
Power endowment	826 (47.94%)	897 (52.06%)	1,723
Total	14,914 (83.07%)	3,039 (16.93%)	17,973

$\chi^2 = 1,700$ ($p < 0.000$)
$\gamma = 0.754$ (adjusted standard error = 0.012)

	Enduring Rivalry		
	No (row percentage)	Yes (row percentage)	Total
No power endowment	14,877 (91.66%)	1,353 (8.34%)	16,230
Power endowment	949 (55.08%)	774 (44.92%)	1,723
Total	15,826 (88.15%)	2,127 (11.85%)	17,953

$\chi^2 = 2,000$ ($p < 0.000$)
$\gamma = 0.799$ (adjusted standard error = 0.010)

	Strategic Rivalry		
	No (row percentage)	Yes (row percentage)	Total
No power endowment	13,013 (80.18%)	3,217 (19.82%)	16,230
Power endowment	693 (40.22%)	1,030 (59.78%)	1,723
Total	13,706 (76.34%)	4,247 (23.66%)	17,953

$\chi^2 = 1,400$ ($p < 0.000$)
$\gamma = 0.715$ (adjusted standard error = 0.013)

Note: Contiguous dyad-years only.

TABLE 8.10. *ICOW power endowments and interstate rivalry, 1816–2001*

	Klein et al. Rivalry		
	No (row percentage)	Yes (row percentage)	Total
No power endowment	14,014 (90.02%)	1,554 (9.98%)	15,568
Power endowment	2,455 (58.33%)	1,754 (41.67%)	4,209
Total	16,469 (83.27%)	3,308 (16.73%)	19,777

$\chi^2 = 2,400$ ($p < 0.000$)
$\gamma = 0.731$ (adjusted standard error = 0.010)

	Enduring Rivalry		
	No (row percentage)	Yes (row percentage)	Total
No power endowment	14,719 (94.55%)	849 (5.45%)	15,568
Power endowment	2,808 (66.71%)	1,401 (33.29%)	4,209
Total	17,527 (88.62%)	2,250 (11.38%)	19,777

$\chi^2 = 2,500$ ($p < 0.000$)
$\gamma = 0.793$ (adjusted standard error = 0.009)

	Strategic Rivalry		
	No (row percentage)	Yes (row percentage)	Total
No power endowment	13,189 (87.63%)	1,862 (12.37%)	15,051
Power endowment	1,618 (39.29%)	2,500 (60.71%)	4,118
Total	14,807 (77.24%)	4,362 (22.76%)	19,169

$\chi^2 = 4,300$ ($p < 0.000$)
$\gamma = 0.833$ (adjusted standard error = 0.006)

Note: Contiguous dyad-years only.

dyad-years when it is (a 202–391% change). In short, we evidence consistent with the expectations that interstate rivalry present more often when dyad members dispute power-endowed territory – as opposed to when they do not.

The second finding from Tables 8.9–8.10 confirms that this positive bivariate relationship is statistically meaningful. As noted in Chapter 6, the chi-squared (χ^2) statistic indicates the likelihood that the two variables under consideration have no relationship to one another (i.e., are independent of one another), given the frequency distribution observed in the data (i.e., how the observations are distributed across the cells within each panel of our tables). The null hypothesis expects that the variables are not related, while the alternative hypothesis expects that they are. As the chi-squared statistic climbs, we reject the null hypothesis with greater certainty. Thus, the large chi-squared statistics that accompany each panel of Tables 8.9–8.10 suggest that it would be extremely unlikely for disputed, power-endowed territory and rivalry to be unrelated. If, for example, these two variables had no relationship to one another, then the probability of our obtaining the frequency distributions displayed in the various panels of Tables 8.9–8.10 is less than 0.000.[15]

In addition, the gamma (γ) statistic measures the strength of the bivariate relationship. A value of 0 indicates no relationship, while -1 and 1 signify a perfect negative and positive relationship, respectively (for more details, see Blalock 1979). Each panel of Tables 8.9–8.10 reports a positive, moderate-to-strong relationship between disputed, power-endowed territory and rivalry. Regardless of how we measure either power-endowed territory or rivalry, the gamma statistic ranges from 0.715 (lower panel, Table 8.9) to 0.833 (lower panel, Table 8.10). We can therefore confidently conclude that, if interstate rivalry exists within a contiguous dyad, it disproportionately does so when the dyad members dispute power-endowed territory. Such a finding not only potentially explains why power-endowed territory facilitates rivalry onset, but also why rivalries might persist (or alternatively, not end). If this territory fosters rivalry, then resolving the territory's status offers one path to rivalry termination (Hypothesis 7.5).

The bivariate analysis presented earlier offers prima facie evidence consistent with our argument, but does not address Hypothesis 7.5 directly. In particular, it misses two aspects of the hypothesis. First, it focuses on rivalry generally, rather than rivalry termination specifically. A correlation between power endowments and rivalry (generally) might hide a null relationship between power endowments and rivalry termination (specifically). We therefore need additional analysis. Chapter 6 demonstrates that disputed, power-endowed territory is correlated with rivalry onset; yet such a finding need not imply that disputed, power-endowed territory reduces the likelihood of rivalry termination as well.

[15] This is derived from a Fisher's exact test. See Blalock (1979).

Tables 8.6–8.8 allow us to address both aspects – and therefore, to assess Hypothesis 7.5. Recall that these tables predict rivalry termination in Klein et al. (Table 8.6), enduring (Table 8.7), and strategic (Table 8.8) rivalries. The latter two models in each table explore the effect of power endowments on rivalry termination, measured separately through the Huth and Allee data (Models 2, 5, and 8) and the ICOW data (Models 3, 6, and 9). A review of these models lends moderate support to Hypothesis 7.5. The presence of power endowments reduces the likelihood of rivalry termination. This conclusion derives from three sources. First, the coefficients attached to the *power-endowment* variable possess a negative sign across every model. Second, these coefficients achieve statistical significance in three of six models (Models 2, 3, and 9). The coefficient in a fourth model obtains statistical significance at the $p < 0.10$ level (Model 8). This give us confidence that the effect we observe is generally real (i.e., not zero); on this score, our confidence is highest for Klein et al. rivalries and lowest for enduring rivalries.

Finally, probability estimates suggest that power endowments exert a noteworthy, substantive effect on rivalry termination as well. The likelihood of rivalry termination falls by 40–57% in Klein et al. rivalries if the rivals dispute power-endowed territory – compared to when they do not (i.e., from 0.049 to 0.021 when using Huth and Allee data and from 0.052 to 0.031 when using ICOW data). These differences are either statistically significant or nearly so (i.e., the 95% confidence intervals associated with the pair-wise estimates for rivals that do and do not dispute power-endowed territory do not overlap).[16] Similarly, the likelihood of rivalry termination is 26–49% lower in enduring rivals and 36–62% lower in strategic rivals when the rivals dispute power endowed territory, as opposed to when they do not. Only one of these differences, however, is statistically significant – the 62% decline in strategic rivalry termination derived from Model 9.

In the end, the evidence all points in the direction that Hypothesis 7.5 predicts. The probability of rivalry termination decreases when rivals dispute power-endowed territory – as opposed to when they do not. Nevertheless, the strength of the evidence admittedly varies. Only three (possibly, four) of six coefficients obtain statistical significance. Moreover, although substantive probability estimates demonstrate that rivalry termination declines when power endowments are present, these declines are only meaningful in two (possibly, three) of six calculations. We therefore conclude that Hypothesis 7.5 receives moderate support.

As elsewhere, we recognize that readers may wonder whether the effect of power endowments on rivalry termination varies over time. Figure 8.7 addresses this question and follows a now familiar format. The figure's panels sit within columns and rows. Each row calculates rivalry termination – *ceteris*

[16] The 95% confidence intervals associated with the estimates derived from Model 3 overlap by 0.002.

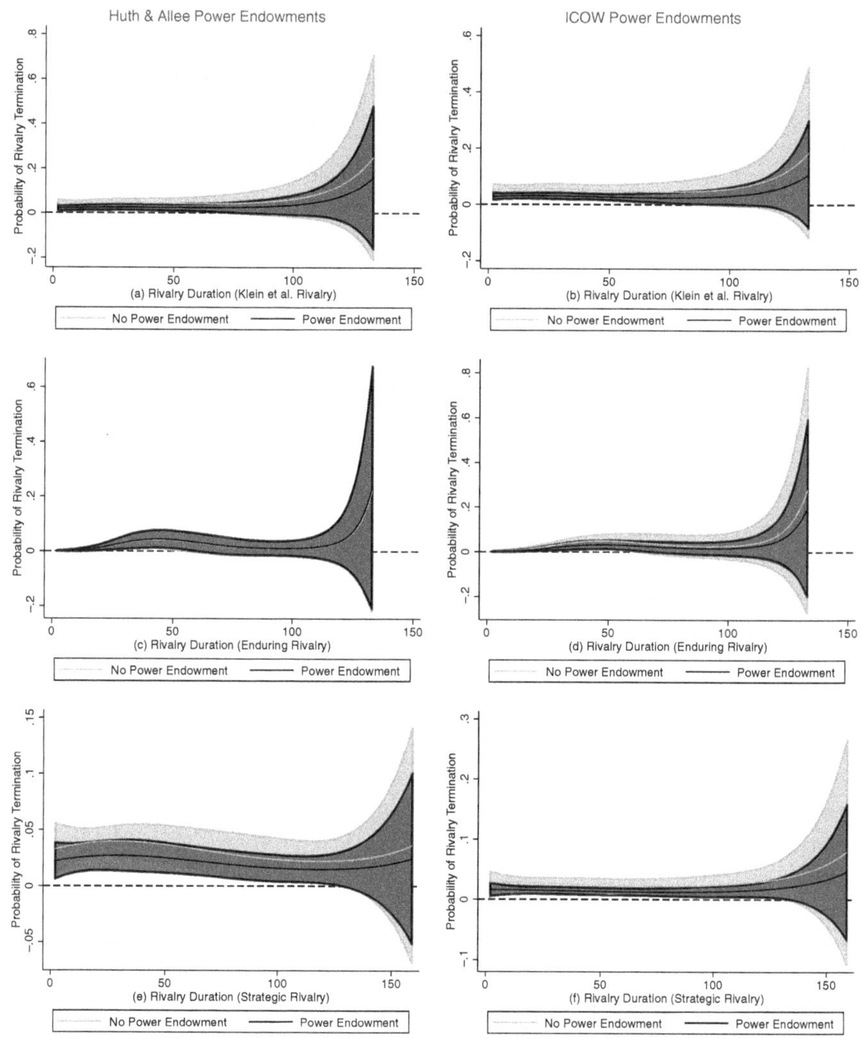

FIGURE 8.7. Power endowments and rivalry termination, 1816–2001

Notes: Results derived from Models 2–3 (Table 8.6), 5–6 (Table 8.7), and 8–9 (Table 8.8). *Y*-axes vary to best illustrate results. All nongraphed variables held at their mean values.

paribus (i.e., with all nonmanipulated variables held at their mean values) – for a distinct rivalry population: Klein et al. (first row), enduring (second row), and strategic (third row) rivalries. Each column, in contrast, uses different power endowment data: Huth and Allee (first column) and ICOW (second column) data. Finally, we capture the difference between rivals that dispute power-endowed territory and those that do not via shading. A darker line (and region) tracks the mean probability estimate (and 95% confidence interval around that estimate) of rivalry termination for the rivals that dispute power-endowed territory, as that probability evolves throughout a rival's lifespan (*x*-axis). A lighter line (and region) then tracks the same information for the rivals lacking such a dispute.[17]

Evidence consistent with our argument will again manifest in two ways: a lighter line that sits vertically above the darker line, and (ideally) a lighter region that sits entirely above the darker region. The former appears in almost every panel of Figure 8.7. The probability that Klein et al. rivalries end, for example, is 42–47% higher if rivals do not dispute power-endowed territory (compared to when they do); for these rivals, the lighter "no power endowment" line consistently sits 42–43% higher than the darker "power endowment" line if we measure power endowments via the Huth and Allee data (panel a) and 46–47% higher if we use the ICOW data instead (panel b).[18] Similarly, the odds that a strategic rivalry ends are 32–45% higher when the rivals do not dispute power-endowed territory (panels e and f). Enduring rivalries, however, display a curious trend. If we use the Huth and Allee data (panel c), then the likelihood that an enduring rivalry ends is 5–6% *lower* when the dyad does not dispute power-endowed territory – contrary to our prediction (Hypothesis 7.5). This may simply be an artifact of the Huth and Allee data's narrower temporal range. If we employ the ICOW data instead (panel d), we obtain a finding similar to the Klein et al. and strategic rivalries. The probability that an enduring rivalry ends is 35–37% higher when strategic rivals do not dispute power-endowed territory – as opposed to when they do.

This evidence consistently supports Hypothesis 7.5. Yet, a second finding from Figure 8.7 undermines its strength: the differences between the nonpower-endowed and power-endowed estimates – in each panel, and at every age of the rivalry under investigation – are never statistically meaningful. In visual terms, the lighter region never sits entirely above the darker region. This indicates substantively that we cannot confidently conclude the differences exist; they may, in fact, be zero.

The cumulative weight of the evidence we present throughout this section lends consistent, moderate support to our main argument (Hypotheses 7.4 and 7.5). Rivalries – however measured – are generally more likely to end when the rivals have settled, as opposed to unsettled, borders. What exactly causes unsettled borders to impede rivalry termination? As in Chapters 5 and 6, we argue that the answer lies with commitment problems, which arise when rivals dispute territory that contains power endowments. The evidence

[17] Those interested in the underlying temporal trends present in the figure may revisit Figure 8.6.

[18] To obtain these percentages, we calculate the difference between the two lines at the rivalry's 1st, 25th, 50th, 75th, and 100th year. Although the difference varies across panels (i.e., depending on the power endowment and rivalry data used), it remains relatively constant *within* each panel, regardless of the rivalry's age – hence, the narrow ranges discussed here.

supports this line of argument. When rivals dispute power-endowed territory, their rivalry is typically more likely to persist (i.e., not end); absent a dispute over power-endowed territory, however, the likelihood rises that the rivalry terminates. Our theoretical supposition therefore gains support: if commitment problems produce rivalry, they likely sustain rivalries as well. Overcoming the commitment problem – that is, settling the borders (on this point, see the previous section of this chapter) – paves the way for rivalries driven by the commitment problem to end.

8.3.3 Pre- and Post-Border Settlement Behavior

Rivalries may not immediately end when borders settle. Nevertheless, our argument predicts that rivals' behavior toward one another will change significantly after border settlement occurs, even if the rivalry itself persists (Hypotheses 7.6–7.8). Tables 8.11–8.13 consider this possibility; these tables examine how each type of rivalry – Klein et al., enduring, and strategic (respectively) – behaves within their international crises (top of the tables) and MIDs (bottom of the tables). In particular, we track a series of crisis-level and MID-level characteristics, comparing what these characteristics look like (on average) in rivals' pre-border-settlement period (first column) to what they look like (on average) in their post-border-settlement period (second column). The final column (*t*-value) then indicates whether the given characteristic differs meaningfully (i.e., statistically) across the pre- and post-border settlement periods (i.e., whether we can distinguish the difference in the two averages from zero).

The data in Tables 8.11–8.13 highlights numerous noteworthy regularities. First, rivals suffer fewer conflicts after border settlement, but this effect is neither precipitous nor consistent. Enduring and strategic rivals, respectively, see a 10% and 18% drop in the annual likelihood that a militarized dispute occurs when moving from the pre- to post-border settlement period. Klein et al. rivalries, in contrast, experience no such decline, and the onset of new international crises changes imperceptibly across the pre- and post-border-settlement periods for all rivalry types (i.e., the *t*-value is statistically insignificant). This evidence weakly supports Hypothesis 7.6. Some rivals begin fewer disputes, but not crises, after border settlement.

The inconsistency of (or caveats associated with) this result might be readily explained. Rivals lock-in their hostile relationship, building their competition and the expectation of militarily confronting one another into their foreign policy apparatus. Through a history of disputatious interactions, rivals learn and institutionalize hostile patterns of behavior (see, for example, Leng 1983; Vasquez 2009). Border settlement loosens that locked-in effect, but may not dislodge it completely – at least not immediately. Changing behavioral patterns requires a watershed moment (e.g., border settlement), the recognition that the relationship has changed fundamentally, a re-orientation of how (former) rivals expect to interact with one another going forward, and the establishment of

TABLE 8.11. *Disputatious behavior in Klein et al. rivalries, 1816–2001*

	Pre-Settlement	Post-Settlement	*t*-value
International crises			
Crisis onset	0.05	0.05	0.0547
Duration			
Overall	160.32	134.47	0.7873
Crisis duration for Disputant A	124.05	98.04	0.8428
Crisis duration for Disputant B	124.90	106.40	0.5950
Trigger	7.05	6.78	0.6287
Gravity of value threat	3.53	2.87	2.9415**
Crisis management technique	6.25	5.55	1.9738*
Centrality of violence	2.49	2.26	1.2130
Severity of violence	2.40	2.07	1.8260*
Extent of violence	2.58	2.21	2.2772*
Number of involved actors	4.84	6.01	−2.0970*
Who approaches global organization	2.56	2.10	1.5972†
Global organization actions	3.71	3.48	0.4213
Ambiguous/definitive outcome	1.36	1.44	−0.9734
Form of outcome	2.89	3.49	−2.3017*
Disputant satisfaction with outcome	2.27	2.36	−0.4111
Outcome effect on tensions	1.57	1.40	2.1638*
Whether mediation occurs	2.55	2.20	1.5415†
Number of mediators	1.59	1.44	1.3914†
Observations: 165 crises			
Militarized interstate disputes			
MID onset	0.29	0.29	−0.0069
Duration			
Maximum duration	225.28	150.75	3.0848**
Minimum duration	215.72	145.84	2.8880**
Maximum duration for Disputant A	215.03	149.62	2.7759**
Maximum duration for Disputant B	223.46	148.81	3.0870**
Reciprocated dispute	0.69	0.58	3.8984**
Fatality level	1.00	0.50	4.8093**
Highest action	14.21	13.75	1.7077*
Hostility level	3.75	3.67	2.1161*
Severity (Diehl/Goertz measure)	71.95	52.83	5.2686**
Dispute outcome	4.74	5.01	−3.5247**
Settlement type	2.56	2.70	−2.7875**
Observations: 1,031 MIDs			

Notes: † $p < 0.10$, * $p < 0.05$, ** $p < 0.01$.

a new, less hostile pattern of behavior. This process may take time, and as it unfolds, rivals likely fall back on the patterns of interaction they know: crises and disputes.

TABLE 8.12. *Disputatious behavior in enduring rivalries, 1816–2001*

	Pre-Settlement	Post-Settlement	*t*-value
International crises			
Crisis onset	0.05	0.05	0.0605
Duration			
Overall	170.65	112.60	1.6631*
Crisis duration for Disputant A	131.80	76.17	1.8905*
Crisis duration for Disputant B	127.58	87.44	1.2930†
Trigger	7.12	6.64	0.9283
Gravity of value threat	3.38	2.94	1.6691*
Crisis management technique	6.22	5.47	1.7764*
Centrality of violence	2.37	2.28	0.3600
Severity of violence	2.25	2.08	0.7993
Extent of violence	2.50	2.19	1.5943†
Number of involved actors	4.72	5.68	−1.4494†
Who approaches global organization	2.53	2.08	1.2981†
Global organization actions	3.80	3.38	0.6497
Ambiguous/definitive outcome	1.35	1.43	−0.9087
Form of outcome	2.82	3.40	−1.8467*
Disputant satisfaction with outcome	2.31	2.15	0.6097
Outcome effect on tensions	1.57	1.405	1.2053
Whether mediation occurs	2.67	2.13	2.0162*
Number of mediators	1.65	1.40	1.7866*
Observations: 112 crises			
Militarized interstate disputes			
MID onset	0.29	0.26	1.8022*
Duration			
Maximum duration	229.66	165.86	2.0417*
Minimum duration	219.79	161.26	1.8690*
Maximum duration for Disputant A	220.34	164.73	1.8210*
Maximum duration for Disputant B	228.13	163.82	2.0553*
Reciprocated dispute	0.68	0.58	2.9851**
Fatality level	0.94	0.52	3.2814**
Highest action	14.08	13.89	0.5531
Hostility level	3.73	3.69	0.7429
Severity (Diehl/Goertz measure)	71.06	53.55	3.8513**
Dispute outcome	4.81	5.01	−2.2098*
Settlement type	2.56	2.70	−2.2135*
Observations: 702 MIDs			

Notes: † $p < 0.10$, * $p < 0.05$, ** $p < 0.01$.

The preceding discussion implies that rivals' behavior does not change across the pre- and post-border settlement periods. Yet *beginning* a crisis or dispute is different than how one behaves during it. Our second main finding illustrates

TABLE 8.13. *Disputatious behavior in strategic (CRT) rivalries, 1816–2001*

	Pre-Settlement	Post-Settlement	*t*-value
International crises			
Crisis onset	0.03	0.04	−1.1062
Duration			
Overall	164.83	118.56	1.4552†
Crisis duration for Disputant A	128.61	73.24	2.1632*
Crisis duration for Disputant B	130.86	82.70	1.7181*
Trigger	7.03	6.51	1.1394
Gravity of value threat	3.44	2.73	3.3386**
Crisis management technique	6.25	5.44	2.1471*
Centrality of violence	2.51	2.19	1.5529†
Severity of violence	2.42	2.04	1.9877*
Extent of violence	2.57	2.15	2.4131**
Number of involved actors	4.97	6.14	−1.9304*
Who approaches global organization	2.29	1.93	1.2450
Global organization actions	3.57	3.03	0.9472
Ambiguous/definitive outcome	1.33	1.42	−1.1426
Form of outcome	2.83	3.55	−2.5598**
Disputant satisfaction with outcome	2.21	2.33	−0.4995
Outcome effect on tensions	1.56	1.42	1.6505†
Whether mediation occurs	2.52	2.33	0.8103
Number of mediators	1.59	1.45	1.1973
Observations: 148 crises			
Militarized interstate disputes			
MID onset	0.17	0.14	2.4339**
Duration			
Maximum duration	236.32	140.55	3.6067**
Minimum duration	226.07	135.06	3.4205**
Maximum duration for Disputant A	224.20	139.45	3.3547**
Maximum duration for Disputant B	232.74	131.73	3.9115**
Reciprocated dispute	0.70	0.67	1.0513
Fatality level	1.05	0.75	2.0329*
Highest action	14.36	13.66	2.0138*
Hostility level	3.78	3.67	2.1863*
Severity (Diehl/Goertz measure)	74.09	61.44	2.7002**
Dispute outcome	4.71	4.94	−2.2432*
Settlement type	2.49	2.62	−1.9963*
Observations: 720 MIDs			

Notes: † $p < 0.10$, * $p < 0.05$, ** $p < 0.01$.

this well: when crisis and disputes occur, they are shorter after border settlement occurs. The international crises in which rivals are involved last (on average) about 160–171 days before border settlement, but only 113–134 days after border settlement (note: the ranges result from looking at all rivalry types simultaneously to simplify discussion). This may over- (or under-)state the matter, however, since crises often involve actors besides the dyad members alone. When we focus only on the rival dyad members (labeled *crisis duration for disputant A and B* in Tables 8.11–8.13), we observe a similar decline – from about 124–132 days pre-border settlement to about 73–106 days post-border settlement. These decreases are statistically significant for enduring and strategic rivals, but not the Klein et al. rivals.

The duration of rivals' MIDs also declines after border settlement. The MID data presents a maximum and minimum duration for each dispute – an artifact of uncertainty about the exact day on which a MID begins or ends (e.g., coders know a given MID ends in October, but not the precise day it ends, thereby producing a thirty-day window in which the dispute could possibly end). Whether we use the maximum or minimum duration, pre-border-settlement MIDs last longer than post-border-settlement MIDs. On average, a MID involving rival states persists for about 216–236 days before border settlement, but only 135–166 days after border settlement (note: the range results from aggregating maximum and minimum MID duration across all rivalry types). Once again, this potentially masks the rivals' behavior; if a MID involves other disputing states, those "others" may drive its duration, rather than the rivals. We consequently restrict attention to the rivals themselves (labeled *maximum duration for disputant A and B* in the lower panels of Tables 8.11–8.13), and doing so yields a similar conclusion.[19] On average, rivals participate in a MID for approximately 215–233 days before border settlement occurs (i.e., between seven and eight months). After border settlement, however, they participate in a MID for approximately 132–165 days (i.e., slightly under five months). This decrease is statistically significant for all rivalry types – both at the dispute-level (i.e., involving all disputing states) and when focusing on the rivals in particular. Such findings, in combination with those on interstate crisis duration, strongly support the expectation captured in Hypothesis 7.7 embodies. When they occur, rivals experience shorter crises and disputes after border settlement, as opposed to before it.

Crisis and dispute duration might decline for a couple of interrelated reasons: a change in the issues under dispute or in the management of the disputed issues. Territorial issues are among the most salient that states can dispute. Border settlement generally resolves them – and with finality – leaving less(er) salient issues behind. Given the lower salience of the remaining issues, states should handle these issues (e.g., foreign policy disagreements or troubles with specific regimes) differently than their border issues (Hensel et al. 2008). In particular,

[19] To save space, we use the maximum MID duration for Disputants A and B, but omit minimum duration. As the dispute-level *maximum* and *minimum duration* values demonstrate (i.e., data involving all disputants), these two estimates lie within five to ten days of each other (on average). The conclusions we reach with the maximum values are therefore similar to those produced with the minimum values.

we expect post-border-settlement disputes to be managed with less violence, even if the involved states still perceive one another as threats, competitors, and enemies (i.e., as rivals). This accords with our third finding: across a number of indicators, rivals behave less violently in the crises and MIDs they experience after border settlement, as opposed to those that occur before it (i.e., post-border-settlement disputes are less severe than pre-border-settlement disputes; Hypothesis 7.8).

We observe a decline in dispute severity through numerous direct and indirect indicators. First, crises begin less violently after border settlement (see *trigger* rows).[20] Prior to border settlement, rivals' average crisis begins with a "nonviolent military act" (e.g., a show or movement of force, which accepts a value of 7–8 on the indicator; see Brecher et al. 2017). The mean crisis after border settlement, in contrast, starts with a nonmilitary act – an internal domestic issue or a verbal challenge to a given regime (e.g., riot, coup, or sabotage; a value of 6–7 on the indicator). Both might be considered nonviolent; yet the former involves the show and display of force, whereas the later does not. In that sense, the post-border settlement crises begin somewhat less violently, although this difference fails to obtain statistical significance.

Second, the salience of the issue driving the crisis declines after border settlement, much as the argument above anticipates (see *gravity of value threat* rows). The threats that trigger interstate crisis among rivals before border settlement typically involve territorial issues or contests over influence (i.e., a value of 3–4 on the indicator). Once border settlement occurs, however, these motivating issues instead involve political threats (e.g., intervening in domestic politics to threaten a regime; a value of 2–3 on the indicator). Political threats still endanger the regime, which explains why they produce an interstate crisis in the first place. Nevertheless, states will find political threats less salient than the possibility of losing a piece of their territory. This alters how they manage the crises that arise.

Third, states rely less often on violence as a primary management technique after border settlement (see *crisis management technique* rows). Crisis management techniques include diplomatic options (e.g., negotiation, mediation, or arbitration), nonmilitary coercion (e.g., withholding aid), nonviolent military acts (e.g., threats or displays of force), and outright violence. Prior to border settlement, rivals' primary crisis management technique falls between nonviolent military actions and violent ones (a value of 6–7 on the indicator).

20 To simplify the discussion that follows, we discuss rivalry in the aggregate (i.e., across all three rivalry types simultaneously). Differences exist in how the indicators behave across rivalry types, particularly in which indicators experience a statistically significant change when comparing the pre- and post-border-settlement periods (see *t*-value columns). This affects the strength of the evidence supporting our hypotheses. It is worth noting, however, that the indicators move in the same direction for all rivalry types, even if they do not obtain statistical significance. This pattern allows us to speak generally. When we cite figures in the text, we present the median value of the three rivalry types.

After border settlement, the primary technique they use moves toward the more diplomatic end of the scale, falling between nonmilitary pressure and nonviolent military actions (a value of 5–6 on the indicator). A more detailed analysis of this indicator (not shown) reveals that rivals achieve this outcome by substituting negotiation for other techniques.[21] Rivals are 2–4 times more likely to negotiate after border settlement, as opposed to before it; yet they do not merely substitute nonviolent techniques (e.g., negotiation) for violent ones. Mediation, another nonviolent technique, is also less likely to occur in Klein et al. and enduring rivals' crises post-border settlement (see *whether mediation occurs* rows), and when it does, it involves fewer third-party mediators (see *number of mediators* rows). We note that this does not occur because offers to mediate dissipate (not shown); rather, rivals bargain directly with one another more often after border settlement and therefore need less mediation – a sign that their relationship has somehow changed.

A fourth set of characteristics looks at the centrality, severity, and extent of violence within rivals' disputes. When rivals use violence in a crisis, *centrality of violence* considers how important decision-makers think that violence is for achieving their goals – ranging from no violence to violence being of minor, major, or pre-eminent importance. This indicator shows a decline across the pre- and post-border-settlement periods, but it is often not statistically significant or noteworthy. In both periods, rivals see violence playing a minor to major role in securing what they want (a value of 2–3 on the indicator). The indicator does shift a bit – from violence being of more major to more minor import across the pre- and post-border-settlement periods (i.e., a move from the higher to the lower 2s). This decline achieves statistical significance for strategic rivals, but proves smaller and insignificant for Klein et al. and enduring rivals.

The *severity of violence* next captures individual crisis actors' most intense use of violence during a crisis. It ranges from no violence to minor confrontations, serious clashes, and full-scale war. The *extent of violence* uses a similar scale to track how crisis actors in the aggregate use violence during a crisis (i.e., overall, rather than "highest level"). Both indicators reveal a similar trend. When violence occurs in rivals' crises prior to border settlement, it peaks (on average) at a level that falls between minor and serious clashes (a value of 2–3 on the indicator). Violence in rivals' post-border-settlement crises sits in a similar range, but shifts closer to a minor clash and away from a serious one. These differences almost always obtain statistical significance – except for within enduring rivalries. We therefore conclude that violence features less prominently in rivals' disputes after they settle their borders.

Similar severity measures exist for MIDs, and an analysis of them yields an identical conclusion: rivals' disputes are generally less severe in the

[21] This variable assumes eight values. When we divide these across two periods (pre- and post-settlement), we necessarily obtain small sample sizes for any one combination (i.e., any one of the sixteen cells). We therefore do not wish to overstate this result.

post-border-settlement phase of their relationship. Fatalities, for example, offer a direct measure of MID severity (see *fatality level* rows). On average, MIDs involve fewer than twenty-five battle-related fatalities (a value of 1 on the indicator), regardless of whether rivals' borders are settled. Yet fatalities are significantly closer to 0 (a value of 0 on the indictor) after border settlement, as opposed to before – a finding that holds across all rivalry types.

Fewer battle-related deaths offer one tangible indicator that MIDs in the post-border-settlement period are less severe. Other indicators reinforce this conclusion. The *highest action* in a MID parallels the *severity of violence* indicator for international crisis. It tracks the most hostile action that rivals use during a MID, and ranges from no military action to threats of force to alerts and shows of force (e.g., mobilization) and, finally, to uses of force (e.g., seizures or blockades). Prior to border settlement, rivals' coercive actions in a MID (on average) peak between occupations of territory and seizures (a value of 14–15 on the indicator); after border settlement, they peak between blockades and occupations of territory instead (a value of 13–14 on the indicator). These actions each constitute a "use of force," but the latter peak is considered slightly less hostile. Despite its small magnitude, however, the difference between the two peaks is statistically significant for Klein et al. and strategic rivalries.

Another way to assess MID hostility collapses the *highest action* scale. If a MID involves either the threat, display, or use of force, what is the likelihood that a MID reaches these various thresholds – which reflect increasing levels of severity? As one might expect, the collapsed scale produces a finding similar to the broader scale (see *hostility level* rows). Hostility within rivals' MIDs always rests (on average) somewhere between a display and use of force (a value of 3–4 on the indicator). Yet their pre-border-settlement MIDs are significantly more hostile than their post-border-settlement MIDs; the former sit closer to the use of force, while the latter occupy a space closer to the display of force. This difference is again statistically significant for Klein et al. and strategic rivalries.

One challenge with the above MID severity measures, however, is their compressed scale; it may be, for example, that enduring rivals experience less severe disputes after border settlement, but the categorizations underlying the above measures do not capture that variation. Mindful of this, Diehl and Goertz (2000) create an expanded severity scale for MIDs (0–200). Their scale confirms that rivals' MIDs are less severe after border settlement – a finding that holds across all three rivalry types, including for enduring rivalries. Prior to border settlement, a rivalry's average MID obtains a severity score of 71.95; this score falls significantly to 53.55 in the post-border-settlement period. What do these scores mean? Any dispute scoring less than 100 contains no fatalities. Thus, MIDs within rivalries (on average) involve no fatalities (see *severity (Diehl/Goertz measure)* rows, in which all reported values are less than 100). A difference in the dispute severity measure across the border settlement periods then depends, in large part, on how rivals treat one another within those MIDs. The data therefore suggest that rivals act significantly less hostile toward one another within the MIDs that begin after border settlement – as opposed to those that begin before it.

The above severity measures all point in a similar direction. To present a thorough analysis of rivals' dispute behavior, however, we also proxy dispute severity via numerous, additional indicators. These indicators fall into three broad categories. The first examines dispute expansion and produces contradictory findings. On the one hand, the number of actors involved in a crisis *increases* significantly after border settlement – from (on average) 4.84 to 6.01 (see *number of involved actors* rows). We can interpret this indicator as a measure of severity. Crises containing more actors are, by definition, more widespread, and common parlance views this spread as one dimension of "severity." The measure therefore suggests that crises become more severe after border settlement. On the other hand, reciprocity in rivals' MIDs falls after border settlement (see *reciprocated dispute* rows). Reciprocation indicates whether the target of an initial threat, display, or use of force takes military action in response (Ghosn, Palmer, and Bremer 2004, 141). On average, rivals reciprocate 69% of their MIDs when their borders are unsettled, but only 58% of MIDs when their borders are settled – a roughly 16% decrease that achieves statistical significance within Klein et al. and enduring rivalries.[22] Under this measure, rivals' disputes become less severe after border settlement.

The second camp of proxy variables considers the involvement of third parties, particularly global organizations. Numerous scholars note that global organizations intervene in the most serious (i.e., severe) conflicts (e.g., see Gartner 2011; Gilligan and Stedman 2003). Prima facie evidence supportive of our argument would therefore show disputes in the theoretically more severe (pre-border-settlement) period receiving greater global organization involvement. We find once again, however, that the results in this camp are mixed. We first investigate which actor asks a global organization to intervene in the crisis (see *who approaches global organization* rows). Prior to border settlement, the request (on average) originates from either the disputants or a third party to the dispute (a value of 2–3 on the indicator); in contrast, after border settlement, the request tends to originate less from third parties and more from the disputants (closer to a value of 2 on the indicator) – a statistically significant shift across all three rivalry populations. Part of this movement likely results from the organization not being approached at all (a value of 1 on the indicator). It consequently seems that rivals either (i) rely less on global organizations in the disputes that occur after border settlement or (ii) recognize the need for assistance in post-border-settlement disputes and request it themselves, rather than waiting for a third party to initiate intervention. Both possibilities signal a shift toward a less hostile relationship (e.g., a willingness to negotiate, especially bilaterally).

[22] Because this is a dichotomous indicator, it can be interpreted as the rough percentage of reciprocated disputes (a value of 1).

We also examine what actions any involved global organization takes in a crisis (see *global organization actions* rows). These actions range from nothing to nonbinding assistance (e.g., fact-finding or mediation) to binding assistance (e.g., adjudication, or our legal approaches) to sanctions to the deployment of forces. As we might expect, global organization typically rely on (the relatively less costly) nonbinding conflict management strategies to manage interstate crises. In particular, their average involvement sits somewhere between fact-finding and good offices (i.e., facilitated negotiations) along the indicator's scale (a value of 3–4 on the indicator). This changes imperceptibly across rivals' pre- and post-border-settlement periods. To the extent that a more severe dispute requires a more costly third-party conflict management effort – that is, a strategy lying more firmly under the third party's control – we see no evidence that rivals' post-border-settlement disputes prove less severe. Of course, if one takes exception with the premise, the conclusion may not follow.

The final camp of proxy variables analyzes dispute outcomes – that is, how disputes end. Outcomes in interstate crises carry four noteworthy characteristics for our analysis. First, they vary in ambiguity. In this case, "ambiguity" equates with stalemate or compromise (i.e., rivals' goals were not fully met at the end of the crisis; see Brecher et al. 2017). Severe crises perhaps produce more ambiguous outcomes. To see why, consider the theoretical characteristics of rivalry relationships in the pre-border settlement period: (i) rivals possess relatively similar power (a definitional characteristic of rivalry[23]), (ii) the stakes are greater than in the post-settlement period because rivals dispute a highly salient (territorial) issue, (iii) territorial divisions are zero-sum, meaning that rivals cannot achieve all their goals unless they defeat the other soundly – an unlikely scenario, given power symmetry – or the adversary concedes entirely – also unlikely, given the high salience of territorial issues, and therefore (iv) rivals' willingness or ability to reach a definitive outcome (i.e., one in which they both perceive that all their goals were met) will be greater before border settlement.[24] Despite such a theoretical possibility, we find no evidence that outcome ambiguity varies perceptibly across the pre- and post-border-settlement periods. Although the average moves slightly from more ambiguous (a value of 1 on the indicator) to more definitive (a value of 2 on the indicator) as we shift from the pre- to post-border-settlement phases of a rivals' relationship – much as the argument outlined above expects – this move remains statistically insignificant for each of the rivalry populations.

Second, a crisis outcome may affect the tension level between rivals. Our analysis reveals that tensions escalate more often in the aftermath of crises within the post-border-settlement period (i.e., the value moves from nearer a

23 Recall that rivals view one another as competitors, which implies a more symmetric (as opposed to asymmetric) relative power distribution. Power alone therefore seems unlikely to drive movement along the definitive/ambiguous continuum of rivals' dispute outcomes.

24 Here, we would emphasize willingness, since relative power will approach symmetry for the rivalry to continue.

value of 2 [reduced tensions] toward a value of 1 [escalated tensions]). This change achieves statistical significance within Klein et al. and strategic rivalries, and admittedly runs counter to our expectation (see *outcome effect on tensions* rows). Why might it occur? One explanation is that rivals exercise extreme caution in the pre-border-settlement phase. Mindful of the high stakes, hostility, and potential for escalation, rivals reduce tensions deliberately after their crises in the pre-border-settlement period. Indeed, Vasquez (2009) hints at such a possibility, noting that many rivals develop a pattern of behavior to reduce uncertainty about one another's actions. Reduced tensions may be part of such a pattern – one designed to prevent crisis escalation from escaping their control. The stakes lessen, however, after border settlement, making higher tensions less dangerous. Moreover, rivals redefine their relationship after border settlement; old patterns of behavior no longer hold, but new ones are not yet in place. These factors cumulatively may promote tension, even as dispute hostility does not directly increase (see the earlier discussion of other indicators).

Third, crisis outcomes vary in form – from a formal agreement to a tacit understanding to an imposed settlement. Across all three rivalry populations, this characteristic demonstrates an odd tendency: crises in the pre-border settlement period sit toward the more formal end of the spectrum, while those in the post-border settlement period reside closer to the imposed end of the spectrum (see *form of outcome* rows). Prior to border settlement, rivals' crises produce (on average) an outcome that falls between a semiformal agreement and a tacit understanding (a value of 2–3 on the indicator). After border settlement, rivals' crises yield average outcomes that rest between a tacit understanding and a unilateral action (i.e., an action that one rival takes without the "voluntary agreement of its adversary"; see Brecher et al. 2017). This suggests less cooperation among rivals in the post-border-settlement period, as rivals rely more heavily on semiformal agreements, unilateral actions, and imposed settlements (additional analysis not shown). Perhaps less salient issues allow them to behave more unilaterally without the fear of dispute escalation. Nevertheless, it is unanticipated.

Finally, benefits (re)distribute in the wake of a crisis, thereby affecting how satisfied rivals are. This satisfaction runs a continuum from mutual satisfaction to asymmetrical satisfaction to mutual dissatisfaction (see *disputant satisfaction with outcomes* rows). Once again, our analysis reveals an odd findings: dissatisfaction with rivals' crisis outcomes increases slightly, but imperceptibly, after border settlement. When a crisis occurs in the pre-border-settlement period, more participants walk away from the crisis feeling satisfied than dissatisfied (a value of 2–3 on indicator). A similar result obtains for crises that begin after border settlement, although the indicator's value shifts closer to the point at which an equal number of participants are satisfied and dissatisfied. This implies that rivals' dissatisfaction with crisis outcomes rises somewhat after border settlement. The difference between the two periods, however, does not achieve statistical significance for any rivalry population.

In addition to crisis outcomes, we consider MID outcomes as well via two measures. The first tracks how MIDs end. It ranges from one-sided victory to one-sided yielding to stalemate to compromise (see *dispute outcome* rows).[25] One might view this scale as a continuum that runs from less to more cooperative, and through such an interpretation, our analysis shows that rivals behave more cooperatively after border settlement. Prior to settling their borders, rivals' MIDs end (on average) somewhere between a one-sided yield and a stalemate (a value of 4–5 on the indictor). In contrast, after rivals settle their borders, their MIDs end (on average) somewhere between a stalemate and a compromise instead (a value of 5–6 on the indicator, but essentially the stalemate value of 5). A closer investigation (not shown) reveals a cooperative trade off; rivals in the post-border-settlement period end MIDs less often via one-sided victory or yielding and more often through stalemate and compromise. We interpret this evidence to be consistent with our general argument. Rather than all (i.e., one-sided victory) or nothing (i.e., one-sided yielding) outcomes, which dominate the pre-border-settlement phase of their relationship, rivals – however measured – significantly shift to more mutual-oriented outcomes after settling their borders. These mutual-oriented outcomes do not guarantee a mutually satisfactory *outcome*; sometimes they are stalemates, in which rivals agree to walk away. They are, nevertheless, not as one-sided.

A second characteristic considers how the MID settles. The possibilities involve a negotiated agreement, an imposed outcome, and neither (i.e., the MID fades without a settlement; see *settlement type* rows). On this measure, rivals display a notable pattern across periods. Before border settlement, a rivalry's average MID settles via an imposed outcome or simply fading (a value of 2–3 on the indicator). A similar result obtains after border settlement, but the indicator's value shifts significantly for all three rivalry populations. In particular, more disputes end by simply fading (additional analysis not shown). One might interpret this in two ways. On the one hand, it is less cooperative; rather than use negotiation to end a MID, rivals simply walk away. On the other hand, it may signify greater cooperation. Rivals are more comfortable with MIDs that end less definitively after border settlement. That comfort may result from disputing issues of lower salience in the post-border-settlement period (i.e., nonterritorial issues), or from a less hostile relationship. Such an interpretation lends our general argument support.

The discussion throughout this section is purposefully thorough. We claim that rivals behave fundamentally differently toward one another after border settlement, even if their rivalry continues. To understand whether border settlement constitutes such a watershed moment in rivals' relationship, we therefore examined myriad dispute characteristics (within both interstate crises

[25] War joining sits past compromise, but additional analysis (not shown) demonstrates that this is a rarer MID outcome and does not alter the conclusions we discuss subsequently.

and MIDs) – in search of differences between how rivals behave in disputes that arise before and after they settle their borders. These indicators point in a similar direction, but not unanimously or with equal magnitude. Readers may therefore wonder: where does the analysis in this section leave us?

In our view, three broad conclusions emerge. First, rivals are no more or less likely to have disputes in the pre-, as opposed to post-, border-settlement period. Although enduring and strategic rivals experience a 10–18% decline in the likelihood of crises across these periods, the decline is never statistically significant. MID onset rates also remain relatively constant across the two periods. Hypothesis 7.6 therefore receives no support. Second, the disputes that occur within rivalries – whether crises or MIDs – are significantly shorter after border settlement occurs. Crisis duration falls from four to five months to slightly less than three months, while MID duration declines from seven to eight months to less than five months. These differences are statistically significant for all three rivalry populations, using a number of duration measures. Hypothesis 7.7 consequently receives strong support.

Third, rivals experience less severe disputes after settling their borders. Direct measures of severity consistently and strongly point toward this conclusion – not only in direction, but also in significance. Each direct measure's difference achieves statistical significance within at least two distinct rivalry populations. Enduring rivalries constitute the exception (when it occurs), but this might be expected. Enduring rivalries are the longest-lasting, most hostile rivalries; if any rivalry population might resist attempts to dislodge its institutionalized patterns of hostile behavior, it would be this one. Such findings – across numerous measures of severity and rivalry populations – lend moderate-to-strong support to Hypothesis 7.8.

Indirect (i.e., proxy) measures of severity also support Hypothesis 7.8, although variance around *these* measures is admittedly greater. We include the proxies of severity to provide a more thorough, triangulated analysis; however, we must temper our expectations about what evidence these proxies can provide. A proxy variable might support a hypothesis (or not) for numerous reasons, including (i) a poor fit between measure and concept (i.e., severity), (ii) intervening or omitted variables, or (iii) a sound theoretical conclusion. It is not always easy to know which factor produces the effect we observe. Thus, we take a simpler approach: if all (or most, or many) proxy measures of severity supply evidence significantly contrary to our argument, we interpret this as a red flag worthy of additional investigation. This, however, does not happen.

8.3.4 Alternative Explanations

The evidence presented throughout this chapter consistently supports our main argument. When unsettled borders create commitment problems (i.e., via power endowed border territory), rivals struggle to settle their borders. The lack of settled borders, in turn, hinders rivalry termination, and further examination confirms that the presence of power endowments in disputed border territory links the unsettled borders to rivalry's persistence.

Despite these conclusions, there exist four alternative arguments to consider. The first proposes that joint democracy facilitates rivalry termination (Hypothesis 7.9). On its face, this argument seems untenable. Democracies behave more peacefully toward one another, so they theoretically enter into rivalries with one another less frequently than nondemocratic states (see Chapter 6; for a null effect, however, see Colaresi, Rasler, and Thompson 2007, 200). Nevertheless, it remains possible that those (rarer) democratic rivals that form – or whose members switch from not both being democratic to both being democratic during the rivalry – face a greater chance that their rivalry ends.

The statistical results decidedly do not support this argument. Klein et al. rivals with two democratic members are 69–87% *less* likely than similar rivals containing at least one nondemocratic partner to end their rivalry (see Models 1–3, Table 8.6).[26] This difference is not only statistically significant, but also runs *counter* to Hypothesis 7.9. Analysis of enduring (see Models 4–6, Table 8.7) and strategic (see Models 7–9, Table 8.8) rivalries produces a similar, albeit weaker, effect. Democratic enduring rivals are 25–53% less likely to end their rivalry than nondemocratic enduring rivals. Likewise, democratic strategic rivals are 17–30% less likely to end their rivalry than nondemocratic strategic rivals. These latter two differences fail to achieve statistical significance, so they may, in effect, be zero; even if this were true, though, Hypothesis 7.9 would receive no support, as opposed to evidence that runs significantly counter to it.[27]

It is also worth noting that democratic rivals are generally not more likely than nondemocratic rivals to settle their borders (see Tables 8.3–8.5; Models 4 and 8 are the exceptions to this statement). Many expect democratic states to excel at conflict management over their nondemocratic counterparts, even in territorial disputes (e.g., see Dixon 1994; Hensel et al. 2008). Yet, consistent with Gibler and Owsiak (2018), we see little evidence of such an effect within rivals' border settlement process. This might be because democratic dyads do not typically have unsettled borders; the emergence of dyadic democracy almost always *follows* dyadic border settlement (Gibler and Owsiak 2018; Owsiak and Vasquez 2019). Regardless of the reason, we conclude that democratic rivals consistently prove no more (or less) competent at border settlement than nondemocratic rivals.

A second alternative explanation for rivalry termination invokes rivals' relative capabilities. As dyad members' capabilities approach parity, their

26 The range derives from discussing multiple models simultaneously, since each model produces distinct probability estimates of rivalry termination. We follow a similar format throughout this section (i.e., focus on ranges that cover multiple models) to simplify and shorten the discussion.

27 Discussion of statistical significance in this section refers to the overlap of the probability estimates' 95% confidence intervals. The statistical significance of the coefficient estimates in Tables 8.6–8.8 (e.g., *joint democracy*), however, is usually identical.

ability both to distinguish who will win a military contest between them and to defeat one another soundly declines. Three effects follow. First, both states compete earnestly for the disputed good, since each stands a decent chance of obtaining it. The result of their competition is not a foregone conclusion. Second, the likelihood of a militarized conflict rises (Fearon 1995). Whereas a substantially weaker state often lacks the ability to convince a substantially stronger one that it will win a military contest they have, states with more equal capabilities can mislead one another more easily. Misrepresentations about capabilities or resolve consequently offer the promise of significant, marginal gains. This incentive to misrepresent the state's position, however, decreases the probability that the involved states avoid military conflict. Finally, given their relative parity, any militarized dispute will likely end in a stalemate, rather than a victory for one side or the other. The dispute therefore festers, recurs, and sours the interstate relationship. In this way, the probability of rivalry termination falls (i.e., the rivalry becomes more likely to persist) as dyad members' capabilities approach parity and rises as these capabilities become more asymmetric (Hypothesis 5.10).

Our analysis uncovers no support for this hypothesis. As Klein et al. rivals move from conditions of extreme parity to extreme asymmetry (i.e., the 5th to 95th percentile of the *capability ratio's* value), the probability of rivalry termination rises 66–153% as the hypothesis expects; yet these changes are never statistically significant. Similar, albeit smaller, increases of 26–32% and 21–60% derive from our models of enduring and strategic rivalry termination respectively; once again, however, these increases never achieve statistical significance. That extreme conditions reveal no effect gives us pause. These conditions represent the best case scenario for the argument. Nevertheless, we are mindful that a variable's effect may vary across its range of values and consequently calculate probability estimates at the 25th, 50th, and 75th percentile values of the *capability ratio* as well. Under no circumstances, though, do we discover probability estimates that achieve statistical significance. Simply put, power parity exerts no discernible, meaningful effect on rivalry termination.

The third alternative explanation for rivalry termination stresses alliance relationships. It argues that dyad members who are allied to one another are more likely to end their rivalry (Hypothesis 7.11). In so doing. it, too, seems odd at first glance. Rivalries and alliances are generally incompatible relationships (Goertz, Diehl, and Balas 2016; Kupchan 2010); it would be unusual, in other words, for the same pair of states to perceive one another mutually as a threat, enemy, and competitor, while also coordinating security policy – however shallowly. More plausibly, an alliance could form during the rivalry and subsequently raise the prospect of rivalry termination.

Such a scenario necessarily envisions fast timing; once the alliance forms, the rivalry probably ends quickly to resolve the incompatibility in the relationship types. Although we suspect the temporal ordering of these events generally runs the other way – that is, states end a rivalry, then form an alliance – we nevertheless consider the argument here. When we do, we find no empirical support for the alliance argument. Rivals whose members are allied to one another do experience a higher likelihood of rivalry termination, but these effects are substantively small and always statistically insignificant. Allied Klein et al. rivals, for example, experience a 27–35% greater likelihood of rivalry termination than similar, nonallied rivals. For enduring and strategic rivals, the increase is smaller and more variable: 7–32% and 14–26%, respectively. The effect alliances exert on rivalry termination may be zero in every single model, which offers extremely weak support to Hypothesis 7.10 at best.

Alliances also do not foster border settlement (see Tables 8.3–8.5). Gibler (1996) demonstrates that some alliance treaties resolve outstanding territorial issues. Through his research, a possible sequence of events emerges. Rivals build an alliance, which then leads to border (i.e., territorial) settlement; that settlement, in turn, terminates the rivalry. If true, then our failure to observe that alliances affect rivalry termination might result from a selection effect; that is, alliances could theoretically alter rivalry termination *indirectly* through border settlement. For this to be true, we would expect allies to settle their borders more easily than nonallies. Tables 8.3–8.5, however, suggest that this possibility has no empirical support. Rivals allied to one another are never more (or less) likely than nonallies to settle their borders.

The final alternative explanation involves ethnic conflict. As we note elsewhere, ethnic conflict features prominently in international relations research, but less so in studies of interstate rivalry. Nevertheless, it is reasonable to argue that campaigns intended to reunite ethnic brethren within the state's borders, along with the possible mistreatment of these brethren at the hands of a neighboring state, foster and sustain interstate rivalry among neighbors (Hypothesis 7.12). We therefore investigate this possibility, but find no support for it. Rivals disputing territory with ethnic value are *more* likely to terminate their rivalry – contrary to what the hypothesis expects (see also the coefficients associated with the *ethnic value* variable in Tables 8.3–8.5). For example, Klein et al. rivals that dispute ethnically valuable territory, as opposed to those that do not, are 6–86% more likely to end their rivalry. Enduring and strategic rivalries experience a similar effect. And none of these probability estimate differences – regardless of how we measure rivalry or the ethnic value of territory – obtains statistical significance. The weight of the evidence therefore runs counter to the hypothesis's claim.

In the end, the various alternative explanations perform poorly relative to our main theoretical story. A contiguous, rival dyad experiences a significantly higher likelihood of rivalry termination when it possesses settled – as opposed to unsettled – borders. This, importantly, derives from the effects of power endowments. Not only are unsettled borders disproportionately likely to involve territory with power endowments, but a contiguous, rival dyad disputing border territory that contains a power endowment also experiences significantly lower odds of rivalry termination than a similar dyad disputing territory that lacks these power endowments. The commitment problem explains why; fearing that border settlement will weaken it and increase its vulnerability, a state chooses to forego border settlement when power endowments are at stake and might shift to its adversary. This leaves unsettled borders – a highly salient issue – to fester, ultimately causing the involved, rival states to continue perceiving one another as threats, enemies, and competitors for a good that each earnestly wants to possess. Unsettled borders, in other words – particularly those with power endowments – cause rivalries to persist.

8.4 CONCLUSION

This chapter confronts various questions that our earlier chapters beg. First, if commitment problems foster unsettled borders that then produce and sustain interstate rivalries among neighboring states, how do rivals surmount this commitment problem hurdle? Second, what happens when they do surmount it? Does their relationship change markedly? Pursuing these answers leads us to revisit the border settlement process (this time, within rivalries specifically), investigate rivalry termination, and study rivals' dispute behavior both before and after they settle their borders. Table 8.14 summarizes the hypotheses we derive from theorizing about these factors, as well as the results of our empirical analyses. It lists each hypothesis, how consistent the regularities reported in this chapter are with it, and the main substantive conclusions we draw about it. The details underlying each conclusion appear throughout the chapter's discussion.

The conclusions listed in Table 8.14 once again integrate to support our larger theoretical story. Rivals face two different problems when bargaining over unsettled borders. The first, an information problem, appears when rivals dispute border territory that lacks power endowments. Repeated conflict management (e.g., negotiation, mediation, and legal approaches) generally helps rivals overcome this obstacle because it clarifies intentions, capabilities, and resolve through an iterative process. The second problem – the commitment problem – arises, in contrast, when rivals dispute border territory that contains power endowments, and it resists most conflict management efforts. A commitment problem results not from incomplete information, but rather the fear that border settlement – through the (re)distribution of territory and, therefore, the power endowments it contains – will be unstable. Conflict management that simply shares greater information among disputants (e.g., negotiation and mediation) cannot assuage this fear, even if used repeatedly; indeed, these tools prove ineffective at resolving rivals' unsettled borders when power endowments are present.

A potential exception arises with legal approaches (i.e., arbitration and adjudication). Because legal approaches ground a settlement in international law, rivals experience significant material and reputation costs if they subsequently try to change the settlement's terms unilaterally. These costs decrease the likelihood that the post-settlement agreement changes, and therefore also

TABLE 8.14. *Hypotheses and conclusions about rivalry termination*

Hypothesis	Evidence	Conclusion
7.1	Moderately supported	Negotiations generally promote border settlement when rivals dispute territory that lacks power endowments, but not when they dispute territory that contains power endowments. Within rivalries, this effect seems to erode over iterated negotiation rounds.
7.2	Moderately supported	Mediation generally promotes border settlement when rivals dispute territory that lacks power endowments, but not when they dispute territory that contains power endowments. This effect erodes within rivalries over repeated mediations.
7.3	Weakly supported	Legal approaches generally promote border settlement when rivals dispute territory that *either* lacks or contains power endowments. Nonetheless, nonpower-endowed territory often settles at significantly higher rates than power-endowed territory – although the effect of legal approaches on border settlement in the presence of power endowments suggests that legal approaches may help rivals overcome the commitment problem too.
7.4	Moderately supported	Rivals that possess settled borders are more likely to end their rivalry than those with unsettled borders. This effect is strongest for Klein et al. rivalries, although some evidence of such an effect appears within enduring and strategic rivalries as well.
7.5	Moderately supported	A bivariate analysis shows that power endowments feature prominently in interstate rivalries. Moreover, a contiguous, rival dyad is more likely to terminate its rivalry in a given year when it is disputing territory that lacks – as opposed to contains – power endowments. This finding varies across models. It seems strongest (and most significant) for Klein et al. and strategic rivalries, but less so (and not significant) for enduring rivalries.
7.6	Not supported	Some rivals (e.g., enduring and strategic rivals) experience slightly fewer interstate crises after – as opposed to before – border settlement, but the decline is not noteworthy (i.e., significant). The probability of MID onset does not change perceptibly in any rivalry population across the pre- and post-border-settlement periods.

Hypothesis	Evidence	Conclusion
7.7	Strongly supported	Rivals' disputes – whether crises or MIDs – are significantly shorter if those disputes occur after, as opposed to before, they settle their borders.
7.8	Moderately supported	Direct measures of severity consistently reveal that rivals' crises and MIDs are less severe after border settlement, compared to before it. Indirect measures of severity paint a more mixed picture, although they rarely point in the opposite direction of what our argument expects. To the extent that we preference the direct measures, the evidence more strongly supports the hypothesis.
7.9	Not supported	Rivals composed of two democratic states are not significantly more likely – and in the case of Klein et al. rivalries, are significantly *less* likely (contrary to the hypothesis's expectation) – than those composed of at least one nondemocratic state to end their rivalry. (Rival, democratic dyads also do not achieve border settlement more easily than their rival, nondemocratic counterparts.)
7.10	Not/weakly supported	The likelihood of rivalry termination rises somewhat as a rival dyad's members achieve less power parity (i.e., more power asymmetry) in their relationship, as the hypothesis predicts. These changes, however, never achieve statistical significance.
7.11	Not supported	The odds that a rivalry ends do not change significantly when rivals are allied (or not) to one another. (Allies also prove no more or less likely to settle their borders.)
7.12	Not/weakly supported	Concerns about the residence and well-bring of ethnic kin living in disputed border territory occasionally raise the likelihood of rivalry termination significantly – contrary to what one would expect theoretically. Indeed, three of six models' coefficients suggest such an effect. When we explore the substantive effects derived from these models, however, we find that ethnic concerns do not significantly alter the likelihood of rivalry termination.

lessen a to-be-weakened state's fear that its adversary will exploit it. As a result, the repeated use of legal approaches significantly fosters border settlement even when rivals dispute power-endowed territory.

Once rivals reach border settlement, the odds then often increase that their rivalry ends. This too is conditional on the presence of commitment problems. Rivals that contest power-endowed territory are *less* likely to end their rivalry than those that dispute nonendowed territory. Findings like these lead us to two overarching conclusions. First, unsettled borders – particularly those involving power endowments – not only create interstate rivalries, but sustain them as well. Although our theoretical argument expects as much, it need not be true empirically. Once a rivalry begins, it demands that the involved states confront their adversary on any and every issue. Rivals, in other words, link multiple issues together, so the resolution of one issue – even if highly salient – would not necessarily foster rivalry termination. Yet we find that the settled status of rivals' borders fundamentally affects their relationship, for bad and good. When the unsettled borders resolve, the relationship transforms from one of higher to lower hostility (i.e., nonrivalry). Second, the most dangerous borders involve power endowments – or the commitment problem – as the causal mechanism underlying our theoretical argument proposes. Unsettled borders generally prove dangerous because states find territorial issues highly salient; the danger increases, though, when the disputed territory contains power endowments. States then eschew settlement for fear that the settlement agreement will be unstable. As the dispute persists, the interstate relationship deteriorates. Bettering the relationship then requires resolving the borders' status, thereby removing the issue from the involved states' foreign policy agenda.

The above discussion suggests that border settlement constitutes a watershed moment in a rival's lifespan – one that holds the promise of fundamentally transforming it. Ending the rivalry and moving to a less hostile, dyadic relationship offers one method of transformation, and we find evidence that it occurs (see earlier discussion). Another method, though, involves significant behavioral changes *within* the rivalry. In other words, rivalries might continue after border settlement; if they do – and if border settlement is the watershed moment we propose it is – then we should see a significant difference in how rivals treat one another after they settle their borders. Our evidence confirms this latter type of transformation as well. Rivals experience roughly the same number of disputes before and after they settle their borders; yet these disputes are of different quality. Compared to those that occur before border settlement, the disputes that rivals experience after border settlement are significantly shorter and less severe across myriad metrics. If, therefore, rivals can clear the bargaining obstacles that impede border settlement – an obtainable, albeit often challenging, achievement – the prospect of greater interstate peace grows.

9

Conclusion

> Territorial [border] disputes have at all times been found one of the most fertile sources of hostility among nations.
>
> A. Hamilton

9.1 INTRODUCTION

China has shared borders with fourteen different states since 1816 (see Table 9.1). It developed rivalries with seven of the neighbors, but not with the other seven. Why did this 50–50 split occur? Multiple factors likely influence such a pattern (e.g., see Fravel 2008; Goertz, Diehl, and Balas 2016); we propose, however, that unsettled borders – particularly those with power endowments capable of triggering a commitment problem – constitute a major, contributing one. Among China's seven rivals, five (71%) dispute(d) power-endowed border territory with it. Conversely, of the seven nonrival neighbors, only three (43%) – Tajikistan, Kyrgyzstan, and Kazakhstan – dispute(d) power-endowed territory with it (i.e., 57% of nonrivals lack(ed) a dispute over power-endowed territory). Our main argument, in other words, performs well when predicting which interstate relationships turn hostile, even in a specific, noteworthy case that spans numerous dyads and time periods (e.g., pre-world wars, Cold War, and post–Cold War).

We recognize, however, that the pattern of rivalry are not perfectly consistent with our argument, and we do not expect them to be. China, for example, develops rivalries with North Korea and Laos – both of which form in the absence of disputed, power-endowed territory (see Goertz, Diehl, and Balas 2016). The North Korean rivalry follows China's official, diplomatic recognition of South Korea in 1992, while the Laotian rivalry stems from each state giving support to guerrilla forces fighting against the other. Exceptions

TABLE 9.1. *Chinese relationships*

Power Endowments	Not Rivals	Rivals
No	Mongolia Korea Bhutan Pakistan	North Korea Laos
Yes	Tajikistan Kyrgyzstan Kazakhstan	Russia India Myanmar Nepal Vietnam

like these underscore that rivalries can (and do) form for nonterritorial reasons as well, a point we return to subsequently.

Similarly, three relationships – with Tajikistan, Kyrgyzstan, and Kazakhstan – do not turn into rivalries, despite a lingering, historical dispute over power-endowed territory. This, too, seems to run counter to our argument. Why would power-endowed territory *not* produce a rivalry in these cases? Fravel (2008, 160–166) offers one potential explanation. China settles its borders with Central Asian neighbors to confront domestic turmoil (e.g., to secure the neighbors' support in combating extremist groups within the border region and permit it to turn its attention inward). According to this argument, internal needs cause cooperation, not competition, to dominate Chinese policy within this geographic and temporal context.

Although possible, a domestic turmoil argument seems incomplete. It does not explain why a similar motivation would not have prompted earlier major concessions to Russia in order to achieve the same goal, especially since domestic turmoil existed frequently along the Chinese–Russian border. To resolve this puzzle, one must therefore augment the domestic argument, and our theoretical story offers a way to do so. First and foremost, it stresses the dyadic interstate relationships involved, as well as their development and history (see also Goertz, Diehl, and Balas 2016; Kupchan 2010). The China–Russia rivalry formed initially around a dispute involving power-endowed territory, much as we would predict. That dispute, along with the hostility it fostered, carried forward in *their* relationship (and persists; see Thompson and Dreyer 2012) but the break-up of the Soviet Union offered the Chinese an opportunity to "reset" relations with its new, neighboring states. The disputed border segments with Tajikistan, Kyrgyzstan, and Kazakhstan, in other words, delinked from China's hostile relationship with Russia, thereby shedding (some) baggage associated with the China–Russia rivalry and becoming part of three relationships that contained no prior, independent history.[1] A unique opportunity therefore emerged, and rounds of border negotiations followed in the mid-1990s. Of course, a serious potential for rivalry still existed between China and the Central Asian states, since they disputed power-endowed territory. That potential never materialized, though; the "reset" relationships did not travel our entire causal pathway to rivalry. The reset in relations, as well as the continuance of hostility with Russia, may help explain why.

Second, and even more consistent with our argument, negotiations with the Central Asian states did not proceed smoothly. Where power-endowed territory came into play (e.g., the Pamir Mountains), negotiations stalled, even though China was willing and (theoretically) strongly incentivized to offer major concessions. As Fravel (2008, 165–166) notes:

> Continuing differences over how to divide the Pamir area prevented the two sides [China and Tajikistan] from signing a formal agreement. China has offered to compromise, but the two sides could not agree on an appropriate division.... [Thus] the Pamirs remained a sticking point.

Our argument anticipates this bargaining difficulty too, and therefore solves a second dilemma that the domestic turmoil argument leaves behind. If (i) China needed to settle its borders to gain internal security and (ii) it was willing to issue major concessions, then why did settlement stall? Two theoretical possibilities exist. The first possibility would be that the domestic turmoil lacked sufficient strength to motivate Chinese concessions (i.e., point i is incorrect). This alone seems unlikely. Domestic turmoil existed at the time and loosely connects to China's territorial bargaining strategy (broadly defined; Fravel 2008). Moreover, China granted large territorial concessions to multiple other states in a short period of time, suggesting that incentives for settlement generally existed. The second possibility would be that China's willingness to concede border territory varied according to the exact territory under dispute (i.e., point ii is not uniformly correct for all disputed border territory). This possibility aligns with our argument. It proposes that the primary bargaining obstacle lay with *what* exactly settlement would divide. China may have been willing to grant some – even many – concessions, but its generosity had limits; it still wanted control over specific, valuable territory.

In the end, our argument properly classifies the majority of China's neighborhood relations (i.e., 9 of 14, or 64%). The misclassifications, however, reveal both the value and shortcomings of our argument, as well as fruitful paths forward for future research. Rivalries can form over nonterritorial issues, a process our argument necessarily cannot explain. Moreover, rivalries do not *always* form when neighboring states dispute power-endowed territory. Our argument, being probabilistic, accepts such an outcome. Yet it raises an

[1] We do not intend to say that China had no relationship with Central Asia prior to the 1990s, only that the earlier relationship necessarily fell under its larger relationship with Russia.

important question: what factors mitigate our argument's causal mechanism? A complete answer must await further study, but we see hints of one in our research. Three (exceptional) cases occur in which China does not develop a rivalry with its neighbor, despite disputing power-endowed territory with it. In all three cases, the neighbor gains independence from a rival (and here, the same one), negotiates quickly with China, and faces difficulty when navigating the distribution of power-endowed territory. The findings we present in earlier chapters anticipate these dynamics. Border settlement succeeds more often early in a (nonrival) dyad's life, even with power-endowed territory at stake (see Chapter 4). Nevertheless, negotiating over territory that contains power endowments presents a unique bargaining challenge with which neighboring states struggle (see Chapters 4 and 8). Why some states overcome this obstacle in the pre-rivalry phase of their relationship, however – as opposed to developing a rivalry because of the obstacle – requires further study.

Revisiting the Chinese case that began the book serves a critical purpose here: it highlights the contribution of our argument, while simultaneously acknowledging the argument's limitations. The remainder of this chapter does the same in much broader strokes. The first part of the chapter summarizes the theoretical argument – from the emergence of neighboring states, to their attempt to delimit borders, to their success at or failure to reach border settlement, to the rivalry that follows if they fail, and finally, to the pathway out of the rivalries that form. That summary ties the theoretical story back together into a larger arc and highlights the major empirical findings that support each component of it. The second part of the chapter then turns to limitations. One book cannot thoroughly cover all facets of an argument, and we do not expect our argument to account for all border settlements, or even all rivalries. We therefore elucidate a number of paths forward for future research, each of which builds on the foundations that we lay in this book. Finally, we end the chapter with a discussion of the policy implications that derive from our work. These implications chart not only how interstate peace can expand, but also where the greatest risk to peace exists and why.

9.2 THE THEORETICAL ARGUMENT AND ITS SUPPORT

The story we tell throughout this book follows an (historical) arc. When states enter the international system, they immediately confront a highly salient issue: how to delimit their mutual borders with neighbors. This issue activates two competing incentives. On the one hand, states pursue delimitation actively and want it to succeed. Absent agreed upon jurisdictional limits, whose sovereign laws govern a given (disputed) area remains unclear. That, in turn, forces states to forego numerous security and economic benefits (e.g., trade; Simmons 2005). To access those benefits, states must reach a border settlement.

On the other hand, states – both the citizenry and, therefore, leaders – find border disputes highly salient (i.e., important). They consequently will not accept just *any* settlement, but instead seek the most favorable set of terms possible. Myriad factors underlie this incentive, including (i) a desire for the specific resources the territory contains (e.g., Bolivian access to the coast); (ii) the pursuit of a larger security agenda, in which states fear that a territorial redistribution renders them more vulnerable to an adversaries' future, Machiavellian designs; (iii) the need for leaders to prevent domestic challengers from ousting them (e.g., through being branded a "traitor" and then thrown from office); (iv) concerns about the state's overall integrity, which might be undermined if territorial concessions to one actor prompt demands for territorial concessions from others (see Walter 2006); and (v) recognition that any settlement will likely persist indefinitely, unless mutually renegotiated. These competing incentives encourage states to bargain over their borders' delimitation – but to bargain hard (Fearon 1998). States, in other words, frequently travel the road to border settlement, but do not easily reach its end. What can we conclude about this journey?

Border settlement follows one of two paths, depending on the bargaining obstacle(s) the disputed territory produces. The failure to agree on how to settle interstate borders generally results from either an information problem or a commitment problem. An information problem occurs when states misrepresent their position, intentions, capability, or resolve. The incentive to engage in such behavior derives directly from rational bargaining theory (Fearon 1995; Hopmann 1996). A state that successfully convinces its adversary that it has greater capabilities and resolve – and intends to use those in pursuit of the disputed good (i.e., territory) – can both demand and in theory receive a larger proportion of the disputed good. All involved states understand this, however, so much of the bargaining process (and therefore, conflict management) involves sifting through misinformation (i) to locate the bargaining range – that is, the various settlements that both sides prefer to contesting the good further – and then (ii) to determine which particular settlement terms within that range to adopt – that is, the exact distribution of the disputed good to accept.

Repeated, nonlegal conflict management – negotiation and mediation – helps overcome the information problem. Indeed, it frequently excels at this task precisely because it confronts misinformation directly. Repeated negotiations, for example, allow states to exchange offers with one another. Through proposals and counterproposals, they advance their interests, test what position(s) each finds acceptable, explore what information is accurate or misrepresented, and (ideally) converge on one of the mutually agreed settlements that lie within the bargaining range. If the negotiation process breaks down – a distinct possibility when disputants struggle to communicate credibly with one another – a mediator's assistance then re-opens or re-enforces the highly needed communication channels. In addition, mediators also (can) verify the accuracy of disputant's positions, suggest settlement terms, and even incentivize a settlement (either generally, or in support of specific settlement terms).

Empirically, an information problem dominates the border settlement process when states dispute territory that lacks a power endowment – that is, when the territory gives its possessor neither a military strategic advantage nor access to highly desirable economic resources (on the alternative, see subsequent discussion). Integrating this with the earlier argument generates a specific proposition: if repeated conflict management overcomes information problems that arise during the border settlement process, then it will foster border settlement only in the absence of power endowments. This is exactly what we find.

The introduction of power endowments, however, reduces the effectiveness of negotiation and mediation markedly. We propose that this occurs because power endowments activate a commitment problem. A commitment problem arises when disputants do not expect an agreement they reach today to be honored in the future. Casual readers might interpret this loosely – that is, they may think that leaders who anticipate one another will have a simple "change of heart," the international context (generally conceived) will change, or that leadership turnover will cause a state to renege (e.g., when President Trump abandoned the 2015 Joint Comprehensive Plan of Action [Iran nuclear deal] that President Obama signed). Yet the commitment problem logic depends on a far more specific mechanism: one actor anticipates a large, rapid, future power shift to benefit its adversary (Powell 2006). It then projects the consequences of that power shift forward in time. A strengthened adversary will hold greater power, allowing it to renege on and re-bargain today's settlement in the future, in order to obtain better terms; in fact, a rational adversary cannot credibly promise not to do this, so the agreement will be unstable – particularly when the involved states bargain over a good that contains a source of power and, therefore, can cause a large, rapid power shift if settlement redistributes that good (i.e., power-endowed territory). To stave off the power shift, the state refuses to reach a settlement today.

Negotiation and mediation prove more futile in such a context because they do not interfere with the commitment problem mechanism. They are ill-equipped, on average, to prevent either the power shift itself or the renegotiation of a settlement's terms during its implementation phase. Legal approaches also cannot prevent a power shift, but they hinder a state's ability to renegotiate settlement terms unilaterally. Legal rulings constitute international law, which states cannot violate without facing sanctions from the wider international community – in both reputational and material terms. This, of course, does not altogether preclude a state's ability to renegotiate a legally reached agreement unilaterally, but it does raise the costs of doing so. It consequently lowers the likelihood that renegotiation occurs, thereby disrupting the commitment problem mechanism and permitting settlement to move forward. *Legal approaches, in other words, promote border settlement when commitment problems impede it (i.e., states dispute power-endowed territory).*

The earlier discussion risks painting legal approaches as a silver bullet for resolving the commitment problem. They are not. States often avoid legal approaches because they impose significant costs on the participants. When using such processes, for example, not only must states incur high material costs (e.g., researching and preparing a legal position, engaging in a process that plays out over months or years, etc.), but they also lose significant control over their dispute's management – now governed by pre-established court statutes – and outcome – now decided entirely by third parties (Gent and Shannon 2011; Owsiak and Mitchell 2019). This, combined with the high salience of the border issue and the intractability of the commitment problem, means that *the likelihood of border settlement declines significantly if a commitment problem exists (i.e., states dispute power-endowed territory).*

Border disputes involving power endowments therefore persist more often than those without power endowments, and as they do, the relationship between the involved neighboring states sours. Their jurisdictional conflict demands attention, but neither state can resolve it – either alone or together. Conquest and concessions fail – the former because each state lacks the strength to impose its preferred outcome decisively on the other, the latter because concessions threaten an unstable settlement that promises future losses.[2] Yet each state understands that it must compete for the territory to prevent becoming more vulnerable to its adversary. The issue consequently dominates the foreign policy agenda of both states and leads each state to view the other as a threat, competitor, and enemy (i.e., rivals). In this way, *unsettled borders – particularly those containing a commitment problem (i.e., power-endowed territory) – promote the formation of interstate rivalry among neighboring states.*

A salient issue, however, does more than just instigate a rivalrous relationship; it theoretically sustains that relationship as well. If true, then resolving that issue promises to transform the interstate relationship – from rivalry to something less hostile (Goertz, Diehl, and Balas 2016). Rivals attempt this regularly, but with mixed results. As with their nonrival counterparts, *negotiation and mediation often promote border settlement when rivals face an information problem (i.e., absent a dispute over power-endowed territory); yet unlike their counterparts, the effectiveness of this conflict management erodes over iterated rounds of conflict management.* The rivalry relationship itself likely explains the discrepancy. Over time, rivals institutionalize their relationship, expecting to encounter hostility from each other for the foreseeable future. That expectation, in turn, undermines information credibility further, and eventually, repeated interactions cannot overcome the incredibility that permeates their exchanges.

Legal approaches offer an exit. When rivals face an information problem, the legal process enhances the credible exchange of information. Disputants participating in such a process must submit developed legal positions, and courts can solicit expert advice or request documentation that supports those positions. Nonrivals need courts less for this purpose; they can achieve the same

[2] Conquest may also fail because the international system prevents it from resolving territorial disputes. See Hathaway and Shapiro (2017).

goal via the iterated use of other conflict management tools they prefer (e.g., negotiation and mediation). For rivals, though, the preferred routes often close, and the courts provide them with an alternative.

Courts also assist rivals facing a commitment problem. Because courts link a settlement to international law (through a legal ruling, or award), they decrease the likelihood that the settlement they produce will be renegotiated unilaterally in the future, thereby interrupting the commitment problem mechanism. *Legal approaches therefore generally promote border settlement within rivalries, regardless of whether or not the rivals dispute power-endowed territory.* Despite this general effect, legal approaches do exert a slightly stronger effect when states dispute nonendowed territory, a fact that bargaining theory anticipates somewhat. An international court possesses more mechanisms to address information, as opposed to commitment, problems. The discovery phase of the legal process clarifies information – and the court ultimately finds both the bargaining range and the settlement terms the disputants will accept. In contrast, the court assuages fears of a settlement's future, unilateral renegotiation, but it does not banish those fears entirely.

Once they obtain border settlement – however they do so – rivals' relationship then transforms significantly. First and foremost, *the likelihood that a rivalry ends is greater when the rivals have settled, as opposed to unsettled, borders.* If we conceptualize all interstate relationships along a continuum from highly hostile (i.e., rivalry) to highly collaborative (i.e., a security community), then a dyad that terminates its rivalry necessarily moves to a less hostile relationship (Goertz, Diehl, and Balas 2016; Kupchan 2010). Further evidence of such a shift appears when we examine how rivals behave toward one another if their rivalry continues after border settlement. *Although disputes (i.e., crises and MIDs) occur with similar frequency in the pre- and post-border settlement phases of rivals' relationship, the disputes that originate after border settlement are significantly shorter and less severe than those that begin before border settlement.* It therefore seems that border settlement constitutes a watershed moment in interstate relations, including within rivalries.

None of this implies that states reach border settlement easily. The commitment problem appears frequently, and when it does, it causes and sustains interstate rivalry. Indeed, *rivals that dispute power-endowed territory are significantly less likely to end their rivalry.* If states – even rivals – settle their borders, however, hostility and conflict decline. The prospects for interstate peace grow to the extent that states confront and overcome the information and commitment problems that plague their bargaining over interstate border delimitation.

9.3 FUTURE RESEARCH

We do not intend our study to be the final word on the subjects of border settlement and rivalry. Mindful of this, future research might build on it along five distinct fronts. First, our work illustrates that scholars do not understand border settlement well. Numerous studies examine the onset, management, and resolution of territorial claims (e.g., see Hensel et al. 2008; Huth and Allee 2002). These studies inform our understanding of border settlement, but not entirely – at least, not in their current form (see Chapter 2). Two advancements would prove particularly valuable: exploring the intersection of disparate claims (especially across different borders) and theorizing border settlement as a process.

Territorial borders are not always independent of one another, although scholars typically analyze them this way. Some borders interlock. For example, Colombia and Brazil resolved most of their territorial border in 1907, but left the southern section unresolved at that time. They did so because the terms by which they might resolve this segment of their mutual border (will) depend on how Colombia resolves its territorial borders with Peru and Ecuador (Huth and Allee 2002, 442). One border's resolution, in other words, affects others. How does this alter the settlement process (if at all)? Does interdependence among borders facilitate or impede settlement? Which interlocked borders do states manage first (or last), and why?

Theorizing the interdependence among distinct borders (or even, claims) proves challenging, but not impossible. Clay and Owsiak (2016), for example, propose a diffusion mechanism. Some borders connect to one another in such a way that the resolution of one border produces a cascade of further settlements (as in the Colombia–Brazil, Colombia–Peru, and Colombia–Ecuador example mentioned earlier). In other cases, though, Clay and Owsiak argue that states use a border settlement with one neighbor to signal the (type of) settlement terms that they generally find acceptable to other neighbors.[3] Studies such as this offer a start, but much remains to be done. Do states with multiple unsettled borders pursue settlements in a specific sequence? Do they handle information problems (i.e., nonpower-endowed territory) before commitment problems? Do they negotiate multiple settlements simultaneously? Does progress along one settlement yields progress along another, and if so, under what conditions?

One challenge to this path forward lies with existing data, which tends to pitch dyadic claims in the aggregate. As an illustration, Huth and Allee (2002, 397) list one territorial claim each between China and Kazakhstan, China and Kyrgyzstan, and China and Tajikistan – claims simply captured as "claims along the border." The Issue Correlates of War Project follows a similar format (although not for all states in the world; see Frederick, Hensel, and Macaulay 2017). Yet these borders contain multiple, interlocking subclaims. Kazakhstan inherits fifteen disputed boundary segments from the

[3] A review of Chinese behavior in the 1960s, as well as large-*n* analysis, suggests this argument has merit. See Clay and Owsiak (2016).

Chinese–Russian relationship, while Kyrgyzstan and Tajikistan inherit an additional seven and three, respectively (Fravel 2008, 160–166).[4]

The problem with this discrepancy (i.e., level of aggregation) may not seem large at first glance, but the narratives we constructed during the research for this project demonstrate that neighboring states often settle their border(s) in pieces. Iran and Afghanistan, for example, proceed through four different partial settlements, resolving segments of their mutual border in 1872, 1889, 1905, and 1935 (Prescott and Triggs 2008, 269–272). This raises a series of conceptual, theoretical, and empirical questions related to claim aggregation. Are border "segments" (however defined) truly part of the same or different "claims" (i.e., how do states interpret them)? If the former, how do states delink certain border segments from others to obtain a partial settlement? Why do segments settle in a particular order and at the time that they do? Does one partial settlement lead to further partial settlements (on this question, see Mattes 2018)? Answers to such questions will only come from theorizing about border settlement as a process – one that directly models and accounts for the interdependence between states' various claims (across borders) and subclaims (within borders).[5]

The empirical analysis presented throughout this book also demonstrates the need for a better understanding of the border settlement process. Our models contain myriad factors that scholars think alter bargaining between states, including (i) conflict management efforts, (ii) whether the disputed border contains power endowments; and (iii) a host of other characteristics (e.g., whether both dyad members qualify as democratic states, or the relative power balance between dyad members). The first two factors correspond with our main theoretical story and perform well. Almost all other factors, however, perform poorly; they either (seemingly) exert no effect on the border settlement process or behave inconsistently across our models (for a similar finding, see also Gibler and Owsiak 2018). This suggests that scholars do not yet have a good grasp of the border settlement process – or that border settlement is itself idiosyncratic (Gibler and Owsiak 2018, 1859–1860). We suspect the former is more likely (i.e., generalizable knowledge can be had), but only further theorizing and analysis will discern whether that is true. At this point, we know

4 Some research has begun disaggregating borders into spatial components. That data addresses the challenge noted here, but were it available, it would not alter our argument or findings, which depend on whether states have *fully* settled (i.e., delimited) their mutual borders under international law. Future research might investigate how border segments settle, as we note here (i.e., use a different dependent variable than the one our study uses). Our argument might predict that states will settle border segments containing a power endowment last (or after nonpower-endowed segments), since these theoretically drive the commitment problem. Conflict management scholars, however, might propose an alternative – namely, that states leave "easier" border segments unresolved until they settle the more difficult ones (i.e., "nothing is settled until everything is settled"). With better data, one might evaluate the robustness of these expectations directly.

5 For a similar critique of the conflict management research, see Owsiak (2014).

only that the factors we expect to influence interstate bargaining do not do so when states bargain over the settlement of their interstate borders. What factors might influence border settlement as a process remain to be seen.

A second avenue for future research elucidates the alternative causal pathways by which interstate rivalries begin and end. Our argument supplies one – albeit, we believe, prominent and noteworthy – explanation for why rivalry occurs. Yet it does not attempt to, and cannot, explain all rivalries. Noncontiguous rivalries, for example, must form because of an alternative logic; lacking shared borders, these rivalries cannot result from the territorial border conflict on which our argument rests (e.g., the United States–Soviet Union or United States–Cuba). Similarly, some contiguous rivalries form after the involved states settle their borders (e.g., Rwanda–Democratic Republic of the Congo (DRC) or Afghanistan–Iran). Our argument does not explain why these rivalries occur either, since it presupposes the existence of unsettled borders to begin the causal mechanism that yields rivalry. Finally – relatedly, and perhaps most obviously – some rivalries simply involve nonterritorial issues, even when the involved states are contiguous. Goertz, Diehl, and Balas (2016) offer an illustration. They classify China and North Korea as rivals during the 1990s. Although this rivalry contains contiguous states engaged in repeated border skirmishes, it does not concern a disputed border; rather, it stems directly from China's willingness to extend official, diplomatic recognition to South Korea in 1992. Such examples illustrate our larger point. There exist numerous causal pathways to interstate rivalry (see also Colaresi, Rasler, and Thompson 2007). Identification of these other pathways – including, importantly, the logic underlying them – promises to advance scholarship and policy prescriptions significantly. When we understand these paths and why they occur, we will gain greater insight into how (if at all) to interrupt them.

A third front for future research investigates a lingering curiosity. Our analysis finds that the likelihood of rivalry termination increases significantly in the wake of border settlement. If the rivalry continues instead, our study reveals that the rivals' behavior toward one another turns significantly less hostile. Why, though, do some rivalries continue after border settlement, while others do not? We argue that the commitment problem constitutes the main obstacle in the border settlement process and fuels interstate rivalry; resolving the border, however states do that, signals that the rivals must have surmounted any commitment problem that stems from the disputed border territory. Thus, a curiosity remains. Absent the motivating cause (i.e., the commitment problem), what sustains rivalry after border settlement, especially if rivalries cost states much to maintain and, therefore, (rational) rivals will want to end them?

Existing studies offer a potential answer: rivalries accumulate issues (Dreyer 2010; Vasquez 2009). Rivals view one another as threats, competitors, and enemies; reorient their foreign policy to confront one another for the foreseeable future; and institutionalize expectations of future hostility. A centripetal-like force, in other words, pulls all of the dyad's disputed issues into its rivalry, which then becomes about something larger – namely, imposing costs on (or impeding the action of) the adversary. If true, then rivals' ability to resolve one issue successfully – even a highly salient one – may not end the rivalry immediately. The institutionalized, hostile foreign policy may instead persist for a while, fueled by the residual, unresolved issues.

Iraq and Iran demonstrate this process well. They formed a rivalry initially over two broad issues: how to delimit their common border and who held more sway in the region (Thompson and Dreyer 2012). The 1975 Algiers Agreement eventually settled the outstanding border issues, including a division of the valuable Shatt al-Arab waterway (Frederick, Hensel, and Macaulay 2017; Huth and Allee 2002). The 1979 Iranian Revolution next promised to resolve questions of influence, introducing an Iranian regime more friendly to Iraq. This promise, however, never materialized. Iran accelerated its support of Shi'ite rebellions throughout the Middle East, thereby threatening Iraq's perceived regional dominance again, while Iraq reopened the previously settled border issues (Frederick, Hensel, and Macaulay 2017; Thompson and Dreyer 2012). The Iran–Iraq war soon followed (1980–1988). At the war's end (in 1990), the two sides restored the 1975 territorial division (i.e., reaffirmed and reinforced border settlement), but the rivalry still persisted.[6]

Why did this happen? By 1975, the Iran–Iraq rivalry concerned more than border territory alone. Questions of regional influence loomed large, and "both sides supported rebellions and secessionist movements in the other state in the early 1970s" – a practice that continued throughout the 1980s and 1990s (Thompson and Dreyer 2012, 164–166). In such a context, border settlement likely raised the probability that rivalry termination would occur, but ultimately proved unable to overcome the rivals' entrenched hostility. Under what conditions might it have done so? This remains an open question, but the Iran–Iraq case points toward a possible answer for future research to explore. States find territorial (border) threats salient because they threaten the regime's power directly (i.e., their sovereignty). Fomenting rebellion similarly threatens the regime's survival, but from within – as opposed to outside – the state. Perhaps, then, rivalry continues after border settlement when a neighbor historically has worked actively to oust its adversary's regime. If true, then a deeper understanding of rivalry dynamics will derive from research that explores the intersection of interstate and intrastate conflict more explicitly.[7]

The fourth avenue for future research dives deeper into how conflict management tools might help disputants overcome the bargaining challenges associated with commitment problems – and relatedly, power endowments. We propose throughout this book that legal approaches succeed where negotiation

[6] For a narrative, see Thompson and Dreyer (2012).

[7] Owsiak, Diehl, and Goertz (2017) argue that both a lack of border delimitation and the fomenting of rebellion (or civil conflict) may lead to a similar outcome: the destabilization of border regions.

and mediation fail because they raise the costs associated with a unilateral, future renegotiation of a border settlement. In other words, they interrupt the commitment problem mechanism and allow settlement to proceed.

Existing research presents an alternative logic for why states use legal approaches: domestic political cover (Allee and Huth 2006; Gent and Shannon 2011). Unsettled borders necessarily involve overlapping, conflicting claims to sovereignty. To reach a settlement, at least one actor will need to concede something. Domestic audiences, however, find these concessions unpalatable – the unacceptable ceding of the homeland to an adversary. Leaders recognize this but also understand the value in reaching a settlement. They consequently hand control of their dispute's management and outcome to a court (or arbiter) in order to shield themselves from domestic backlash. Settlement then proceeds because the courts decide what concessions each side will make – and because leaders avoid responsibility for making those concessions.

The logics associated with our argument and the domestic political cover argument contradict. In the first (ours), leaders worry that a concession today will be deleterious because it threatens to make the state more vulnerable to adversaries in the (near) future. In the second, leaders do not fear a large, rapid, future power shift in the adversary's favor, but rather the domestic consequences of moving settlement forward (but see also Powell 2006). Both processes lead to the same empirical outcome – the use of a legal process to lock-in a border settlement – but for different reasons. Future research might attempt to disentangle which of the two logics dominate. The domestic cover argument, in particular, raises a key question. An interstate dispute enters the legal process only if the involved states acquiesce (at some point) to the court's or arbiter's authority to hear the dispute. Compliance also depends on the state itself, rather than a third-party enforcer. Publics that would punish a leader for concessions presumably know all this; so it is unclear why these same publics would not also punish a leader who either allows a highly salient dispute to enter the legal process in the first place or who agrees to comply with a court ruling, especially with valuable territory at stake (e.g., power endowments).[8]

Tracing the process through which leaders submit cases to legal bodies promises to hold some answers. Do leaders, for example, submit cases to courts and arbiters because domestic groups block their negotiating authority or, alternatively, because they want the benefits of a more stable settlement that the courts provide? Do domestic groups truly not foresee the consequences of their state submitting to a legal body – that is, that the court might force the state to give concessions to an adversary or that compliance with a settlement would be expected? To the extent that domestic publics do not anticipate these

[8] Theoretically, the domestic publics that find concessions unpalatable prefer noncompliance with a court's ruling, even if that noncompliance carries other costs (e.g., material or reputational sanctions). After all, these publics prefer the costs of a continued, unresolved border dispute to the benefits that resolution holds, as demonstrated through their opposition to concessions.

effects, the domestic cover argument holds greater merit. To the extent they do not, the argument seems more suspect.

The evidence required to answer such questions will be difficult to obtain. Nevertheless, it would be worthwhile to pursue. The domestic political cover argument dominates the discussion of why states use legal approaches to manage their contentious issues. We find, however, that legal approaches succeed at managing power-endowed territory – the exact territory that domestic publics should, in theory, least want to enter the legal process. This puzzle begs further examination, and focusing on it promises to change, condition, or revise what we know about how and why legal approaches operate in interstate conflict management.

The final avenue for future research revises and extends our argument to maritime borders. We decide to restrict our attention to land borders in this book because scholars demonstrate conclusively that states treat land and maritime borders (or claims) differently (Hensel et al. 2008; Owsiak and Mitchell 2019). The argument we present, however, could be extended to maritime borders after additional theorizing (on bargaining over maritime borders, see Asgeirsdottir and Steinwand 2018). Many maritime spaces contain power endowments (e.g., natural resources or strategic value). These could theoretically yield commitment problems too, but perhaps only under certain circumstances. For example, access to oil reserves may provoke fears of a potential power shift (e.g., see the Guyana–Suriname rivalry, which is partly fueled by a dispute about who possesses sovereignty over a border maritime space that contains oil reserves; Goertz, Diehl, and Balas 2016). In contrast, fishing rights, migratory fish stocks – whose exact location is not stable and whose value does not easily convert into rapid power shifts – and navigational concerns – partially assuaged via the United Nations Convention on the Law of the Sea (UNCLOS) – may not.

The so-called Cod Wars between the United Kingdom and Iceland illustrate the differences occupying the maritime domain well. The United Kingdom and Iceland enter a brief rivalry from 1958 to 1976 as a result of Iceland extending its (fishing) maritime boundary outward after World War II – first to four, then to twelve, then to fifty, and finally to two hundred miles (Goertz, Diehl, and Balas 2016; Jóhannesson 2004). The United Kingdom never believed that this would produce a large, rapid, future shift in power, at least not one that would make it vulnerable to continued Icelandic demands (i.e., the United Kingdom always understood that it would be more powerful). Rather, the British fishing industry wanted access to the disputed waters for its continued economic livelihood. At the same time, UNCLOS negotiations worked to standardize global claims. Eventually (in 1976), the United Kingdom accepted the two hundred mile limit, imposed a similar one around its own territories, and the rivalry ended. The dispute, therefore, hinged as much on what the global norm for maritime space should be, as on the specifics of the Icelandic boundaries.

Maritime disputes also differ in their recourse to legal processes. UNCLOS outlines an elaborate dispute resolution mechanism, complete with arbitration channels and courts; creates a new court (i.e., the International Tribunal for the Law of the Sea); and compels states to use legal processes when other conflict management efforts fail. This should alter bargaining dynamics. If, for example, legal processes excel at overcoming the commitment problem (as we argue) *and* states can initiate legal processes unilaterally (as they can under UNCLOS), then bargaining over maritime borders will diverge from that bargaining over land borders in two ways. First, overcoming commitment problems will be (relatively) easier when they underlie maritime, as opposed to land, borders. States individually possess the tools needed to overcome the commitment problem in their maritime border disputes, for a single state may unilaterally activate the legal process in that context. Guyana, for example, initiated arbitration proceedings against Suriname in 2004 to address their oil-rich maritime border; the Permanent Court of Arbitration issued a ruling in that case in 2007, settling the maritime border and ending the rivalry (Goertz, Diehl, and Balas 2016). This process moved forward at the behest of one rival.

Second (and relatedly), rational, strategic states that see potential legal processes looming on the horizon should bargain differently in the shadow of those processes (Mitchell and Owsiak 2017; Mnookin and Kornhauser 1979). Growing case law (over 90 to date) allows states to forecast potential court rulings in their own cases. Armed with this information, those states that want to retain control over their dispute's management and outcome – and retain flexibility in settlement terms – may more easily reach settlement outside the courtroom.

These, of course, are probabilistic claims. That bargaining over maritime borders adopts a different flavor than that over land borders – one that more readily overcomes commitment problems – does not imply that maritime border bargaining lacks any challenges. Indeed, the 2013–2016 arbitration that the Philippines initiated against China over the South China Sea reminds us as much (e.g., China refused to participate in the arbitration process at all, even going so far as to return the tribunal's correspondence to it). Yet it does indicate that extending our argument to maritime borders will require additional theorizing. Scholars will, in particular, need to account for the unique characteristics that govern bargaining over interstate maritime borders and to think more systematically about the distinct bargaining challenges that appear in the maritime context. Despite these differences, a similar argument could operate there. How it manifests remains to be theorized and studied.

9.4 POLICY IMPLICATIONS

The argument and evidence we present throughout this book, if correct, suggest four main policy implications. First, border disputes that contain power-endowed territory require more than negotiation and mediation to resolve.

Conflict hot spots throughout the world often involve rivals actively disputing border territory that contains power endowments (e.g., Belize–Guatemala, Russia–China, Saudi Arabia–Yemen, Syria–Israel, China–India, North Korea–South Korea, etc.). These rivals regularly negotiate to settle their border's delimitation, and from time to time, third-party mediators assist them. Yet our analysis suggests that various efforts will struggle to obtain border settlement, primarily because they fail to address the main, underlying bargaining obstacle – the commitment problem.

A second, related implication follows the first: when rivals dispute power-endowed territory, channel that dispute into a legal conflict management process (e.g., arbitration or adjudication) to move settlement forward.[9] The failure of negotiation and mediation to settle disputes over power-endowed territory results from a mismatch between those conflict management tools, on the one hand, and the underlying commitment problem logic that fuels the disputes, on the other. To reach a settlement in these disputes, one must intervene directly in the commitment problem mechanism. Two possibilities exist: either prevent the large, rapid, future power shift from occurring or impede the strengthened state's ability to renegotiate the settlement unilaterally in the future. No conflict management approach, to our knowledge, will accomplish the former possibility. Border delimitation will necessarily (re)distribute the power-endowed border territory and, therefore, cause the power shift that states anticipate. Legal approaches, however, address the latter possibility well – albeit imperfectly. Because they ground a border settlement in an international arbitral or court ruling, legal approaches significantly raise the costs of a unilateral, future renegotiation (e.g., through material and reputational consequences). This may not preclude a renegotiation from occurring altogether, but does substantially reduce its likelihood. In so doing, it assuages – even if it does not eliminate – the weakened states' fear that a signed settlement today will be unstable tomorrow, thereby raising the probability that rivals sign a settlement that delimits their mutual border.

The challenge, of course, is that negotiation and mediation are (the most) popular choice of conflict management tool for disputants and third parties alike. Disputants want to retain control over the management and outcome of their disputes, particularly salient ones like border delimitation. Negotiation – and to a lesser extent, mediation – allow them to do this. Similarly, third parties prefer that disputants resolve conflicts among themselves when possible (i.e., via negotiation). If that fails, they may then get involved, but they, too, prefer to use mediation because it is the least costly conflict management tool available to them (see Owsiak 2014). Mediation allows third parties to avoid responsibility for whether a settlement ultimately occurs. That responsibility lies, by mediation's design, with the disputants, which is one reason why disputants

[9] This implication assumes that policy-makers aim to settle the dispute. Those who prefer not to settle the dispute might avoid legal approaches instead.

prefer it to other third-party approaches. Moreover, mediation requires third parties to commit fewer resources than alternative conflict management tools (e.g., legal approaches, sanctions, or peace operations; see Greig, Owsiak, and Diehl 2019). These preferences cumulatively push against the channeling of disputes into legal processes and explain why disputants and third parties use negotiation and mediation repeatedly, even when those tools fail. Overcoming such preferences will be difficult, but worthwhile, for the border delimitation process.

The third policy implication derived from our study elucidates policy toward conflict management within territorially based rivalries: focus efforts on resolving the rivals' unsettled borders, for this promises the greatest return on resource investment. Rivalries often snowball, gathering multiple issues as the relationship turns hostile and institutionalizes (Dreyer 2010; Vasquez 2009). One might therefore wonder how best to help rivals escape their entrenched relationship. Which issues might be managed first? Which issues, if resolved, provide the largest payoff? Our study offers a suggestion. Of all the issues available, unsettled borders fuel a notable number of prominent, interstate rivalries, especially when those borders contain power endowments that produce a commitment problem. Prioritizing the settlement of these borders promises a large payoff for those interested in peace. It removes a key, underlying fuel source for the rivalry, and in so doing, increases the likelihood that the rivalry will end. Even if the rivalry continues after such a settlement, though, the rivals will behave significantly less hostilely toward one another. Given limited resources and the numerous issues vying for the international community's attention (both within rivalries and throughout the world), it might therefore focus particularly on rivals' unsettled borders. Although difficult to achieve, a settlement of these borders yields a large gain on behalf of interstate peace.

The fourth implication captures a harbinger of danger: for the foreseeable future, the Asian region will be particularly conflict-prone, especially around India and China. If unsettled borders threaten interstate relationships – for example, by introducing the possibility of long-lasting, entrenched hostility – then they indicate a noteworthy source of actual or latent interstate conflict. When we review the seventeen land borders that remain to be settled in the world, a pattern emerges (see Table 2.1). More of the unsettled borders lie in Asia than in any other region (47%, or 8 of 17). In fact, Asia has *two to three times* more unsettled borders than the region(s) with the next highest number of unsettled borders (i.e., the Americas and Africa, which hold three unsettled borders each). And of the eight unsettled, Asian borders, five involve either China or India. To put that in perspective, China and India together account for 63% (5 of 8) of the region's unsettled borders or 29% of *the world's* unsettled borders (5 of 17).

Cumulatively, statistics like these suggest that the Asian region – particularly around India and China – possesses more actual or latent interstate conflict (potential) than any other region. We note that others reach a similar conclusion, but via a different route. Many of those writing about a "rising China," petulant Russia, or rogue North Korean regime stress these states' relationships with the United States. Some, for example, fear that China's growing strength will eventually cause it to challenge the global order that the United States established after World War II.[10] These fears may be exaggerated (see Chan 2017; Ikenberry 2011). Nevertheless, they illustrate the broader belief that any significant conflict stemming from Asia relates to positional (i.e., [regional] hegemonic) disagreements between individual Asian states and the United States.

We reach a similar conclusion about the dangerousness of the Asian region, but our argument shifts the focus from the global to the regional level, with particular attention given to the relationships between neighboring states who share unsettled borders. It predicts that: (i) the danger is spatial (i.e., territorial), not positional (Thompson and Dreyer 2012); (ii) the major source of conflict lies within the Asian region, not between it and other regions; (iii) minor states feature prominently in conflict predictions, and (iv) the United States, although likely to play a supporting role (e.g., as an ally), will not be a primary disputant in many situations. China looms large in these predictions, but only because of its numerous unsettled borders. Its potential hegemonic conflict with the United States, although perhaps important, shifts to the back burner; it will not be the source of *immediate* conflict in Asia.

Finally, and more broadly, the argument we present carries implications for the potential, future stability of the international system. The territorial integrity norm – that is, the widely accepted idea that interstate borders should not change via force or conquest – provides stability, enhances dyadic and systemic peace, and affects bargaining dynamics.[11] Through it, borders currently remain immutable once negotiated, unless a mutual renegotiation among the involved states adjusts them. International law underwrites this immutability, which explains both why we conceptualize border settlement as an international legal issue (see Chapter 2) and why legal approaches may possess the unique ability to assist states with overcoming their territorially based commitment problems (see Chapters 3 and 4).

International law, however, evolves over time (see Shaw 2014). For example, although the territorial integrity norm operates strongly today, this has not always been the case. Borders historically emerged and changed via alternative norms, such as dynastic secession or marriage (e.g., see the France–Italy negotiations over Nice and Savoy in the mid-nineteenth century),[12] conquest (e.g., the expansion of France under Napoleon), the balance of power (e.g., Europe's

[10] For an overview and critique of this argument, see Chan (2017).

[11] On these various points, see Fearon (1998), Zacher (2001), Goertz, Diehl, and Balas (2016), Hathaway and Shapiro (2017), and Smith (2018).

[12] Napoleon III relied on the norm of dynastic marriage to legitimize and facilitate the transfer of Nice and Savoy from Italy to France during the Italian Wars of Independence (see Coppa 1992). In the Plombieres Agreement, Napoleon III negotiated for his cousin, Jerome, to marry

readjustment in the wake of the Napoleonic Wars),[13] and compensation (e.g., the basis for German claims to land in Africa should it make concessions to France in Morocco in the early twentieth century; see Richardson 1994). These alternative norms have gone out of fashion, particularly conquest (see Hathaway and Shapiro 2017), but that reminds us that norms (can) change. Much as financial advisors warn that past performance does not indicate a stock's future trajectory, the fact that the territorial integrity norm strengthened throughout the twentieth century does not imply that it will continue strengthening – or perhaps more importantly, not weaken.

At first glance, the above sounds like speculation (at best) or fear-mongering (at worst). Yet we see increasing evidence of states challenging the international legal system, including with respect to the norms governing the stability of interstate borders. Two modern examples illustrate the point. The first is the Russian annexation of Crimea in 2014. Russia argues that ethnic Russians living in Crimea faced serious human rights abuses prior to 2014 and therefore gained the right to "remedial self-determination" (i.e., to declare independence from Ukraine; for a thorough legal analysis, see Grant 2015). The human rights abuses, in other words, re-opened the borders. They granted those in Crimea the right to hold a referendum about their future status, which then led to the region's separation from Ukraine, an expressed desire to join Russia, and (re)incorporation into the Russian homeland.

Although the Russian position sounds permissible under – and even seems grounded in – international law, it may not be. Two main questions arise. First, under what conditions do sub-state actors acquire the right to "remedial self-determination" (i.e., secession)? This question indirectly appeared before the ICJ in 2008.[14] At that time, the General Assembly asked the Court to issue an advisory opinion on the validity of Kosovo's declaration of independence. Participants in the proceedings discussed the possibility that such a remedial right existed in Kosovo, as well as the general conditions under which it might exist. The Court opinion, however, sidestepped the matter entirely; it noted that the right to self-determination had evolved over the twentieth century, that "radically different views were expressed by those taking part in the proceedings and expressing a position on the question," and that the remedial self-determination question lay beyond the scope of the original question that the General Assembly asked it (International Court of Justice 2010, 438). Thus, although some potential answers exist – for example, that secession (or remedial self-determination) must be a matter of last resort, even in situations involving human rights abuses, or that secession must follow a

into the House of Savoy (i.e., Princess Clotilde, the daughter of King Victor Emmanuel II of Sardinia). This, and the transfer of his desired territories, went hand-in-hand; France required both for Piedmont–Sardinia to secure it as an ally against Austria.

13 On the elasticity of this term, however, see Haas (1953).

14 All documentation associated with this case appears on the ICJ website at `www.icj-cij.org/en/case/141` (last accessed March 8, 2019).

specific procedure (e.g., a legitimate, democratic decision of the people) – the Court did not express an opinion about those answers.[15]

Second, given that a remedial right to self-determination exists, under what conditions (if any) can third-party states (e.g., Russia) intervene with armed force in support of that right? The international community continues to work out the general answer to this question. As Bellamy (2015) notes, it recognizes the need to defend peoples against mass atrocities (i.e., the Responsibility to Protect norm) but has not fully determined who specifically has the duty (if anyone) to provide that protection and how (e.g., whether and when coercion can be used). Or to borrow Bellamy's phrasing more directly, we agree on the need and (perhaps) a solution, but not how to implement that solution.

Russia's behavior in Crimea may reflect a genuine desire to implement the broadly sketched international solution. Even then, however, problems remain. Armed intervention in support of ethnic Russians may be legally at odds with Russia's behavior in Crimea, for "[j]ustifications for an armed intervention, even if accepted, are not justifications for the forcible acquisition of territory" (Grant 2015, 77). That is, although Russian actions to assist ethnic Russians *may* be legally defensible, the annexation (i.e., political events) that followed may not be. Combined with data that questions how widespread human rights violations were, highlights that similar rights violations continued after annexation, and indicates that the Crimean vote for separation from Ukraine and unification with Russia did not follow a free and fair process, the situation looks as though Russia pitted two international legal norms – self-determination and territorial integrity – against one another to achieve its desired political end. It used international law along one dimension to push the limits of international law along another.[16]

Chinese behavior in the South China Sea offers a second, similar illustration, albeit in the maritime context. In 1995, China began building structures on and around Mischief Reef.[17] Between 2013–2015, it subsequently engaged in land reclamation projects there, resulting in the emergence of new, artificial "islands." China maintains that these land masses constitute proper islands under UNCLOS and, therefore, afford it maritime rights. If true, then a (re)distribution of the disputed territory in the South China Sea may logically follow – to China's advantage and its neighbors' disadvantage.

[15] For a larger discussion of this point, see Grant (2015). The answers listed here reflect the international community's conservatism with respect to changing interstate borders. That is, the international community understands that both extenuating circumstances may demand changes to borders via nonmutual renegotiation (in violation of the territorial integrity norm) and the stability of the international system requires that these circumstances be circumscribed as much as possible.

[16] This trade off has long existed. Smith (2018), for example, chronicles how major states navigated it during the Paris Peace Conference of 1919.

[17] The disputed issues in the South China Sea involve more than Mischief Reef.

The Philippines adopts a different position. It argues that Mischief Reef (i) is not a proper island under UNCLOS, (ii) lays within the Philippines's waters, (iii) contains "artificial" Chinese structures to which UNCLOS affords no rights, and (iv) therefore does not offer China any benefit under UNCLOS. China would instead need to negotiate any benefits associated with the land masses in question through direct negotiations with the Philippines. On the basis of this position (in addition to other related, disputed issues) – and to contest what it views as Chinese encroachments into its maritime space – the Philippines filed arbitration proceedings against China in 2013, arguing that UNCLOS renders the above Chinese actions unlawful. China refused to acknowledge the tribunal's jurisdiction in the issues being contested, however, and therefore did not participate in the proceedings at all. Nevertheless, the tribunal found that it had jurisdiction, tried to ascertain the Chinese position despite China's absence, and issued a ruling in 2016. That ruling affirmed the Philippines's position.[18]

The Russian annexation of Crimean and Chinese behavior in the South China Sea share a few curious features. In each case, a prominent, major power challenged the widely accepted laws and norms that govern the delimitation of interstate borders.[19] Each challenge also involved a revisionist state that exploited gray(er) areas within existing international law to push its preferred policy. Both Russia and China framed their actions as defensible (or at least, justifiable) under international law; Russia invoked a norm that the international community widely champions, while China referenced UNCLOS terminology, rights, and reservations as it expanded its hold in the South China Sea. Each used international law to test the boundaries of international law. Finally, both states eventually resorted to unilateral action to achieve their aims – either coercion (in the case of Russia) or ignoring the international legal system (in the case of China).

Such challenges affect the system marginally at the moment.[20] Yet a specter looms on the horizon. Border settlement brings peace – and indeed, its achievement is often helped – *because* of the existing international legal system. After border settlement occurs, borders remain stable under international law (i.e., immutable, except under certain, cooperative or extenuating conditions; Shaw 2014).[21] That stability, in turn, removes a highly salient, conflict-prone issue from neighboring states' foreign policy agendas, allowing their relationship to proceed along a significantly less hostile path. To the extent, however, that border stability results from international law, then challenges the international legal system – particularly those directly related to interstate borders – should raise alarms among those desirable of a more peaceful world. Norms hold

[18] All documentation associated with this case appears on the Permanent Court of Arbitration website at `https://pca-cpa.org/en/cases/7/` (last accessed March 8, 2019).

[19] For a prediction of this behavior in the Chinese context, see Ikenberry (2011, 346–347).

[20] On the conditions of marginality, see also Ikenberry (2011) and Chan (2017).

[21] For an alternative view, see Gibler (2012), who sees stability as a function of the borders' characteristics.

because they are accepted and followed; when that is no longer true, the norms change. In this case of interstate borders, when the existing norms (and the laws underlying them) no longer hold, the likelihood rises that border disputes reopen, thereby introducing a series of conflict fault lines across the globe. That promises to reintroduce border negotiations, reactivate commitment problems, and usher in a new era of greater interstate hostility.

Bibliography

Abramson, Scott F. and David B. Carter. 2016. "The Historical Origins of Territorial Disputes." *American Political Science Review* 110(4):675–698.

Allee, Todd L. and Paul K. Huth. 2006. "Legitimizing Dispute Settlement: International Legal Rulings as Domestic Political Cover." *American Political Science Review* 100(2):219–234.

Arena, Philip and Scott Wolford. 2012. "Arms, Intelligence, and War." *International Studies Quarterly* 56:351–365.

Asgeirsdottir, Aslaug and Martin C. Steinwand. 2018. "Distributive Outcomes in Contested Maritime Areas: The Role of Inside Options in Settling Competing Claims." *Journal of Conflict Resolution* 62(6):1284–1313.

Axelrod, Robert. 1984. *The Evolution of Cooperation*. Cambridge, MA: Basic Books.

Barnett, Michael and Martha Finnemore. 2004. *Rules for the World: International Organizations in Global Politics*. Cornell: Cornell University Press.

Beardsley, Kyle. 2008. "Agreement without Peace? International Mediation and Time Inconsistency Problems." *American Journal of Political Science* 52(4):723–740.

2011. *The Mediation Dilemma*. Cornell: Cornell University Press.

Beardsley, Kyle and Nigel Lo. 2014. "Third-Party Conflict Management and the Willingness to Make Concessions." *Journal of Conflict Resolution* 58(2):363–392.

Bell, P. M. H. 2007. *The Origins of the Second World War in Europe*. 3rd ed. New York: Pearson Longman.

Bellamy, Alex J. 2015. "The Responsibility to Protect Turns Ten." *Ethics and International Affairs* 29(2):161–185.

Bendor, Jonathan, Roderick M. Kramer, and Suzanne Stout. 1991. "When in Doubt ...Cooperation in a Noisy Prisoner's Dilemma." *Journal of Conflict Resolution* 35(4):691–719.

Bendor, Jonathan and Piotr Swistak. 1997. "The Evolutionary Stability of Cooperation." *American Political Science Review* 91(2):290–307.

Bennett, D. Scott. 1996. "Security, Bargaining, and the End of Interstate Rivalry." *International Studies Quarterly* 40(2):157–183.

1997. "Measuring Rivalry Termination, 1816–1992." *Journal of Conflict Resolution* 41(2):227–254.
1998. "Integrating and Testing Models of Rivalry Duration." *American Journal of Political Science* 42(4):1200–1232.
Bennett, D. Scott and Allan C. Stam. 2000. "EUGene: A Conceptual Manual." *International Interactions* 26(2):179–204.
Bercovitch, Jacob and Paul F. Diehl. 1997. "Conflict Management of Enduring Rivalries: The Frequency, Timing, and Short-Term Impact of Mediation." *International Interactions* 22(4):299–320.
Bercovitch, Jacob and Richard Jackson. 2009. *Conflict Resolution in the Twenty-First Century*. Ann Arbor: University of Michigan Press.
Biger, Gideon. 1995. *The Encyclopedia of International Boundaries*. New York: Facts on File.
Bilder, Richard B. 1987. "International Dispute Settlement and the Role of International Adjudication." *Emory Journal of International Dispute Resolution* 1(2):131–173.
Bils, Peter and William Spaniel. 1917. "Policy Bargaining and Militarized Conflict." *Journal of Theoretical Politics* 29(4):647–678.
Blalock, Jr., Hubert M. 1979. *Social Statistics*. Rev. 2nd ed. New York: McGraw-Hill.
Blum, Gabriella. 2007. *Islands of Agreement*. Cambridge: Harvard University Press.
Bo, Pedro Dal. 2005. "Cooperation under the Shadow of the Future: Experimental Evidence from Infinitely Repeated Games." *American Economic Review* 95(5): 1591–1604.
Boulding, Kenneth E. 1978. *Stable Peace*. Austin: University of Texas Press.
Box-Steffensmeier, Janet M. and Bradford S. Jones. 2004. *Event History Modeling*. Cambridge: Cambridge University Press.
Braithwaite, Alex and Douglas Lemke. 2011. "Unpacking Escalation." *Conflict Management and Peace Science* 28(2):111–123.
Braumoeller, Bear F. 2004. "Hypothesis Testing and Multiplicative Interaction Terms." *International Organization* 58(4):807–820.
Brecher, Michael and Jonathan Wilkenfeld. 2000. *A Study of Crisis*. Ann Arbor: University of Michigan Press.
Brecher, Michael, Jonathan Wilkenfeld, Kyle Beardsley, Patrick James, and David Quinn. 2017. "International Crisis Behavior Data Codebook, Version 12." `http://sites.duke.edu/icbdata/data-collections/`.
Bremer, Stuart A. 1992. "Dangerous Dyads – Conditions Affecting the Likelihood of Interstate War, 1816–1965." *Journal of Conflict Resolution* 36(2):309–341.
Brewster, Rachel. 2009. "The Limits of Reputation on Compliance." *International Theory* 1(2):323–333.
Brownlie, Ian. 1979. *African Boundaries: A Legal and Diplomatic Encyclopaedia*. London: C. Hurst and Co.
Bueno de Mesquita, Bruce, James D. Morrow, Randolph M. Siverson, and Alastair Smith. 1999. "An Institutional Explanation of the Democratic Peace." *American Journal of Political Science* 93(4):791–807.
Bueno de Mesquita, Bruce, Alastair Smith, Randolph M. Siverson, and James D. Morrow. 2003. *The Logic of Political Survival*. Cambridge, MA: MIT Press.
Busch, Marc L. 2007. "Overlapping Institutions, Forum Shopping, and Dispute Settlement in International Trade." *International Organization* 61(4):735–761.

Busch, Marc L. and Eric Reinhardt. 2002. The Evolution of GATT/WTO Dispute Settlement. In *Trade Policy Research*, ed. John M. Curtis and Dan Ciuriak. Ottawa: Canadian Foreign Affairs and International Trade, pp. 143–184.

Carroll, Robert J. and Brenton Kenkell. 2019. "Predictions, Proxies, and Power." *American Journal of Political Science* 63(3):577–593.

Carter, David B. and Henk E. Goemans. 2011. "The Making of the Territorial Order: New Borders and the Emergence of Interstate Conflict." *International Organization* 65(2):275–309.

Carter, David B. and Curtis S. Signorino. 2010. "Back to the Future: Modeling Time Dependence in Binary Data." *Political Analysis* 18(3):271–292.

Chadefaux, Thomas. 2011. "Bargaining over Power: When Do Shifts in Power Lead to War?" *International Theory* 3(2):228–253.

Chan, Steve. 2017. *Trust and Distrust in Sino-American Relations: Challenge and Opportunity*. Amherst, NY: Cambria Press.

Chayes, Abram and Antonia H. Chayes. 1993. "On Compliance." *International Organization* 47(2):175–205.

Chiozza, Giacomo and H. E. Goemans. 2011. *Leaders and International Conflict*. Cambridge: Cambridge University Press.

Clarke, Kevin A. and David M. Primo. 2012. *A Model Discipline: Political Science and the Logic of Representations*. Oxford: Oxford University Press.

Clay, K. Chad and Andrew P. Owsiak. 2016. "The Diffusion of International Border Agreements." *Journal of Politics* 78(2):427–442.

Cohen, Raymond. 1991. *Communicating across Cultures: Communication Obstacles in International Diplomacy*. Washington, DC: United States Institute of Peace.

Colaresi, Michael P. 2004. "When Doves Cry: International Rivalry, Unreciprocated Cooperation, and Leadership Turnover." *American Journal of Political Science* 48(3):555–570.

Colaresi, Michael, Karen Rasler, and William R. Thompson. 2007. *Strategic Rivalries in World Politics: Position, Space and Conflict Escalation*. Cambridge: Cambridge University Press.

Colaresi, Michael and William R. Thompson. 2002. "Strategic Rivalries, Protracted Conflict, and Crisis Escalation." *Journal of Peace Research* 39(3):263–287.

Coppa, Frank J. 1992. *The Origins of the Italian Wars of Independence*. London: Longman.

Cornwell, Derekh D. F. and Michael P. Colaresi. 2002. "Holy Trinities, Rivalry Termination, and Conflict." *International Interactions* 28(4):325–354.

Correlates of War Project. 2008. *State System Membership List, v2008.1*. `http://correlatesofwar.org`.

Cox, Eric W. 2010. *Why Enduring Rivalries Do-or Don't-End*. Boulder, CO: Lynne Rienner.

Crescenzi, Mark J. C., Kelly M. Kadera, Sara McLaughlin Mitchell, and Clayton L. Thyne. 2011. "A Supply Side Theory of Mediation." *International Studies Quarterly* 55(4):1069–1094.

Cukwurah, A. O. 1967. *The Settlement of Boundary Disputes in International Law*. Manchester: Manchester University Press.

Dal Bo, Ernest and Robert Powell. 2009. "A Model of Spoils Politics." *American Journal of Political Science* 53(1):207–222.

Day, Alan J. 1987. *Border and Territorial Disputes*. 2nd ed. Essex: Longman.

Debs, Andre and H. E. Goemans. 2010. "Regime Type, the Fate of Leaders, and War." *American Political Science Review* 104(3):430–445.

Diehl, Paul F. and Gary Goertz. 2000. *War and Peace in International Rivalry*. Ann Arbor: University of Michigan Press.

2012. The Rivalry Process: How Rivalries Are Sustained and Terminated. In *What Do We Know about War?*, ed. John A. Vasquez. 2nd ed. Lanham, MD: Rowman & Littlefield, pp. 83–109.

Diehl, Paul F. and Thorin M. Wright. 2016. "A Conditional Defense of the Dyadic Approach." *International Studies Quarterly* 60(2):363–368.

Diener, Alexander C. and Joshua Hagen. 2012. *Borders: A Very Short Introduction*. New York: Oxford University Press.

Dixon, William J. 1994. "Democracy and the Peaceful Settlement of International Conflict." *American Political Science Review* 88(1):14–32.

Downs, George W. and Michael A. Jones. 2002. "Reputation, Compliance, and International Law." *The Journal of Legal Studies* 31(S1):S95–S114.

Downs, George W., David M. Rocke, and Peter N. Barsoom. 1996. "Is the Good News about Compliance Good News about Cooperation?" *International Organization* 50(3):379–406.

Dreyer, David R. 2010. "Issue Conflict Accumulation and the Dynamics of Strategic Rivalry." *International Studies Quarterly* 54(3):779–795.

Druckman, Daniel and James A. Wall. 2017. "A Treasure Trove of Insights: Sixty Years of JCR Research on Negotiation and Mediation." *Journal of Conflict Resolution* 61(9):1898–1924.

Fearon, James D. 1994a. "Domestic Political Audiences and the Escalation of International Disputes." *American Political Science Review* 88(3):577–592.

1994b. "Signaling vs. the Balance of Power and Interests." *Journal of Conflict Resolution* 38:236–269.

1995. "Rationalist Explanations for War." *International Organization* 49(3):379–414.

1996. "Bargaining over Objects That Influence Future Bargaining Power."

1997. "Signaling Foreign Policy Interests: Tying Hands versus Sinking Costs." *Journal of Conflict Resolution* 41(1):68–90.

1998. "Bargaining, Enforcement, and International Cooperation." *International Organization* 52(2):269–305.

Feste, Karen A. 1991. *Plans for Peace*. New York: Praeger.

Fey, Mark and Kristopher W. Ramsay. 2010. "When Is Shuttle Diplomacy Worth the Commute? Information Sharing through Mediation." *World Politics* 62(4): 529–560.

Fisher, Roger, William Ury, and Bruce Patton. 1991. *Getting to Yes*. New York: Penguin.

Fortna, Virginia Page. 2003. "Scraps of Paper? Agreements and the Durability of Peace." *International Organization* 57(2):337–372.

Fravel, M. Taylor. 2008. *Strong Border, Secure Nation*. Princeton: Princeton University Press.

Frazier, Derrick V. and William J. Dixon. 2006. "Third-Party Intermediaries and Negotiated Settlements, 1946–2000." *International Interactions* 32(4):385–408.

Frederick, Bryan A., Paul R. Hensel, and Christopher Macaulay. 2017. "The Issue Correlates of War Territorial Claims Data, 1816–2001." *Journal of Peace Research* 54(1):99–108.

Gartner, Scott S. 2011. "Signs of Trouble: Regional Organization Mediation and Civil War Agreement Durability." *Journal of Politics* 73(2):380–390.
Gartzke, Erik, Quan Li, and Charles Boehmer. 2001. "Investing in the Peace: Economic Interdependence and International Conflict." *International Organization* 55(2):391–438.
Gent, Stephen E. and Megan Shannon. 2010. "The Effectiveness of International Arbitration and Adjudication: Getting into a Bind." *Journal of Politics* 72(2): 366–380.
2011. "Decision Control and the Pursuit of Binding Conflict Management: Choosing the Ties That Bind." *Journal of Conflict Resolution* 55(5):710–734.
Ghosn, Faten. 2010. "Getting to the Table and Getting to Yes: An Analysis of International Negotiations." *International Studies Quarterly* 54(4):1055–1072.
Ghosn, Faten, Glenn Palmer, and Stuart A. Bremer. 2004. "The MID3 Data Set, 1993–2001: Procedures, Coding Rules, and Description." *Conflict Management and Peace Science* 21(2):133–154.
Gibler, Douglas M. 1996. "Alliances That Never Balance: The Territorial Settlement Treaty." *Conflict Management and Peace Science* 15:75–97.
1997. "Control the Issues, Control the Conflict: The Effects of Alliances That Settle Territorial Issues on Interstate Rivalries." *International Interactions* 22:341–368.
2007. "Bordering on Peace: Democracy, Territorial Issues, and Conflict." *International Studies Quarterly* 51:509–532.
2012. *The Territorial Peace: Borders, State Development, and International Conflict.* Cambridge: Cambridge University Press.
Gibler, Douglas M. and Steven V. Miller. 2014. "External Territorial Threat, State Capacity, and Civil War." *Journal of Peace Research* 51(5):634–646.
Gibler, Douglas M. and Andrew P. Owsiak. 2018. "Democracy and the Settlement of International Borders, 1919–2000." *Journal of Conflict Resolution* 62(9): 1847–1875.
Gibler, Douglas M. and Jaroslav Tir. 2014. "Territorial Peace and Democratic Clustering." *Journal of Politics* 76(1):27–40.
Gilligan, Michael and S. John Stedman. 2003. "Where Do the Peacekeepers Go?" *International Studies Review* 5(4):37–54.
Gleditsch, Nils Petter, Kathryn Furlong, Havard Hegre, Bethany Lacina, and Taylor Owen. 2006. "Conflicts over Shared Rivers: Resource Scarcity or Fuzzy Boundaries." *Political Geography* 25(4):361–382.
Goemans, Hein E. 2000. *War and Punishment: The Causes of War Termination and the First World War.* Princeton: Princeton University Press.
Goemans, Hein E. and Kenneth A. Schultz. 2017. "The Politics of Territorial Claims: A Geospatial Approach Applied to Africa." *International Organization* 71(1):31–64.
Goertz, Gary and Paul F. Diehl. 1993. "Enduring Rivalries: Theoretical Constructs and Empirical Patterns." *International Studies Quarterly* 37(2):147–171.
1995. "The Initiation and Termination of Enduring Rivalries: The Impact of Political Shocks." *American Journal of Political Science* 39(1):30–52.
2002. "Treaties and Conflict Management in Enduring Rivalries." *International Negotiation* 7(3):379–398.
Goertz, Gary, Paul F. Diehl, and Alexandru Balas. 2016. *The Puzzle of Peace.* Oxford: Oxford University Press.

Goertz, Gary and James Mahoney. 2012. *A Tale of Two Cultures: Qualitative and Quantitative Research in the Social Sciences*. Princeton: Princeton University Press.
Goldsmith, Jack L. and Eric A. Posner. 2006. *The Limits of International Law*. Oxford: Oxford University Press.
Grant, Thomas D. 2015. "Annexation of Crimea." *American Journal of International Law* 109(1):68–95.
Greene, William H. 2012. *Econometric Analysis*. 7th ed. Boston: Prentice Hall.
Greig, J. Michael. 2001. "Moments of Opportunity: Recognizing Conditions of Ripeness for International Mediation between Enduring Rivals." *The Journal of Conflict Resolution* 45(6):691–718.
2005. "Stepping into the Fray: When Do Mediators Mediate?" *American Journal of Political Science* 49(2):249–266.
Greig, J. Michael and Paul F. Diehl. 2006. "Softening Up: Making Conflicts More Amenable to Diplomacy." *International Interactions* 32(4):355–384.
2012. *International Mediation*. Cambridge: Polity.
Greig, J. Michael, Andrew P. Owsiak, and Paul F. Diehl. 2019. *International Conflict Management*. Cambridge: Polity.
Greig, J. Michael and Patrick M. Regan. 2008. "When Do They Say Yes? An Analysis of the Willingness to Offer and Accept Mediation in Civil Wars." *International Studies Quarterly* 52(4):759–781.
Guzman, Andrew T. 2002. "A Compliance-Based Theory of International Law." *California Law Review* 90(6):1825–1888.
2008. *How International Law Works*. Oxford: Oxford University Press.
Haas, Ernst B. 1953. "The Balance of Power: Prescription, Concept, or Propaganda?" *World Politics* 5(4):442–477.
Hathaway, Oona A. and Scott J. Shapiro. 2017. *The Internationalists: How a Radical Plan to Outlaw War Remade the World*. New York: Simon & Schuster.
Hensel, Paul R. 1994. "One Thing Leads to Another – Recurrent Militarized Disputes in Latin-America, 1816–1986." *Journal of Peace Research* 31(3):281–297.
1996. "Charting a Course to Conflict: Territorial Issues and Interstate Conflict, 1816–1992." *Conflict Management and Peace Science* 15(1):43–73.
1999. Charting a Course to Conflict: Territorial Issues and Interstate Conflict, 1816–1992. In *A Road Map to War: Territorial Dimensions of International Conflict*, ed. Paul F. Diehl. Nashville, TN: Vanderbilt University Press, pp. 115–146.
2000. Territory, Theory, and Evidence on Geography and Conflict. In *What Do We Know about War?*, ed. John A. Vasquez. Lanham, MD: Rowman & Littlefield, pp. 57–84.
2001. "Contentious Issues and World Politics: The Management of Territorial Claims in the Americas, 1816–1992." *International Studies Quarterly* 45(1):81–109.
Hensel, Paul R., Gary Goertz, and Paul F. Diehl. 2000. "The Democratic Peace and Rivalries." *The Journal of Politics* 62(4):1173–1188.
Hensel, Paul R., Sara McLaughlin Mitchell, Thomas E. Sowers, and Clayton L. Thyne. 2008. "Bones of Contention: Comparing Territorial, Maritime, and River Issues." *Journal of Conflict Resolution* 52(1):117–143.
Hoffman, Aaron M. 2002. "A Conceptualization of Trust in International Relations." *European Journal of International Relations* 8(3):375–401.
Holsti, Kalevi J. 1991. *Peace and War: Armed Conflicts and International Order 1648–1989*. Cambridge: Cambridge University Press.

Honaker, James and Gary King. 2010. "What to Do about Missing Values in Time-Series Cross-Section Data." *American Journal of Political Science* 54(2):561–581.

Hopmann, P. Terrence. 1996. *The Negotiation Process and the Resolution of International Conflicts*. Columbia: University of South Carolina Press.

Horowitz, Michael C., Paul Poast, and Allan C. Stam. 2017. "Domestic Signaling of Commitment Credibility: Military Recruitment and Alliance Formation." *Journal of Conflict Resolution* 61(8):1682–1710.

Huth, Paul K. 1996. *Standing Your Ground: Territorial Disputes and International Conflict*. Ann Arbor: University of Michigan Press.

Huth, Paul K. and Todd L. Allee. 2002. *The Democratic Peace and Territorial Conflict in the Twentieth Century*. Cambridge: Cambridge University Press.

Huth, Paul K., Sarah E. Croco, and Benjamin J. Appel. 2013. "Bringing Law to the Table: Legal Claims, Focal Points, and the Settlement of Territorial Disputes since 1945." *American Journal of Political Science* 57(1):90–103.

Ikenberry, G. John. 2011. *Liberal Leviathan*. Princeton: Princeton University Press.

Ireland, Gordon. 1938. *Boundaries, Possessions, and Conflicts in South America*. New York: Octagon Books.

1971. *Boundaries, Possessions, and Conflicts in Central and North America and the Caribbean*. New York: Octagon Books.

James, Patrick, Johann Park, and Seung-Whan Choi. 2006. "Democracy and Conflict Management: Territorial Claims in the Western Hemisphere Revisited." *International Studies Quarterly* 50(4):803–818.

Jóhannesson, Gudni Thorlacius. 2004. "How 'Cod War' Came: The Origins of the Anglo-Icelandic Fisheries Dispute, 1958–61." *Historical Research* 77(198): 543–574.

Kegley, Charles W., Jr. and Gregory A. Raymond. 1990. *When Trust Breaks Down: Alliance Norms and World Politics*. Columbia: University of South Carolina Press.

Keohane, Robert O. 1984. *After Hegemony: Cooperation and Discord in the World Political Economy*. Princeton: Princeton University Press.

King, Gary, James Honaker, Anne Joseph, and Kenneth Scheve. 2001. "Analyzing Incomplete Political Science Data: An Alternative Algorithm for Multiple Imputation." *American Political Science Review* 95(1):49–69.

Klein, James P., Gary Goertz, and Paul F. Diehl. 2006. "The New Rivalry Dataset: Procedures and Patterns." *Journal of Peace Research* 43(3):331–348.

Klein, Natalie. 2011. *Maritime Security and the Law of the Sea*. Oxford: Oxford University Press.

Kocs, Stephen A. 1995. "Territorial Disputes and Interstate War, 1945–1987." *Journal of Politics* 57(1):159–175.

Kornprobst, Markus. 2002. "The Management of Border Disputes in African Regional Sub-systems: Comparing West Africa and the Horn of Africa." *Journal of Modern African Studies* 40(3):369–393.

Kraska, James. 2011. *Maritime Power and the Law of the Sea*. Oxford: Oxford University Press.

Kupchan, Charles A. 2010. *How Enemies become Friends*. Princeton: Princeton University Press.

Kydd, Andrew. 2000. "Arms Races and Arms Control: Modeling the Hawk Perspective." *American Journal of Political Science* 44(2):222–238.

2003. "Which Side Are You On: Bias, Credibility, and Mediation." *American Journal of Political Science* 47(4):597–611.

2007. *Trust and Mistrust in International Relations*. Princeton: Princeton University Press.

Lamb, Alastair. 1964. "The Sino-Pakistani Boundary Agreement of 2 March 1963." *Australian Outlook* 18(3):299–312.

Lebow, Richard Ned. 1996. *The Art of Bargaining*. Baltimore: Johns Hopkins University Press.

Lee, Hoon and Sara McLaughlin Mitchell. 2012. "Foreign Direct Investment and Territorial Disputes." *Journal of Conflict Resolution* 56(4):675–703.

Leeds, Brett Ashley, Jeffrey M. Ritter, and Sara McLaughlin Mitchell. 2002. "Alliance Treaty Obligations and Provisions, 1815–1944." *International Interactions* 28:237–260.

Leng, Russell J. 1983. "When Will They Ever Learn? Coercive Bargaining in Recurrent Crises." *The Journal of Conflict Resolution* 27(3):379–419.

Lissitzyn, Oliver J. 1967. "Treaties and Changed Circumstances (Rebus Sic Stantibus)." *American Journal of International Law* 61(4):895–922.

Long, J. Scott and Jeremy Freese. 2006. *Regression Models for Categorical Dependent Variables Using Stata*. 2nd ed. College Station, TX: Stata Press.

MacMillan, Margaret. 2001. *Paris 1919*. New York: Random House.

Maoz, Zeev. 1989. "Joining the Club of Nations: Political Development and International Conflict, 1816–1976." *International Studies Quarterly* 33(2):199–231.

Maoz, Zeev and Ben D. Mor. 2002a. *Bound by Struggle*. Ann Arbor: University of Michigan Press.

2002b. *Bound by Struggle: The Strategic Evolution of Enduring International Rivalries*. Ann Arbor: University of Michigan Press.

Maoz, Zeev and Bruce Russett. 1993. "Normative and Structural Causes of Democratic Peace, 1946–1986." *The American Political Science Review* 87(3):624–638.

Marshall, Monty G. and Keith Jaggers. 2009. "Political Regime Characteristics and Transitions, 1800–2006. Polity IV Project."

Mattes, Michaela. 2018. "'Chipping Away at the Issues': Piecemeal Dispute Resolution and Territorial Conflict." *Journal of Conflict Resolution* 62(1):94–118.

Mattes, Michaela and Burcu Savun. 2009. "Fostering Peace after Civil War: Commitment Problems and Agreement Design." *International Studies Quarterly* 53(1): 737–759.

McGinnis, Michael D. and John T. Williams. 2001. *Compound Dilemmas*. Ann Arbor: University of Michigan Press.

Mearsheimer, John J. 1994/1995. "The False Promise of International Institutions." *International Security* 19(3):5–49.

Melin, Molly M. 2011. "The Impact of State Relationships on If, When, and How Conflict Management Occurs." *International Studies Quarterly* 55(3):691–715.

2013. "When States Mediate." *Penn State Journal of Law and International Affairs* 2(1):78–90.

Melin, Molly M. and Isak Svensson. 2009. "Incentives for Talking: Accepting Mediation in International and Civil Wars." *International Interactions* 35(3):249–271.

Merrills, J. G. 2005. *International Dispute Settlement*. 4th ed. Cambridge: Cambridge University Press.

Mitchell, Sara McLaughlin. 2012. Norms and the Democratic Peace. In *What Do We Know about War?*, ed. John A. Vasquez. 2nd ed. Lanham, MD: Rowman & Littlefield, pp. 167–188.

Mitchell, Sara McLaughlin and Andrew P. Owsiak. 2017. The International Court of Justice. In *Routledge Handbook of Judicial Behavior*, ed. Robert M. Howard and Kirk A. Randazzo. London: Routledge, pp. 445–463.

Mitchell, Sara McLaughlin and Brandon C. Prins. 2004. "Rivalry and Diversionary Uses of Force." *Journal of Conflict Resolution* 48(6):937–961.

Mitchell, Sara McLaughlin and Emilia J. Powell. 2011. *Domestic Law Goes Global: Legal Traditions and International Courts*. Cambridge: Cambridge University Press.

Mnookin, Robert H. and Lewis Kornhauser. 1979. "Bargaining in the Shadow of the Law: The Case of Divorce." *Yale Law Journal* 88(5):950–997.

Morey, Daniel S. 2011. "When War Brings Peace: A Dynamic Model of the Rivalry Process." *American Journal of Political Science* 55(2):263–275.

Morgenthau, Hans. [1948]1985. *Politics among Nations: The Struggle for Power and Peace*. 5th ed. New York: Knopf.

Morrow, James D. 1991. "Alliances and Asymmetry: An Alternative to the Capability Aggregation Model of Alliances." *American Journal of Political Science* 35(4): 904–933.

1999. "How Could Trade Affect Conflict." *Journal of Peace Research* 36(4):481–489.

2000. "Alliances: Why Write Them Down?" *American Review of Political Science* 3:63–83.

Most, Benjamin A. and Harvey Starr. 1989. *Inquiry, Logic, and International Politics*. Columbia: University of South Carolina Press.

Owsiak, Andrew P. 2012. "Signing Up for Peace: International Boundary Agreements, Democracy, and Militarized Interstate Disputes." *International Studies Quarterly* 56(1):51–66.

2013. "Democratization and International Border Agreements." *Journal of Politics* 75(3):717–729.

2014. "Conflict Management Trajectories in Militarized Interstate Disputes: A Conceptual Framework and Theoretical Foundations." *International Studies Review* 16(1):50–78.

2019. "Foundations for Integrating the Democratic and Territorial Peace Arguments." *Conflict Management and Peace Science* 36(1):63–87.

Owsiak, Andrew P., Allison Cuttner, and Brent Buck. 2018. "The International Border Agreements Dataset." *Conflict Management and Peace Science* 35(5):559–576.

Owsiak, Andrew P., Paul F. Diehl, and Gary Goertz. 2017. "Border Settlement and the Movement toward and from Negative Peace." *Conflict Management and Peace Science* 34(2):176–193.

Owsiak, Andrew P. and Derrick V. Frazier. 2014. "The Conflict Management Efforts of Allies in Interstate Disputes." *Foreign Policy Analysis* 10(3):243–264.

Owsiak, Andrew P. and Sara McLaughlin Mitchell. 2019. "Conflict Management in Land, River, and Maritime Claims." *Political Science Research and Methods* 7(1):43–61.

Owsiak, Andrew P. and John A. Vasquez. 2019. "The Cart and the Horse Redux: The Timing of Border Settlement and Joint Democracy." *British Journal of Political Science* 49(1):339–354.

Palmer, Glenn, Vito D'Orazio, Michael Kenwick, and Matthew Lane. 2015. "The MID4 Dataset, 2002–2010: Procedures, Coding Rules and Description." *Conflict Management and Peace Science* 32(2):222–242.

Park, Johann and Michael Colaresi. 2014. "Safe across the Border: The Continued Significant of the Democratic Peace When Controlling for Stable Borders." *International Studies Quarterly* 58(1):118–125.

Park, Johann and Patrick James. 2015. "Democracy, Territory, and Armed Conflict, 1919–1995." *Foreign Policy Analysis* 11(1):85–107.

Partell, Peter J. and Glenn Palmer. 1999. "Audience Costs and Interstate Crises: An Empirical Assessment of Fearon's Model of Dispute Outcomes." *International Studies Quarterly* 43(1):389–405.

Posner, Eric A. 2014. *The Twilight of Human Rights Law*. Oxford: Oxford University Press.

Powell, Emilia J. and Krista E. Wiegand. 2010. "Legal Systems and Peaceful Attempts to Resolve Territorial Disputes." *Conflict Management and Peace Science* 27(2): 129–151.

2014. "Strategic Selection: Political and Legal Mechanisms of Territorial Dispute Resolution." *Journal of Peace Research* 51(3):361–374.

Powell, Robert. 2006. "War as a Commitment Problem." *International Organization* 60(Winter):169–203.

Prescott, Victor and Clive Schofield. 2004. *The Maritime Political Boundaries of the World*. 2nd ed. Leiden, The Netherlands: Martinus Nijhoff Publishers.

Prescott, Victor and Gillian D. Triggs. 2008. *International Frontiers and Boundaries: Law, Politics and Geography*. Leiden, The Netherlands: Martinus Nijhoff Publishers.

Princen, Thomas. 1992. *Intermediaries in International Conflict*. Princeton: Princeton University Press.

Prins, Brandon C. and Ursula E. Daxecker. 2008. "Committed to Peace? Liberal Institutions and the Termination of Rivalry." *British Journal of Political Science* 38(1):17–34.

Quackenbush, Stephen L. 2010. "Territorial Issues and Recurrent Conflict." *Conflict Management and Peace Science* 27(3):239–252.

Ramsbotham, Oliver, Tom Woodhouse, and Hugh Miall. 2011. *Contemporary Conflict Resolution*. Cambridge: Polity.

Rasler, Karen and William R. Thompson. 2011. "Borders, Rivalry, Democracy and Conflict in the European Region, 1816–1994." *Conflict Management and Peace Science* 28(3):280–302.

2012. War Making and State Making: How and Where Does It Fit into a Bigger Picture? In *What Do We Know about War?*, ed. John A. Vasquez. 2nd ed. Lanham, MD: Rowman & Littlefield, pp. 237–256.

Rauchhaus, Robert W. 2006. "Asymmetric Information, Mediation, and Conflict Management." *World Politics* 58(2):207–241.

Reed, William. 2003. "Information and Economic Interdependence." *Journal of Conflict Resolution* 47(1):54–71.

Reich, Arie. 2017. "The Effectiveness of the WTO Dispute Settlement System: A Statistical Analysis." *European University Institute Working Papers, 2017/11* .

Reiter, Dan. 1995. "Exploding the Powder Keg Myth: Preemptive Wars Almost Never Happen." *International Security* 20(2):5–34.

Rich, Norman. 1992. *Great Power Diplomacy 1814–1914*. Boston: McGraw-Hill.
Richardson, James L. 1994. *Crisis Diplomacy*. Cambridge: Cambridge University Press.
Richmond, Oliver. 1998. "Devious Objectives and the Disputants' View of International Mediation: A Theoretical Framework." *Journal of Peace Research* 35(6):707–722.
Rider, Toby J. 2009. "Understanding Arms Race Onset: Rivalry, Threat, and Territorial Competition." *Journal of Politics* 72(2):693–703.
2013. "Uncertainty, Salient Stakes, and the Causes of Conventional Arms Races." *International Studies Quarterly* 57(3):580–591.
Rosato, Sebastian. 2003. "The Flawed Logic of Democratic Peace Theory." *American Political Science Review* 97(4):585–602.
Russett, Bruce and John R. Oneal. 2001. *Triangulating Peace: Democracy, Interdependence, and International Organizations*. New York: W.W. Norton.
Sarkees, Meredith Reid and Frank W. Wayman. 2010. *Resort to War: 1816–2007*. Washington, DC: CQ Press.
Schelling, Thomas C. 1960. *The Strategy of Conflict*. Cambridge, MA: Harvard University Press.
1966. *Arms and Influence*. New Haven: Yale University Press.
Schultz, Kenneth A. 1998. "Domestic Opposition and Signaling in International Crises." *American Political Science Review* 92(4):829–844.
2001. "Looking for Audience Costs." *Journal of Conflict Resolution* 45(1):32–60.
Schultz, Kenneth A. and Henk E. Goemans. 2019. "Aims, Claims, and the Bargaining Model of War." *International Theory* 11:344–374.
Scott, James B. 1922. "The Swiss Decision in the Boundary Dispute between Colombia and Venezuela." *American Journal of International Law* 16(3):428–431.
Senese, Paul D. and John A. Vasquez. 2008. *The Steps to War*. Princeton: Princeton University Press.
Sharma, Surya P. 1997. *Territorial Acquisition, Disputes and International Law*. The Hague: Martinus Nijhoff Publishers.
Shaw, Malcolm N. 1982. "Territory in International Law." *Netherlands Yearbook of International Law* 13:61–91.
2008. *International Law*. 6th ed. Cambridge: Cambridge University Press.
2014. *International Law*. 7th ed. Cambridge: Cambridge University Press.
Simmons, Beth A. 2002. "Capacity, Commitment, and Compliance: International Institutions and Territorial Disputes." *Journal of Conflict Resolution* 46(6):829–856.
2005. "Rules over Real Estate: Trade, Territorial Conflict, and International Borders as Institution." *Journal of Conflict Resolution* 49(6):823–848.
2009. *Mobilizing for Human Rights: International Law in Domestic Politics*. New York: Cambridge University Press.
Simmons, Beth A. and Allison Danner. 2010. "Credible Commitments and the International Criminal Court." *International Organization* 64(2):225–256.
Simmons, Beth A., Frank Dobbin, and Geoffrey Garrett. 2008. Introduction: The Diffusion of Liberalization. In *The Global Diffusion of Markets and Democracy*. Cambridge: Cambridge University Press.
Singer, David J., Stuart A. Bremer, and John Stuckey. 1972. Capability Distribution, Uncertainty, and Major Power Wars, 1820–1965. In *Peace, War, and Numbers*, ed. Bruce M. Russett. Beverly Hills: Sage, pp. 19–48.
Slantchev, Branislav L. 2003. "The Principle of Convergence in Wartime Negotiations." *American Political Science Review* 97(4):621–632.

2011. *Military Threats: The Cost of Coercion and the Price of Peace*. Cambridge University Press.
2005. "Military Coercion in Interstate Crises." *American Political Science Review* 99(4):533–547.
Smith, Alastair. 1995. "Alliance Formation and War." *International Studies Quarterly* 39(4):405–425.
Smith, Leonard V. 2018. *Sovereignty at the Paris Peace Conference of 1919*. Oxford: Oxford University Press.
Spivak, Michael. 1994. *Calculus*. 3rd ed. Cambridge: Cambridge University Press.
Spruyt, Hendrik. 1994. *The Sovereign State and Its Competitors*. Princeton: Princeton University Press.
2005. *Ending Empire: Contested Sovereignty and Territorial Partition*. Ithaca: Cornell University Press.
Stinnett, Douglas M. and Paul F. Diehl. 2001. "The Path(s) to Rivalry: Behavioral and Structural Explanations of Rivalry Development." *The Journal of Politics* 63(3):717–740.
Stinnett, Douglas M., Jaroslav Tir, Philip Schafer, Paul F. Diehl, and Charles S. Gochman. 2002. "The Correlates of War (COW) Project Direct Contiguity Data, Version 3." *Conflict Management and Peace Science* 19(2):59–67.
Sumner, Brian T. 2003. "Territorial Disputes at the International Court of Justice." *2004* 53(6):1779–1812.
Svensson, Isak. 2009. "Who Brings Which Peace? Neutral versus Biased Mediation and Institutional Peace Arrangements in Civil Wars." *Journal of Conflict Resolution* 53(3):446–469.
Tang, Shiping. 2018. Understanding Ethnic Conflict: Four Waves and Beyond. In *The Oxford Encyclopedia of Empirical International Relations Theory*, ed. William R. Thompson. Vol. 4. Oxford University Press, pp. 435–447.
Thompson, William R. 1995. "Principal Rivalries." *The Journal of Conflict Resolution* 39(2):195–223.
Thompson, William R. and David R. Dreyer. 2012. *Handbook of International Rivalries, 1494–2010*. Washington, DC: CQ Press.
Tilly, Charles. 1992. *Coercion, Capital, and European States, AD 990–1992*. Cambridge, MA: Blackwell.
Tir, Jaroslav and Paul F. Diehl. 2002. "Geographic Dimensions of Enduring Rivalries." *Political Geography* 21(2):263–286.
Tir, Jaroslav and John A. Vasquez. 2010. Geography and Territory. In *The International Studies Encyclopedia (ISE)*, ed. Robert A. Denemark. Vol. V. Hoboken, NJ: Wiley-Blackwell Publishing.
United Nations. 1969. *Vienna Convention on the Law of Treaties*. New York: United Nations.
International Court of Justice. 2010. Accordance of International Law of the Unilateral Declaration of Independence in Respect of Kosovo. In *Reports of Judgments, Advisory Opinions and Orders*, ed. International Court of Justice. The Hague: United Nations, pp. 403–453.
United States Department of State. 1964. *International Boundary Study No. 42: Burma-China Boundary*. Washington, DC: Department of State.
1966. *International Boundary Study No. 62: Colombia-Panama Boundary*. Washington, DC: Department of State.

1968. *International Boundary Study No. 85: China-Pakistan*. Washington, DC: Department of State.
1969. *International Boundary Study No. 89: Afghanistan-China Boundary*. Washington, DC: Department of State.
Valeriano, Brandon. 2012. Becoming Rivals: The Process of Rivalry Development. In *What Do We Know about War?* 2nd ed. Rowman & Littlefield, pp. 63–82.
Vasquez, John A. 1993. *The War Puzzle*. Cambridge: Cambridge University Press.
1995. "Why Do Neighbors Fight? Proximity, Interaction, or Territoriality." *Journal of Peace Research* 32(3):277–293.
1996. "Distinguishing Rivals That Go to War from Those That Do Not: A Quantitative Comparative Case Study of the Two Paths to War." *International Studies Quarterly* 40(4):531–558.
2009. *The War Puzzle Revisited*. Cambridge: Cambridge University Press.
Vasquez, John A. and Marie T. Henehan. 2001. "Territorial Disputes and the Probability of War, 1816–1992." *Journal of Peace Research* 38(2):123–138.
Vasquez, John and Christopher S. Leskiw. 2001. "The Origins and War Proneness of Interstate Rivalries." *American Review of Political Science* 4:295–316.
Wagner, R. Harrison. 2007. *War and the State*. Michigan University Press.
Walter, Barbara F. 1997. "The Critical Barrier to Civil War Settlement." *International Organization* 51(3):335–364.
2002. *Committing to Peace*. Princeton: Princeton University Press.
2006. "Building Reputation: Why Governments Fight Some Separatists but Not Others." *American Journal of Political Science* 50(2):313–330.
Weeks, Jessica L. 2008. "Autocratic Audience Costs: Regime Type and Signaling Resolve." *International Organization* 62(1):35–64.
Weisiger, Alex. 2013. *Logics of War: Explanations for Limited and Unlimited Conflicts*. Cornell: Cornell University Press.
Werner, Suzanne. 1999a. "Choosing Demands Strategically: The Distribution of Power, the Distribution of Benefits, and the Risk of Conflict." *Journal of Conflict Resolution* 43(6):705–726.
1999b. "The Precarious Nature of Peace: Resolving the Issues, Enforcing the Settlement, and Renegotiating the Terms." *American Journal of Political Science* 43(3):912–934.
Werner, Suzanne and Amy Yuen. 2005. "Making and Keeping Peace." *International Organization* 59(2):261–292.
Whittam, Daphne E. 1961. "The Sino-Burmese Boundary Treaty." *Pacific Affairs* 34(2):174–183.
Wiegand, Krista E. 2011. *Enduring Territorial Disputes: Strategies of Bargaining, Coercive Diplomacy, and Settlement*. Athens: University of Georgia Press.
Zacher, Mark W. 2001. "The Territorial Integrity Norm: International Boundaries and the Use of Force." *International Organization* 55(2):215–250.
Zartner, Dana. 2014. *Courts, Codes, and Custom: Legal Tradition and State Policy toward International Human Rights and Environmental Law*. Oxford: Oxford University Press.
Zawahri, Neda A. and Sara McLaughlin Mitchell. 2011. "Fragmented Governance of International Rivers." *International Studies Quarterly* 55(3):835–858.

Index

Lightning Source UK Ltd.
Milton Keynes UK
UKHW022301271022
411233UK00011B/121

9 781108 794541